Principles and Practice of
STRUCTURAL EQUATION MODELING

METHODOLOGY IN THE SOCIAL SCIENCES
David A. Kenny, *Series Editor*

PRINCIPLES AND PRACTICE OF
STRUCTURAL EQUATION MODELING
Rex B. Kline

SPECTRAL ANALYSIS OF
TIME-SERIES DATA
Rebecca M. Warner

PRINCIPLES AND PRACTICE OF

Structural Equation Modeling

REX B. KLINE
Concordia University
Montréal

Series Editor's Note by David A. Kenny

THE GUILFORD PRESS
New York   London

QA278 .K5851998

Kline, Rex B.

Principles and practice
of structural equation

© 1998 The Guilford Press
A Division of Guilford Publications, Inc.
72 Spring Street, New York, NY 10012
http://www.guilford.com

Printed in the United States of America

This book is printed on acid-free paper.

Last digit is print number: 9 8 7 6 5 4 3 2

Library of Congress Cataloging-in-Publication Data
Kline, Rex B.
    Principles and practice of structural equation modeling / Rex B.
Kline.
        p.   cm. — (Methodology in the social sciences)
    ·Includes bibliographical references and index.
    ISBN 1-57230-336-0 (hardcover). — ISBN 1-57230-337-9 (pbk.)
    1. Multivariate analysis.   2. Social sciences—Statistical
methods.   I. Title.   II. Series.
QA278.K585   1998
519.5'35—dc21   97-46642
                                                              CIP

For my parents
JUNE I. CHADWICK and WILLIAM C. KLINE

Series Editor's Note

I am proud to introduce *Principles and Practice of Structural Equation Modeling* by Rex B. Kline as the inaugural book in The Guilford Press series "Methodology in the Social Sciences." The book is an intelligent, practical, and detailed introduction of a method that has become essential in the social and behavioral sciences.

Structural equation modeling (SEM) is an analytic tool that is entering into middle adulthood. Its parentage is clear: Sewall Wright is the father, but Otis Dudley Duncan served as an able stepparent during its early years. As a young child it wondered about, but never really knew, the pleasures of latent variables. It had a difficult, awkward adolescent period in which it clung to the computer program LISREL as an identity marker. It owes a great deal to Peter Bentler and Ken Bollen, who served as mentors in its late adolescence. It is now mature, but is still exploring new features of its personality.

There are many ways to index that SEM is an important method. Many universities have courses on the topic, there are over 10 computer programs that estimate such models, and there is extensive discussion of the method on the Internet. But by far the best index is that researchers use the method. It is virtually impossible to pick up an issue of an empirical journal in the social sciences and not find at least one paper that uses SEM. Researchers love SEM because it addresses the questions they want answered. Perhaps more than any other technique, SEM "thinks" about research as researchers do.

It is no surprise that a new method has its critics. Some who criticize the method do so out of ignorance; that is, they do not really understand SEM. Of course, these criticisms can be dismissed. But others criticize SEM because they worry that the technique is misapplied. These are not really criticisms but rather reasonable suggestions about when and how the method should be used. We need to heed these caveats. Finally, some criticize the method because they are envious of the enthusiasm that practitioners have for SEM, and they feel jealous that their own esoteric methods are neglected. These critics just do not see that the questions they are asking are largely irrelevant to the needs of researchers.

I cannot help but compare this book to my own *Correlation and Causality* (Kenny, 1979). There are numerous similarities: Both books are written for the practitioner and they avoid the many formulas and minutiae of statistical esoteric. Both present practical guides to the research consumer and are replete with examples that span the wide range of the social and behavioral sciences. However, this book's examples—from clinical psychology, education, cognitive science, behavioral medicine, and developmental psychology, to name just a few—surpass mine in both number and quality. Both books elaborate the potential as well as the limitations of SEM. It is critical to understand when not to use SEM and to recognize when the technique is being abused.

I wrote my book when SEM was in its early adolescence, whereas this book considers SEM as a mature adult. Rex Kline was faced with a much more challenging task and he has done remarkably well. He clearly and concisely presents many modern topics such as measures of model fit, alternative fit functions, the detection of model misspecification, and the estimation of models in multiple samples, as well as the multiplicity of computer programs now available. Somehow he has managed to explain difficult concepts in such a way that both novices can understand and experts can still learn something new.

I see this book as a clear successor to *Correlation and Causality* and am proud that I have played a small role in initiating its birth. I often have been asked to revise my book. There is no need to do so with the publication of *Principles and Practice of Structural Equation Modeling.*

DAVID A. KENNY
University of Connecticut, Storrs

Preface and Acknowledgments

Part of this book is based on workshops about structural equation modeling (SEM) presented from 1991 to 1996 as part of the American Psychological Association's Continuing Education Academic/Scientific Seminars. The talented men and women who attended these workshops did not do so because they loved statistics. Instead, because they loved their research, they spent their weekends learning about statistics in cities (New York, Los Angeles, Toronto, etc.) that offer many more entertaining activities. These workshop attendees, established researchers and students alike, saw SEM as a means to the end of being able to test hypotheses that are difficult if not impossible to evaluate with other analytical methods. It is these types of people for whom this book is written. Consequently, the presentation style of this book emphasizes the application of SEM to actual research problems over discussion of general mathematical issues. Other works that better explain the statistical neuroanatomy of SEM are cited throughout this book, and these sources should be consulted by those interested in such presentations. Also, fundamental principles of SEM are presented here in words and figures and not matrix algebra. Matrix algebra can convey a lot of information in a fairly small amount of space, but one must already be familiar with linear algebra to translate the message.

Although this book is written for applied researchers and not statisticians and assumes only familiarity with very basic statistical concepts (e.g., correlation and regression), complex topics are not avoided. For example, some of the applications of SEM demonstrated here are fairly complicated. However, the same is often true when interesting hypotheses are tested with data from actual research projects. The reward for perseverance through the more difficult parts of this book will, I hope, be an increased awareness of the possibilities for addressing new kinds of questions with SEM.

It was a privilege to write this book under the stewardship of the Series Editor, Dr. David A. Kenny. One of my first introductions to SEM was through his 1979 book, *Correlation and Causality*, a clear and concise work the style of which I tried to emulate in my own humble way in the writing of this book. Dr. Kenny offered numerous suggestions about how to improve the clarity of the text, often in the form of notes that began "Why don't you just say . . . ?", which were then followed by a summary that was much more concise and focused than my original version. Thank you, Dave, for all of your help.

SmallWaters Corporation (Chicago), Multivariate Software (Encino, CA), and Scientific Software International (SSI; Chicago) generously contributed copies of (respectively) Amos, EQS, and LISREL for the descriptions of these model-fitting programs that appear in Chapter 11. I would like to personally thank Dr. Werner Wothke of SmallWaters, Dr. Peter Bentler of Multivariate Software, and Leo Stam of SSI for their help and comments on drafts of this chapter.

The staff of The Guilford Press were very helpful from the beginning of this project to its conclusion. I would like to thank individually Rochelle Serwator and Judith Grauman. Special thanks goes to Bert N. Zelman, of Publishers Workshop, Inc., who copyedited the original (and technically complicated) manuscript. His many helpful suggestions and attention to detail much enhanced the quality of this book. Also thanks to Editor-in-Chief Seymour Weingarten for giving me this opportunity in the first place.

And, finally, to M: Consider these words by Albert Schweitzer: "Truth has no special time of its own. Its hour is now—always." Soar high and stand in the light.

REX B. KLINE
Concordia University, Montréal

Contents

II. CORE SEM TECHNIQUES

PART ONE

FUNDAMENTAL CONCEPTS

CHAPTER ONE

Introduction

Be ready, heart, for parting, new endeavor
To find new light that old ties cannot give
In all beginnings dwells a magic force
          —HERMANN HESSE (1943/1969)

1.1 Foreword

This book is intended to serve as a guide to the principles, assumptions, strengths, limitations, and application of structural equation modeling (SEM) for researchers and students who do not have extensive quantitative backgrounds. Some familiarity with basic concepts such as correlation is assumed, but higher levels of statistical knowledge are not required before reading this book. Accordingly, the presentation is conceptually rather than mathematically oriented, the use of formulas and symbols is kept to a minimum, and many examples are offered of the application of SEM to a wide variety of research problems. It is hoped that readers who complete this book will have acquired the skills necessary to begin to use SEM in their own research.

1.2 Plan of the Book

SEM is a very broad topic and every aspect of it cannot be covered comprehensively in a single volume. With this reality in mind, the main goals of this book are to introduce the fundamental concepts that underlie most facets of SEM and some more advanced techniques that allow additional kinds of hyptheses to be tested. A learning-by-doing approach is strongly encouraged and is facilitated by two things. First, the data for every example reviewed in this book are summarized in tables, which allows the reader to recreate any of the analyses discussed here. Second, the last chapter of this book is about the features and syntax of three widely used computer programs for SEM: Amos, EQS, and LISREL. (The term "model-fitting program" is used throughout this book to refer to programs for SEM.) Readers who at present have no experience using a model-fitting program or use other programs are not at any disadvantage, however, because the presentation in this book of fundamental concepts in SEM is not based upon a particular software package. (More about this point later.)

Part I introduces ideas and vocabulary that are essential to understanding the general rationale of SEM. The latter part of the present chapter is about characteristics that all facets of SEM have in common. The main goal of Chapter 2 is to review basic statistical principles that form the foundation for learning more about SEM. Topics such as bivariate and multivariate correlation and regression, the rationale of significance testing, and other fundamental statistical concepts are covered in Chapter 2. Readers with more advanced backgrounds may be able to simply skim through this chapter. Chapter 3 builds a conceptual context for SEM relative to other, more conventional kinds of statistical methods such as multiple regression and the analysis of variance (ANOVA). Assumptions and examples of the types of research questions that can (and cannot) be evaluated with different types of analytical methods are considered. Chapter 4 deals with the screening and preparation of data for SEM, a topic so important that it is considered before any specific techniques are described in detail. Ways to identify and rectify potential problems due to things like non-normal distributions, missing data, and outliers are covered in that chapter.

Part II consists of four chapters devoted to basic SEM methods. The majority of SEMs described in the research literature involve these fundamental techniques. Chapters 5 and 6 are about path analysis. Path analysis is the original SEM technique, and path models concern only observed variables. The conceptual foundations of path analysis and the evaluation of basic path models are covered in Chapter 5; Chapter 6 deals with more complex types of path models and the topic of multiple group analyses. The next two chapters are about models in which latent variables are represented. Chapter 7 deals with fundamental principles of the distinction between latent and observed variables in SEM and the technique of confirmatory factor analysis (CFA). Chapter 8 extends these ideas to "hybrid" structural equation models that have features of both path models and factor analysis models. It is possible to evaluate a wide variety of hypotheses with these core SEM techniques, as is demonstrated with numerous examples.

Part III covers three subjects. Chapter 9 is concerned with avoiding mistakes. This chapter is written as a "how not to" manual that summarizes ways that researchers can mislead themselves with SEM. Although most of these points are mentioned earlier in the book in the context of particular SEM techniques, they are considered altogether in that chapter. Chapter 10 provides an overview of advanced methods in SEM. Although these advanced techniques cannot be covered in detail in a single chapter, this review is intended to at least make the reader aware of other possibilities in SEM and provide pertinent references. Some of the topics covered in Chapter 10 include the estimation of nonlinear effects, the analysis of means in SEM, and SEM-based ways to analyze incomplete data. The last chapter of the book (11) reviews three software packages for SEM: Amos, EQS, and LISREL.

Most of the chapters after this one offer lists of recommended readings. These suggested readings are not intended to be exhaustive; instead, they were selected for the clarity of their presentations and potential usefulness as stepping stones for further study.

1.3   Notation

As with other statistical techniques, there is no "gold standard" for notation in SEM. Although the symbol set associated with the LISREL program is probably the most widely used in books and journal articles about SEM, it features a profusion of double-subscripted Greek letters (e.g., Φ_{11}, Λ_{31}, etc.) and matrix algebra that can be confusing to follow unless the reader has memorized the entire system. Instead, a minimum number of alphabetic characters are used to represent various aspects of SEM such as observed versus latent variables and error terms. Also, to avoid double notation, no distinction is made between population values and sample statistics. It is assumed that readers are already aware of this difference and know that sample data can only be considered as estimates of population values.

1.4   Computer Programs for SEM

Computer programs are important tools for the conduct of SEM. About 25 years ago, LISREL (Linear Structural Relationships)—which is currently in its eighth version (Jöreskog & Sörbom, 1993, 1996a)—was essentially the only widely available SEM program. The situation is very different now, however, as there are many other choices of model-fitting programs, including Amos (Analysis of Moment Structures; Arbuckle, 1997), CALIS (Covariance Analysis and Linear Structural Equations; Hartmann, 1992), EQS (Equations; Bentler, 1995), LISCOMP (Linear Structural Equations with a Comprehensive Measurement Model; Muthén, 1987), RAMONA (Reticular Action Model or Near Approximation; Browne, Mels, & Cowan, 1994), and SEPATH (SEM and Path Analysis; Steiger, 1995), among others.[1] For this reason, the presentation of concepts in this book is not linked to a particular computer package. Instead, essential principles of SEM that users of *any* model-fitting program must understand are emphasized. In this way, this book is more like a guide to writing style and composition than a handbook about how to use a particular word processor. The aforementioned chapter (11) about Amos, EQS, and LISREL should be helpful to readers who intend to use one of these programs for their own analyses.

A special comment is warranted about model-fitting programs. For two reasons, these types of programs were traditionally difficult to use. Part of the problem was that model-fitting programs usually required users to generate a lot of rather arcane code for each analysis, a time consuming, tedious, and highly error-prone process. The other part of the difficulty was that these programs tended to be available only on mainframe computers, which typically required batch-file-type programming with stark command-line interfaces. The increasing availability of powerful microprocessors and large amounts of memory and storage on affordable personal computers has dramatically changed both of these situations, however. Specifically, statistical software programs for personal computers that are based on graphical user interfaces can be much easier to user than their character-based predecessors, and this near-revolution in "user friendliness" is appearing in model-fitting programs.

As an example of the issues just mentioned, consider a feature of the most recent versions of Amos, EQS, and LISREL for personal computers. Users of each package can still choose to write code in each program's matrix algebra- or equations-based syntax. As an alternative, however, they can draw their model on the screen. The programs then translate the figure into lines of code, which are then used to generate

---

[1]The following SEM site on the World Wide Web offers information about model-fitting programs: HTTP://AVARICE.GSM.UCI.EDU./~JOELWEST/SEM/INDEX.HTML.

the output. Thus, the user need not know very much about the writing of program code in order to conduct a very sophisticated type of statistical analysis. Similar types of interfaces that generate program code "behind the scenes" will undoubtedly soon be common among model-fitting programs. Thus, the importance of highly technical programming skills for the conduct of SEM is likely to quickly diminish. For researchers who have a good understanding of the fundamental concepts of SEM, this development can only be a boon—anything that reduces the drudgery and gets one to the results quicker is a clear benefit. The arrival of "push-button modeling" has potential drawbacks, however. For example, no- or low-effort programming could encourage the use of SEM in an uninformed or careless way. It is thus more important than ever to be familiar with the conceptual bases of SEM. Computer programs, however easy to use, should only be the tools of knowledge and not its master.

1.5   Statistical Journeys

Learning to use and understand a new set of statistical procedures is like making a long journey through a strange land. Such journeys require a substantial commitment of time, patience, and a willingness to tolerate the frustration of some initial uncertainty and inevitable trial and error. But this is a journey that you do not have to make alone. Think of this book as a travel atlas or even as someone to talk to you about language and customs, what to see and what to avoid, and what's coming over the horizon. It is hoped that the combination of a conceptually based approach, numerous examples, and the occasional bit of useful advice presented in this book will help to make this particular journey a little easier, maybe even enjoyable. And remember: the first steps of a long journey—statistical or otherwise—can be among the most difficult . . . but this feat you have already accomplished. Let's begin with an overview of properties common to almost all SEM techniques.

1.6   Family Values

The term *structural equation modeling* (SEM) does not designate a single statistical technique but instead refers to a family of related procedures. Other terms such as *covariance structure analysis, covariance structure modeling,* or *analysis of covariance structures* are also used in the literature to classify these various techniques together under a single label. These terms are essentially interchangeable, but—for clarity's sake—only the first will be used throughout this book. Another term that readers may have encountered is *causal modeling,* which is used mainly in association with the technique of path analysis. This expression may be somewhat dated, however, as it seems to appear less often in the literature nowadays. Although much of the next few chapters concerns various kinds of basic SEM methods, summarized below are some things that most of them have in common. These shared characteristics are first enumerated and then discussed in detail in the following paragraphs:

1. SEM is a priori and requires researchers to think in terms of models. But a priori does not mean exclusively confirmatory. Many applications of SEM are a blend of exploratory and confirmatory analyses.
2. SEM allows the explicit representation of a distinction between observed and latent variables, which makes it possible for researchers to test a wide variety of hypotheses.
3. The basic statistic in SEM is the covariance. It is possible, however, to analyze other types of data such as means.
4. SEM is not just for nonexperimental (correlational) data. Instead, it is a very flexible analytical tool that can be applied to data from experiments, too.
5. Many standard statistical procedures like multiple regression, canonical correlation, factor analysis, and ANOVA can be viewed as special cases of SEM.
6. SEM is a large-sample technique.
7. It is possible to test many different types of effects for statistical significance in SEM, but the role of significance testing in the overall analysis may be less important than for more standard techniques.

1. *SEM is a priori.* Computer programs used for SEM require researchers to provide a lot of information about things such as which variables are assumed to affect others and the directionalities of these effects. These a priori specifications reflect the researcher's hypotheses, and in total they make up the model to be evaluated in the analysis. In this sense, SEM could be viewed as confirmatory. That is, the model is a given at the beginning of the analysis, and whether it is supported by the data is the main question to be answered. But as often happens in SEM, the data may be inconsistent with the model, which means that the researcher must either abandon the model or modify the hypotheses on which it is based. The former option is

rather drastic. In practice, researchers more often opt for the second choice, which means that the analysis now has a more exploratory tenor as revised models are tested with the same data. A related point concerns the adjective "exploratory," which is often associated with procedures like multiple regression or exploratory factor analysis. So-called exploratory techniques can also be used to test a priori hypotheses. For example, researchers can specify the order in which predictor variables are entered into a regression equation; they can also instruct a computer program that performs exploratory factor analysis to extract a specified number of factors. Thus, readers should not interpret the terms "confirmatory" and "exploratory" as applied to statistical techniques—SEM or otherwise—in an absolute way.

Jöreskog (1993) expressed the aforementioned ideas more formally by distinguishing among (1) *strictly confirmatory*, (2) *alternative models*, and (3) *model-generating* applications of SEM. The first refers to when the researcher has a single model that is accepted or rejected based on its correspondence to the data. There are few occasions, however, when the scope of model testing is so narrow. The second context may be more frequent than the first but is still restricted to situations where more than one a priori model is available. The last context, model generation, is probably the most common and occurs when an initial model does not fit the data and is modified by the researcher. The altered model is then tested again with the same data. The goal of this process is more to "discover" a model with two properties: it makes theoretical sense and its statistical correspondence to the data is reasonable.

2. *Observed and latent variables.* Some standard statistical procedures do not offer a convenient way to differentiate between observed and latent variables. For example, ANOVA and multiple regression are concerned with (respectively) means and intercorrelations among observed variables, but neither procedure offers a straightforward way to test hypotheses at a higher level of abstraction. For example, a researcher may believe that dependent variables Y_1, Y_2, and Y_3 tap some common domain that is distinct from the one assessed by Y_4 and Y_5. There is no simple, direct way to represent this specific hypothesis in multiple regression or ANOVA. On the other hand, factor analysis programs such as those available in widely used, general statistical packages such as SPSS (Statistical Package for the Social Sciences), BMDP (Biomedical Data Processing), SAS (Statistical Analytical System), or SYSTAT (System for Statistics) seem at first glance to address this issue. After all, a factor is something akin to a hypothetical, latent variable, is it not? Well, not really, at least not as represented by some widely used factor analysis algorithms in general statisti-

cal packages. Although the distinction between observed and latent variables will be discussed in more detail later in the book, an overview is offered below:

   a. It is not necessary to have latent variables in your models. The evaluation of models that contain only observed variables is certainly possible in SEM.
   b. There is more than one type of latent variable, each of which reflects different assumptions about the relation between observed and latent variables.
   c. Latent variables in SEM can represent a wide range of phenomena. For example, theoretical constructs about characteristics of persons (e.g., anxiety, phonological processing, verbal reasoning), of higher-level units of analysis (characteristics of geographic areas), or of measures such as method effects (e.g., self-report vs. projective) can all be represented in SEM as latent variables.
   d. The observed–latent distinction also provides a way to take account of imperfect reliability of measures. This is not to say that SEM can be used as a way to compensate for gross psychometric flaws. It cannot—no technique can—but this aspect of SEM can lend a more realistic quality to an analysis.

   3. *Covariances at center stage, but means too.* Although basic principles of correlations and covariances are covered in more detail in the next chapter, a covariance is briefly defined here. The covariance between two variables, X and Y, is as follows:

$$cov_{XY} = r_{XY} \, SD_X \, SD_Y, \tag{1.1}$$

where r_{XY} is the Pearson correlation between X and Y, and SD_X and SD_Y are their standard deviations. A covariance thus represents the strength of the association between X and Y and their variabilities. Sometimes a covariance is referred to as an unstandardized correlation because it has no bounds on its upper or lower values. For example, covariance values of, say, –1,003.26 or 1,562.71 are possible. In contrast, the value of a Pearson correlation can range only from –1 to +1. Although this characteristic of correlations makes for easy interpretation, a covariance conveys more information as a single-number statistic than a correlation.

   To say that the covariance is the basic statistic of SEM means that there are two main goals of the analysis: to understand patterns of correlations among a set of variables, and to explain as much of their variance as possible with the model specified by the researcher. The next several chapters are devoted to outlining the rationale behind these goals, but at this point it can be said that essentially all applications of SEM concern these ends. But some researchers, especially those who use ANOVA as their main analytical tool, have the impression that SEM is concerned *solely* with covariances. Although this perception is understandable because so much of the SEM literature is devoted to the analysis of covariances instead of means, it is in fact too narrow. SEM is a actually a very flexible analytical approach that can incorporate the types of effects traditionally associated with ANOVA, including between-group and within-group (e.g., repeated measures) mean comparisons. It is also possible in SEM to test for group mean differences on latent variables, something that is not really feasible with standard ANOVA.

4. *SEM can be applied to nonexperimental and experimental data.* Another common view of SEM is that it is appropriate only for nonexperimental data. The heavy emphasis on covariances in the SEM literature may be related to this perception, but the foregoing discussion should suggest that this belief is without foundation. For example, between-group comparisons conducted within an SEM framework could involve experimental conditions to which subjects are randomly assigned. Suppose that all subjects in a study are asked to perform a challenging visual–motor task such as mirror drawing. Some of these subjects are randomly assigned to a condition in which they are told that their task performance reflects their intelligence; the rest of the subjects are assigned to a condition in which they are instructed that the task is of trivial importance. Also suppose that the researcher uses four self-report measures of anxiety, two of which are believed to assess state anxiety and the other two trait anxiety. SEM techniques could be used to compare the means of two groups of subjects across the anxiety questionnaires and test the hypothesis that the four questionnaires measure two underlying constructs, state and trait anxiety. ANOVA could be used to compare group means, but it lacks a direct way to distinguish between observed measures and underlying constructs. SEM techniques can also be used in studies that have a mix of experimental and nonexperimental features, as would occur, say, if subjects with various psychiatric diagnoses were randomly selected to receive different types of medications.

5. *The SEM family also includes many standard statistical procedures.* About 30 or so years ago, researchers started to realize that multiple regression and ANOVA are actually the same technique. More specifically, ANOVA is a specific case of multiple regression, and both

of these procedures are members of what is known as the general linear model. The general linear model also includes the multivariate extensions of multiple regression and ANOVA—canonical correlation and multivariate analysis of variance (MANOVA), respectively—as well as exploratory factor analysis. All of these techniques—the whole of the general linear model, in fact—are in turn special instances of SEM. Thus, the generality of SEM hinted at in the preceding paragraphs is very broad. In fact, many of the labels we have in our statistical vocabularies are merely conveniences that allow us to quickly associate something with the analysis (e.g., ANOVA: means from one dependent variable are analyzed; MANOVA: means from two or more dependent variables are analyzed; multiple regression: there are two or more predictors of a criterion variable). They may not, however, designate real differences in the underlying conceptual or quantitative paradigm. Although the theme of connections between techniques is elaborated in Chapter 3, it's safe to say here that the SEM family is one of the most inclusive statistical procedures used within the social sciences.

6. *SEM is a large-sample technique.* It is generally understood among statisticians that SEM requires large sample sizes. Because several factors affect sample size requirements in SEM, however, it is difficult to give a simple answer to the question of how large of a sample is large enough. For example, the evaluation of complex models requires more subjects than does the evaluation of simpler models. More complex models involve the estimation of more statistical effects, and thus larger samples are necessary in order for the results to be reasonably stable. The type of estimation algorithm used in the analysis also affects sample size requirements. There is more than one type of estimation method for SEM, and some of these methods may need very large samples due to the assumptions they make (or do not make) about the data.

Because sample size is such an important issue in research, however, some very rough guidelines are offered now. With less than 100 cases, almost any type of SEM analysis may be untenable unless a very simple model is evaluated. Such simple models may be so bare-bones as to be uninteresting, however. For descriptive purposes, sample sizes less than 100 could be considered "small." Between 100 and 200 subjects—a "medium" sample size—is a better minimum, but again this is not an absolute because things like model complexity must also be considered. Sample sizes that exceed 200 cases could be considered "large." Another, more empirical guideline about sample size is from Breckler (1990), who surveyed 72 studies published in personality and social psychology journals in which some type of

SEM was conducted. The median sample size across these studies was 198, approximately "medium" according to the aforementioned guidelines. The range of sample sizes reported by Breckler was from 40 to 8,650 cases; a total of 18 studies (25%) had sample sizes greater than 500, but 16 studies (22%) had fewer than 100 subjects, or "small" sample sizes.

7. *Significance testing.* Significance testing is a central part of many statistical techniques. In ANOVA, for example, there are many procedures for testing the significance of mean comparisons, including post hoc tests, planned comparisons, and trend tests, among others. A great many effects can also be tested for significance in SEM, ranging from things such as the variance of a single variable up to entire models evaluated across multiple groups of subjects. There are two reasons, however, why the results of significance testing may be less relevant in SEM than for other types of techniques.

First, SEM allows the evaluation of entire models, which brings a more macro-level perspective to the analysis rather than a more micro-level one. Although tests of individual effects represented in a model may be of interest, at some point the researcher must make a decision about the whole model: should it be rejected?—modified?— if so, how? Thus, there is some sense in SEM that the view of the entire landscape (the whole model) has precedence over that of specific details (individual effects).

The second reason why significance testing may play a smaller role in SEM concerns the large sample requirement discussed above. With most types of significance tests, it is possible to have results that are "highly significant" (e.g., $p < .0001$) but trivial in absolute magnitude when the sample size is large. By the same token, virtually all effects that are not nil will be statistically significant given a large enough sample. For instance, a correlation of .03 is not significant at the .01 level when $N = 100$, but the same correlation (.03) is significant when $N = 10,000$. Although most researchers do not work with samples so large, it is still possible that some quite small effects could be statistically significant in SEM analyses with even moderate sample sizes. Suggestions for the conduct of significance testing in SEM that address the issues mentioned here will be discussed at various points throughout the book.

1.7 Family History

No discussion of family values would be complete without some history. Don't worry, though—the home movies and slide projector are not coming out of the closet, as this overview is brief. Because SEM is a collection of related techniques, it does not have a single source. Part of its origins date to the turn of the century with the development of what we now call exploratory factor analysis, usually credited to Charles Spearman (1904). Only a few years later, Sewall Wright (1921, 1934), a geneticist, developed the basics of path analysis, which was later introduced by various authors to researchers in other disciplines such as sociology, economics, and eventually psychology (e.g., Blalock, 1964; Duncan, 1966; Dunlap & Cureton, 1930). These measurement (factor analysis) and structural (path analysis) approaches were integrated in the early 1970s in the work of basically three authors, K. G. Jöreskog, J. W. Keesling, and D. E. Wiley (e.g., Jöreskog, 1973; Wiley, 1973), into a framework that Bentler (1980) called the JKW model. One of the first widely available computer programs able to analyze models based on the JKW framework (now called SEM) was LISREL, developed by K. G. Jöreskog and D. Sörbom in the 1970s. The 1980s and 1990s have witnessed the development of many more computer programs and a rapid expansion of the use of SEM techniques in diverse areas such as sports medicine, developmental psychology, and behavioral genetics.

1.8 Summary

Characteristics essential to the SEM family were considered in this chapter, including its a priori nature, the potential to differentiate between observed and latent variables, the ability to analyze covariances as well as means, and the requirement for large samples. SEM is an extremely flexible set of techniques that are applicable to both experimental and nonexperimental data. The ideas introduced in this chapter set the stage for reviewing basic statistical principles that underlie SEM, the subject of the next chapter.

CHAPTER TWO

Basic Statistical Concepts

Chance only favors invention for minds which are prepared for discoveries by patient study and persevering efforts.
—LOUIS PASTEUR

2.1 Foreword

One should bring to a journey of learning about SEM prerequisite knowledge about two topics: (1) bivariate and multiple correlation and regression, and (2) the general logic of significance testing. These and related fundamental statistical concepts are the focus of this chapter. This presentation assumes that the reader has had at least one undergraduate-level course in statistics in the social sciences. For readers with this background, some parts of the presentations about bivariate correlation and regression and significance testing should be a review. Although the topic of multiple correlation and regression may be new for some readers, its similarities to bivariate correlation and regression are emphasized. Readers should note, however, that the topic of multiple regression is a very broad one to which whole books are devoted. More advanced works about multiple regression are listed in the recommended readings section at the end of the chapter, and these works should be consulted for more detailed reviews. Also discussed in this chapter is terminology for variables analyzed in SEM, general requirements for their level of measurement, and the concept of standardization and its advantages and disadvantages. Altogether the topics covered here should help to prepare readers for their upcoming journey.

2.2   Variable Labels

In their most basic form, experimental and nonexperimental studies concern the relation between two variables. In experimental studies, these two variables are often called the *independent variable* and the *dependent variable*. The independent variable is manipulated by the researcher and its effect on the dependent variable is observed. In nonexperimental research, the terms *predictor* and *criterion* tend to be used instead of (respectively) independent variable and dependent variable. This usage is especially common with the method of regression. The connotation of the term "predictor" is that the variable may not be experimentally manipulable.

Somewhat different names for variables are used in SEM. The term *exogenous variable* is often used instead of "predictor" or "independent variable." The word "exogenous" is from Greek and means "of external origin." Accordingly, the causes of exogenous variables are not represented in structural equation models. Instead, they are assumed to affect other variables in the model. Exogenous variables can be either experimental or nonexperimental. *Endogenous variables,* on the other hand, are represented as the effects of other variables in the model, which is consistent with the Greek meaning of this word, "of internal origin." In this sense, the connotation of endogenous is similar to that of dependent variable or criterion, but endogenous variables in SEM can also be represented as causes of other endogenous variables. Other special names for variables may be used for models that distinguish between observed and latent variables. (Recall that not all types of models in SEM feature this distinction.) Latent variables may be referred to as *factors* or *constructs*. An observed variable that is presumed to measure a latent variable may be called a *manifest variable* or, more commonly, an *indicator*. Because scores on indicators are typically assumed to be caused in part by the latent variables that are presumed to underlie them, indicators are generally considered endogenous.

2.3   Level of Measurement

Variables analyzed in SEM are typically continuous and at the interval or ratio level of measurement. These variables also tend to be total scores that are summed across individual items or composites that are sums of other variables. Desirable properties for a continuous variable include a distribution that is approximately normal and a range of scores sufficiently broad to reasonably distinguish among individual cases. The screening of continuous variables is discussed in Chapter 4.

There are some exceptions to the general requirement for interval- or ratio-level variables. For instance, it is possible to analyze categorical (nominal) variables that represent group membership. These categorical variables can be either experimental (e.g., treatment vs. control group) or nonexperimental (e.g., gender). One possibility is to represent a categorical variable as an exogenous variable that affects other variables in a structural equation model that is tested within a single sample. Another way to analyze a categorical variable in SEM is to evaluate a whole model across independent samples, each of which represents one level of the categorical variable. Such analyses are *multiple group* analyses. Numerous examples of multiple group analyses are presented later in the book. There are also some more specialized methods in SEM that permit the analysis of dichotomous or ordinal variables that are conceptualized as indicators of an underlying continuous latent variable. Such methods may require large samples or special software, though. Methods for categorical or ordinal indicators are described in Chapter 7. Other types of models may feature outcome variables represented as dichotomous latent variables, such as mastery versus nonmastery of some skill. Models with latent dichotomous or categorical variables are discussed in Chapter 10.

2.4 Standardized and Unstandardized Variables

Standardization means that a variable has been transformed so that its average is zero and its standard deviation is 1. The most common way to standardize a variable X is to convert its raw scores to z scores. The z score for a raw score on X is computed as follows:

$$z = \frac{X - M}{SD},\qquad(2.1)$$

where M is the mean and SD the standard deviation. The standard deviation is based on squared deviations of raw scores from the mean and the number of cases, N:

$$SD = \sqrt{\frac{\Sigma(X - M)^2}{N - 1}}.\qquad(2.2)$$

There is another form of the standard deviation that has N in the denominator instead of $(N - 1)$, but it is more appropriate for large samples or as a population statistic. Equation 2.2 is sometimes called the unbiased standard deviation because it adjusts for the tendency of sample SDs to be too small relative to the population value. The variance of X, s^2, equals its squared standard deviation.

Standardization gives all variables the same scale, which means that scores from standardized variables can all be interpreted in the same way. For example, a z score of 1.0 on variable X and a z score of 1.0 on variable Y both mean the same thing: they are one standard deviation above their respective means. Statistical results calculated with standardized variables are called *standardized estimates*. The values of standardized estimates usually range from –1 to + 1 (not always, though, as is demonstrated later) and are interpreted in the same way for all variables. For example, a Pearson correlation (described in more detail later) is calculated with variables in standardized form and its values cannot fall outside of the range –1 to + 1. A correlation between X and Y of, say, .50, means the same thing as a correlation of .50 between X and any other variable.

Unstandardized estimates are derived with unstandardized variables, that is, variables in their original metrics (scales) rather than expressed as z scores. The values of unstandardized estimates are not all limited to the same range. Their ranges are instead determined by the original metrics of the unstandardized variables. Thus, unstandardized estimates cannot be directly compared across variables with different scales. A covariance is an example of an unstandardized estimate. It is, in fact, an unstandardized form of the Pearson correlation. As defined in the previous chapter, the covariance between two variables, X and Y, is the product of their Pearson correlation and their standard deviations in their original metrics, or $cov_{XY} = r_{XY} SD_X SD_Y$. If variables Y and W have different scales, then the values of cov_{XY} and cov_{XW} are not directly comparable as is demonstrated in the accompanying table. Even though the Pearson correlations between X and Y and between X and W in this table are identical (.50), cov_{XY} and cov_{XW} are unequal because Y and W have different standard deviations (10 and 20, respectively).

	X	Y	W	Correlations	Covariances
SD	5	10	20	$r_{XY} = r_{XW} = .50$	$cov_{XY} = .50(5)(10) = 25$ $cov_{XW} = .50(5)(20) = 50$

Although researchers generally prefer standardized estimates, there is a strong preference in the SEM literature for unstandardized estimates. One reason is that most estimation procedures for SEM assume the analysis of unstandardized variables. It is possible with such procedures that some types of estimates such as results of tests of statistical significance may not be correct when standardized variables are analyzed. There are also situations where standardized estimates are inappropriate. These include (1) a multiple group analysis with samples that differ in their variabilities; (2) longitudinal measurement of variables that show increasing (or decreasing) variability over time; and (3) instances when the original metrics of the variables are meaningful rather than arbitrary (e.g., number of readmissions to a hospital, years to complete a degree, salaries in dollars). In all three situations, important information may be lost when variables are standardized. For example, suppose that X is measured on four occasions and that its variance is greater each time. When X is standardized, its variance will equal 1.0 at every occasion, which masks the increasing range of individual differences over time.

In examples of the application of SEM presented later in the book, both standardized and unstandardized estimates are presented whenever it makes sense to do so. Although interpretation of standardized estimates is easier to master, for the reasons just cited readers should not rely exclusively on them.

2.5   Bivariate Correlation and Regression

Correlation

Suppose that X and Y are both continuous, interval-level variables. The Pearson product–moment correlation coefficient between them, r_{XY}, is computed with X and Y in standardized form:

$$r_{XY} = \frac{\Sigma(z_X)(z_Y)}{N - 1}. \qquad (2.3)$$

The correlation r_{XY} is thus calculated by multiplying the z scores on X and Y for every case and then dividing by the number of cases minus 1. Values of r_{XY} range from -1 (perfect negative relation) to $+1$ (perfect positive relation). If r_{XY} is zero, then X and Y are unrelated. The squared correlation coefficient, r_{XY}^2, indicates the proportion of variance in Y accounted for by X (and vice versa). If r_{XY} is .50, for example, then X and Y share 25% of their variance in common.

The covariance between X and Y, cov_{XY}, is calculated with unstandardized variables. Readers already know that $cov_{XY} = r_{XY} SD_X SD_Y$ and that, unlike r_{XY}, the values of cov_{XY} are not limited to a standardized range. The covariance can also be expressed as a function of the raw scores on X and Y:

$$cov_{XY} = \frac{\Sigma(X - M_X)(Y - M_Y)}{N - 1}, \qquad (2.4)$$

where $(X - M_X)$ and $(Y - M_Y)$ are deviations of each subject's raw scores on X and Y from the respective sample means. Contrast Equation 2.4 for the covariance, which is based on products of raw deviation scores from the mean, with Equation 2.3 for the correlation, which is based on products of standardized deviation scores from the mean.[1]

As an example of the calculation of r_{XY} and cov_{XY}, consider the data for five cases presented at the top of Table 2.1. Listed for each case are raw scores on X and Y and z score equivalents of each raw score. Calculation of r_{XY} according to Equation 2.3 is demonstrated in the table. For these data, r_{XY} is .60. The squared correlation is $.60^2$, or .36, which means that X and Y share 36% of their variance in common. Although computation of cov_{XY} with the raw scores according to Equation 2.4 is not demonstrated in the table (readers are encouraged to do so), its value can also be obtained more directly by multiplying r_{XY} by SD_X and SD_Y, or $.60(6.21)(4.69) = 17.48$.

There are variations of the Pearson correlation for observed variables that are either categorical or ordinal. For example, a Pearson correlation between a dichotomous variable and a continuous one (e.g., gender and weight) is called a *point–biserial correlation* (r_{pb}); between two dichotomous variables (e.g., treatment/control and no relapse/relapsed), a *phi coefficient* (ϕ); and *Spearman's rank order correlation* (also called Spearman's rho, ρ) is for two ordinal variables (e.g., ranks assigned by different judges). There are also numerous other non-Pearson coefficients that estimate associations between different kinds of variables, but it is mainly r_{XY} and r_{pb} that are analyzed in SEM. (The analysis of some of these non-Pearson correlations for categorical or ordinal indicators of underlying latent variables that are assumed to be continuous is discussed in Chapter 7.)

Regression

Whereas correlation (and covariance) concerns association, regression is based more on prediction. In regression, one variable is designated as the predictor (X) and the other as the criterion (Y). Based on their association, the computer constructs a regression equation that generates a predicted score on the criterion (often represented by the symbol $\hat{Y}$) given a score on the predictor. This process is also described as regressing Y on X. (If X is the criterion, then the description "regressing X on Y" applies.) The regression equation for unstandardized variables is as follows:

---

[1]Equations 2.3 and 2.4 assume the use of Equation 2.2 to calculate SD, which has $(N - 1)$ in the denominator. If SD is calculated with N in the denominator, then Equations 2.2 and 2.3 also have N in their denominators instead of $(N - 1)$.

TABLE 2.1. Demonstration of Bivariate Correlation and Regression

	Observed scores					Predicted scores	
	Unstandardized		Standardized			Unstan-dardized	Stan-dardized
Case	X	Y	z_X	z_Y	$(z_X)(z_Y)$	$\hat{Y}$	$\hat{z}_Y$
A	3	24	−1.29	−.21	.27	21.40	−.77
B	8	20	−.48	−1.07	.51	23.65	−.29
C	10	22	−.16	−.64	.10	24.55	−.10
D	15	32	.65	1.49	.97	26.80	.39
E	19	27	1.29	.43	.55	28.60	.77
					$\Sigma = 2.40$		

Descriptive statistics

M	11	25	0	0	—	25	0
SD	6.21	4.69	1.00	1.00	—	2.79	.60
s^2	38.56	22.00	1.00	1.00	—	7.80	.36

Pearson correlation

$$r_{XY} = \Sigma(z_X)(z_Y)/(N - 1) = 2.40/4 = .60$$
$$r_{XY}^2 = .60^2 = .36$$

Covariance

$$cov_{XY} = r_{XY} SD_X SD_Y = .60(6.21)(4.69) = 17.48$$

Raw score regression line

$$\hat{Y} = B(X) + A = .45(X) + 20.05:$$
$$B = r_{XY}(SD_Y/SD_X) = .60(4.19/5.55) = .45$$
$$A = M_Y - B_X(M_X) = 25 - .45(11) = 20.05$$
$$r_{XY}^2 = s_{\hat{Y}}^2/s_Y^2 = 7.80/22.00 = .36$$

Standardized score regression line

$$\hat{z}_Y = r_{XY}(z_X) = .60(z_X)$$
$$r_{XY}^2 = s_{\hat{z}_Y}^2 = .36$$

Note. There is some slight rounding error in the above calculations due to the use of only two decimal places.

$$\hat{Y} = B(X) + A, \tag{2.5}$$

which defines a straight line. The slope of this regression line is indi-cated by B, and its intercept by A. The intercept A is the value of $\hat{Y}$ generated by the regression line when X equals zero. In the output of regression programs, the value of the intercept may be labeled as the "constant." The term B is called the *unstandardized regression coeffi-cient*. (The term "regression weight" is sometimes used instead of "regression coefficient.") Its value indicates the expected increase in the criterion, Y, as a function of the predictor, X. For example, if B equals 2.30, it means that an increase in X of one point is associated with an increase of 2.30 points in Y. Unstandardized regression coefficients less than zero (e.g., -2.30) have a similar interpretation except that they indicate an expected decrease in the criterion given an increase of one point in the predictor. However, note two things about an unstandardized regression coefficient: First, its value in part reflects the original metrics of X and Y. (More about this point below.) Thus, if the metric of either variable is changed (e.g., X is measured in centimeters instead of inches), then the value of B also changes. Second, because B is an unstandardized statistic, its values are not limited to a particular range. For example, it may be possible to derive values of B such as -13.58 or $1,546.79$. For both of these reasons, a large numerical value of B does not necessarily mean that X is an "important" or "strong" predictor of Y.

The values of B and A for a particular regression line are those that satisfy the *least squares criterion,* which means that the sum of squared differences between actual criterion scores and predicted scores yielded by the regression line, or $\Sigma(Y - \hat{Y})^2$, is as small as possible. The difference between an actual and a predicted score, or $(Y - \hat{Y})$, is called a *residual*. If $r_{XY} = 1.00$ (or -1.00; i.e., the relation is perfect), then the residual for every case is zero. If the association between X and Y is not perfect—with real data, the absolute value of r_{XY} is almost always less than 1—then some of the residuals differ from zero. Because residuals reflect the part of Y that X cannot be explained, they are uncorrelated with X ($r_{X(Y-\hat{Y})} = 0$). Also, the sum of the variances of the predicted scores ($s_{\hat{Y}}^2$) and the residuals ($s_{(Y-\hat{Y})}^2$) exactly equals the variance of the observed scores, or

$$s_Y^2 = s_{\hat{Y}}^2 + s_{(Y-\hat{Y})}^2 = s_Y^2(r_{XY}^2) + s_Y^2(1 - r_{XY}^2). \qquad (2.6)$$

The unstandardized regression coefficient for predicting Y from X, B, is related to r_{XY} and the standard deviations of X and Y as follows:

$$B = r_{XY}(SD_Y/SD_X). \qquad (2.7)$$

Thus B is analogous to a covariance in that it reflects the correlation between X and Y and their variabilities in the original metrics of each variable. (Recall that $cov_{XY} = r_{XY} SD_X SD_Y$.) The intercept of the regression line for predicting Y from X, A, is related to both the unstandardized regression coefficient and the means of X and Y:

$$A = M_Y - B(M_X). \tag{2.8}$$

When X and Y are standardized, their means equal zero and their standard deviations are 1, which simplifies the regression equation for generating a predicted z score on Y ($\hat{z}_Y$), given an observed z score on X, to the following:

$$\hat{z}_Y = r_{XY}(z_X). \tag{2.9}$$

Equation 2.9 also describes a straight line but one with a slope equal to r_{XY} and an intercept equal to zero. (Because the means of z_X and z_Y are zero, the intercept is also zero.) For two variables in standardized form, the correlation between them is also the *standardized regression coefficient*. For example, if a subject's z score on X is 1.00 (i.e., one standard deviation above the mean) and r_{XY} is .75, then $\hat{z}_Y$ for this case is .75(1.00), or .75 (i.e, three-quarters of a standard deviation above the mean on Y). A standardized regression coefficient thus indicates the expected increase in Y in standard deviation units given an increase in X of one full standard deviation. Unlike the unstandardized regression coefficient B, the value of the standardized coefficient (r_{XY}) is unaffected by changes in the scale of either X or Y. If the metric of X is changed from inches to centimeters, for instance, the value of its standardized regression coefficient remains the same.

Calculation of the regression equations and predicted scores for Y is demonstrated with the data in Table 2.1. The raw score regression line for these data is

$$\hat{Y} = .45(X) + 20.05.$$

Thus, scores on Y are expected to increase by .45 points for every increase in X of one whole point. If X is parental IQ and Y is child IQ, for example, then every one-point increase in parental IQ leads to a predicted increase in child IQ of .45 points. The intercept for the above regression equation, 20.05, is the value of $\hat{Y}$ when X is zero. Also outlined in Table 2.1 is another way to express the concept of explained variance: note that r_{XY} for these data is .60 and that r_{XY}^2 is .36; also note that the ratio of the variance of the unstandardized predicted scores over the variance of the observed scores, or $s_{\hat{Y}}^2/s_Y^2 =$

7.80/22.00, equals the squared correlation, .36. Thus, r_{XY}^2 is literally the proportion of Y's variability that is explainable by X in the form of predicted scores generated from the latter.

The regression line for predicting Y from X in standardized form for the data of Table 2.1 is

$$\hat{z}_Y = .60(z_X).$$

Thus, an increase in X of one full standard deviation is associated with an expected increase in Y of .60 standard deviations. To show the relation between the standardized and unstandardized regression coefficients for these data, an increase in X of one standard deviation in raw score terms equals 6.21 points ($SD_X = 6.21$). This much raw score change in X is, according to the unstandardized regression coefficient for these data (.45), associated with a change in Y of .45(6.21) = 2.79 points. Because the standard deviation for Y is 4.69, a change of 2.79 raw scores points is equivalent to a change of 2.79/4.69, or .60 standard deviations, which equals the standardized regression coefficient. Also presented in Table 2.1 is another way to represent the proportion of explained variance but this time in terms of the standardized variables. Note the variance of the predicted z scores, $s_{\hat{z}_Y}^2$, equals .36, which is r_{XY}^2 for these data. Because the observed z scores on Y have a variance of 1, the ratio of the variance of the predicted over observed z scores on Y is .36, which equals the squared Pearson correlation for these data.

Readers are encouraged to work through all of the derivations for the data of Table 2.1 as a check of their understanding. Left as exercises are computations of the residual scores for these data in unstandardized $(Y - \hat{Y})$ and standardized form $(z_Y - \hat{z}_Y)$, the variances of the residuals and how these values relate to the variance of Y in unstandardized and standardized form (e.g., Equation 2.6), and their respective correlations with X and z_X. (Both correlations should equal zero within the limits of rounding error.)

Assumptions

The assumptions of bivariate correlation and regression are listed below. These assumptions also apply to multiple correlation and regression:

1. The relation between X and Y is linear.
2. The residuals have a mean of zero and are independent, nor-

mally distributed, and have variances that are uniform across the levels of X. (The latter is known as *homoscedasticity*.)

The assumption of linearity is discussed in the next section. The requirements listed under 2 above are necessary for significance testing of regression coefficients. Among these requirements, the assumption of independence is probably the most crucial. Independence means that error in predicting Y from X for one case is unrelated to that of another case. For example, the independence assumption may be violated if students copied answers from each other while completing a test. The independence assumption may also be violated if Y is measured on more than one occasion. The residuals of repeated measures variables tend to be *autocorrelated*, which means that whatever leads to unpredictability on one occasion is related to the same on another occasion. Violation of the independence assumption compromises the accuracy of tests of significance. (Significance tests are covered later.) The normality and homoscedasticity assumptions are less critical. For example, results of significance tests of regression coefficients are relatively robust against moderate violations of these requirements. The regression modules of many general statistical packages offer options for empirically checking the independence, normality, and homoescasticity of the residuals. Readers are referred to Cohen and Cohen (1983, pp. 125–130), Pedhazur (1982, pp. 36–39), and Tabachnick and Fidell (1996, pp. 136–139, 174–178) for examples of the screening of residuals in regression analyses.

2.6   Factors That Affect the Magnitudes of Correlations

Because the covariance is the basic datum of SEM and the correlation is part of the covariance, it is important to be aware of factors that affect the magnitudes of correlations. That is, although the values of r_{XY} theoretically range from –1 to +1, its actual range can be narrowed closer to zero under certain conditions, listed below (these same conditions also affect the magnitudes of multiple correlations, which are discussed later):

1. *Linearity.* The correlation coefficient r_{XY} reflects only linear relations. If the relation between X and Y is nonlinear, then r_{XY} could be about zero. (More about linearity below.)
2. *Variability.* If the variability of either X or Y is relatively nar-

row (restricted), then r_{XY} may be small. A greater range of individual differences allows for potentially larger correlations.

3. *Relative shapes of distributions.* If the shapes of the frequency distributions of X and Y are very different (e.g., one variable is negatively skewed and the other positively skewed), then the maximum absolute value of r_{XY} may be constrained. Evaluation of the shapes of frequency distributions and the related issue of outliers (extreme scores) is covered in Chapter 4.

4. *Reliability.* The absolute value of r_{XY} tends to decline as the measurement of either X or Y is less reliable. The topic of reliability is discussed in Chapter 7.

5. *Validity.* Validity concerns in part the hypothetical constructs measured by X and Y. As X and Y measure either the same construct or ones that covary, the absolute value of r_{XY} tends to increase. Validity is considered in more detail in Chapter 7.

Presented in Figure 2.1 are examples of linear and nonlinear relations between X and Y. Figure 2.1(a) shows a positive linear relation: as X increases, so does Y. Furthermore, the rate of the increase is uniform across X. There are two general kinds of nonlinear relations, curvilinear and interactive. Two examples of *curvilinear relations* between X and Y are presented in Figure 2.1(b). The one plotted with the solid line is a quadratic relation in which scores on Y first increase and then decrease as scores on X rise. If X is anxiety and Y is performance, for example, then this quadratic relation would indicate that only moderate levels of anxiety facilitate performance. The curvilinear relation plotted with the dashed line is cubic because it changes direction twice: first scores on Y increase, then decrease, then increase again as the level of X increases.

A second kind of nonlinear relation is an *interactive relation* (also called an *interaction effect*), an example of which is illustrated in Figure 2.1(c). Unlike curvilinear relations, interactive relations involve at least three variables. If the relation of X to Y changes as a function of a third variable W, then an interaction effect is indicated. Figure 2.1(c) shows the relations between X and Y for subjects who have high versus low scores on a third variable W. (Variable W could also be a dichotomous variable that represents group membership such as gender.) Although the relation between X and Y is linear at both levels of W, its direction changes from positive at high levels on W to negative at low levels. As an example of an interaction effect, suppose that X in Figure 2.1(c) is motivation, Y is effort, and W is the expectancy that effort will lead to success. For subjects who expect that their efforts have a high chance of paying off (high scores on W),

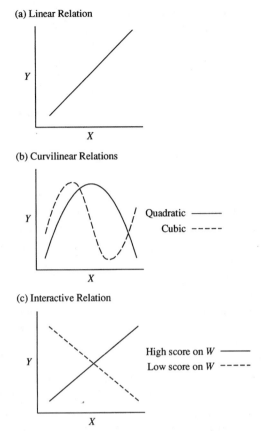

FIGURE 2.1. Examples of (a) linear and (b) curvilinear relations between X and Y and (c) an interactive relation of X and W to Y.

motivation and effort (X and Y) may be positively related. For subjects who do not expect their efforts to be fruitful (low scores on W), the relation between motivation and effort may be negative (i.e., those who are motivated are even less likely to try). In this sense, W, expectancy, could be called a *moderator variable* because it moderates the relation between X and Y, motivation and effort. The term *moderator effect* is sometimes used to refer to an interaction effect.

If one were to compute Pearson correlations between X and Y for graphs (b) or (c) of Figure 2.1, the values of r_{XY} would be about zero. These results are potentially misleading because both graphs (b) and (c) show strong albeit nonlinear relations between X and Y. Although correlations (and thus covariances) do not reflect nonlinear relations, it is nevertheless possible to represent nonlinear relations, either curvilinear or interactive, in a regression equation. The technique of multiple regression (reviewed later) is required to do so, however. It is also necessary to create special variables that represent nonlinear effects and include them in the regression equation. The same basic method used in multiple regression to analyze nonlinear effects is also used in SEM. Unlike multiple regression, though, SEM allows the analysis of nonlinear relations of both observed and latent variables. The analysis of nonlinear effects in SEM is an advanced topic that is discussed in Chapter 10.

It is also important to be aware of factors that do *not* affect the magnitude of r_{XY}. The means of X and Y (M_X and M_Y) have no bearing on r_{XY} (or on cov_{XY}). Look again at the raw scores of Table 2.1. Suppose that a constant of 10 points is added to the scores of X for every subject. Although the mean of X is increased by 10 points (from 11 to 21), the value of r_{XY} (.60) does not change nor does that of SD_X (6.21). Thus, a statistical analysis that involves only covariances is insensitive to changes in means. In many data analyses, however, it is of utmost interest to take means into account. For example, when groups are compared or when a variable is measured longitudinally, information about means may be critical. Fortunately, there is a way in SEM to analyze means in addition to covariances. It involves representing an intercept term in a structural equation model. Recall that the intercept (A) of a regression equation for unstandardized variables reflects the means of all variables (see Equations 2.8 and 2.12). The inclusion of intercept terms in structural equation models as a way to analyze means is described in Chapter 10.

Another factor that does not affect the magnitude of r_{XY} is N, the sample size. This assumes that N is not extremely small. For instance, with only two cases r_{XY} must be either –1 or +1 if X and Y are not exactly equal for both cases. Apart from extremely small numbers of cases, N per se does not affect the absolute magnitude of r_{XY}. Sample size does affect other aspects of r_{XY} such as its sampling error and level of statistical significance; both concepts are discussed later in section 2.9.

2.7 Partial Correlation

The concept of an interactive effect introduces the idea that a third variable W can influence the observed correlation between X and Y. The technique of *partial correlation* also takes a third variable into account, but it concerns a different kind of phenomenon, *spuriousness*. To illustrate the concept of spuriousness, consider the correlations summarized in the accompanying table for three variables measured among children. Although the correlation between shoe size and vocabulary breadth is fairly substantial (r_{XY} = .50), it is hardly surprising because both are probably caused by a third variable, W, age (i.e, maturation). If the observed relation between X and Y is due entirely to one or more common causes, then their association is said to be spurious.

	X	Y	W
X shoe size	—		
Y vocabulary breadth	.50	—	
W age	.80	.60	—

As its name suggests, the technique of partial correlation involves partialing out the effect of a third variable, W, from both X and Y and reestimating their association. The expressions "controlling for W" or "holding W constant" describe partial correlation. These same expressions are sometimes used in experimental studies, but note that partial correlation is based on a statistical correction. The partial correlation in this example is represented by the symbol $r_{XY \cdot W}$. The subscript of $r_{XY \cdot W}$ indicates that W has been partialed out of both X and Y. The formula for partial correlation is

$$r_{XY \cdot W} = \frac{r_{XY} - r_{XW} r_{YW}}{\sqrt{(1 - r_{XW}^2)(1 - r_{YW}^2)}}. \tag{2.10}$$

The numerator in the above equation reflects one aspect of statistically holding W constant: r_{XW} and r_{YW} are literally subtracted out of r_{XY}. The denominator adjusts the total standardized variance of X and Y by subtracting out the portions of each explained by W (e.g., $(1 - r_{XW}^2)$). Applied to the correlations presented above, the partial correlation between shoe size (X) and vocabulary breadth (Y) controlling for age (W) is

$$r_{XY \cdot W} = \frac{.50 - (.80)(.60)}{\sqrt{(1 - .80^2)(1 - .60^2)}} = \frac{.02}{.48} = .04.$$

Because the association between X and Y essentially disappears when W is controlled (r_{XY} = .50 vs. $r_{XY \cdot W}$ = .04), their observed relation as indicated by r_{XY} may be a spurious one.

Equation 2.10 for partial correlation can be extended to control for two or more external variables. For example, the higher-order partial correlation $r_{XY \cdot UW}$ estimates the relation between X and Y with U

and W partialed out of both. There is a related coefficient called a *part correlation* or a *semipartial correlation* that partials external variables out of either X or Y but not both. An example of part correlation is not presented here, but it works on the same basic principle as partial correlation. See Cohen and Cohen (1983) and Pedhazur (1982) for more information about partial and part correlation. Also, SEM readily allows the representation and estimation of possible spurious associations due to one or more common causes, something that is introduced in Chapter 3.

2.8   Multiple Correlation and Regression

Basic Concepts

Multiple correlation and regression are extensions of bivariate correlation and regression that allow for two or more predictors of a single criterion. One of the main features of multiple correlation/regression (from this point described simply as multiple regression) is that it corrects for intercorrelations among the predictors. Suppose that the bivariate correlations between predictors X_1 and X_2 and the criterion Y are respectively .40 and .50. If the correlation between X_1 and X_2 is zero, then their squared correlations with Y can be added together ($.40^2 + .50^2 = .16 + .25 = .41$) to yield the total proportion of Y's variance explained by them. In the more likely event that X_1 and X_2 covary, then adding their squared bivariate correlations with Y yields a total proportion that is too high. This is so because some of the variance of Y explained by each of the predictors overlaps (is redundant) due to their intercorrelation.

The results of a multiple regression analysis yield two general types of estimates: (1) of the total proportion of criterion variance explained by all predictors, and (2) of the relative importance of each predictor. Both types of estimates are adjusted for correlated predictors. We'll approach the concepts that underlie multiple regression first from the perspective of unstandardized variables. It is assumed in the following discussion that there are two predictor variables, but the concepts outlined below also apply when there are three or more predictors.

A multiple correlation is often represented by the symbol $R_{Y \cdot 12}$ (the subscript indicates that Y is predicted by X_1 and X_2). A multiple correlation is simply a Pearson correlation between actual scores on Y and predicted scores ($\hat{Y}$); that is, $R_{Y \cdot 12} = r_{Y\hat{Y}}$. The squared multiple correlation, $R_{Y \cdot 12}^2$, indicates the overall proportion of variance in Y explained by both of its predictors. Unlike Pearson correlations, though, multiple correlations theoretically range from 0 to 1. Note that the same factors that can restrict the observed values of Pearson correlations also affect $R_{Y.12}$ (section 2.6).

Predicted raw scores ($\hat{Y}$s) are generated in multiple regression with an equation that has the same general form as in bivariate regression but includes an additional predictor:

$$\hat{Y} = B_1(X_1) + B_2(X_2) + A. \qquad (2.11)$$

The above regression equation does not describe a straight line; instead, it defines a plane with a slope respective to X_1 of B_1, a slope respective to X_2 of B_2, and an intercept of A. The Bs in Equation 2.11 are the unstandardized regression coefficients. As in bivariate regression, the values of the Bs and the intercept (A) in multiple regression are those that satisfy the least squares criterion in a particular sample (i.e., $\Sigma(Y - \hat{Y})^2$ is as small as possible). The intercept in Equation 2.11, A, is similar to its bivariate counterpart (see Equation 2.7) in that it equals $\hat{Y}$ when both predictors are zero and can be expressed as a function of the unstandardized coefficients and the means of all variables. With two predictors, the intercept, A, is

$$A = M_Y - B_1(M_1) - B_2(M_2). \qquad (2.12)$$

Unstandardized regression coefficients B_1 and B_2 of Equation 2.11 indicate the expected raw score increase in Y given an increase of a single point in one predictor while we are controlling for the other. For example, if $B_1 = 5.40$ and $B_2 = 3.65$, then Y is expected to increase by 5.40 points given a change in X_1 of one point, with X_2 held constant; likewise, a one-point increase in X_2 predicts a 3.65 point change in Y while we are controlling for X_1. Because unstandardized regression coefficients reflect the scales of their respective predictors, the values of Bs from predictors with different raw score metrics are not directly comparable.

For standardized variables, the regression equation for generating predicted z scores on Y, $\hat{z}_Y$, is as follows:

$$\hat{z}_Y = \beta_1(z_1) + \beta_2(z_2), \qquad (2.13)$$

where z_1 and z_2 are z scores on X_1 and X_2, and β_1 and β_2 are the standardized regression coefficients, which are also called *beta weights*. Beta weights indicate expected increase in Y in standard deviation units controlling for the other predictors. Because the standard deviations of standardized variables are all 1.0, the values of beta weights can be directly compared across the predictors. For example, if β_1 equals .40, it means that Y is expected to increase by .40 standard deviations given an increase in X_1 of one full standard deviation controlling for X_2; the term β_2 has an analogous meaning except that X_1 is held constant. Because beta weights are corrected for intercorrelations among the predictors, their absolute values are usually less than the corresponding Pearson correlations of the predictors with the criterion. This is not always true, however. Absolute values of beta weights can exceed the corresponding correlations. It is also possible for the absolute values of beta weights to be greater than 1.0. When either occurs, a *suppression* effect is indicated. Suppression is described later.

When there are only two predictors, the values of β_1 and β_2 are related to the observed correlations as follows:

$$\beta_1 = \frac{r_{Y1} - r_{Y2}r_{12}}{1 - r_{12}^2} \quad \text{and} \quad \beta_2 = \frac{r_{Y2} - r_{Y1}r_{12}}{1 - r_{12}^2}, \tag{2.14}$$

where r_{Y1}, r_{Y2}, and r_{12} are correlations among the criterion and predictors. Beta weights are analogous to partial correlations in that both correct for a third variable (see Equation 2.10), but beta weights are not correlations. (Recall that the absolute values of βs can exceed 1. Also compare Equations 2.14 and 2.10.) Note that if the predictors are independent ($r_{12} = 0$), then each beta weight equals the corresponding correlation (i.e., there is no adjustment for correlated predictors). When there are more than two predictors in the equation, the formulas for the beta weights are more complicated but follow the same basic principles.

The squared multiple correlation can also be expressed as a function of the beta weights and the correlations of the predictors with the criterion. With two predictors, we have

$$R_{Y\cdot12}^2 = \beta_1(r_{Y1}) + \beta_2(r_{Y2}). \tag{2.15}$$

The role of beta weights as corrections for the other predictor is also apparent in the above formula. Note that if $r_{12} = 0$, then $\beta_1 = r_{Y1}$ and $\beta_2 = r_{Y2}$ in Equation 2.14, which implies that the squared multiple correlation is simply the sum of the squared Pearson correlations, $r_{Y1}^2 + r_{Y2}^2$. If $r_{12} \neq 0$, as when the predictors covary, then β_1 and β_2 do not equal the corresponding correlations and $R_{Y\cdot12}^2$ is not the simple sum of r_{Y1}^2 and r_{Y2}^2 (it is less).

The relation between unstandardized and standardized regression coefficients in multiple regression is analogous to that in bivariate regression. For example, the unstandardized coefficient for X_1 is related to its beta weight as follows:

$$B_1 = \beta_1(SD_Y/SD_1), \qquad (2.16)$$

where SD_1 is X_1's standard deviation. (Compare Equations 2.16 and 2.7.)

Presented in the upper part of Table 2.2 is a set of observed scores for five cases. In this table X_1 and Y have the same values as X and Y of Table 2.1. Variable X_2 in Table 2.2 is new and is the second predictor of Y. Reported below the observed scores in the table are values of descriptive statistics for all three variables including their intercorrelations. Note that r_{Y1}, the Pearson correlation between X_1 and Y, is .60, the same as for the data in Table 2.1.

The raw scores from Table 2.2 were analyzed with a multiple regression program, and part of the output from this analysis is reported in the middle of Table 2.2. The overall multiple correlation between the predictors and the criterion is .80, which means that 64% of Y's variance is explained by X_1 and X_2. Also note that this proportion is less than the sum of their squared Pearson correlations with Y: $.64 < .60^2 + .75^2 = .93$. This occurs because the predictors covary, which is taken into account in the calculation of $R^2_{Y.12}$ (Equation 2.14). Reported as an unstandardized estimate in the middle of Table 2.2 is the constant (i.e., the intercept), which is 10.77 for these data. The unstandardized regression coefficients for X_1 and X_2 are respectively .24 and .19. If X_1 increases by one point, then Y is predicted to increase by .24 points while we are controlling for X_2; likewise, scores on Y are expected to increase by .19 points given a one-point increase in X_2 while we are controlling for X_1. However, because X_1 and X_2 have different raw score metrics ($SD_1 = 6.21$, $SD_2 = 14.58$), the values of their unstandardized regression coefficients are not directly comparable. To gauge the relative importance of X_1 and X_2 to the prediction of Y, one can instead compare their beta weights, which are respectively .32 and .60. These values indicate that the relative predictive power of X_2 is about twice that of X_1. That is, a change in X_2 of one standard deviation leads to an expected increase in Y of .60 standard deviations while we are controlling for X_1. In contrast, a similar change in X_1 with X_2 held constant increases scores on Y by only .32 standard deviations. Also note that each beta weight is less than the corresponding Pearson correlations of the predictor with the criterion ($\beta_1 = .32$, $r_{Y1} = 60$; $\beta_2 = .60$, $r_{Y2} = .75$).

Reported in the bottom part of Table 2.2 are various calculations

TABLE 2.2. Demonstration of Multiple Correlation and Regression

	Observed scores						Predicted scores	
	Unstandardized			Standardized			Unstan-dardized	Stan-dardized
Case	X_1	X_2	Y	z_1	z_2	z_Y	$\hat{Y}$	$\hat{z}_Y$
A	3	65	24	−1.29	.34	−.21	24.04	−.26
B	8	50	20	−.48	−.69	−1.07	22.36	−.70
C	10	40	22	−.16	−1.37	−.64	20.91	−1.09
D	15	70	32	.65	.69	1.49	27.91	.77
E	19	75	27	1.29	1.03	.43	29.84	1.29

Descriptive statistics

M	11	60	25	0	0	0	25	0
SD	6.21	14.58	4.69	1.00	1.00	1.00	3.76	.80
s^2	38.56	212.50	22.00	1.00	1.00	1.00	14.14	.64

Correlations: $r_{12} = .47$, $r_{Y1} = .60$, $r_{Y2} = .75$, $r_{Y\hat{Y}} = .80$

Output from a regression program

	Regression weights			
Variable	Unstandardized	Standardized (beta weight)	$R_{Y \cdot 12}$	$R_{Y \cdot 12}^2$
X_1	.24	.32	.80	.64
X_2	.19	.60		
Constant	10.77			

Multiple correlation

$$R_{Y \cdot 12} = r_{Y\hat{Y}} = .80$$
$$R_{Y \cdot 12}^2 = .80^2 = \beta_1(r_1) + \beta_2(r_{Y2}) = .32(.60) + .60(.75) = .64$$
$$= s_{\hat{Y}}^2/s_Y^2 = 14.14/22.00 = .64$$
$$= s_{\hat{z}_Y}^2 = .64$$

Beta weights

$$\beta_1 = (r_{Y1} - r_{Y2}\, r_{12})/(1 - r_{12}^2) = [.60 - .75(.47)]/(1 - .47^2) = .25/.78 = .32$$
$$\beta_2 = (r_{Y2} - r_{Y1}\, r_{12})/(1 - r_{12}^2) = [.75 - .60(.47)]/(1 - .47^2) = .47/.78 = .60$$

Standardized score regression equation

$$\hat{z}_Y = \beta_1(z_1) + \beta_2(z_2) = .32(z_1) + .60(z_2)$$

Raw score regression equation

$$\hat{Y} = B_1(X_1) + B_2(X_2) + A = .24(X_1) + .19(X_2) + 10.77:$$
$$B_1 = \beta_1(SD_Y/SD_1) = .32(4.69/6.21) = .24$$
$$B_2 = \beta_2(SD_Y/SD_2) = .60(4.69/14.58) = .19$$
$$A = M_Y - B_1(M_1) - B_2(M_2) = 25 - .24(11) - .19(60) = 10.77^a$$

[a]There is noticeable rounding error in this calculation due to the use of only two decimal places. Using three decimal places (i.e., .242 for B_1 and .193 for B_2) brings the value calculated by hand closer to 10.77.

for $R_{Y·12}$ and $R_{Y·12}^2$, standardized and unstandardized regression coefficients, regression equations, and predicted scores. These calculations illustrate the concepts discussed in this section. They also highlight some of similarities between bivariate and multiple correlation and regression. For instance, the squared multiple correlation, $R_{Y·12}^2$, is expressed in Table 2.2 as the ratio of the variance of raw predicted criterion scores over the variance of the observed raw criterion scores, which is the same basic relation for r_{XY}^2 that is outlined in Table 2.1. Altogether there is a lot of information summarized in Table 2.2. Readers are encouraged to work through these calculations as a check on their understanding of the basic concepts of multiple regression.

The Problem of Omitted Variables

Sometimes researchers use multiple regression in a strictly predictive sense, which means that they are mainly interested in determining the overall predictive power of a set of a variables against some criterion. In such cases, the overall R (or R^2, the percent of explained variance) is the primary statistic of interest. For a strictly predictive application of multiple regression, about all one really needs to be concerned about are whether the statistical assumptions are met (linearity; independent and homoscedastic residuals with means of zero; section 2.5). However, there are other, broader uses of multiple regression that involve the interpretation of regression coefficients of individual predictors. This usually occurs in one of two contexts. The first is when the researcher does not have hypotheses about causality but wishes to look at regression coefficients as estimates of the "true" relation of each predictor to the criterion holding the other predictors constant. The second context is when the researcher wishes to evaluate hypotheses about causality among observed variables and uses multiple regression to estimate a path model. Although this particular application of multiple regression is described in Chapter 5, it has in common with the first, noncausal context the interpretation of individual regression coefficients.

Whenever it is important to interpret regression coefficients, one needs to be concerned about the potential problem of omitted variables. An omitted variable accounts for some unique proportion of the variance of the criterion but is not included in the analysis. The omission of a relevant variable from a regression equation is a type of *specification error* that may occur due to a lack of knowledge about all of the predictors of some criterion. The potential consequences of omitted variables are outlined below for the case of multiple regression used in a noncausal context, but readers should note that many of the same issues are relevant when multiple regression is used to estimate a path model. The specification error of omitted causal variables in path analysis is considered in Chapter 5.

Suppose that variables X_1 and X_2 both covary with Y, the criterion variable. The Pearson correlations are as follows: $r_{Y1} = .40$, $r_{Y2} = .60$. A researcher measures only X_1 and uses it as the sole predictor of Y in a bivariate regression. The standardized regression coefficient for X_1—the *included variable* in this analysis—equals the Pearson correlation r_{Y1}, or .40 (Equation 2.9). If the researcher in this example had the foresight to also measure X_2 (the *omitted variable*) and enter it along with X_1 as a predictor of Y, then the standardized regression coefficient for X_1 (the beta weight, β_1) in this multiple regression analysis may not equal .40, the value of r_{Y1}. If not, then r_{Y1} as a standardized coefficient with X_1 as the only predictor of Y is biased relative to β_1, which is derived with both X_1 and X_2 in the equation. *However— and this is an important point—the amount of this potential bias varies with the correlation between the included variable X_1 and the omitted variable X_2.* Specifically, if the included and omitted variables are uncorrelated ($r_{12} = 0$), then there is no bias because the value of the included variable's regression coefficient is the same regardless of whether the omitted variable is in the equation ($r_{Y1} = \beta_1$). As the absolute value of their correlation increases ($r_{12} \neq 0$), though, the amount of bias due to the omission of X_2 from the regression equation becomes greater.

To illustrate these points about bias due to omitted variables, consider the results of the three regressions summarized in the accompanying table. In all three cases, X_2 is considered the omitted variable. (The same principles hold if X_1 is viewed as the omitted variable.) Also constant across all three cases are the Pearson correlations between X_1 and X_2 and the criterion Y: $r_{Y1} = .40$, $r_{Y2} = .60$. The only thing that varies across the three analyses is the value of r_{12}, the correlation between the included and the omitted variables. Reported for each analysis are the overall multiple correlation ($R_{Y.12}$) and the beta weights for the regression of Y on X_1 and X_2 (β_1, β_2); readers are encouraged to use Equations 2.14 and 2.15 to reproduce these values. For each case, compare the two values in boldface, r_{Y1} and β_1. The difference between these values indicates the amount of the bias in X_1's bivariate standardized regression coefficient (r_{Y1}) due to the omission of X_2 from the equation. Note that when the omitted variable X_2 is uncorrelated with the included variable X_1 (case 1, $r_{12} = 0$), there is no bias; that is, the standardized regression coefficient for X_1 is the same regardless of whether X_2 is in the equation ($r_{Y1} = \beta_1 = .40$). However, when r_{12} is .20 instead of zero (case 2), then β_1 is lower than r_{Y1}, .29 versus .40, respectively. This occurs because β_1 controls for the correlation between X_1 and X_2 whereas r_{Y1} does not. Thus, r_{Y1} here *overestimates* the association between X_1 and Y relative to β_1. In case 3 in the table, the correlation between X_1 and X_2 is even higher ($r_{12} = .40$), which for these data results in even more bias in the value of r_{Y1} relative to that of β_1 (.40 vs. .19, respectively).

| | | Pearson | Regression with both predictors | |
Case	Predictor	r with Y	β	$R_{Y \cdot 12}$
1 $r_{12} = 0$	X_1 included	.40	.40	.72
	X_2 omitted	.60	.60	
2 $r_{12} = .20$	X_1 included	.40	.29	.66
	X_2 omitted	.60	.54	
3 $r_{12} = .40$	X_1 included	.40	.19	.62
	X_2 omitted	.60	.52	

Omitting a variable that is correlated with others in the equation does not always result in regression coefficients that overestimate the relation of included predictors to the criterion. For example, if X_1 is the included variable and X_2 the omitted variable, it is also possible for the absolute value of r_{Y1} to be *less than* that of β_1 (i.e., r_{Y1} *underestimates* the relation indicated by β_1) or even for r_{Y1} and β_1 to have different signs. Both of these situations indicate a suppression effect, which is described momentarily. It should be noted, though, that overestimation due to the omission of a variable probably occurs more often than underestimation (suppression). Also, the pattern of bias may be more complicated when there are multiple included and omitted variables (e.g., overestimation for some included predictors; underestimation for others). Although the direction of the bias depends upon the specific intercorrelations, the absolute magnitude of the bias tends to increase as included and excluded variables are more highly correlated. See Bollen (1989, chap. 3) and Kenny (1979, pp. 62–65) for additional examples of bias due to omitted variables.

There is another that way that the omitted variable problem can be viewed. Recall that one of the principles of least squares derivation of predicted scores ($\hat{Y}$) is that the residuals ($Y - \hat{Y}$)—the part of each subject's score that is not explained—are uncorrelated with the predictors (e.g., Equation 2.6). As a result, the regression coefficients are derived under the condition that omitted variables that may account for residual Y variance are assumed to be unrelated to variables in the equation. As discussed above, if this presumption is warranted, then there is no bias. If not, however, then individual regression coefficients may be too high or too low (over- or underestimation). The consequence of least squares estimation that unexplained variance is unrelated to the predictors has implications for the use of multiple regression to estimate path models, a topic discussed in Chapter 5.

Variables are typically excluded because they are not measured by the researcher. Thus, it is difficult to know by how much and in what direction the regression coefficients of included predictors may be biased. Mauro (1990) devised a statistical procedure to estimate bias due to what he lightheartedly called the heartbreak of LOVE (left-out variables error). Briefly described, Mauro's procedure requires that the researcher indicate a range of correlations between a hypothetical omitted predictor and an included predictor already in the equation. Given such estimates, Mauro's technique indicates the magnitudes of the correlations between the omitted predictor and the criterion that would be required to substantially alter the estimate of the regression coefficient of the included predictor if the excluded predictor were also in the equation. Some potential correlations between the excluded predictor and the criterion may be mathematically implausible, which rules out their consideration. Other values could suggest that bias due to omission of the excluded predictor is either negligible or more substantial. The accuracy of these estimates depends upon the researcher's initial assumptions about correlations between the included and omitted predictors, but Mauro's technique also accommodates a range of estimates instead of just a single value. The specific mechanics of this technique are not described here, but Mauro presents examples of its application to the study of the perceived justice of an adjudicative process and factors that predict capital sentencing.

Even with procedures like Mauro's, it is unrealistic to expect the researcher to know and be able to measure all the relevant predictors of a criterion. In this sense, most regression equations are probably misspecified to some degree. If omitted predictors are essentially uncorrelated with included predictors, then the consequences of a specification error may be slight. If not, then the consequences of a misspecified regression equation are more serious. The main way to avoid a serious specification error is through a careful review of extant theory and research, which may decrease the potential number of omitted predictors.

Suppression

Suppression occurs when either the absolute value of a predictor's beta weight is greater than its Pearson correlation with the criterion (e.g., $\beta_1 = .60$, $r_{Y1} = .40$) or when the two have different signs (e.g., $\beta_1 = .10$, $r_{Y1} = -.30$). Suppression thus refers to the finding that the relation of a predictor to a criterion once corrected for its intercorrelation with other predictors is quite different from that suggested by its simple correlation with the criterion. An example of suppression is presented in the accompanying table. Note there that the correlation between psychotherapy and suicide attempts is positive ($r_{Y1} = .19$), which suggests that the effects of therapy are harmful (more therapy, more attempts). Less surprising are the positive correlations between depression and suicide attempts ($r_{Y2} = .49$) and between depression and psychotherapy ($r_{12} = .70$). So people who are depressed, who are already at higher risk for suicide attempts, should not go to psychotherapy because being in therapy is also positively related to suicide attempts, right?

r_{12}	Predictor	r with Y (suicide attempts)	Regression with both predictors	
			β	$R_{Y \cdot 12}$
.70	X_1 psychotherapy	.19	−.30	.54
	X_2 depression	.49	.70	—

Well, no, and the reason is suppression. When both therapy and depression are predictors of suicide in a regression equation, the beta weight for therapy is negative ($\beta_1 = -.30$), which has the *opposite* sign of its correlation with the criterion ($r_{Y1} = .19$). Also, the beta weight for depression is *greater* than its correlation with suicide, $\beta_2 = .70$, $r_{Y2} = .49$. Both results are due to controlling for the other predictor (i.e., r_{12}). Here, people who are more depressed are also more likely to be in therapy. Depressed people are also more likely to attempt to harm themselves. Correcting for these associations in the multiple regression analysis reveals that the relation of psychotherapy to suicide attempts is actually negative once depressed is controlled. Also, the relation of depression to suicide attempts is even stronger once the beneficial effects of psychotherapy are held constant. Omit either psychotherapy or depression as a predictor of suicide attempts, and the results with the other remaining predictor are potentially misleading about its true relation to the criterion.

r_{12}	Predictor	r with Y (outcome)	Regression with both predictors	
			β	$R_{Y \cdot 12}$
.50	X_1 adjustment	.60	.80	.69
	X_2 social desirability	.00	−.40	—

As a second example of suppression, consider the correlations and beta weights presented in the accompanying table. Note there that adjustment is related to outcome ($r_{Y1} = .60$) but the measure of social desirability (the tendency to present oneself in a favorable but unrealistic light) is not ($r_{Y2} = 0$). When their association ($r_{12} = .50$) is controlled in a multiple regression analysis, however, both variables have nonzero beta weights ($\beta_1 = .80$, $\beta_2 = -.40$). These beta weights suggest that (1) adjustment is even a better predictor of outcome when we are controlling for a social desirability response set, and (2) this response set is negatively related to outcome once adjustment is partialed out. This example demonstrates that correlations of zero can mask true predictive relations once other variables are controlled. For more information about suppression, readers are referred to Smith, Ager, and Williams (1992).

The Role of Multiple Regression in SEM

Multiple regression is a widely used data-analytic method that is enormously flexible. As mentioned, it is possible with multiple regression to analyze nonlinear effects (curvilinear or interactive; more about this topic in Chapter 10). This property in combination with the capability to represent categorical variables (e.g., a control group vs. several treatment groups) as predictors implies that essentially any type of analysis of variance (ANOVA) can be performed with multiple regression. Thus, multiple regression, which is sometimes viewed as a "correlational" technique for nonexperimental data, can also be applied to analysis of means in experimental or nonexperimental studies. (A similar, overly narrow perception of SEM was mentioned in Chapter 1.)

However flexible the technique of multiple regression, its role in SEM is rather limited. Multiple regression is very useful in data screening (discussed in Chapter 4). Multiple regression can also be used in path analysis to analyze some but not all kinds of path models. If a structural equation model has either latent variables or assumes that certain residuals are correlated, then multiple regression cannot be used to estimate the model. Other kinds of estimation methods described later in the book—especially maximum likelihood estimation—are used much more often in SEM. Understanding the basic ideas of multiple regression discussed in this section, though, will provide readers with an useful cognitive "bridge" with which to cross over to other methods that are used more often in SEM.

2.9 Significance Testing

General Rationale

Many types of data analyses including SEM have an inferential as well as a descriptive focus. Inferential analyses concern the testing of hypotheses about population *parameters* with sample statistics. A parameter is some characteristic of a whole population such as a mean or a variance. Sample statistics, on the other hand, only estimate population parameters. Especially in the social sciences, a widely used tool for evaluating hypotheses about population parameters with sample estimates are tests of statistical significance. Most applications of significance tests usually concern whether the value of a sample statistic differs significantly from zero. For example, a value of r_{XY} in a particular sample may be .35. Is this sample correlation sufficiently greater than zero to be able to conclude at some level of probability that the population correlation is also greater than zero? As a second example, suppose that the mean score of the treatment group on the outcome measure is 10 points higher than that of the control group. Is this difference large enough to reasonably conclude that the treatment and control conditions really differ in the population? Although the procedure for testing whether a sample mean differs significantly from zero is described below, the same general logic underlies significance testing for other types of sample statistics such as variances and regression coefficients.

Suppose that X is a continuous variable measured in a sample with N cases, the mean (M) is 20, and the standard deviation (SD) is 15. To test whether this sample mean differs significantly from zero, one forms the ratio M/SE_M, where SE_M is the *standard error of the mean*. The SE_M is related to the standard deviation and the sample size as follows:

$$SE_M = SD/\sqrt{N}. \qquad (2.17)$$

Whereas SD indicates the variability of cases around the sample mean, SE_M estimates the variability of sample means (each derived from the scores of N cases) around the population mean.[2] Another way to describe SE_M is that it reflects the amount of sampling error among the means of independent samples. Under the assumption that the population mean is zero and that sample means are normally distributed around the population mean, SE_M is interpreted as is any standard deviation in a normal curve. For example, approximately 68% of the sample means are expected to fall within the range plus and minus one SE_M from the population mean, and about 95% of the sample means should fall within two SE_Ms from the population mean.

In large samples, the ratio M/SE_M is interpreted as a z statistic in a normal curve with a mean of zero and a standard deviation of SE_M. A rule of thumb for large samples is that if the absolute value of this ratio exceeds 2, then the sample mean differs significantly from zero at the .05 level of significance for a two-tailed test. The precise absolute value of z for the .05 level is 1.96. The .01 level of significance for a two-tailed test requires a higher absolute value of z, 2.58. Because tests of the significance of other types of sample statistics such as variances and regression coefficients have the same general form (i.e., the statistic divided by its standard error), the same large sample rule of thumb about significance at the .05 level applies. Within small samples, the ratio statistic/SE_M is a t statistic instead of a z statistic, which necessitates the use of special tables to determine critical values of t for significance at the .05 or .01 levels. Within large samples, t and z for the same parameter estimate are essentially equal.

Let's return to our example where $M = 20$ and $SD = 15$. If $N = 25$, then SE_M is 15 divided by the square root of 25, or 15/5 = 3. The ratio M/SE_M is 20/3 = 6.67. Because the sample size is small, this ratio is interpreted as a t statistic. Consulting a table of critical values of t for a sample size of 20 (i.e., degrees of freedom = 19) indicates that an absolute value of 2.09 is required for significance at the .05 level and an absolute value of 2.86 is required for the .01 level (both values are for a two-tailed test). Because the ratio of M/SE_M here (6.67) exceeds both tabled values, we conclude that the sample mean of 20 differs significantly from zero at the .01 level of significance.

Now let's increase the sample size to 400 cases. The value of SE_M, with SD divided by the square root of N, is now 15/20 = .75. Note that this value of SE_M is smaller than when N is 25 (.75 vs. 3). The smaller value of SE_M with a larger sample also yields a greater value of M/SE_M, which for $N = 400$ is 20/.75 = 26.67. (For $N = 25$, M/SE_M is 6.67.) Because the sample size is large, this ratio (26.67) is interpreted

[2]Equation 2.17 assumes the use of Equation 2.2 to calculate SD.

as a z statistic. This z statistic obviously exceeds the value required for significance at the .01 level.

This effect of sample size demonstrated above—larger samples lead to lower standard errors and greater values of M/SE_M—has four implications:

1. There is more sampling error with small samples than with large samples. Thus, statistical estimates calculated within small samples tend to be less stable than within larger samples.
2. Tests of significance tend to lead to rejection of the null hypothesis of no difference more often in larger samples than in smaller ones given the same value of a sample statistic.
3. A hypothesis with a sample statistic of trivial absolute magnitude that is not statistically significant in a small sample could be significant in a larger sample.
4. When a population parameter is actually different from zero (i.e., there is a real effect), significance tests conducted in large samples are said to be more *powerful* because they are more likely to be significant, which leads to the correct decision (i.e., the null hypothesis is rejected.)

It is worthwhile to briefly mention other factors that affect the power of a test of significance besides the sample size and the magnitude of a real effect in the population. These include (1) the general design of the study such as the representation of an independent variable as a between- or within-subject factor (e.g., respectively, independent vs. dependent samples); (2) the particular test of significance used; (3) the level of significance at which the null hypothesis is rejected (e.g., .05 or .01); and (4) the directionality of the test of the alternative hypothesis (i.e., one- or two-tailed test). The following combination of the four factors just mentioned lead to the greatest power: a within-subject design, a parametric test statistic (e.g., t or F) rather than a nonparametric statistic (e.g., the Mann–Whitney U), the .05 level of significance, and a one-tailed (directional) test of the alternative hypothesis.

Significance Testing in SEM

Significance testing of individual sample statistics in SEM has the same general form as just described. That is, the ratio of a sample statistic over its standard error tests whether the statistic is statistically different from zero. It also possible in SEM to conduct significance tests of entire models. Particular types of significance tests are described throughout the book for each SEM technique.

Readers should keep in mind three things about significance tests in SEM. First, because SEM is a large-sample technique, it may happen more often than in other kinds of analyses that small effects are statistically significant. Ways to guard against this possibility are suggested at various points throughout the book. Second, because most model-fitting programs assume the analysis of unstandardized variables, they usually report results of significance tests only for unstandardized estimates. Users of model-fitting programs often assume that results of significance tests of unstandardized estimates apply to the standardized estimates. For samples that are large and representative, this assumption may not be problematic. Readers should realize, however, that the significance level of an unstandardized estimate does not automatically apply to its standardized counterpart. Third, model-fitting programs that assume the analysis of unstandardized variables may derive incorrect standard errors when standardized variables are analyzed. The reasons for this potential inaccuracy are technical (e.g., Bollen, 1989, pp. 123–126; Boomsma, 1983; Cudeck, 1989; Loehlin, 1992, pp. 75–76), but standard errors are the denominators of significance tests. Although there are procedures to correct for potential bias in the calculation of standard errors for standardized variables (e.g., Bentler & Lee, 1983; Browne, 1982), they are not widely implemented in model-fitting programs. The SEPATH (Steiger, 1995) and RAMONA (Browne et al., 1994) programs are exceptions.

2.10 Summary

This chapter reviewed fundamental statistical concepts that underlie many aspects of SEM. Included among these concepts is the terminology for variables in SEM. Latent and observed variables are usually designated as exogenous or endogenous. The causes of exogenous variables are not represented in structural equation models; in contrast, endogenous variables are specified as caused by other variables. Variables analyzed in SEM are usually continuous and at least at the interval level of measurement. It is also possible to analyze categorical variables that represent group membership, but usually only as exogenous variables.

Many of the concepts of correlation and regression are central to the rationale of SEM. One of these ideas is that of statistical control— the partialing out of one or more variables from other variables, a standard feature of almost all models analyzed in SEM. Partialing provides one of the bases for testing hypotheses about observed correlations. For example, partial correlation, which controls for the effects of an external variable on X and Y, provides a test of spuriousness. That is, if the relation between X and Y disappears when the external variable is partialed out of both, then the external variable may be a common cause of X and Y. The technique of multiple regression performs a somewhat different type of statistical adjustment: Estimates of the relation of predictors to a criterion are corrected for their intercorrelations. The results of a multiple regression analysis can indicate that the relation of a predictor X to the criterion Y when the other predictors are controlled is different than suggested by r_{XY}. In some cases known as suppression, the sign of the estimate of the adjusted relation of X to Y may differ from that of r_{XY} or r_{XY} can be zero even though the adjusted relation of X to Y is not zero. One lesson of the techniques of partial correlation and multiple correlation is that the values of observed correlations may mask true relations between variable once intercorrelations with other variables are controlled. This is a fundamental concept in SEM.

Another lesson of multiple regression is the importance of including all relevant predictors of a criterion in a regression equation. Specifically, the omission of predictors that are correlated with those included in the equation is a type of specification error that may result in bias. The nature of this bias is that the regression coefficients for the included predictors may not reflect their relations with the criterion that would be revealed if the omitted predictors were also in the equation. The magnitude of this bias is greater as correlations between included and omitted predictors increase. If an omitted predictor is uncorrelated with included predictors, however, then there is no bias. Although it is unrealistic to expect the researcher to measure all relevant predictors or even know what they are, the number of omitted predictors may be reduced by review of extant theory and empirical research. A statistical procedure by Mauro (1990), described earlier, may also be useful for evaluating potential bias due to omitted predictors.

The general form of the test of whether a sample statistic differs significantly from zero is the same in SEM as in other statistical methods. With a large number of cases, the ratio of a sample statistic over its standard error is interpreted as a z test. If the absolute value of z is greater than 2, then the sample statistic differs from zero at the .05 level of significance. Model-fitting programs usually report tests of significance only for unstandardized estimates. Although users of model-fitting programs often assume that these results also apply to the standardized estimates, this is not guaranteed. Also, significance tests may not be accurate when standardized variables are analyzed.

The fundamental concepts discussed in this chapter set the stage for the overview of techniques in the SEM family and their relations to more standard statistical methods presented in the next chapter.

2.11   Recommended Readings

General Statistical Concepts

The books listed below provide comprehensive, undergraduate-level presentations of concepts such as correlation, regression, and significance testing.

Gravetter, F. J., & Wallnau, L. B. (1996). *Statistics for the behavioral sciences* (4th ed.). New York: West.

Minium, E. E., King, B. M., & Bear. G. (1993). *Statistical reasoning in psychology and education* (3rd ed.). New York: John Wiley.

Multiple Regression

The Cohen and Cohen (1983) and Pedhazur (1982) texts listed below are devoted to multiple regression and provide in-depth coverage of many of its applications. The work by Licht (1995) provides a chapter-length overview of the technique. The text by Keppel and Zedeck (1989) cover univariate data analysis from the perspective of both multiple regression and ANOVA. Chapters 4 and 5 of Nunnally and Bernstein (1994) provide excellent reviews of regression procedures.

Cohen, J., & Cohen, P. (1983). *Applied multiple regression/correlation for the behavioral sciences* (2nd ed.). Hillsdale, NJ: Erlbaum.

Keppel, G., & Zedeck, S. (1989). *Data analysis for research designs.* New York: Freeman.

Licht, M. H. (1995). Multiple regression and correlation. In L. G. Grimm & P. R. Yarnold (Eds.), *Reading and understanding multivariate statistics* (pp. 19–64). Washington, DC: American Psychological Association.

Nunally, J. C., & Bernstein, I. H. (1994). *Psychometric theory* (3rd ed.). New York: McGraw-Hill.

Pedhazur, E. J. (1982). *Multiple regression in behavioral research* (2nd ed.). New York: Holt, Rinehart & Winston.

CHAPTER THREE

SEM Family Tree

Great knowledge sees all in one.
Small knowledge breaks down into the many.
　—Chuang Tzu, fourth or third century B.C.,
　　China (in Merton, 1965, p. 40)

3.1　Foreword

The core SEM techniques—path analysis, confirmatory factor analysis, and the evaluation of hybrid models with features of both path and factor models—are reviewed in this chapter. Much of this presentation is organized around actual research examples. Data analysis options for each example are considered from two perspectives: first from that of standard statistical procedures, and then from that of one of the core SEM techniques. Assumptions, requirements, and limitations of the various analytical options are examined. In the spirit of the quotation that appears at the beginning of this chapter, the main goal of this chapter is to build a broader context for SEM, one that gives the reader a better sense of the connections between core SEM techniques and other analytical methods with which he or she may be more familiar. Before the research examples are presented, the symbols that are used in diagrams of models throughout this book are introduced.

3.2　Symbols for Model Diagrams

The expression "a picture is worth a thousand words" is a very apt one for SEM. Researchers who use SEM techniques often use diagrams to illustrate their hypotheses and summarize the results of the analysis. The ability to interpret and construct model diagrams is thus an important skill. There is a potential complication, though, one that was mentioned in Chapter 1: there is no single notational system in SEM, and this is also true for the diagrammatic presentation of models. Fortunately, some symbols are so widely used that they are essentially standard. Only a limited number of hypotheses can be represented with these standard symbols, however, so it is sometimes necessary to use other symbols for which there is less consensus.

Presented in Table 3.1 are the symbols that are used in model diagrams in this book. These symbols represent things such as types of variables, presumed causal or noncausal relations, or residual terms (unexplained variance). It is not important now that you understand all the symbols or definitions presented in the table because most are described in more detail later in this chapter. Symbols that are more or less standard in the SEM literature are designated in the table. Among these are the representation of observed variables with squares or rectangles, latent variables with circles or ellipses, presumed direct causal effects with a line and one arrowhead that points from cause to effect ($\rightarrow$), two such lines with arrowheads pointing in opposite directions to depict presumed reciprocal causality ($\rightleftarrows$), and a curved line with two arrowheads to depict the weaker assumption that two variables are simply correlated ($\curvearrowright$; for typographic convenience, this double-headed arrow appears as $\leftrightarrow$ in the text throughout this book though it is curved in the figures). Additional symbols for model diagrams are introduced in Chapter 10, which deals with advanced SEM techniques.

3.3   Steps of SEM

Although SEM is actually a family of techniques that address different kinds of hypotheses, they all share the same basic sequence in which the analysis is conducted. These steps are listed and briefly described below. Later chapters elaborate specific issues of each step for particular SEM techniques:

1. *Specify* the model, which means that the researcher's hypotheses are expressed in the form of a structural equation model. Although many researchers begin the process of specification by drawing a diagram of the model using at least the standard symbols presented in Table 3.1, the model can also be described as a series of equations. These equations define the model's parameters, which correspond to presumed relations among observed or latent variables that the computer eventually estimates with sample data.

TABLE 3.1. Symbols for Diagrams of Structural Equation Models

Category	Symbol	Standard?	Definition
Variables			
Observed	□	Yes	Variables measured by the researcher. Other terms: *manifest variable* or *indicator* when represented as measuring a latent variable. Rectangles are also used to represent observed variables.
Latent	○	Yes	An unobserved, hypothetical construct. Other term: *factor*. Ellipses instead of circles are also used in diagrams.
Relations between variables			
Direct effect	→	Yes	For example, $X \to Y$: X is presumed to affect Y in a unidirectional way.
Reciprocal effect	⇄	Yes	For example, $Y_1 \rightleftarrows Y_2$: The influence between Y_1 and Y_2 is bidirectional. Other term: *feedback loop*.
Correlation or covariance	↭	Yes	For example, $X_1 \leftrightarrow X_2$: Two variables are assumed to covary, but there is no more specific hypothesis about how this correlation arises. Other term: *unanalyzed association*.
Residual variances			
Disturbance	D	No	For example, $X \to Y \leftarrow D$: Variance in Y unexplained by a variable (X) that is presumed to affect it.
Measurement error	E	No	For example, $A \to X \leftarrow E$, where X is an observed variable that is presumed to measure A, a latent variable; E is variance in X unexplained by A.

2. Determine whether the model is *identified*. A model is identified if it is theoretically possible for the computer to derive a unique estimate of every model parameter. Different types of structural equation models must meet certain requirements in order to be identified. If a model fails to meet requirements for its identification, attempts to estimate it may not be successful.

3. *Select measures* of the variables represented in the model and *collect the data.*
4. *Analyze* the model. This step typically involves using a model-fitting program to derive estimates of the model's parameters with the data. As mentioned in Chapter 2, multiple regression is useful only for the most basic type of model in path analysis. Other, more sophisticated methods such as maximum likelihood are typically used to estimate the model.
5. *Evaluate model fit,* which means to determine how adequately the model accounts for the data. Perhaps more often than not, researchers' initial models do not fit the data very well. When (not if) this happens to you, then:
6. *Respecify* the model and evaluate the fit of the revised model to the same data (i.e., return to step 1). As with a model's initial specification, its respecification should be guided by the researcher's hypotheses.

The next three sections describe research examples that are used to introduce the core SEM techniques. Each example is also considered in greater detail in later chapters devoted to each technique.

3.4   Path Analysis: A Structural Model of Delinquency

This first example is based on a recent investigation by Lynam, Moffit, and Stouthamer-Loeber (1993), who hypothesized that delinquency among adolescent males varies as a function of social class, motivation, and verbal ability. They also hypothesized that scholastic achievement is affected by the same three variables and that achievement also affects delinquency. For example, adolescents with poor verbal ability may be more likely to drop out of school, which may contribute to delinquency through things such as reduced employment prospects or more unsupervised time on the streets. Note that achievement is accorded a special role in Lynam and associates' hypotheses in that it is viewed as both as a cause of delinquency and as an effect that is presumed to be influenced by other variables (social class, motivation, verbal ability). Lynam et al. had no specific hypotheses about causal relations among social class, motivation, and verbal ability—these variables were simply assumed to covary. Lynam et al. assessed each of these variables with a single measure within samples of African-American and white male adolescents. For example, the teachers of these boys completed a rating scale about overall scholastic achievement. The boys were also administered an IQ test to assess their general verbal skills, and observers of the IQ evaluations completed ratings about the boys' levels of motivation.

A standard statistical technique that could be used here is multiple regression. Two separate analyses could be conducted, the first with achievement as the criterion and social class, motivation, and verbal ability as the predictors; delinquency could be the criterion in a second analysis, with all four other variables as predictors. Each regression would yield R^2 values that indicate the proportions of explained variance and regression coefficients that reflect the relative importance of each predictor (section 2.8). But note that achievement cannot be represented in multiple regression as both a predictor *and* a criterion in the same analysis—it must be either one or the other. A similar limitation is apparent with another statistical technique called *canonical correlation,* which is a multivariate extension of multiple regression that analyzes multiple predictor and criterion variables. One way to apply canonical correlation to this problem is to specify social class, motivation, and verbal ability as predictors and achievement and delinquency as criteria. Although the results of such an analysis would indicate the total proportion of variance in this set of two criterion variables explained by the three predictors, treating achievement solely as a criterion ignores its hypothesized role as something that affects delinquency. (Readers can find more information about canonical correlation in Stevens, 1992, and Tabachnick & Fidell, 1996.)

The technique of path analysis from the SEM family provides a way around the aforementioned limitations. Path analysis is a possible technique for when there is only a single observed measure of each theoretical variable and the researcher has a priori hypotheses about causal relations among these variables. The starting point for path analysis is specification of a *structural model* that represents the causal hypotheses. Consider the model presented in Figure 3.1, which represents one of the path models specified by Lynam et al. (1993). In this model, social class, motivation, and verbal ability are specified as exogenous variables, which usually appear on the left side of a path model as in Figure 3.1. Recall from the previous chapter (section 2.2) that the causes of exogenous variables are unknown and thus are not represented in structural models. Accordingly, associations among exogenous variables are typically *unanalyzed;* that is, they are simply assumed to covary because whatever causes them is unknown. Note that every pair of exogenous variables in Figure 3.1 is connected by the symbol for an unanalyzed association (↔).

The other two observed variables in the path model of Figure 3.1,

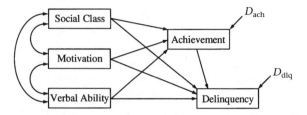

FIGURE 3.1. A path model of delinquency.

achievement and delinquency, are endogenous. Unlike exogenous variables, presumed causes of these endogenous variables are explicitly represented in the model. For example, Lynam et al. specified that achievement is affected by the exogenous variables, which is represented in Figure 3.1 by the three straight lines with single arrowheads that point to achievement. These lines represent *direct effects,* which in a path model depict causal effects that are presumed to "flow" from the observed variable on the left to the one on the right of the arrowhead. Statistical estimates of direct effects are called *path coefficients.* Path coefficients are interpreted as regression coefficients are in multiple regression (section 2.8), which means that they control for correlations among multiple presumed causes of an endogenous variable. For example, the path coefficient for the direct effect of motivation on achievement in Figure 3.1 is corrected for the correlation of motivation with social class and verbal ability.

Now look at the second endogenous variable in the path model of Figure 3.1—delinquency. All three exogenous variables are specified as direct causes of delinquency. Achievement is also specified as a cause of delinquency, which gives achievement a dual role as, in the language of regression, both a predictor and a criterion. This dual role is described in path analysis as an *indirect effect* or a *mediator effect.* Indirect effects involve one or more intervening variables that "transmit" some of the causal effects of prior variables onto subsequent variables. (Intervening variables in indirect effects are also called *mediator variables.*) The possibility mentioned in the first paragraph of this section that verbal ability affects delinquency through scholastic achievement is an example of an indirect effect. This indirect effect and two others of motivation and social class through achievement on delinquency are represented in the path model of Figure 3.1. Just as direct causal effects are estimated in a path analysis, so too are indirect causal effects.

Another standard feature of path models is the representation of hypothesized spurious associations. Observe that achievement and delinquency in Figure 3.1 are specified to have three common causes. For instance, social class is specified as a cause of both endogenous variables. The path coefficient for the direct effect of achievement on delinquency thus controls for their presumed common causes. Like a partial correlation (section 2.7), if the value of this path coefficient is close to zero, then the observed correlation between achievement and delinquency may reflect solely a spurious association. On the other hand, if the value of this path coefficient is substantial, then the hypothesis of spuriousness is rejected. Together with the ability to estimate direct and indirect effects and to control for correlations among presumed causal variables, path analysis can be viewed as a way to "decompose" observed correlations into their constitute parts, spurious and nonspurious (causal). A path model is thus said to fit the data if these decompositions can reproduce the observed correlations.

In adition to the lines in Figure 3.1 that represent direct effects on achievement and delinquency from other observed variables, note that lines also point to each endogenous variable from terms designated with an uppercase D, which are *disturbances*. Every endogenous variable in a path model has a disturbance. The term D_{ach} in Figure 3.1 represents variance in achievement unaccounted for by the three exogenous variables specified as its causes; D_{dlq} has a similar meaning, but it represents variance unexplained by the four presumed causes of delinquency. Disturbances are analogous to residuals in regression but have a connotation based more in causal modeling than just prediction. Thoeretically, disturbances represent all causes of an endogenous variable that are omitted from the model. For example, there are almost certainly other causes of scholastic achievement than social class, motivation, and verbal ability—factors such as student–teacher rapport and parental involvement in education, among others, quickly spring to mind. A disturbance can be seen as a "proxy" or composite variable that represents all unmeasured causes, and the line that points from a disturbance to an endogenous variable represents the combined effects of all the omitted causes of that variable. Because the nature and number of these omitted causes is unknown as far as the model is concerned, disturbances can also be viewed as unmeasured exogenous variables.

As mentioned in the previous section, any structural equation model can be expressed as a series of equations. An example of how the path model of Figure 3.1 would be described in the equations-based syntax of the Amos model-fitting program (Arbuckle, 1997) is presented below. Note that Amos is also capable of automatically generating these equations after the user draws a diagram of the model in its graphics mode. (Amos is described in more detail in Chapter 11.)

```
$Structure
  social_class <> motivation
  social_class <> verbal_ability
  motivation <> verbal_abilility
  achievement = social_class + motivation +
                verbal_ability + (1) d_ach
  delinquency = social_class + motivation +
                verbal_ability + achievement + (1) d_dlq
```

The first three lines under $Structure above designate the unanalyzed associations between the exogenous variables of Figure 3.1, and the last four lines specify the observed variables that have direct effects on the endogenous variables, achievement and delinquency, and define their disturbances.

Lynam et al. (1993) conducted a multiple-group path analysis in which they evaluated the model of Figure 3.1 across samples of African-American and white male adolescents. The purpose of their multisample analysis was to evaluate an interactive effect of race. As described in the previous chapter (section 2.6), an interaction effect occurs when the relation between two variables changes across the levels of a third variable. In Lynam and associates' analysis, race was this "third variable," and they evaluated whether the relations specified in the path model of Figure 3.1 were moderated by race. Lynam et al. found that the direct effect of achievement on delinquency was virtually nil for white subjects. For these subjects, verbal ability was the strongest predictor of delinquency among the remaining variables. For the African-American group, however, achievement was the only variable with a sizable direct effect on delinquency. Also, verbal ability was related to delinquency for African-American males only indirectly through achievement. Based on these results, Lynam et al. speculated that school may be a more important source of structure and support for African-American adolescents in the prevention of delinquency than for white adolescents. A more detailed description of this multiple-group path analysis is presented in Chapter 6.

A final comment before we go on to the next example. Lynam and colleagues' analysis concerned both a mediator variable (achievement) and a moderator variable (race). Although these terms and the related ones of mediator effect (indirect effect) and moderator effect (interaction effect) sound alike and all concern a "third variable" phenomenon, they are not the same thing. A mediator variable like achievement in Figure 3.1 is specified to be part of a causal chain that is affected by a prior variable and in turn affects a subsequent one. Mediator variables are always endogenous. In contrast, the variable race in Lynam and colleagues' analysis is more like an exogenous variable in that it is not specified to be caused by any of the observed variables. Indeed, it would be illogical to suggest that any of the variables in Figure 3.1 cause race. We'll return to the topics of mediator and moderator variables/effects later in the book. Also, articles by Baron and Kenny (1986) and James and Brett (1984) about the distinction between mediators and moderators in structural models are highly recommended.

3.5   Confirmatory Factor Analysis: A Measurement Model of Cognitive Processes

The Kaufman Assessment Battery for Children (K-ABC; A. S. Kaufman & N. L. Kaufman, 1983) is an individually administered test for 2½- to 12½-year-olds that is based on a theoretical model of cognitive ability. Part of the test is intended to measure two hypothetical constructs, sequential processing and simultaneous processing: the first refers to the analysis of stimuli in a particular order; the second, to more holistic, integrative, less order-dependent reasoning. Hypothetical constructs like these or others like *intelligence* or *need for affiliation* are not directly observable. Instead, they can only be inferred or measured indirectly through observed variables (indicators). For two reasons, however, it is probably unrealistic to expect that a hypothetical construct could be adequately measured by a single indicator. First, scores on most measures are not completely free from the effects of random error (e.g., inadvertent scoring mistakes), which means that they are not perfectly reliable. Second, not all of the systematic, non-error portions of an indicator's variance may reflect the construct that the researcher wishes to assess (e.g., a questionnaire is susceptible to a social desirability response set), which means that the measure is not perfectly valid. (Reliability and validity are discussed in Chapter 7.)

One way around the aforementioned problems of measuring a construct with a single indicator is to use multiple indicators. A set of measures tends to be more reliable than any individual one. Also, multiple indicators may each assess a somewhat different facet of the construct, which enhances validity. Along these lines, the authors of the K-ABC devised three tasks intended to measure some aspect of sequential processing. All three tasks require the correct recall of the order in which either words or numbers are spoken or a series of hand movements is demonstrated. All three tasks concern sequences, but they vary in stimuli (words, numbers, movements) and sensory modes of input (aural, visual) and response (oral, motoric). These three tasks make up the K-ABC's Sequential Processing scale. The K-ABC's authors also constructed five other tasks intended to measure simultaneous processing. Each of these tasks requires that the child grasp a "gestalt" but within somewhat different formats and sets of stimuli. For instance, one task uses a puzzle-like format in which the child manipulates objects, and another consists of visual patterns that must be memorized. These five tasks make up the K-ABC's Simultaneous Processing scale. None of these eight tasks is expected to be synonymous with its underlying construct, but together they may offer more reliable and valid measurement than can any individual task.

Suppose that a researcher wishes to evaluate whether these eight K-ABC subtests measure two domains that correspond to its Sequential Processing and Simultaneous Processing scales. Some type of factor analysis would be a logical choice. Considered first is exploratory factor analysis (EFA), for which computer programs are readily available in many statistical packages. The term "EFA" actually refers to a set of procedures that include centroid, principal components, and principal axis factor analysis, among others, that differ in the statistical criteria used to derive factors. Specific EFA procedures are not reviewed here in detail; interested readers can find recommended readings about this topic listed at the end of the chapter. Instead, some general characteristics of EFA and potential limitations concerning this research example are considered below.

EFA has three core features:

1. The potential number of factors ranges from one up to the number of observed variables, but most EFA programs allow users to request a particular number.
2. All of the observed variables in EFA are allowed to correlate with every factor. Hence the term "exploratory," which means that the researcher has little direct influence on the correspondence between indicators and factors.
3. A given EFA solution (e.g., two factors) usually requires rotation to make the factors more interpretable. Very briefly, rotation changes the correlations between the factors and the indicators so the pattern of values is more distinct. There is more than one type of rotation option, but perhaps the most

important decision is whether the rotated factors will be un-correlated (orthogonal) or correlated (oblique).

One sensible way to apply EFA to this problem is to (1) instruct the computer to derive two factors that are allowed to correlate (cognitive abilities typically covary), and (2) look at the estimated relations between the K-ABC's subtests and the two factors. Strong associations between the K-ABC's three Sequential Processing scale subtests and one factor and between its five Simultaneous Processing scale tasks and the other factor would support the conceptual model of the K-ABC.

Presented in Figure 3.2 is a representation of EFA using the symbols listed in Table 3.1. This model is a *measurement model* that depicts relations between indicators and underlying factors. The two factors in this model are each represented by a symbol for a latent variable, an ellipse. The curved line that connects the ellipses in the figure represents a presumed correlation (in standardized form) or covariance (unstandardized) between the factors. This symbol has the same meaning as in path analysis in that it designates an unanalyzed association. Here, there is no hypothesis that one of these cognitive ability factors causes the other; instead; they are simply assumed to covary. In this way, the two factors in Figure 3.2 are analogous to exogenous variables in a path model.

Also analogous to their counterparts in path analysis are the lines in Figure 3.2 that point from the factors to the indicators, which represent direct effects—but here of the factors on the indicators.[1] Conceptually, these direct effects represent causal effects of the latent variables on the indicators, that is, the extent to which the factor is reflected in the scores of the indicator. In this sense, a measurement model can be viewed as a structural model of presumed causal effects of latent variables on observed scores. Whereas estimates of direct effects in path analysis are called path coefficients, the corresponding term in factor analysis for such estimates is *factor loading*. In EFA, factor loadings are typically Pearson correlations between the observed variables and the factors. If the loadings of, say, the Hand Movements task of Figure 3.2 on the two factors are (respectively) .75 and .10, then it is clear that scores on this subtest strongly covary with the first factor but are essentially unrelated to the second.

---

[1]The representation in Figure 3.2 does not describe the EFA technique of principal components, in which the factors are simple linear combinations of the observed variables. A figure for this technique would more appropriately feature lines that point from the indicators to the factors.

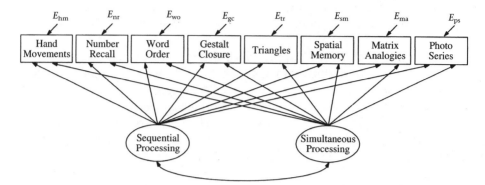

FIGURE 3.2. An exploratory factor analysis model.

The terms in Figure 3.2 designated with uppercase *Es* are *measurement errors*, which represent *unique variance*, a factor analytic term for indicator variance unexplained by the factors. Like disturbances in path models, measurement errors are proxy variables for all sources of residual variance that are not explicitly represented in the model. Two types of unique variance are represented by *E* terms: random error (unreliability) and all sources of systematic (nonrandom) variance not due to the factors. Examples of the latter include effects due to a particular measurement method (e.g., self-report vs. projective formats), the source of the information (e.g., the subject vs. other informants such as coworkers), or the particular stimuli (pictures, words, etc.) that make up the task. For example, the Hand Movements task of the K-ABC is the only one of the eight that involves the reproduction of movements demonstrated by the examiner. Thus, some of the variability of this task's scores may be specific due to its particular format rather than to a presumed underlying cognitive process.

An even more precise test of whether these eight subtests measure two factors that correspond to their placement on the K-ABC's Sequential Processing scale or Simultaneous Processing scale is afforded by confirmatory factor analysis (CFA). Unlike EFA, CFA allows the researcher to specify and test measurement models that are more a priori. For example, consider the CFA measurement model of the K-ABC presented in Figure 3.3. Note that each indicator in this model is specified to measure (load on) a single latent variable. Also note that the correspondence of indicators to factors in Figure 3.3 exactly matches the placement of these eight tasks on the K-ABC's Sequential Processing or Simultaneous Processing scale. In contrast, standard EFA does not permit the researcher to specify that an indicator loads on only one factor. (Contrast Figures 3.2 and 3.3.)

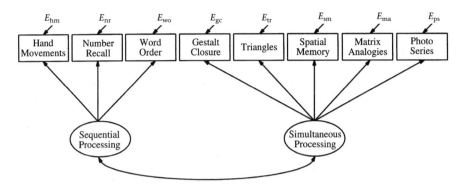

FIGURE 3.3 A confirmatory factor analysis model.

An example of how the measurement model of Figure 3.3 would be expressed as series of equations in the syntax of the EQS model-fitting program (Bentler, 1995) is presented below. Like the Amos program, EQS can automatically generate these equations after the user draws the model on the screen. (More information about EQS is presented in Chapter 11.)

```
/LABELS
  V1 = HANDMOVE; V2 = NUMBER;    V3 = WORDORD;
  V4 = GESTALT;  V5 = TRIANGLE; V6 = MATRIX;
  V7 = SPATIAL;  V8 = PHOTOSER; F1 = SEQUENT; F2 = SIMULT;
/EQUATIONS
  V1 =  F1 + E1; V2 = *F1 + E2; V3 = *F1 + E3;
  V4 =  F2 + E4; V5 = *F2 + E5; V6 = *F2 + E6;
  V7 = *F2 + E7; V8 = *F2 + E8;
/VARIANCES
  F1 = *; F2 = *;
/COVARIANCES
  F1,F2 = *;
```

Very briefly described, variable names are assigned above under the /LABELS command. Lines in the /EQUATIONS section define the loadings of each indicator (designated as Vs) on its underlying factor (Fs) and associate an error of measurement term (E) with each indicator. The two factors, sequential (F1) and simultaneous (F2), are specified as exogenous under the /VARIANCES section. Their presumed unanalyzed association is specified under the /COVARIANCES heading.

As implied by the EQS code presented above, the results of a CFA of a measurement model include estimates of correlations between the factors, loadings of the indicators on their respective factors, and the amount of measurement error (unique variance) of each indicator. If the researcher's a priori measurement model is reasonably correct, then one should see the following pattern of results: (1) Indicators specified to measure a common underlying factor all have relatively high loadings on that factor, and (2) estimated correlations between the factors are not excessively high (e.g., >.85). The former result indicates *convergent validity,* and the latter *discriminant validity.* Discriminant validity refers to the distinctiveness of the factors measured by different sets of indicators. For instance, if the estimated correlation between the sequential and simultaneous factors of the model in Figure 3.3 is .95, then the eight indicators can hardly be said to measure two distinct cognitive processes. (Convergent and discriminant validity and other aspects of validity are discussed in more detail in Chapter 7.) If the results of a CFA do not support the researcher's a priori hypotheses, then the measurement model can be respecified and reanalyzed.

Results of numerous EFA and CFA studies of the K-ABC generally support the two-factor model of Figure 3.3 (e.g., Kamphaus & Reynolds, 1987; Kline, Guilmette, Snyder, & Castellanos, 1994). The fit of this model to the sample data analyzed in Chapter 7 is, however, only mediocre. How the model of Figure 3.3 could be respecified to improve its fit to these data is demonstrated in Chapter 7. Also presented in that chapter is the analysis of the measurement model of Figure 3.3 across independent samples of African-American and white children. Results of a multisample CFA indicate whether a set of indicators seems to measure the same constructs in each group.

3.6 A Hybrid Model: Familial Risk Factors for Psychopathology and Child Adjustment

Within a sample of junior and senior high school students and their parents, Worland, Weeks, Janes, and Strock (1984) studied the relation of familial risk factors for psychopathology to student cognitive ability, scholastic performance, and classroom adjustment. Measures of familial risk included degree of parental psychopathology (schizophrenia or affective disorder, other psychiatric or medical disorder, or none) and family socioeconomic status (SES). Student cognitive ability and scholastic skills were assessed with an IQ test and a battery of achievement measures. The IQ test yielded three scores (verbal, visual–spatial, memory), as did the achievement battery (reading, arithmetic, spelling). The students' teachers completed a questionnaire about classroom adjustment with four scales: scholastic motivation, harmony of social relations, emotional stability, and extroversion. Worland et al. hypothesized that familial risk for psychopathology affects classroom adjustment only indirectly first through cognitive ability and then through scholastic achievement (e.g., high risk → low ability → poor achievement → problematic classroom adjustment).

Worland and colleagues' use of multiple measures of each domain implies a measurement model—here, one with four factors each assessed with either two (familial risk), three (cognitive ability, achievement), or four (classroom adjustment) indicators. Using CFA, one could test whether the 12 indicators in this study indeed seem to measure four factors. Results of a CFA would also yield estimates of correlations among these four factors. However, Worland et al. did not simply assume that these four factors are correlated. Instead, they hypothesized a specific pattern of direct and indirect causal relations among them. CFA estimates only unanalyzed associations among factors, not direct causal effects. Presumed causal effects can be specified and tested in path analysis, but this technique analyzes observed variables, not latent variables.

What is needed here is an analytic approach that combines features of CFA and path analysis. It is possible in SEM to specify a hybrid model that has a structural component (like a path model) and a measurement component (like a factor model). Consider the model presented in Figure 3.4 specified to reflect Worland and colleagues' hypotheses. The measurement part of this hybrid model concerns an a priori pattern of loadings of the indicators on the factors, just as in a CFA model. The structural portion of the model involves direct effects among the four latent variables. Here, the familial risk factor is specified as exogenous and the other three factors as endogenous.

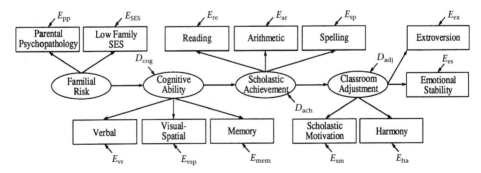

FIGURE 3.4. A hybrid model of familial risk for psychopathology and child adjustment.

The cognitive ability latent variable is specified to mediate the effect of familial risk on scholastic achievement, which in turns mediates the effect of cognitive ability on classroom adjustment, just as hypothesized by Worland et al. The evaluation of a hybrid model is thus akin to conducting a path analysis but with latent variables instead of observed variables.

Note another feature of the hybrid model of Figure 3.4: it has both measurement errors *and* disturbances. Each indicator in the model has its own measurement error term, just as in a CFA model. Like a path model, the endogenous factors in Figure 3.4 each have a disturbance, but these disturbances reflect omitted causes of latent rather than observed variables. The representation of both kinds of residual terms in a hybrid model allows measurement error in the indicators to be estimated apart from direct or indirect causal effects among the factors. The expression that "SEM takes reliability into account" refers to this characteristic of hybrid (and CFA measurement) models. As we'll see in Chapter 7, this description is a bit simplistic because measurement error terms reflect more than just unreliability. However, estimation of structural relations in path models, which do not have latent constructs and thus have no measurement error terms, does not directly control for measurement error. The ability to do so with a hybrid model in the evaluation of presumed causal relations is thus an important advantage over a path model.

The specification of the hybrid model of Figure 3.4 as a series of equations in the SIMPLIS language of the LISREL program (Jöreskog & Sörbom, 1993) is listed below. LISREL also allows a model to be specified by drawing it on the screen instead of writing equations. (LISREL and its SIMPLIS language are described in Chapter 11.)

```
Observed Variables
 PARPSYCH  FAMSES  VERBAL  VISUAL  MEMORY
 READ  ARITH  SPELL  SCHOLMOT  HARMONY  EMOTSTAB  EXTROVER
Latent Variables:  Famrisk  Cognitiv  Achieve  Classadj
Relationships
 PARPSYCH  FAMSES = Famrisk
 VERBAL  VISUAL  MEMORY = Cognitiv
 READ  ARITH  SPELL = Achieve
 SCHOLMOT  HARMONY  EMOTSTAB  EXTROVER = Classadj
 Cognitiv = Famrisk
 Achieve = Cognitiv
 Classadj = Achieve
```

Briefly described, the first four lines in the above program code label the indicators and the factors. The a priori relations between the observed and latent variables are specified under the heading "Relation-ships." The first four lines in this section define the loadings of the indicators on their respective factors, which specifies the measurement portion of the model. The last three lines of code specify the presumed structural relations among the latent variables. As per Worland and colleagues' hypotheses, direct effects are specified only between adjacent pairs of constructs (i.e., Famrisk $\rightarrow$ Cognitiv $\rightarrow$ Achieve $\rightarrow$ Classadj).

The results of the analysis of the hybrid model of Figure 3.4 with Worland and colleagues' data are described in detail in Chapter 8. Briefly summarized, this model is ultimately rejected because its fit to the data is poor. There are two problems with this model. First, the measurement portion of the model is incorrect. Although the familial risk and classroom adjustment factors are relatively distinct, the cognitive ability and scholastic achievement factors are not. This lack of discriminant validity between the latter two factors suggests that the indicators in Figure 3.4 really measure fewer than four factors. The second problem is that the measurement error terms of the three indicators of the cognitive ability factor and of the three indicators of the scholastic achievement factor appear to be related. This pattern suggests that the unique variances of these respective sets of indicators may reflect something in common such as method effects specific to the IQ and achievement tests used by Worland et al. A respecified model that addresses both of these problems has reasonable fit to the data, and results of its analysis generally support Worland and associates' hypothesis about a mediated effect of familial risk for psychopathology on classroom adjustment through child cognitive/academic skills.

3.7   Overview of Techniques

As is demonstrated in Part II of this book, path, factor, or hybrid models can be specified to test a wide variety of hypotheses about how variables are presumed to relate to each other. Discussed in Chapter 10 (in Part III) are ways that these basic types of models can be extended to represent additional kinds of statistical effects including, among others, curvilinear or interaction effects, group mean differences, or changes over time in longitidinal studies, all on either observed or latent variables. Thus, most standard types of statistical methods such as multiple regression or the analysis of variance (ANOVA) can be thought of as special cases of SEM. Presented in Table 3.2 is a summary of the relation between standard statistical

TABLE 3.2. Overview of Standard Statistical Methods and
SEM Techniques

Procedure	Description
Standard techniques	
Canonical correlation	Multiple exogenous and endogenous observed variables.
MANOVA (multivariate analysis of variance)	A special case of canonical correlation: multiple exogenous variables that usually represent group membership; multiple endogenous observed variables.
Multiple regression	A special case of canonical correlation: multiple exogenous observed variables but only a single endogenous observed variable.
ANOVA (analysis of variance)	A special case of multiple regression: multiple exogenous variables that usually represent group membership; a single endogenous observed variable.
EFA (exploratory factor analysis)	Explicit distinction between observed (indicator) and latent variables: multiple exogenous latent factors and indicator variables that are considered endogenous. The researcher has no direct influence over the linkage between indicators and factors.
SEM	
Hybrid models	Combined measurement and structural models: multiple exogenous and endogenous variables that can be either latent or observed.
Path analysis	A subset of hybrid models that concerns only observed variables and structural models: multiple exogenous and endogenous variables; endogenous variables can affect one another.
CFA (confirmatory factor analysis)	A subset of hybrid models that concern only measurement models: explicit distinction between observed (indicator) and latent variables; multiple exogenous latent variables. The researcher specifies the linkage between factors and indicators.
All SEM techniques	Mean scores can be analyzed as well as entire models across multiple groups.

techniques and types of SEM procedures but expressed in the language of SEM. Techniques in each category are ordered from most to least general; procedures that are specific instances of others are also indicated in the table. Note that the analysis of hybrid structural equation models together with the capability to analyze group mean differences represent the most general and flexible of all the procedures listed in Table 3.2.

3.8   Summary

Many examples of the types of research questions that can be addressed with the core SEM techniques were considered in this chapter. Path analysis allows researchers to specify and test structural models that reflect a priori assumptions about spurious associations and direct or indirect causal effects among observed variables. Measurement models that represent a priori hypotheses about relations between indicators and latent factors can be evaluated with the technique of CFA. Hybrid models in which hypotheses about both structural relations and measurement are represented can also be tested. In addition, any type of structural equation model can be evaluated across multiple groups. This feature and the ability to analyze means of either observed or latent variables makes SEM a very flexible tool for the analysis of experimental or nonexperimental data.

Before specific SEM techniques are described in detail, the very important subject of the screening and preparation of the data is considered in the next chapter.

3.9   Recommended Readings

Introductions to Basic SEM Techniques

These chapter- or article-length presentations offer introductions to path analysis, EFA or CFA, or hybrid structural equation models.

Bryant, F. B., & Yarnold, P. R. (1995). Principal components analysis and exploratory and confirmatory factor analysis. In L. G. Grimm & P. R. Yarnold (Eds.), *Reading and understanding multivariate statistics* (pp. 99–136). Washington, DC: American Psychological Association.

Cole, D. A. (1987). Utility of confirmatory factor analysis in test validation research. *Journal of Consulting and Clinical Psychology, 55,* 584–594.

Klem, L. (1995). Path analysis. In L. G. Grimm & P. R. Yarnold (Eds.), *Reading and understanding multivariate statistics* (pp. 65–98). Washington, DC: American Psychological Association.

Kline, R. B. (1991). Latent variable path analysis in clinical research: A beginner's tour guide. *Journal of Clinical Psychology, 47,* 471–484.

Morris, R. J., Bergan, J. R., & Fulginiti, J. V. (1991). Structural equation modeling in clinical assessment research with children. *Journal of Consulting and Clinical Psychology, 59,* 371–379.

Nesselroade, J. R. (1995). Exploratory factor analysis with latent variables and the study of processes of development and change. In A. von Eye & C. C. Clogg (Eds.), *Latent variables analysis* (pp. 131–154). Thousand Oaks, CA: Sage.

Tabachnick, B. G., & Fidell, L. S. (1996). *Using multivariate statistics.* New York: Harper Collins. (See chap. 14.)

Annotated Bibliographies of Theoretical and Technical Works in SEM

The following bibliographies provide invaluable summaries of recent work in SEM.

Austin, J. T., & Calderón, R. F. (1996). Theoretical and technical contributions to structural equation modeling: An updated bibliography. *Structural Equation Modeling, 3,* 105–175.

Austin, J. T., & Wolfe, L. M. (1991). Annotated bibliography of structural equation modeling: Technical work. *British Journal of Mathematical and Statistical Psychology, 44,* 93–132.

CHAPTER FOUR

Data Preparation and Screening

It is the ideas about the data that count, it is they that provide the cement, the integration. . . . No amount of fancy statistical acrobatics will undo the harm that may result by using an ill-conceived theory, or a caricature of a theory.
—ELAZAR J. PEDHAZUR (1982, p. 230)

4.1 Foreword

This chapter is about preparation of the data for SEM. There are two reasons why this topic is crucial. First, the most widely used estimation procedures for SEM require certain assumptions of the data, especially about their distributional characteristics. Unlike similar requirements of other techniques that can be violated with relative impunity—the normality assumption of ANOVA, for instance—the same is not generally true in SEM. Second, data-related problems can cause model-fitting programs to fail to yield a solution or to "crash." A researcher who has not carefully screened the data may mistakenly believe that the model is at fault, and an unnecessary trip down the path of frustration commences if alternative models are then evaluated with the same blemished data.

Considered first are the two main options about the form in which data can be submitted to a model-fitting program—either a raw data file or some type of matrix summary of the data such as a correlation matrix or a covariance matrix. Readers may be surprised to learn that the raw data themselves are not necessary for many types of SEM. The same is also true, however, for other types of statistical techniques. For example, it is possible to calculate some types of ANOVA using only group means and standard deviations, and a computer can conduct an exploratory factor analysis given only a correlation matrix.

The second major topic of this chapter concerns the screening of the raw data before they or a matrix summary of them are analyzed. Two broad categories of problems are discussed: (1) that including case-related issues such as the accuracy of data input, missing observations, and outliers; and (2) that including distributional/relational issues such as normality, linearity, and homoscedasticity. The application of many of the procedures described in this chapter to the screening of a large data set is also demonstrated. Readers should note, however, that it is not possible to thoroughly cover all aspects of data screening in a single chapter. Indeed, entire books have been written on some of these topics such as the treatment of missing data. Overall, this chapter is intended as a brief introduction, one that points out some of the basic options for dealing with data-related problems. More advanced works are cited throughout, and these works should be consulted for more information.

4.2   Form of the Input Data

Model-fitting programs typically accept either a raw data file or a matrix summary of the data. If a raw data file is submitted, then the program will create its own matrix, which is then analyzed. In choosing between a raw data file and a matrix summary, the researcher should consider the following issues:

1. There are three occasions when it is necessary that the raw data are submitted to a model-fitting program instead of a matrix summary of them. The first is when an estimation method is used that does not assume that the data are normally distributed. Such methods control for non-normality by estimating the degree of skew or kurtosis in the raw data. These special methods are described in Chapter 5. The second is when non-normal data are analyzed with a more standard estimation method (i.e., one that assumes normality, like maximum likelihood) but test statistics are calculated that correct for non-normality. Corrected test statistics for normal distribution methods are reviewed in Chapter 7. The third occasion is when a model is analyzed within a single sample using a special method that accommodates cases with missing observations, which is described in Chapter 10. For SEMs that do not involve any of these special meth-

ods—and most do not—either the raw data or a matrix summary of them can be analyzed.

2. Although the capabilities of model-fitting programs to manage raw data are rapidly improving, general statistical packages like SPSS, BMDP, SAS, or SYSTAT usually offer more options for things like the handling of cases with missing observations, the computation of composite variables (e.g., a total score), and the selection of cases. Also, general statistical programs can usually write matrix summaries of the data to an output file, which can then be read into a model-fitting program.

3. Matrix input offers a potential economy over raw data files, especially for large samples. Suppose that 1,000 subjects are measured on 10 variables. The raw data file may be 1,000 lines (or more) in length, but a covariance matrix, for instance, might be only 10 lines long.

4. Many journal articles about the results of SEM procedures contain enough information (e.g., correlations and standard deviations) to create a matrix summary of the data, which can then be submitted to a model-fitting program. Thus, readers of such papers can either replicate the analyses or analyze alternative models not considered by the original author(s) without having access to the raw data. See MacCallum, Wegener, Uchino, and Fabriger (1993) and Hershberger (1994) for examples of this capability. Also, readers can replicate analyses described in this book using the matrix summaries that accompany each example.

If means are not analyzed in a structural equation model (more about means momentarily), there are two basic types of summaries of raw data—correlation matrices and covariance matrices. For example, presented in Table 4.1 are the raw data for 10 cases on four variables. The correlation matrix and the covariance matrix for these four variables are presented in the table below the raw data. Note that the diagonal entries of the covariance matrix are variances and that the off-diagonal entries, the covariances, are the products of correlations and standard deviations. For example, the entry 21.64 in the covariance matrix is $cov_{\text{age, IQ}}$, which is $r_{\text{age, IQ}} \, SD_{\text{age}} \, SD_{\text{IQ}} = .21(9.85)(9.25)$. The diagonal of the correlation matrix also contains variances, but these entries are all the same value (1.00) because the variables are standardized when correlations are calculated (section 2.4). Both the correlation matrix and the covariance matrix are in lower diagonal form, which means that only unique values of correlations or covariances are reported in the lower left-hand side of the matrix. Model-fitting

TABLE 4.1. Matrix Summaries of Raw Data

Raw data

Case	Age	IQ	Anxiety	Adjustment
A	41	117	55	510
B	29	109	62	645
C	33	102	41	454
D	27	99	65	557
E	24	110	71	492
F	51	121	52	712
G	45	100	38	687
H	21	113	50	391
I	37	91	45	489
J	26	101	65	500
M	33.40	106.30	54.40	543.70
SD	9.85	9.25	11.16	105.08
s^2	96.93	85.57	124.49	11,041.34

Matrix summaries without means[a]

Correlation				Covariance			
1.00				96.93			
.21	1.00			18.87	85.57		
−.54	.21	1.00		−59.73	21.64	124.49	
.69	.19	−.08	1.00	708.80	180.77	−88.53	11,041.34

Matrix summaries with means[a]

Version (a) r, SD, M				Version (b) cov, M			
1.00				96.93			
.21	1.00			18.87	85.57		
−.54	.21	1.00		−59.73	21.64	124.49	
.69	.19	−.08	1.00	708.80	180.77	−88.53	11,041.34
9.85	9.25	11.16	105.08	33.40	106.30	54.40	543.70
33.40	106.30	54.40	543.70				

[a]The variables in the matrices are in same order as in the raw data.

programs typically accept lower diagonal matrices as an alternative to full ones with (redundant) entries above and below the diagonal. Also, most model-fitting programs can "assemble" a covariance matrix given the correlations and standard deviations.

Which type of matrix, correlation or covariance, is the most appropriate? Correlation matrices have potential drawbacks. As mentioned in Chapter 2, most estimation procedures in SEM assume the analysis of unstandardized variables. In fact, some model-fitting programs give warning messages if the user requests the analysis of a cor-

relation matrix. There is also the possibility that the results of significance tests may not be correct when standardized variables are analyzed (section 2.9). It is generally safer to analyze a covariance matrix.
Considering the potential shortcomings of correlation matrices, covariance matrices are generally more appropriate summaries of raw
data. Accordingly, covariances matrices are analyzed for most of the
examples presented in this book. The only exceptions are when the
authors of the original works did not report standard deviations,
which means that it was impossible to analyze a covariance matrix.

Matrix summaries of raw data must consist of the covariances
and means of the observed variables whenever means are analyzed in
SEM, a subject that is discussed in Chapter 10. Presented at the bottom of Table 4.1 are two examples of matrix summaries that include
means. Version (a) on the left features (respectively) correlations,
standard deviations, and means; version (b) on the right has covariances and means. Both matrices convey the same information.

Three other issues warrant comment. First, if you are using raw
data to estimate a model in which means are not analyzed (i.e., all of
the models in this book except those described in Chapter 10), then
technically the scores in the data file should be deviation scores from
the mean. For variable X, for instance, mean deviation scores for each
subject have the form $(X - M)$ where M is the mean of X. The mean of
these deviation scores is zero, but they have the same standard deviation as the original scores. The analysis of deviation scores from the
mean is consistent with the assumption that means are irrelevant
(i.e., they all equal zero) when only covariances are analyzed. The derivation of deviations scores from the mean is sometimes described as
centering the data. Second, even if your SEM model does not concern
means, you should report the means of all observed variables in the
written summary of the results. You may not be interested in analyzing the means, but someone else may be. Third, there is special type
of matrix summary that is called an *augmented moments matrix* or a
cross-products moments matrix. The entries in an augmented moment
matrix are average cross-products of the raw scores on two variables.
For example, the entry for variables X and Y in such a matrix is the
average value of the product $X \times Y$ for all subjects. This type of matrix
summary is not used very often, but some model-fitting programs
such as LISREL accept augmented moment matrices as input data. For
examples of the analysis of augmented moment matrices, see McArdle and Epstein (1987) and Jöreskog and Yang (1996).

Before either a raw data file is analyzed or a matrix summary of
the data is created, the original data should be screened for the problems considered in the following sections.

4.3   Accuracy of Data Entry

It is very easy to make a mistake while inputting scores of individual cases or entries of a correlation matrix or a covariance matrix into a computer file. Some suggestions to ensure accuracy include independent data entry by two different persons—the resulting files can be compared[1]—and checking a listing of the computer file against the original records. These tactics are not always practical for very large samples, however, nor are they useful when data files come from another source (e.g., archival information, computerized medical records). Screening of such data sets can nevertheless be conducted through examination of basic descriptive statistics (e.g., means, standard deviations, ranges) or of frequency distributions. Values that are out of range or improperly coded can often be detected with such simple checks.

4.4   Missing Data

Patterns of Incomplete Data

Missing observations are a fact of life in many areas of research. They often occur due to factors beyond the control of the researcher such as equipment failure, the failure of subjects to respond to a question, or their attrition from a study. Other times, though, missing observations may be planned; that is, they are part of the research design. Suppose that a questionnaire is so long that it is impractical to administer it in a single session. Instead of arranging multiple testing sessions for subjects of a single sample, only parts of the whole questionnaire can be administered on one occasion to different subsamples. Another example is when a relatively inexpensive measure is used with the entire sample whereas another, more expensive procedure is administered to a much smaller group of randomly selected subjects.

When observations are missing due to unplanned events, there are two questions that the researcher must address. First, how much of the data are missing? Unfortunately, there is no clear guideline about how much missing data is too much. For instance, Cohen and Cohen (1983) suggested that 5% or even 10% missing data on a particular variable is not large, but the seriousness of greater proportions

---

[1]The "document compare" feature of many word processors provides a handy way to compare two data files and identify the specific locations of discrepancies.

is more ambiguous. Obviously, the usefulness of a variable with the majority of its scores missing may be suspect. But perhaps even more important than the absolute percentage of missing data are the implications of the second question: is the pattern of missing observations random or systematic? Rubin (1976) and others in the statistical literature distinguish between data that are *missing at random* (MAR) versus those for which the pattern of loss is systematic, or *nonignorable*. MAR means that the probability of the presence versus absence of scores on some variable is unrelated to subjects' true status on that variable. In other words, whatever process causes missing observations operates at random, which implies that subjects with missing observations differ only by chance from those who have scores on that variable. Thus, results based on data from subjects with nonmissing observations should generalize to those with missing data. Data loss that is systematic, on the other hand, implies just the opposite: cases with missing observations differ systematically from those with scores on that variable. Thus, the pattern of data loss is nonignorable because results based on the latter group of subjects may not generalize to those for whom the scores are missing.

An example illustrates the difference between data loss that is MAR versus systematic (nonignorable). Suppose that health status is assessed over time in a longitudinal study. If subjects who are less healthy are more likely to drop out of the study, then the pattern of missing observations is systematic because data loss varies with actual health. Results based on the healthier subjects who remain in the study may thus not generalize back to the original population from which they were selected. If subjects drop out of the study for reasons unrelated to their health, however, then the data loss pattern is MAR and subjects who remain in the study are a random subsample of all cases. There is another pattern of missing observations that is called *missing completely at random* (MCAR), but MCAR is just a stronger assumption about the randomness of the data loss than is MAR. Like MAR, the notion of MCAR means that the process of data loss on some variable is unrelated to subjects' true status on that variable. However, MCAR also means that the presence or absence of scores on a variable is unrelated to subjects' scores on *other* variables in the data set. In contrast, MAR allows for this possibility.

When systematic, nonignorable data loss is apparent, the specific nature of it needs to be understood so that the results can be appropriately interpreted. In the example cited above about loss of subjects from a longitudinal study about health, the finding that subjects who eventually drop out of the study are less healthy than subjects who are retained at the first measurement occasion would suggest that the pattern of data loss may not be random. Unfortunately, it is not always easy to determine whether the data loss pattern is random or systematic. For example, if subjects in a longitudinal health study become sicker *between* follow-up evaluations and then drop out of the study, it may not be apparent that attrition is related to health status. It may be even more difficult to discern the nature of the missing data pattern in nonlongitudinal studies in which each variable is measured only once. For more information about procedures to evaluate the randomness of patterns of missing observation, readers are referred to Little and Rubin (1987).

It is also crucial for readers to realize that if it is apparent that the missing data pattern is not random, then there is no statistical "fix" that will remedy the problem. In fact, all five of the options for dealing with missing observations briefly described below assume that the pattern of data loss is random. Three of these options are available in most types of data analyses including SEM and require the stronger assumption of MCAR. These options are listwise deletion, pairwise deletion, and replacement of missing observations with estimated scores. The other two options are based on SEM approaches to the analysis of incomplete data, and they require only the somewhat less stringent assumption of MAR. None of these five techniques, however, can somehow nullify potential bias in results based on analyses of nonmissing scores when the pattern of data loss is systematic.

It seems that researchers neglect too often to inform their readers about how missing observations were handled in the analysis, much less how the generalizability of the results may be affected. For example, Roth (1994) recently examined 134 analyses in 75 studies published in two psychology journals. A total of 86 of these analyses were conducted with data that contained missing values, but in over a third of the cases (31, or 36%) the authors did not report how they dealt with missing observations.

With these issues about missing data in mind, let's consider ways to deal with this problem.

Procedures to Handle Missing Observations

With standard statistical techniques (e.g., multiple regression, ANOVA), there are basically three ways to deal with missing observations: select one of two options that instructs the computer how to delete cases with missing data (listwise deletion, pairwise deletion) or replace (impute) the missing observations with estimated scores.

These three methods are also available in SEM, but SEM offers two additional ways to analyze incomplete data that do not require the deletion of cases or the derivation of estimated scores. These SEM-based methods are discussed in Chapter 10; only the three standard methods are described below.

The *imputation* of missing observations with estimated scores is reviewed first. There are basically three ways to calculate estimated scores. One is to substitute missing observations on a particular variable with the overall sample average (or group mean if subjects are classified into groups) on that variable. For example, if the average IQ for the whole sample is 90, then this value is substituted for a missing IQ score. Mean substitution has the advantage of simplicity, but it is not sensitive to subjects' patterns of scores on other variables. A regression-based estimate is a second alternative. In this approach, a missing observation is replaced with a predicted score generated for each subject by using multiple regression based on nonmissing scores on other variables. Regression-based substitution takes account of a subject's set of scores, but it is not feasible if a variable with missing observations does not covary at least moderately with other variables in the data set. Several statistical programs offer mean- or regression-based substitution as options. A third alternative is pattern matching—that is, the replacement of a missing observation with a score from another case with a similar profile of scores across other variables—but this option is not widely available in statistical packages. One exception is PRELIS2 (Jöreskog & Sörbom, 1996b), a data preparation program associated with LISREL that performs pattern matching. The application of any of these methods to generate estimated scores seems most sensible when the proportion of missing data is low (e.g., <10%) and scattered across several different variables. In longitudinal studies in which missing observations are due to subject attrition, however, imputation with estimated scores may be inappropriate. Additional information about imputation of missing observations is available in Raymond and Roberts (1987) and Ward and Clark (1991).

Deletion of cases with missing data is an alternative to imputation. Unless instructed otherwise, statistical programs generally use one of two options as their default way to delete cases with missing observations. The first is *listwise deletion*, which means that cases with missing observations on any variable in an analysis are excluded from all computations. Thus, the effective sample size with listwise deletion includes only cases with complete records, and this number can be substantially smaller than the original N if missing observations are scattered across many subjects. An advantage of listwise deletion, though, is that all analyses are conducted with the same cases. Not so with *pairwise deletion,* in which cases are excluded only if they have missing data on the variables involved in a particular computation. For example, a case with missing data on only X will be omitted from the derivation of the covariance between X and Y, but the case is included when the covariance between Y and W is calculated. Thus, pairwise deletion uses all possible cases for each calculation, which means the effective sample size can vary from analysis to analysis. This feature of pairwise deletion presents a potential drawback for SEM (or for any other multivariate procedure such as MANOVA), which is explained below.

Suppose that a researcher uses a general statistical program to produce a covariance matrix summary of a raw data file with 300 cases in which there are missing observations. Also suppose that the researcher opted for pairwise deletion of cases with missing data. Depending upon the pattern of missing observations, each element of the covariance matrix could be based on different subsets of subjects. For example, if 280 subjects have nonmissing scores on X and Y, then the effective sample size for the covariance between X and Y is this number. If fewer or more subjects have valid scores on X and W, however, then the effective sample size for the covariance between X and W will not be 280. When individual values in a covariance matrix are based on different numbers of cases, it is possible that some of the values may be mathematically out of range; that is, it would be impossible to derive them if the covariances were all calculated using data from the same subjects (e.g., with listwise deletion). One way to look at this phenomenon is at the level of Pearson correlations, which are one part of a covariance. Specifically, given three variables X, Y, and W, the value of the Pearson correlation between X and Y must fall within the following range:

$$r_{XW}r_{YW} \pm \sqrt{(1 - r_{XW}^2)(1 - r_{YW}^2)}. \tag{4.1}$$

If $r_{XW} = .60$ and $r_{YW} = .40$, for example, then the value of r_{XY} must be within the range $.24 \pm .73$ (i.e., $-.49$ to $.97$)—any other value would be out of bounds.

If an out-of-bounds correlation is part of a covariance matrix, then the matrix is *nonpositive definite,* which means that certain mathematical operations with the matrix such as division (i.e., inverting the matrix) will fail due to things like denominators that equal zero. Another term for a correlation or covariance matrix with out-of-bounds values is that it is *singular.* Some computer programs issue warning messages after they try unsuccessfully to analyze a covariance matrix with out-of-bounds values, and these messages may refer to singularity or nonpositive definiteness. Other symptoms of a covariance matrix with out-of-bounds values that may be reported in program output are a matrix determinant that is zero or negative eigenvalues. The latter are variance estimates, and variances cannot logically be less than zero. When the sample size is constant for all calculations, such as when listwise rather than pairwise deletion is used, then out-of-range correlations (and covariances) cannot occur. However, these is another problem, multicollinearity, that can also result in a nonpositive definite correlation or covariance matrix. Multicollinearity is the subject of the next section.

Some comprehensive works about missing data that cover issues raised in this section include those by Bourque and Clark (1992), Dodge (1985), and Little and Rubin (1982, 1989). Also, the BMDPAM (Description and Estimation of Missing Data) module of BMDP and the Missing Values Analysis module of SPSS are specifically intended for the analysis of patterns of missing data.

4.5 Multicollinearity

It was just mentioned that pairwise deletion can result in nonpositive definite covariances matrices with mathematically out-of-bounds values that cause estimation with a computer to fail. Multicollinearity is the other major reason why a sample covariance matrix may be nonpositive definite. Multicollinearity occurs when intercorrelations among some variables are so high that certain mathematical operations are either impossible or the results are unstable because some denominators are very close to zero. Sometimes multicollinearity occurs because what appears to be separate variables actually measure the same thing. Suppose that the correlation between age and vocabulary breadth within a sample of children is .90, which indicates that these two variables are redundant. Either one or the other could be included in the analysis, but it makes little sense to include both in the same analysis because they are essentially identical.

Researchers can also inadvertently cause multicollinearity when composite variables and their constituent variables are included in the same analysis. Suppose that a questionnaire has 10 items and that a researcher creates a composite variable that is the total score across all the items. Although the bivariate correlations between the total and each of the individual items may not be very high, the multiple correlation between the total score and the 10 items must equal 1.00, which is multicollinearity in its most extreme form.

It's easy to spot bivariate multicollinearity simply by inspecting the correlation matrix. If the absolute values of any the correlations exceed, say, .85, then the two variables may be redundant. Multicollinearity on a multivariate level is not so straightforward to detect. Recall the example mentioned above of the 10-item questionnaire, in which none of the bivariate correlations of the individual items with the total score necessarily equal 1.00. One method to detect multicollinearity on the multivariate level is to calculate squared multiple correlations (R^2) between each variable and all the rest; R^2s that are greater than about .90 suggest multicollinearity. A related statistic is called *tolerance*, which equals 1 minus the squared multiple correlation between a variable and all the rest. If a variance has a tolerance of 1%, then 1% of its variance is not redundant with all the other variables. Tolerance values less than 10% may indicate a multicollinearity problem. Another, less well-known statistic is the variance inflation factor (VIF):

$$\text{VIF} = \frac{1}{1 - R^2}.$$ (4.2)

The VIF is the ratio of a variable's total variance in standardized terms to its unique variance. Myers (1990) suggests that if the first is more than 10 times greater than the second, that is, VIF > 10, then the variable may be redundant with others.

There are two basic ways to deal with multicollinearity: eliminate variables or combine redundant ones into a composite variable. For example, if X and Y are very highly correlated, one could be dropped or their scores could be summed to form a single new variable. The latter tactic has the advantage of preserving the information of both variables, but note that a total score must replace both X and Y in the analysis.

A recent chapter by Wothke (1993) is recommended that deals with causes of nonpositive definitive sample covariances matrices (e.g., pairwise vs. listwise deletion of cases with incomplete data; multicollinearity) and related estimation problems in SEM.

4.6 Outliers

Univariate Outliers

Outliers are cases with scores that are very different from the rest. A case can be a *univariate outlier* if it has an extreme score on a single variable. Although there is no absolute definition of "extreme," a common rule of thumb is that scores more than three standard deviations away from the mean may be outliers. A case can also be a *multivariate outlier,* which means that it either has extreme scores on two or more variables or its configuration of scores is unusual. For instance, a case may have scores between two and three standard deviations above the means on all variables. Although none of the individual scores may be considered extreme, the case could be a multivariate outlier if this pattern is atypical in the sample.

Multivariate Outliers

Univariate outliers are easy to find by inspecting frequency distributions of z scores. The detection of multivariate outliers without extreme individual scores is more difficult, but there are several options. For example, some model-fitting programs identify individual cases that contribute the most to multivariate non-normality; such cases may be multivariate outliers. (Multivariate normality is described in the next section.) For example, the EQS model-fitting program reports the value of indexes of multivariate kurtosis developed by Mardia (1970) for individual cases that contribute the most to multivariate kurtosis. In order for cases to be screened by a model-fitting program, though, a raw data file must be analyzed instead of a matrix summary of the data (section 4.2).

Other ways to find possible multivariate outliers can be conducted with general statistical packages. One is based on a statistic called the *Mahalanobis distance,* which indicates the multivariate distance between the scores of an individual case and the sample means. (The latter are often called "centroids.") If the Mahalanobis distance for a case equals zero, then all the subject's scores equal their respective means. Within large samples, squared Mahalanobis distances are interpretable as chi-square (χ^2) statistics with degrees of freedom equal to the number of variables. By comparing the squared Mahalanobis distance of a particular case against the appropriate critical value of χ^2, one can determine whether the case differs significantly from all the rest. Some authors (e.g., Tabachnick & Fidell, 1996) suggest using a conservative level of significance (e.g., $p < .001$) for this comparison. For example, suppose that the squared Mahalanobis distance for a particular case in a data set with 10 variables is 37.89. The critical value of $\chi^2(10)$ at the .001 level is 29.59; thus, this case differs significantly from the others at this level of significance. Examples of the use of the Mahalanobis distance statistic to find potential multivariate outliers are available in

Stevens (1992, pp. 12–18, 110–120) and Tabachnick and Fidell (1996, pp. 94–104, 109–125). Also, one can use programs like the Regression module of SPSS, the BMDPAM and BMDP7M programs of BMDP, or the GLM (General Linear Model) program of SYSTAT, among others, to calculate Mahalanobis distances.

Additional ways to detect multivariate outliers include the following: Some regression programs have extensive capabilities for detecting outliers. Although some of these methods like ones based on residuals are more univariate in nature because they concern a single variable (the criterion), others concern outliers on a set of predictors. For example, two statistics, one called Cook's distance (Cook, 1977) and another known as leverage (or sometimes called a "hat element"; Hoaglin & Welsch, 1978), can also be used to locate potential multivariate outliers. Readers are referred to Stevens (1992, pp. 107–120) for introductions to these and other methods. A text about outliers by Barnett and Lewis (1978) offers more comprehensive information.

Options for Dealing with Outliers

Because outliers can be caused by data entry mistakes—for example, "999" instead of "99" is entered—the accuracy of extreme scores should be checked. If the scores for an outlier are valid, though, then the researcher should consider two basic possibilities: the case is from a different population than the other subjects, or it is just an extreme case within the same population. This differentiation is not always straightforward, however, and sometimes it may be virtually impossible, such as when archival data are analyzed. The basic options for dealing with outliers are to do nothing, drop these cases from the sample, or modify their scores so they have less influence on the analysis. The second choice means a smaller sample size, which may be of trivial concern in a large sample with a handful of outliers or may be a greater problem in a smaller sample with many outliers. The effect of including or excluding outliers can be evaluated by running the analysis both ways. If the results are dramatically different, then both sets of findings should be reported in the written summary of the results.

Extreme scores of univariate outliers can be changed to equal the next most extreme score, for instance, or to a value that is three standard deviations away from the mean. Another way is to transform the scores with a mathematical operation in the hope that the new distribution is more normal, which may bring outliers closer to the mean. (Transformations are discussed in the next section.) Modifying univariate outliers through score substitutions or transformations tends to reduce the number of multivariate outliers, at least ones with extreme scores on more than one variable. Multivariate outliers with unusual patterns of scores but no extreme individual ones present a tougher problem: should they remain in the sample or be dropped? One suggestion by Tabachnick and Fidell (1996) may be helpful: results of contrasts of the outlier cases against the remaining subjects across all the variables may indicate the particular combination of the latter that distinguish these two groups of subjects. Such information may help the researchers to identify variables that may be candidates for transformation or to better understand the characteristics of the cases to which the overall results may not generalize. For more information, readers are referred to Barnett and Lewis (1978) and Bacon (1995).

4.7 Normality

Univariate Normality

Estimation procedures that are widely used in SEM typically assume normal distributions for continuous variables. Non-normality can occur on two levels. The first is univariate, which concerns the distributions of the individual variables. *Skew* and *kurtosis* are two ways that a distribution can be non-normal, and they can occur either separately or together in a single variable. Unlike normal distributions, which are symmetrical about their means, those that are skewed are asymmetrical because they have most of the cases either below the mean (positive skew) or above it (negative skew). Kurtosis means a relative excess of cases in the tails of a distribution relative to a normal curve. Positive kurtosis indicates a peaked distribution with long, thin tails; negative kurtosis implies a flatter distribution, also with too many cases in the tails. (The terms "leptokurtic" and "platykurtic" are sometimes used to describe distributions with positive or negative kurtosis, respectively.)

Extreme skew is easy to spot by inspecting frequency distributions; normal probability plots, which show the relation of actual z scores to ones expected in a normal curve, are useful for spotting both skew and kurtosis. Most statistical packages—and some model-fitting programs when a raw data file is analyzed—also print numerical indexes of univariate skew and kurtosis, and the following two are probably the most widely used:

$$\text{Skew} = \frac{\Sigma(X - M)^3}{SD^3} \quad \text{and} \quad \text{Kurtosis} = \frac{\Sigma(X - M)^4}{SD^4}, \quad (4.3)$$

where SD^3 and SD^4 are the standard deviations of X raised to the third or fourth power.

The sign of the univariate skew index indicates the direction of the skew, positive or negative; zero indicates a symmetrical distribution. The index of univariate kurtosis provides comparable information: values less than zero indicate negative kurtosis (flat, too many tail cases); values greater than zero suggest positive kurtosis (peaked with long tails); and zero means no kurtosis. Many statistical programs also print significance tests of univariate skew and kurtosis indexes, but these tests may not be very useful with large samples because even slight departures from normality can yield significant results.

An alternative to significance tests of univariate skew and kurtosis indexes is to interpret their absolute values, but there are few clear guidelines about how much non-normality is problematic. Some suggestions can be offered, though, that are based on computer simulation ("Monte Carlo") studies of estimation methods used for SEM (e.g., Chou & Bentler, 1995; Hu, Bentler, & Kano, 1992; West, Finch, & Curran, 1995). Data sets with absolute values of univariate skew indexes greater than 3.0 seem to be described as "extremely" skewed by some authors of these studies. There appears to be less consensus about kurtosis, however; absolute values of the univariate kurtosis index from 8.0 to over 20.0 have been described as indicating "extreme" kurtosis. A conservative compromise, then, seems to be that absolute values of the kurtosis index greater than 10.0 may suggest a problem and values greater than 20.0 may indicate a more serious one.

Multivariate Normality

The second level of non-normality is multivariate. *Multivariate normality* is a common assumption of the data in SEM, and it means that (1) all the univariate distributions are normal; (2) the joint distributions of any combination of the variables are also normal; and (3) all bivariate scatterplots are linear and homoscedastic. (Linearity and homoscedasticity are described below in section 4.8.) Because it is impractical to examine the joint frequency distributions of three or more variables, it is difficult to assess all aspects of multivariate normality. Fortunately, most instances of multivariate non-normality are detectable through the inspection of univariate distributions. Deletion of cases that are univariate or multivariate outliers or modification of their scores may also enhance multivariate normality. Some computer programs also print the values of indexes of multivariate skew or kurtosis by Mardia (1970). The normalized versions of Mardia's coefficients are interpreted as z scores, but these z statistics could be significant in a large sample with only small departures from multivariate normality.

Transformations

One way to deal with non-normal univariate distributions (and thereby address multivariate non-normality) is with *transformations*, which means that the original scores are converted with a mathematical operation to new ones that may be more normally distributed. Because transformations alter the shape of the distribution, they can be useful for dealing with outliers, too. For instance, transformations that normalize positively skewed distributions such as square root ($X_{\text{transformed}} = X_t = \sqrt{X}$), logarithmic (e.g., $X_t = \log_{10} X$ or $\log_e X$), or inverse functions ($X_t = 1/X$) tend to pull outlying scores closer to the center of the distribution. Examples of other transformations include the same three just mentioned but applied to the original scores subtracted from a constant that equals the highest score plus 1, which may remedy negative skew. Odd root (e.g., $X_t = \sqrt[3]{X}$) and sine functions that tend to bring outliers in from both tails of the distribution toward the mean, and odd power polynomial (e.g., $X_t = X^3$) and so-called folded root transformations (e.g., $X_t = \sqrt{2X} - 2(1 - X)$), may help for negative kurtosis (too many cases in the tails).

There are many other types of transformations, and this is one of their potential problems. That is, it may be necessary to try several different transformations before finding one that works for a particular distribution. The shapes of some distributions may be so non-normal, however, that essentially no transformation will work. This is especially true for J- or L-shaped distributions (severe negative or positive skew, respectively) wherein most subjects score at the extremes. Also, transformation means that the variable's original metric is lost and that interpretation of the results must be made in the metric of the transformed scores. If the original metric is arbitrary, then this may not be problematic; otherwise, loss of the original measurement scale could be a sacrifice. Readers can find more detailed presentations about transformations in Armitage and Berry (1987), Hartwig and Dearing (1979), and Mosteller and Tukey (1977).

4.8   Linearity and Homoscedasticity

Linearity and homoscedasticity are two aspects of multivariate normality that can be evaluated through the inspection of bivariate scatterplots. A homoscedastic scatterplot is one in which the scores of, say, Y (the criterion) are evenly distributed along the length of the regression line that describes its relation to X (the predictor). Heteroscedasticity can be caused by non-normality in X or Y or by more random error (unreliability) at some levels of X or Y than at others. For example, a cognitive test may not reliably measure the skills of low-ability subjects but has adequate reliability for higher-ability subjects. A transformation may remedy heteroscedasticity due to non-normality but may not be helpful for heteroscedasticity due to differential reliability. Also, some heteroscedastic relations are expected, especially for developmental variables. For example, age is related to height, but the range of individual differences in height increases from childhood to adolescence.

Linearity was discussed in Chapter 2 as one of the factors that affect the magnitudes of Pearson correlations, as were the two kinds of nonlinear relations, curvilinear and interactive (section 2.6). Very briefly reviewed, an interactive relation in its most basic form occurs when the relation between X and Y changes across the levels of a third variable, W. Although strong bivariate curvilinear relations may be readily detected by looking at scatterplots, there is no comparably easy way to visually scan for interactive effects. Although one could possibly examine scatterplots for X and Y for different levels of scores on W, this is not generally a practical solution, especially with a large number of variables. Instead, researchers tend to rely more on theory and their own judgment about when to test for interactive effects among particular sets of variables. The estimation of curvilinear and interactive effects of observed and latent variables in SEM is discussed in Chapter 10.

4.9   Other Screening Issues

Grouped versus Ungrouped Data

Grouped data sets are ones in which subjects are classified into discrete groups (gender, treatment condition, etc.), usually with the intention of treating group membership as an exogenous variable. Data that are ungrouped implies just the opposite—that the cases are considered to belong to a single, undifferentiated sample. If the data are grouped, then the evaluation of case-related problems like outliers or distributional/relational characteristics such as normality or linearity should be conducted within each group. For example, group average scores should be used for mean substitutions of missing observations instead of the overall sample means. An example of the screening of grouped data is presented later. For additional examples, see Tabachnick and Fidell (1996, chap. 4).

Relative Variances

Another issue of data screening concerns the relative magnitudes of the variances. As is described in Chapter 5, some estimation methods used in SEM are iterative, which means that initial estimates are derived and then modified through subsequent cycles of recalculations. The goal of iterative estimation is to derive better estimates at each stage, ones that improve the overall fit of the model to the data. When the improvements from step to step become very small, iterative estimation stops. However, if the estimates do not converge to stable values, then the process may fail. One possible cause of failure of iterative estimation are variances of observed variables that are very different in magnitude (e.g., $s_X^2 = 1,200.00$, $s_Y^2 = 0.12$). When the computer adjusts the estimates from one step to the next in an iterative process, the sizes of these changes may be huge for variables with small variances but trivial for others with large variances. Consequently, the entire set of estimates may head toward worse rather than better fit of the model to the data.

To prevent this problem, variables with extremely low or high variances can be rescaled by multiplying their scores by a constant. Multiplication of scores on X by, say, 5 will increase X's variance by 5^2, or 25-fold; likewise, multiplication by 1/5 will reduce its variance by 1/25. Note that rescaling a variable this way changes its mean and variance but not its correlation with other variables. Although there is no absolute rule, a conservative suggestion would be to consider rescaling when the ratio of the largest to the smallest variance is greater than 10.

4.10   Example of Data Screening

The results of the analysis of a hybrid structural equation model with the data described in this section is reported in Chapter 8, but their screening is described here. At the beginning of the school year

(Time 1), a total of 494 students in grades 6, 7, and 8 in four different schools were administered a measure of alcohol-related expectancies. Six of seven scales on the measure reflect expectations that alcohol has beneficial effects on behavior (e.g., enhances relaxation, improves sociability); the seventh is about the degree of expected negative consequences like cognitive deterioration. High scores on all seven scales indicate stronger beliefs in each area. The students were also administered a four-part measure about the quantity and frequency of their drinking, related problems (e.g., fights with peers or arguments with parents), and the number of intoxications within the last year. (Readers are referred to Kline, 1996, for more information about the sample and measures.) The same measures were readministered at the end of the school year (Time 2), but only 408 of the original 494 students (83%) were available for retesting.

The most obvious potential problem with these data concerns the pattern of missing observations. That is, is attrition related to the students' alcohol expectancies or levels of drinking? If so, then the pattern of data loss is not random. To address this question, students who were retained in the study were compared to those who were not retained across all Time 1 variables. A dichotomous variable coded "1" for "not retained" ($N = 86$) and "2" for "retained" ($N = 408$) was correlated with each of the seven expectancy and four drinking scales. Although none of these correlations were large, some were statistically significant. For example, nonretained students reported more drinking-related problems and intoxications ($r = .20$ and .15, respectively), greater quantity and frequency of drinking (both $rs = .09$), and weaker expectancies about negative effects of alcohol ($r = -.15$). Although these results are based only on Time 1 observations, they suggest that Time 2 data may underestimate the drinking levels among these students. Although the degree of this underestimation may not be large, the overall data loss pattern appears to be systematic rather than missing at random.

Summarized in Table 4.2 are the results of univariate screening of the expectancy and drinking variables by gender for the students tested at both times. Reported for each variable are values of univariate skew and kurtosis indexes, squared multiple correlations (R^2), the number of scores more than three standard deviations away from the mean, test–retest correlations from Time 1 to Time 2, and the internal consistency reliability coefficients (r_{xx}). (Reliability is discussed in Chapter 7, section 7.3.)

Although there are relatively few extreme scores in this sample and the values of all squared multiple correlations are less than .90, other problems are apparent, which are reported in boldface in Table

TABLE 4.2. Univariate Screening of Expectancy and Drinking Variables

Variable	Expectancy							Drinking			
	1	2	3	4	5	6	7	Q	F	P	I
Girls (N = 204; with listwise deletion, N = 199)											
Test–retest r	.60	.70	.42	.56	.45	.45	.64	.57	.51	**.15**	.42
Time 1											
Skew	.14	.67	1.26	−.61	**−3.07**	−.24	−.80	.51	.90	**8.60**	**4.32**
Kurtosis	−.73	−.03	1.78	−.32	**16.39**	−.82	−.12	−.13	1.47	**79.56**	**19.96**
No. of outliers	0	1	3	0	3	0	0	0	0	3	6
R^2	.65	.63	.42	.56	.42	.41	.64	.69	.68	.29	.41
r_{xx}	.76	.72	**.39**	.70	.70	**.40**	.77	.64	.61	.77	NA
Time 2											
Skew	.14	.71	1.72	−.50	−2.56	−.53	−.85	.65	1.06	**8.66**	**4.43**
Kurtosis	−.96	.11	4.16	−.91	9.64	−.70	−.16	.15	2.34	**86.60**	**22.48**
No. of outliers	0	1	4	0	6	0	1	0	10	3	4
R^2	.64	.63	.39	.59	.37	.45	.67	.79	.79	.38	.34
r_{xx}	.83	.69	.53	.77	.73	.53	.81	.61	.62	.68	NA
Boys (N = 204; with listwise deletion, N = 193)											
Test–retest r	.70	.67	.32	.63	.57	.42	.60	.53	.45	**.11**	.60
Time 1											
Skew	.13	.54	1.14	−.45	−1.67	−.38	−.71	.42	.75	**5.52**	2.92
Kurtosis	−.73	−.25	.81	−.63	3.00	−.66	−.29	−.62	−.06	**33.38**	7.78
No. of outliers	0	0	3	0	6	0	0	0	0	4	9
R^2	.65	.64	.42	.58	.49	.43	.60	.64	.61	.23	.50
r_{xx}	.74	.74	.54	.67	.76	**.33**	.73	.71	.68	.82	NA
Time 2											
Skew	−.01	.46	1.31	−.48	−1.67	−.40	−.65	.46	.88	**5.50**	3.01
Kurtosis	−.79	−.42	1.78	−.83	2.66	−.85	−.42	.78	.29	**32.28**	8.31
No. of outliers	0	0	4	0	5	0	0	0	0	6	10
R^2	.73	.60	.41	.62	.48	.44	.69	.72	.69	.32	.66
r_{xx}	.79	.73	.62	.74	.74	**.50**	.79	.70	.73	.80	NA

Note. Values in boldface indicate potential problems such as absolute value of the skew index >3 or kurtosis index >10, internal consistency reliability <.50, or test–retest r < .30. r_{xx}, internal consistency reliability (alpha); NA, not applicable because this measure has a single item. Expectancy scales: 1, Global Positive; 2, Enhances Sociability; 3, Improves Cognitive–Motor Skills; 4, Enhances Sexuality; 5, Deteriorates Cognitive-Behavior; 6, Increases Arousal; 7, Promotes Relaxation. Drinking scales: Q, Quantity; F, Frequency; P, Problems; I, Intoxications.

4.2. For example, there may be severe positive skew and kurtosis in the distributions of two of the drinking variables, the numbers of problems and intoxications. Inspection of the frequency distributions of these variables clearly indicated why this is so: a total of 95% of the girls and 86% of the boys reported zero problems due to drinking; also, 82% of the girls and 78% of boys reported that they were not intoxicated within the last year. Although these percentages are not unexpected given the relatively young age of the subjects, it is not likely that any transformation will normalize variables with such narrow ranges of individual differences. There is an additional complication with the drinking problems variable: its test–retest correlations are very low for both groups (girls, $r = .15$; boys, $r = .11$), but these results could be due to restricted ranges. Considering all of these difficulties, the drinking problem and intoxication variables were excluded from subsequent analyses.

Other problems concern two expectancy scales–one about the belief that alcohol improves cognitive and motor skills (column 3 in Table 4.2), and the other about increase in arousal (column 6). Three of four (Times 1 and 2) internal consistency reliability coefficients are $\leq .40$; the fourth is only .54. The test–retest correlations of these same expectancy scales are also relatively low, all $\leq .45$. Based on these results, these two variables may be very susceptible to random measurement error. Consequently, these variables were also excluded from further analyses.

The next data screening step concerned outliers. The relatively few univariate outliers were converted to values three standard deviations away from their respective means. After this change, potential multivariate outliers were identified with the Mahalanobis distance statistic. With five expectancy scales (2 omitted) and two drinking measures (two omitted), the degrees of freedom for the Mahalanobis distance statistics are 14 (seven variables, two times) and the critical value of $\chi^2(14)$ at the .001 level is 36.12. Within the male sample, there were two cases with squared Mahalanobis distances that exceeded 36.12; a total of three cases were significantly different from the others in the female sample. Because these numbers of cases are quite small—about 1% of each group—they can be dropped from the sample with little concern about loss of information.

The final step concerned missing observations among the 403 remaining subjects. Listwise deletion of any case with one or more missing observations resulted in an overall sample size of 392 complete protocols (199 girls, 193 boys), which is 97% of the total. Thus, the overall proportion of cases with missing observations is relatively small. Also, missing observations did not seem to occur for any particular set of variables. Instead, they seemed to occur throughout the questionnaire and were the result of subjects not responding to individual items. Because the overall number of missing observations among these subjects was so small and their pattern seemed random, mean scores calculated separately by gender were used to replace them. With all of these modifications—the deletion of variables with severe distributional anomalies or poor reliability, the setting of univariate outliers to less extreme values, the deletion of likely multivariate outliers, and the imputation of missing observations among subjects who were retained at Time 2—the raw data were deemed ready for analysis.

4.11 Summary

Two sayings are pertinent about the topic of data screening: "An ounce of prevention is worth a pound of cure"; and: "There's never time to do it right in the first place but there's always time to do it over." And over and over . . . but not if you devote the worthwhile effort to the detection of data-related problems in the first place.

The first step in screening is to check the accuracy of data input by comparing the data file to the original records or inspecting basic descriptive statistics like minimum and maximum values. Other basic descriptive information for each variable such as the numbers of cases, frequency distributions, and values of indexes of univariate skew and kurtosis address issues of missing observations, outliers, and normality. Other characteristics of the data such as the degree of multicollinearity and linearity in their relations to one another can be addressed by inspecting bivariate correlations and scatterplots. Although there are more sophisticated multivariate indexes of data-related problems such as non-normality (e.g., Mardia's statistics), outliers (e.g., Mahalanobis distance), and multicollinearity (e.g., squared multiple correlations), review of the more basic information just described can detect some obvious problems. Ways to deal with each type of data-related problem are briefly summarized below.

Options for handling missing observations—listwise or pairwise deletion, imputation, and two SEM-based methods described in Chapter 10—all assume that the pattern of data loss is random. If not, then none of these procedures can remedy possible bias in the results. Although pairwise deletion uses all available cases for each calculation, correlation or covariance matrices derived using pairwise deletion can be nonpositive definite (singular), which means the matrix contains out-of-bounds values that cause computer estimation to fail. Another cause of nonpositive definiteness is multicollinearity, which refers to very high correlations (e.g., >.85) between two or more variables. Variables so redundant with others should be either combined into a composite with them or excluded from the analysis.

The most widely used estimation procedures in SEM assume that the distributions are multivariate normal, which means in part that all of the univariate distributions are normal and all bivariate relations are linear and homoscedastic. Univariate distributions that are obviously non-normal may be remedied by a transformation, but the variable's original scale is lost. Selection of a transformation that normalizes a distribution sometimes requires trial and error. Outliers can also contribute to multivariate non-normality. Univariate outliers have extreme scores on a single variable; multivariate outliers have atypical patterns of scores across several variables. If outlier cases seem to come from a different population than that of the rest of the cases, then outliers should probably be dropped from the sample. If they appear to be simply cases with unusual scores within the same population, then basic options include conducting the analysis with and without the outliers or making their scores less extreme.

Nonlinear relations between variables are not a problem per se. Nonlinear relations can be estimated in the data analysis, but they must be represented with special variables created by the researcher. Strong curvilinear relations between two variables may be easy to detect by inspecting scatterplots. There is no comparably straightforward way to look for interactive relations, however. Instead, the researcher must usually rely on theory to know which variables may be involved in interactive relations. The estimation of nonlinear effects in SEM is discussed in Chapter 10.

After the data are screened, they can be submitted to a model-fitting program in one of two forms: a raw data file or a matrix summary of the data. The analysis of the raw data is necessary when a specialized estimation procedure is used such as one that fits a model to incomplete raw scores. In most SEMs, though, the analysis can be conducted with a matrix summary of the data. The analysis of a correlation matrix is not recommended in part because the most commonly used estimation procedures in SEM assume that the variables are unstandardized. Covariance matrices (or correlation matrices with the standard deviations) are generally more appropriate. If means are analyzed in a SEM then both covariances and means must be submitted to a model-fitting program. The analysis of means in SEM is considered in Chapter 10.

We are now ready to consider basic SEM techniques in detail in

Part II of this book. Path analysis is considered in Chapters 5 and 6. The basic concepts of path analysis are then extended to the technique of confirmatory factor analysis (CFA; Chapter 7) and to analysis of hybrid models with both measurement and structural components (Chapter 8).

4.12   Recommended Readings

Some of the works cited earlier are quite specialized, but the ones listed here offer very useful starting points for learning more about data management. The first work cited below is more oriented toward data collection and organization; Tabachnick and Fidell (1996, chap. 4) deals specifically with data screening; and the article by Roth provides a good general introduction to the problem of missing data.

Bourque, L. B., & Clark, V. A. (1992). *Processing data: The survey example.* Newbury Park, CA: Sage.

Roth, P. L. (1994). Missing data: A conceptual review for applied psychologists. *Personnel Psychology, 47,* 537–560.

Tabachnick, B. D., & Fidell, L. S. (1996). *Using multivariate statistics* (3rd ed.). New York: HarperCollins.

PART TWO

CORE SEM TECHNIQUES

CHAPTER FIVE

Structural Models with Observed Variables and Path Analysis: I. Fundamentals, Recursive Models

Lie in ambush behind appearances, patiently, and strive to subject them to laws. Thus may you open up roads through chaos and help the spirit on its course.
—Nikos Kazantzakis (1959/1963, p. 227)

5.1 Foreword

This chapter introduces path analysis, which is the original SEM technique and concerns structural models with observed variables. For both of these reasons—its relative seniority in the SEM family and lack of a direct way to represent latent variables—path analysis is sometimes viewed as a less interesting or facile procedure than other varieties of SEM. But there are two reasons why this impression is both unfortunate and mistaken. First, sometimes researchers use only a single measure of each variable they are studying. Whether by design or by default due to factors like limitations of resources or time, the representation in models of latent constructs measured by multiple observed variables is not always possible. Second, it is important to know about the basic principles of path analysis because many of these same ideas hold for more complicated kinds of models. For instance, the evaluation of the structural portion of a hybrid model is essentially a path analysis conducted with estimated covariances among the latent variables. *Readers who master the fundamentals of path analysis will be better able to understand and critique a wider variety of structural equation models.*

This is the first of two chapters devoted to the evaluation of structural models with observed variables, or "path models" for short. Discussed in this chapter are general requirements for inferring causality from correlation, the goals of a path analysis, and the evaluation of recursive path models, the most common type in the social science literature. Also introduced in this chapter are concepts and methods that apply to the analysis of *any* type of structural equation model—path, factor, or hybrid. These include the issue of identification, the most widely used estimation method in SEM (maximum likelihood, ML), and general strategies for testing models. Consequently, a lot of material is presented in this chapter. Patient and diligent study of it, however, will help readers to more efficiently learn about other SEM techniques described later in the book. Chapter 6 is about nonrecursive path models and multiple group path analysis.

5.2   Correlation and Causation

Requirements for Estimating a Causal Effect

Path analysis involves the evaluation of presumed causal relations among observed variables. However, the basic datum of path analysis—and all SEM techniques—is the covariance, which includes correlation: $cov_{XY} = r_{XY} SD_X SD_Y$. The reader is probably familiar with the expression "correlation does not imply causation," which is often heard in introductory statistics or research methods courses. This mantra-like adage is an apt one because although a substantial correlation could indicate a causal relation, variables can also be associated in ways that have nothing to do with causality. The path analytic approach to the study of causation with correlations is as follows. Using the "building blocks" described in section 5.3, the researcher specifies a model that attempts to explain why X and Y (and other variables) are correlated. Part of this explanation may include presumed causal effects (e.g., X causes Y). Other parts of the explanation may reflect presumed noncausal relations such as a spurious association between X and Y due to common causes. The overall goal of a path analysis is to estimate causal versus noncausal aspects of observed correlations.

Part of the evaluation of a path model involves assessing how well it accounts for the data; that is, the observed correlations or co-variances. If the model is not rejected, however, the researcher cannot automatically conclude that the hypotheses about causality are correct. That is, failure to reject a path model (or any other type of structural equation model) does not prove that it is correct. The inference of causality requires more than just acceptable correspondence between the model and the data. To reasonably infer that X is a cause of Y, all of the following conditions must be met:

1. There is time precedence; that is, X precedes Y in time.
2. The direction of the causal relation is correctly specified; that is, X causes Y instead of the reverse or that X and Y cause each other. (The latter refers to reciprocal causation.)
3. The relation between X and Y does not dissappear when external variables such as common causes of both are held constant (partialed out).

Considered altogether, the three conditions just listed are a very tall order. Longitudinal designs allow for time lags between the measurement of X and Y (condition 1 above). The hypothesis that X causes Y would be bolstered if the magnitude of their association is substantial and X is measured before Y. However, note that measurement of X before Y does not by itself prove a causal relation even if their correlation is high. This is because the expected value of r_{XY} may not be zero even if Y causes X and the effect (X) is measured before the cause (Y) (condition 2 above; see Bollen, 1989, pp. 61–65). Even if X does indeed cause Y, the magnitude of their observed correlation may be low if the interval between their measurement is either too short (e.g., effects on Y take time to materialize) or too long (e.g., the effects are temporary and have dissipated).

Despite the problems just described, the assessment of variables at different times at least provides a measurement framework consistent with the specification and evaluation of directional causal effects. However, longitudinal designs pose potential difficulties such as subject attrition and the need for additional resources (e.g., Elias & Robbins, 1991; Judd & Kenny, 1981). Probably due to these reasons, most path analytic studies feature concurrent rather than longitudinal measurement. When the variables are concurrently measured, it is not possible to demonstrate time precedence. Therefore, the researcher needs a very clear, substantive rationale for specifying that X causes Y instead of the reverse or that X and Y mutually influence each other when all variables are measured at the same time. (More about this crucial point later.)

The third condition listed above for inferring that X causes Y applies to longitudinal and nonlongitudinal studies alike. This requirement involves controlling for common causes and correlations between X and other causes of Y. The experimental manipulation of variables is one way to control for such effects, but many variables for reasons of nature (e.g., gender) or ethics (e.g., smoking among humans) are not manipulable in the laboratory. Statistical control such as that represented by partial correlation or multiple regression is the other way to address the third condition listed earlier. However, both experimental and nonexperimental approaches to address this requirement are susceptible to the omission of relevant variables. The potential biasing effects of omitting variables from regression equations (section 2.8) is one example. A true experiment in which the researcher has not measured causal variables that are confounded with a manipulated independent variable is another example of a left-out variable error.

It is only from a solid base of knowledge about theory and research that one can even begin to address these requirements for inferring causation from correlation. Although facility with the statistical details of path analysis and other forms of SEM is essential, it is not a substitute for what could justifiably be called wisdom about one's research area. This point is emphasized time and again not only in this chapter but throughout the rest of the book.

Probablistic versus Deterministic Models of Causality

Briefly reviewed, the causes of exogenous variables are not represented in path models. In contrast, endogenous variables are specified as caused by exogenous variables or other endogenous variables. Every endogenous variable has a disturbance, which represents variance unexplained by other observed variables in the model. A disturbance can also be seen as an unmeasured exogenous variable that represents all omitted causes of the endogenous variable. Path models thus assume that causality is probablistic rather than deterministic. Deterministic models assume a one-to-one correspondence between cause and effect: given a change in the causal variables, the same consequence is observed in all cases of the affected variable. Disturbances allow for changes in affected variables to occur at some probability less than 1.

Kenny (1979) suggested that disturbances are also compatible with the view that some portion of the unexplained variance is fundamentally unknowable because it reflects, for lack of a better term, free will—the ability of people to act on occasion outside of external influences on them. Of course, disturbances could also be seen as not incompatible with a more mechanistic view of human nature: that it is theoretically possible to specify every cause of some behavior and thus perfectly predict it. Although the latter view is a rather extreme one among scientists and nonscientists alike, there is nothing about path analysis per se that commits the researcher to a mechanistic or deterministic view of human behavior.

With these ideas in mind, let's consider some issues in the specification of path models whether they are recursive or nonrecursive.

5.3   Specification of Path Models

What to Include

The is perhaps the most basic specification issue: Given some phenomenon of interest—health status, unemployment, delinquency, etc.—what are all of the variables that affect it? The literature for relatively new research areas can be very limited, so decisions about what to include in the model sometimes need to be guided more by the researcher's experience and intuition than by published works. Consultation with experts in the field about possible model specifications may also be helpful. In more established areas, however, sometimes there is *too much* information. That is, there may be so many potential causal variables mentioned in the literature that it is virtually impossible to include them all. To deal with this situation, the researcher must again rely on his or her judgment to set priorities about which variables are the most crucial.

The specification error of omitting causal variables from a path model has the same potential consequence as omitting predictors from a regression equation (section 2.8): estimates of causal effects of variables included in the model are biased if there are omitted causal variables that covary with those in the model. The direction of this bias could be either underestimation of true causal effects or overestimation, depending upon the correlations between included and excluded variables. Note that underestimation probably occurs more often than overestimation, but the absolute magnitude of the bias increases as these correlations are higher. However, just as it is unrealistic to expect that all relevant predictors are included in a regression analysis, the same is true about including all causal variables in a path model. Given that most path models may be misspecified in this regard, the best way to minimize potential bias is preventative:

make an omitted variable an included one through careful review of extant theory and research.

How to Measure the Theoretical Variable

The selection of measures is a recurrent research problem. This problem is especially crucial in path analysis because all of the measurement eggs of a theoretical variable are placed in the one basket of its single observed measure. It is therefore crucial that measures have good psychometric characteristics. One essential characteristic is that the amount of measurement error is as small as possible. There are two general sources of measurement error, random and systematic. Inadvertent clerical errors in scoring, luck in guessing the correct alternative in a multiple-choice test, and temporary states of examinees such as fatigue are all examples of random error. Tests that are relatively free of random measurement error are called *reliable*. Systematic measurement error may affect all observations equally or some more than others. An improperly calibrated scale that underestimates everyone's weight by 5 pounds is an example of a systematic error that affects all scores by the same amount. A scale that underestimates the weight of heavier individuals more than lighter ones is an example of a systematic bias that affects some scores more than others. Measures that are relatively free from both random and systematic error may be called *valid*. The evaluation of reliability and validity is considered in more detail in section 7.3.

It is especially important in path analysis to use measures with good psychometric characteristics. One assumption of the technique (among others described later) is that the exogenous variables are measured without error. Although this assumption is not required of the endogenous variables, the general consequence of error-prone measures of either exogenous or endogenous variables in path analysis is that the statistical estimates of presumed causal effects may be biased. The nature of this potential bias is different, however, for exogenous and endogenous variables. The consequences of measurement error in path analysis are discussed later (section 5.11) after prerequisite concepts are introduced.

Building Blocks

In this overview of elements of path models, X refers to exogenous variables, Y to endogenous variables, D to disturbances, $\rightarrow$ to direct casual effects, $\rightleftarrows$ to reciprocal effects, and $\leftrightarrow$ to unanalyzed associations. An account of why observed variables are correlated with a path model can reflect two kinds of causal relations or two kinds of noncausal associations. The first kind of causal relation reflects presumed unidirectional influence and includes direct effects of one variable on another (e.g., $X \rightarrow Y$) or indirect effects through one or more mediating variables (e.g., $X \rightarrow Y_1 \rightarrow Y_2$). The second type of causal relation concerns feedback loops, either direct or indirect: direct feedback effects involve only two variables in a reciprocal causal relation (e.g., $Y_1 \rightleftarrows Y_2$); indirect loops involve three or more variables (e.g., $Y_1 \rightarrow Y_2 \rightarrow Y_3 \rightarrow Y_1$). Feedback loops represent mutual influence among variables that are concurrently measured. As an example of a possible feedback relation, consider general vocabulary breadth and reading achievement: a broader vocabulary may facilitate reading, but reading may also result in a bigger vocabulary; thus, these variables may both cause and affect each other.

The two kinds of noncausal relations that can be represented in path models are unanalyzed associations and spurious associations. Most path models with more than one observed exogenous variable assume unanalyzed associations between them (e.g., $X_1 \leftrightarrow X_2$). An unanalyzed association means just that: the two variables are assumed to covary, but the reasons why they covary—do they affect each other? do they have common causes?—are unknown. It is also possible to represent in path models unanalyzed associations between disturbances. Recall that disturbances represent all omitted causes of endogenous variables and in this sense can be seen as unmeasured exogenous variables. An unanalyzed association between a pair of disturbances is called a *disturbance correlation* (for standardized variables) or a *disturbance covariance* (for unstandardized variables). The term "disturbance correlation" is used from this point on to refer to unanalyzed associations between disturbances regardless of whether the variables are standardized or not. A disturbance correlation is represented by the standard symbol for an unanalyzed association (e.g., $D_1 \leftrightarrow D_2$) and reflects the assumption that the endogenous variables share at least one common omitted cause. Accordingly, the *absence* of the symbol for an unanalyzed association between two disturbances reflects the presumption of independence of unmeasured causes. Unlike unanalyzed associations between exogenous variables, which are routinely represented in path models, the inclusion of disturbance correlations in a structural model is not so simple. The reasons why are elaborated later, but for now it is sufficient to know that correlated disturbances are not automatically included in path models.

One other point about disturbances and unanalyzed associations:

if observed exogenous variables have unanalyzed associations and disturbances can have them too, can a disturbance have an unanalyzed association with an exogenous variable (e.g., $X \leftrightarrow D$)? Theoretically, it can, and such a correlation would imply the presence of an omitted variable (e.g., W) that causes both the exogenous variable X and the endogenous variable Y. In other words, part of the covariance of X and Y is spurious due to a common cause. However, it is usually assumed in SEM that the exogenous variables and the disturbances are unrelated. (For an example of the estimation of $X \leftrightarrow D$ and conditions required to do so, see Kenny, 1979, pp. 93–95). Part of the reason for this assumption is statistical. Specifically, when multiple regression is used to estimate a recursive path model, then it must be assumed that the exogenous variables and the disturbances are uncorrelated. (How to use multiple regression to estimate recursive models and related assumptions is discussed later.) Another reason is more conceptual: assuming the independence of disturbances and exogenous variables permits the estimation of causal effects of the latter (e.g., $X \rightarrow Y$), holding omitted causal variables constant. Recall that the derivation of regression coefficients accomplishes the same thing but among observed variables (section 2.8). The assumption of uncorrelated Xs and Ds provides what Bollen (1989) calls "pseudo-isolation" of X from all other causes of Y that are unmeasured and thus omitted from the model. This is a strong assumption, one that is probably violated in most SEMs. As discussed earlier, though, the seriousness of violating this assumption increases with the absolute magnitudes of the correlations between excluded and included variables, which once again highlights the importance of accurate specification.

Spurious associations in path models are represented by specifying common causes. For example, if X is specified as a cause of both Y_1 and Y_2 ($X \rightarrow Y_1$, $X \rightarrow Y_2$), then at least part of the observed correlation between these two endogenous variables is presumed to be spurious. If the model contains no other direct or indirect causal effect between these variables (e.g., $Y_1 \rightarrow Y_2$), then the entire association between them is presumed to be spurious. Spurious associations can also involve multiple common causes.

Directionality

The specification of the directionalities of presumed casual effects is a crucial part of a path analysis. The measurement of some variables before others in a longitudinal study provides one means to specify directionality. When variables are concurrently measured, then the specification of directionality requires a clear rationale. Sometimes common sense can narrow the possibilities. If Y_1 is parental IQ and Y_2 is child IQ, for instance, then the specification of $Y_1 \rightarrow Y_2$ may be more plausible than either $Y_2 \rightarrow Y_1$ or $Y_1 \rightleftarrows Y_2$. Many other times, though, the specification of directionality must be guided by theory or results of empirical research. For example, recall the path model of delinquency by Lynam, Moffitt, and Stouthamer-Loeber (1993) introduced in Chapter 3 (section 3.4; Figure 3.1). Lynam et al. specified that verbal ability affects delinquency, but both variables were concurrently measured, which raises the question: why this particular direction? Is it not also plausible that through things like withdrawal from school, drug use, or head injuries from fights delinquent behavior could affect verbal ability? The arguments offered by Lynam et al. for their specification of verbal ability $\rightarrow$ delinquency over the reverse included the following: their subjects were relatively young (about 12 years old), which may rule out delinquent careers long enough to impair their verbal skills; they also cited results of prospective research that suggest that low verbal ability precedes antisocial acts. These particular arguments have been criticized—see Block (1995) and the response by Lynam and Moffitt (1995)—but at least they exemplify the types of reasons that researchers should provide for their specifications of directionality.

What if a researcher is fundamentally uncertain about the directionalities of effects among the variables? There are basically three options: (1) forego path analysis in favor of techniques that require fewer a priori assumptions like multiple regression or canonical correlation; (2) specify and test alternative path models, each with different directionalities; or (3) include reciprocal effects in the model as a way to cover both possibilities (e.g., $Y_1 \rightleftarrows Y_2$). The last two alternatives may seem appealing to someone who is keen to conduct a path analysis, but neither is a magical solution. In fact, the first choice may be preferable. As is demonstrated later, it is possible in path analysis—or with any SEM technique—that different models may fit the same data equally well. When (not if!) this occurs, there is no statistical basis for choosing one model over the another. Also, the inclusion of reciprocal effects is not a simple matter. The addition of even one reciprocal effect to a model makes it nonrecursive, which makes the model more difficult to analyze. (More about this point later.) Thus, there are potential costs to the inclusion of reciprocal effects in a path model as a "fudge factor" against uncertainty about directionality.

Model Complexity

Given the problems about directionality just discussed, why not make life easier for yourself and specify a path model wherein everything causes everything else? There is a problem with doing so because there is a limit on how many statistical effects—parameters—can be represented in a path model. This limit is determined by the number of *observations,* which is *not* the sample size (number of cases) but instead is the number of variances and covariances among the observed variables. A quick way to count the number of observations is as follows:

$$\text{Number of observations} = \frac{v(v+1)}{2}, \tag{5.1}$$

where v is the number of observed variables. For example, suppose that the there are four observed variables in a path model. Using Equation 5.1 yields 4(5)/2, or 10; thus, there are 10 observations altogether. Note that this number includes only the *unique* entries in a covariance matrix of four variables. That is, only entries above or below the diagonal (i.e., the covariances) are counted and added to the number of entries in the diagonal, which are the variances. The number of observations remains the same regardless of the sample size. If four variables are measured for 100, 300, or 1,000 subjects, the number of observations is still 10. Thus, adding more subjects does not increase the number of observations; only adding *variables* can do so.

   The number of observations for a path model sets the upper limit for the number of parameters that it may contain. Specifically, *the number of model parameters cannot exceed the number of observations.* A model may have fewer parameters than observations, but no more. There is general rule for counting the number of parameters of a path model, and it is as follows:

   The total number of variances and covariances (i.e., unanalyzed associations) of exogenous variables that are either observed or unmeasured (i.e., disturbances) and direct effects on endogenous variables from other observed variables equals the number of parameters.

Recall that disturbances can be seen as unmeasured exogenous variables that can covary with each other (but not generally with the observed exogenous variables). Because the causes of measured or unmeasured exogenous variables are not represented in a path models, they are considered free to vary. Endogenous variables, on the other hand, are represented as caused by other variables including their own disturbances. Thus, they are not free to vary and covary. Instead, the path model as a whole attempts to account for variances of the endogenous variables and why they covary with each other. Thus, the variances and covariances of the endogenous variables are not considered model parameters. Direct effects on endogenous variables from other observed variables (exogenous or endogenous), however, require statistical estimates and thus are model parameters.

Although the reasons are outlined later, a model with more parameters than observations is too statistically complex for empirical analysis. Such models are not identified, which means that it is mathematically impossible to derive unique estimates of each of its parameters. The most likely symptom of this problem is that a model-fitting program may "crash" or terminate its run with error messages. Analogous situations occur in multiple regression when there are more predictors than cases or in exploratory factor analysis when there are more items than cases: the computer cannot conduct the analysis because the model is too complex to be estimated with the available observations.

5.4   Types of Path Models

There are two basic kinds of path models, recursive and nonrecursive. Of the two, *recursive models* are the most straightforward and have two basic features: their disturbances are uncorrelated, and all causal effects are unidirectional. *Nonrecursive models* have feedback loops or may have correlated disturbances. Consider models (a) and (b) of Figure 5.1. Model (a) is recursive because its disturbances are independent and no variable is both a cause and an effect of another variable. For example, Y_1 and X_2 are specified as direct causes of Y_2, X_1 is an indirect cause of Y_2 through Y_1, but Y_2 has no direct effect back onto one of its presumed causes. In contrast, model (b) is nonrecursive because it has a direct feedback loop in which Y_1 and Y_2 are specified as causes and effects of each other ($Y_1 \rightleftarrows Y_2$). Model (b) also has a disturbance correlation. (Note that models with indirect feedback loops such as $Y_1 \rightarrow Y_2 \rightarrow Y_3 \rightarrow Y_1$ are also nonrecursive.)

There is another type of path model, one that has unidirectional effects and correlated disturbances, two examples of which are presented as models (c) and (d) of Figure 5.1. Unfortunately, the classification of such models in the SEM literature is not consistent. Some authors call these models nonrecursive, but others use the term *partially recursive*. But more important than the label for these models is the distinction made in the figure. Although the reasons

(a) Recursive

(b) Nonrecursive

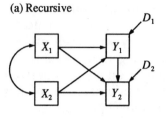

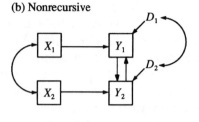

Partially Recursive Models

(c) Without Direct Effects among *Y*s
(Considered Recursive)

(d) With Direct Effects among *Y*s
(Considered Nonrecursive)

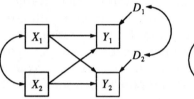

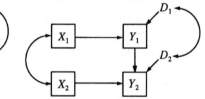

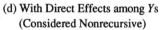

FIGURE 5.1. Examples of recursive, nonrecursive, and partially recursive path models.

are explained later, partially recursive models in which correlated disturbances appear *without* direct effects among the endogenous variables (model (c) in Figure 5.1) can be treated in their analysis just like recursive models. In contrast, partially recursive models where the correlated disturbances occur *with* direct effects among the endogenous variables (model (d) in Figure 5.1) require more specialized estimation procedures. Accordingly, all ensuing references to recursive and nonrecursive models include, respectively, partially recursive models without and with direct effects among the endogenous variables.

The distinction between recursive and nonrecursive models has several implications, some conceptual and others practical. The assumptions of recursive models that all causal effects are unidirectional and that the disturbances are independent when there are direct effects among the endogenous variables greatly simplify the statistical demands for their analysis. Specifically, multiple regression can be used to estimate recursive models. Many social scientists are familiar with multiple regression, and computer programs with regression modules are widely available. The same assumptions of recursive models that ease the analytical burden are also very restrictive, however. For example, causal effects that are not unidirectional (e.g., as in a feedback loop) or disturbances that are correlated in a model with direct effects between the endogenous variables (e.g., model (d) of Figure 5.1) cannot be represented in a recursive model. Although these types of effects can be represented in nonrecursive models, such models cannot be analyzed with multiple regression. Nonrecursive models require more specialized statistical methods and may also require additional assumptions. Also, the likelihood of a problem in the analysis of a nonrecursive model is much greater than for a recursive model. (One of these problems is that of identification, which is discussed in section 5.5.) Perhaps due to such difficulties, one sees relatively few nonrecursive models in the social science literature. But in some disciplines, especially economics, they are much more common, which suggests that the challenges of nonrecursive models are not unmanageable. Nonrecursive path models are discussed in detail in Chapter 6.

Before we continue, let's apply the rules for counting observations (Equation 5.1) and parameters to the four path models of Figure 5.1. Because there are four observed variables in every model, the number of observations for each is $4(5)/2 = 10$. Summarized in the accompanying table are the numbers and types of parameters for each model. Note there that all four models meet the requirement for at least as many observations as parameters. Also note that a reciprocal effect (e.g., $Y_1 \rightleftarrows Y_2$ of model (b) of Figure 5.1) counts as two direct effects. Readers are encouraged to match the parameters listed in the table against the corresponding path models of Figure 5.1.

| | Type of parameter | | | |
| | Exogenous variables | | Direct effects on | |
Model	Variances	Covariances	endogenous variables	Total
(a) Recursive	X_1, X_2 D_1, D_2	$X_1 \leftrightarrow X_2$	$X_1 \rightarrow Y_1$ $\quad X_2 \rightarrow Y_1$ $X_1 \rightarrow Y_2$ $\quad X_2 \rightarrow Y_2$ $Y_1 \rightarrow Y_2$	10
(b) Nonrecursive	X_1, X_2 D_1, D_2	$X_1 \leftrightarrow X_2$ $D_1 \leftrightarrow D_2$	$X_1 \rightarrow Y_1$ $\quad X_2 \rightarrow Y_2$ $Y_1 \rightarrow Y_2$ $\quad Y_2 \rightarrow Y_1$	10
(c) Partially recursive (considered recursive)	X_1, X_2 D_1, D_2	$X_1 \leftrightarrow X_2$ $D_1 \leftrightarrow D_2$	$X_1 \rightarrow Y_1$ $\quad X_2 \rightarrow Y_1$ $X_1 \rightarrow Y_2$ $\quad X_2 \rightarrow Y_2$	10
(d) Partially recursive (considered nonrecursive)	X_1, X_2 D_1, D_2	$X_1 \leftrightarrow X_2$ $D_1 \leftrightarrow D_2$	$X_1 \rightarrow Y_1$ $\quad X_2 \rightarrow Y_2$ $Y_1 \rightarrow Y_2$	9

5.5   Principles of Identification

If life were simple and just, a researcher could proceed directly from specification to collection of the data to estimation. Unfortunately, just as life is sometimes unfair, the analysis of a path model is not always so straightforward. The problem that potentially complicates the evaluation of a path model—or any other type of structural equation model—is that of *identification*. A model is said to be identified if it is *theoretically* possible to calculate a unique estimate of every one of its parameters. If not, then the model is not identified. The word "theoretically" emphasizes identification as a property of the model and not of the data. For example, if a model is not identified, then some of its parameters are not uniquely estimable, and this remains so regardless of the sample size (100, 10,000, etc). Therefore, models that are not identified should be respecified; otherwise, attempts to analyze them may be fruitless.

A basic requirement for identification was mentioned in the previous section: there must be at least as many observations as model parameters. Models that violate this requirement are not identified; specifically, they are described as *underidentified*. As an example of how a deficit of observations leads to nonidentification, consider the following equation:

$$a + b = 6.$$

Look at this equation as a model, the "6" as an observation (i.e., a datum), and a and b as parameters. Because this model has more parameters (2) than observations (1), it is impossible to find unique estimates for a and b. In fact, there are an infinite number of solutions, including ($a = 4$, $b = 2$), ($a = 8$, $b = -2$), and so on, all of which satisfy the above equation. The same thing happens when a computer tries to derive unique estimates for the parameters of an underidentified path model: it is mathematically impossible to do so, and thus the attempt fails.

It is impossible to specify a recursive path model with more parameters than observations. Look again at model (a) of Figure 5.1. This recursive model already has as many parameters as observations (10). However, it is not possible to add another parameter to this model and still have it be recursive. For example, the addition of a disturbance correlation or a direct effect from Y_2 to Y_1 (which results in a direct feedback loop) to this model would make it nonrecursive. It can also be shown that due to their particular characteristics, recursive path models are always identified (e.g., Bollen, 1989, pp. 95–98).

Thus, although it is *theoretically* possible (that word again) to derive unique estimates of the parameters of recursive path models, their analysis can still be foiled by other types of difficulties. (Remember, life isn't fair.) Data-related problems are one such difficulty. For example, multicollinearity can result in what Kenny (1979) described as *empirical underidentification:* if two observed variables are very highly correlated (e.g., $r_{XY} = .90$), then practically speaking they are the same variable, which reduces the effective number of observations below the value indicated by Equation 5.1 (i.e., $v(v + 1)/2$). The analysis of a recursive model can also be foiled if the user of a model-fitting program specifies inaccurate initial estimates of model parameters. This problem concerns the issue of *starting values,* which is discussed later. The good news here is that neither of these potential problems is due to the inherent features of a recursive model. The first (multicollinearity) can be addressed through data screening (section 4.5); the second (bad starting values), through additional runs with a model-fitting program with better initial estimates.

The situation for nonrecursive path models is much more complicated. First, it is possible to inadvertently specify a nonrecursive model with more parameters than observations. Look at model (b) of Figure 5.1, which is nonrecursive. Although it appears that this model has "room" for two more direct effects ($X_1 \rightarrow Y_2$, $X_2 \rightarrow Y_1$), model (b) in the figure already has as many parameters as observations (10). Second, particular configurations of effects in a nonrecursive path model can make it nonidentified even if there are as many observations as parameters. As a simple example of how a model with equal numbers of parameters and observations can nevertheless fail to have a unique solution, consider the following two equations:

$$a + b = 6,$$

$$3a + 3b = 18.$$

Again, look at both of these equations as a single model, the total scores as observations, and a and b as parameters. Although this model has two observations and two parameters, it does have not a unique solution. In fact, there are an infinite number of solutions that satisfy both equations (e.g., ($a = 4$, $b = 2$), ($a = 8$, $b = -2$), etc.). The above two-observation, two-parameter model is underidentified due to an inherent characteristic: the second equation above ($3a + 3b = 18$) is not unique. Instead, it is simply three times the first equation ($a + b = 6$), which means that it cannot narrow the range of solutions that satisfy the first equation.

Although the example just presented oversimplifies the identification issue for nonrecursive path models, it points out one of the difficulties in their analysis: a nonrecursive model with at least as many observations as parameters is not necessarily identified. Fortunately, there are ways that a researcher can determine whether some (but not all) types of nonrecursive models are identified. These procedures are described in Chapter 6, but it is worthwhile to make the following point now: adding exogenous variables is one way to remedy an identification problem of a nonrecursive path model, but this can typically only be done *before* the data are collected. *Thus, it is crucial to evaluate whether a nonrecursive path model is identified right after it is specified and before the study is conducted.*

Two other terms require definition: just-identification and overidentification. A *just-identified* model has equal numbers of parameters and observations *and* is identified. (Just-identified models are sometimes called *saturated models*.) For the reasons just discussed, a nonrecursive model with equal numbers of parameters and observations is not necessarily identified, so the term "just-identified" does not automatically apply to it. It does, however, apply to recursive models with the same property. As a demonstration of just-identification, consider the following two equations as a model with two observations (6 and 10) and two parameters (*a* and *b*). Also note that the second equation is unique; that is, it is not just a simple product of the first:

$$a + b = 6,$$

$$2a + b = 10.$$

This two-observation, two-parameter model has a single solution ($a = 4$, $b = 2$); therefore, it is just-identified. Also notice something else about this just-identified model: given estimates of its parameters, it can perfectly reproduce the observations (i.e., the total scores 6 and 10). The same thing is true for just-identified path models: not only do they theoretically have unique solutions, but given such they will also perfectly fit the data. The implication of this characteristic for the testing of path models is discussed later.

A path model can also have fewer parameters than observations. If such models are also identified (true for a recursive model; perhaps not for a nonrecursive one), then they are called *overidentified*. As an example of parameter estimation for an overidentified model, consider the set of equations below with three observations (6, 10, and 12) and two parameters (*a* and *b*):

$$a + b = 6,$$

$$2a + b = 10,$$

$$3a + b = 12.$$

Try as you might, you will be unable to find values of a and b that satisfy all three equations. For instance, the solution ($a = 4$, $b = 2$) works only for the first two; ($a = 2$, $b = 6$) satisfies only the last two; and ($a = 3$, $b = 3$) satisfies only the first and third. At first glance, the absence of a solution seems paradoxical, but there is a way to solve this problem: the imposition of a statistical criterion on the solution leads to unique estimates for the parameters of an overidentified model. An example of such for the three equations just presented could be: *Find values of* a *and* b *that are positive and yield totals such that the sum of the squared differences between the observations (6, 10, and 12) and these totals is as small as possible.* Applying this criterion to the estimation of parameters a and b yields a solution that not only yields the smallest total squared difference (.67) but is also unique (using only one decimal place, we obtain $a = 3.0$ and $b = 3.3$). Note, however, that this solution does not perfectly reproduce the observations (6, 10, and 12):

$$3.0 + 3.3 = 6.3,$$

$$2(3.0) + 3.3 = 9.3,$$

$$3(3.0) + 3.3 = 12.3.$$

Thus, although it is possible to find a unique solution for overidentified models, it may not perfectly reproduce the observations. By the same token, an overidentified path model may not perfectly fit the data. Although this characteristic may at first seem like a drawback, it has an important role in model testing, one that is explored later.

5.6   The Role of Sample Size

As already mentioned, the number of cases has no bearing on whether a path model is identified. What, then, is the role of sample size in path analysis—and in all other SEM techniques? Basically the same as for other kinds of statistical methods: results derived within larger samples have less sampling error and are more likely to be statistically significant than within smaller samples (section 2.9). The next logical question is this: how large a sample is required in path analysis in order for the results to be reasonably stable? Some guidelines about absolute sample size were offered in Chapter 1 (small, $N <$ 100; medium, N between 100 and 200; large, $N > 200$). An additional consideration is the complexity of the path model. That is, more complex models—those with more parameters—require larger samples than do more parsimonious models in order for the estimates to be comparably stable. Thus, a sample size of 200 or even much larger Ns may be insufficient for a very complicated path model.

Although there are no absolute standards in the SEM literature about the relation between sample size and model complexity, the following recommendations are offered: a desirable goal is to have the ratio of the number of subjects to the number of model parameters be 20:1; a 10:1 ratio, however, may be a more realistic target. Thus, a model with 10 parameters should have a minimum sample size of 100 cases. If the subject/parameter ratio is less than 5:1, the statistical stability of the results may be doubtful.

5.7   Overview of Estimation Options

There are basically two options for the analysis of recursive path models: (1) multiple regression or (2) estimation with a model-fitting program. The latter typically offers users the choice of different procedures, the most widely used of which is maximum likelihood (ML) estimation. For just-identified recursive path models, multiple regression and ML yield identical estimates of direct effects (path coefficients); estimates of disturbance variances may vary slightly because the two procedures use somewhat different denominators in these terms. Values of path coefficients for overidentified recursive models may be slightly different, but the two procedures generally yield similar results within large samples (i.e., their estimates are asymptotic).

Notwithstanding the similarity of results yielded by multiple regression and ML for recursive path models, there are three reasons why it is well worth the effort to learn how to use a model-fitting program. First, there are numerous statistical indexes of the overall fit of the model to the data that are available in the output of model-fitting programs that are not generated by regression programs. These fit indexes are very useful for testing certain types of hypotheses, especially those that involve the comparison of models. Second, there are several types of results that are automatically calculated by model-fitting programs that must be derived by hand when one uses a regression program. For simple models, these hand calculations are not too burdensome a chore. For complex models, though, it's a real advantage to let the computer do the work. Finally, the role of multiple regression as an estimation tool in SEM is limited essentially to recursive path models. In contrast, nonrecursive path models and models with latent variables (e.g., measurement and hybrid models) can be analyzed with ML. Indeed, it would be no exaggeration to describe ML estimation as the motor of SEM. (You are the driver.) Chapter 11 about Amos, EQS, and LISREL should be helpful for readers who have no prior experience with model-fitting programs.

Next, sections 5.8 and 5.9 respectively concern the estimation of recursive path models with multiple regression and with the ML method of a model-fitting program. Estimation options for nonrecursive path models are discussed in Chapter 6.

5.8   Estimation of Recursive Path Models with Multiple Regression

Derivation of Basic Estimates

The parameters of a recursive path model are the variances and covariances of the observed exogenous variables and of the disturbances and direct effects on the endogenous variables from other observed variables (section 5.3). The general steps for using multiple regression to derive standardized and unstandardized estimates of each type of parameter are summarized below. An example follows:

1. *Variances and covariances (unanalyzed associations) of the observed exogenous variables.* These are simply the observed values in the sample. For example, the standardized estimate of an unanalyzed association between two observed exogenous variables is their Pearson correlation and the unstandardized estimate is their covariance.
2. *Direct effects on the endogenous variables from other observed variables.* Find the first endogenous variable. Enter all variables specified to directly affect it as predictors in a regression equation. The beta weights from this analysis are the standardized path coefficients. The unstandardized regression coefficients are the unstandardized path coefficients. *Repeat this step for each of the remaining endogenous variables.*

3. *Variances of the disturbances.* Record the squared multiple correlations (R^2) from the analyses described in step 2. Subtraction of these squared correlations from 1 (i.e., $1 - R^2$) gives the proportions of unexplained variance.[1] The unstandardized estimate of the disturbance variance for endogenous variable Y, D, equals the product $(1 - R^2)s_Y^2$, which is an error variance in the original metric of Y. Note also that the ratio of the unstandardized variance of D over the observed variance of Y equals $(1 - R^2)$, the proportion of unexplained variance. In standardized form, the variance of D is 1.0, as is the variance of any standardized variable. However, in diagrams of path models in which the standardized solution is presented, disturbances are sometimes reported as proportions of unexplained variance. Options for presenting standardized estimates about disturbances in path diagrams are demonstrated later.

4. *Covariances (unanalyzed associations) of the disturbances.* This step concerns only partially recursive models without direct effects between the endogenous variables (e.g., model (c) of Figure 5.1). Kenny (1979) showed that the standardized estimate of a disturbance correlation in such a model is simply the partial correlation between the endogenous variables controlling for their common causes. For example, the partial correlation $r_{Y_1Y_2 \cdot X_1X_2}$ estimates the disturbance correlation for model (c) of Figure 5.1. The unstandardized estimate of this disturbance covariance is the partial covariance $r_{Y_1Y_2 \cdot X_1X_2} SD_{Y_1} SD_{Y_2}$. Readers are referred to Kenny (1979, pp. 52–61) for additional examples.

Roth, Wiebe, Fillingim, and Shay (1989) studied the relation of exercise, psychological hardiness, physical fitness, and level of stress to the frequency of health-related problems within a sample of 373 university students. Psychological "hardiness" refers to dispositional traits such as resiliency and willingness to look for opportunities in difficult situations. Roth et al. conceptualized exercise and hardiness

---

[1]An alternative in these calculations is to use shrinkage-corrected (adjusted) R^2s as estimates of the proportions of explained variance. Adjusted R^2 values are often reported in the output of regression programs. They are typically less than the observed R^2s because their values are corrected for the tendency of sample R^2s to be larger than the population value. However, adjusted R^2s can be negative, especially if the unadjusted R^2 is low and the sample size is small. With small samples, it is preferable to use adjusted R^2 values; with large samples, the two are usually so similar that it may make no appreciable difference.

as exogenous variables that affect fitness and stress, which in turn affect health. Also, Roth et al. believed that all of the effects of exercise and hardiness on illness are mediated by (respectively) fitness and stress. The recursive path model presented in Figure 5.2(a) is specified to represent these hypotheses. Note that the paths depicted with dashed lines in the figure were predicted by Roth et al. to be zero. These paths are included in the model in order to directly test these predictions.

Presented in the upper part of Table 5.1 is matrix summary of the data analyzed by Roth et al. (Note that *low* scores on the hardiness measure used by Roth et al. indicate *greater* hardiness. In order to avoid confusion due to negative correlations, the signs of the correlations that involve the hardiness measure were reversed before they were recorded in the table.) A covariance matrix constructed

TABLE 5.1. Analysis of a Recursive Path Model of Factor of Illness with Multiple Regression

Correlations, means, and standard deviations (Roth et al., 1989; $N = 373$ university students)

Variable	1	2	3	4	5
1. Exercise	—				
2. Hardiness	−.03	—			
3. Fitness	.39	.07	—		
4. Stress	−.05	−.23	−.13	—	
5. Illness	−.08	−.16	−.29	.34	—
M	40.90	0.00	67.10	4.80	716.70
SD	66.50	3.80	18.40	6.70	624.80

Regressions to generate path coefficients and disturbance variances

Criterion	Predictors	Regression coefficients		Standardized	R^2	$(1-R^2)$
		Unstandardized[a]				
1. Fitness	Exercise	.11**	(.01)	.39	.16**	.84
	Hardiness	.39	(.23)	.08		
2. Stress	Exercise	−.01	(.01)	−.01	.07**	.93
	Hardiness	−.39**	(.09)	−.22		
	Fitness	−.04*	(.02)	−.11		
3. Illness	Exercise	.32	(.48)	.03	.18**	.82
	Hardiness	−12.14	(7.98)	−.07		
	Fitness	−8.84**	(1.75)	−.26		
	Stress	27.12**	(4.55)	.29		

[a]The values in parentheses are standard errors.
*$p < .05$; **$p < .01$.

from the correlations and standard deviations of Table 5.1 was read into a general statistical package (e.g., SPSS, BMDP) and analyzed by a multiple regression program. A total of three multiple regressions were conducted to generate estimates of direct effects and disturbance variances. Results of these analyses are summarized in the lower part of Table 5.1, and they include the regression coefficients, the R^2s values, and the proportions of unexplained variance for each endogenous variable $(1 - R^2)$. Note that results of significance tests (which were conducted by the regression program) are reported in the table only for the unstandardized regression coefficients and not for the standardized coefficients (beta weights). For reasons discussed earlier (section 2.9), the significance levels of unstandardized estimates may apply to the standardized estimates, but that is not guaranteed.

Let's consider the standardized estimates first. The estimate of the unanalyzed association between the exogenous variables exercise and hardiness is simply their observed correlation, –.03. The beta weights listed in Table 5.1 are the standardized path coefficients. For example, the values .39 and .08 are the standardized path coefficients for the respective direct effects of exercise and hardiness on fitness. Standardized path coefficients are interpreted in the same way as beta weights. For example, the standardized path coefficient of .39 for the direct effect exercise → fitness means that fitness is expected to improve by .39 standard deviations given a change in exercise of one full standard deviation when the researcher is controlling for hardiness. As another example, the standardized path coefficient for the direct effect fitness → illness is –.26, which means that illness is predicted to decline by .26 standard deviations given a change in fitness of one standard deviation and no change on other variables also specified to affect illness (exercise, hardiness, stress). Also reported in Table 5.1 are the proportions of unexplained variance for each endogenous variable. For example, the proportion of unexplained variance of the illness variable is 82% $(1 - R^2 = 1 - .18)$. The proportion of unexplained variance for fitness is .84 and for stress is .93. The proportions of *explained* variance across the endogenous variables thus ranges from 7% for stress to 18% for illness.

All values of the standardized solution are presented in their appropriate places in the model in Figure 5.2(b). However, note two special things about the presentation of the standardized estimates in the figure. First, the variances of the observed exogenous variables exercise and hardiness are considered model parameters, but their standardized variances (1.0) are not reported in the figure. It is fairly standard practice in path analysis to report only the correlation (or

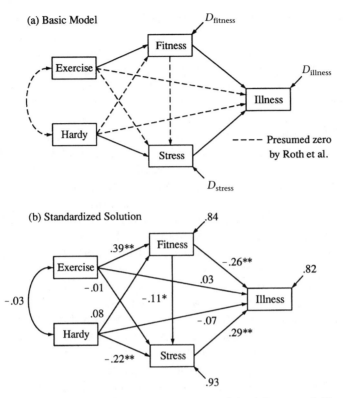

FIGURE 5.2. (a) A just-identified recursive model of factors of illness. (b) This model with standardized estimates. *$p < .05$; **$p < .01$.

covariance for the unstandardized solution) of observed exogenous variables but not their variances in the diagram of a path model. Second, even though the standardized estimates of disturbance variances equal 1.0, note that the values reported in the figure for the disturbances are proportions of unexplained variance. For example, the representation in Figure 5.2(b) "Fitness ← .84" for the disturbance of this endogenous variable means that 84% of the variance of fitness is unexplained, which equals the value of $(1 - R^2)$ for this variable (Table 5.1). The other depictions of disturbances in Figure 5.2(b) have similar meanings. The remaining numerical values in the figure are the standardized path coefficients. For practice, readers should match the beta weights listed in Table 5.1 against the path coefficients presented in Figure 5.2(b).

A common question about standardized path coefficients is this: what indicates a "large" direct effect?—a "small" one? Significance tests of their unstandardized counterparts do not really provide answers to this question. Results of significance tests reflect not only the absolute magnitudes of path coefficients but also factors such as the sample size and intercorrelations among the variables. The interpretation of the absolute values of standardized path coefficients is an alternative, but there are few guidelines about what is a "large" versus a "small" effect. Some suggestions are offered in Appendix 5.A at the end of this chapter, but they can be briefly summarized here: Standardized path coefficients with absolute values less than .10 may indicate a "small" effect; values around .30, a "medium" effect; and those greater than .50, a "large" effect. See Appendix 5.A for more details and cautions about these recommendations.

Let's return to Figure 5.2 for a brief summary of the results so far, based on the standardized estimates. Higher levels of exercise and hardiness are associated with better fitness, and all three generally predict lower levels of stress and illness. With one exception, standardized path coefficients for direct effects hypothesized by Roth et al. to be nil have absolute values less than .10. The exception involves the direct effect fitness → stress, for which the path coefficient is –.11. Overall, these results suggest that it may be possible to trim this model by eliminating some paths, which is demonstrated later.

Before the unstandardized solution for this problem is considered, a second way to report standardized estimates about disturbances in path diagrams is demonstrated. Consider Figure 5.3, which contains just the illness variable from the full path model of the previous figure. Figure 5.3(a) represents the disturbance expressed as the proportion of unexplained variance (.82), just as before. The alternative representation in Figure 5.3(b) retains the symbol for the disturbance (D) and has a number along the arrow that points to the illness variable, much like a path coefficient. In fact, this number *is* a path coefficient, one that indicates the direct effect of the standardized disturbance on the endogenous variable and is called a *residual path coefficient*. For recursive

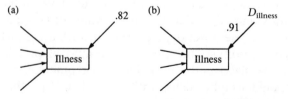

FIGURE 5.3. Two ways to present a standardized estimate of a disturbance in a path diagram: (a) percentage of unexplained variance; (b) residual path coefficient.

path models, residual path coefficients are interpreted as Pearson correlations between an endogenous variable and its disturbance. The basis for this interpretation lies in measurement theory, from which it can be shown that the correlation between the unexplained portion of a variable and the whole variable equals the square root of the unexplained variance (e.g., Nunnally & Bernstein, 1994, pp. 144–146). For example, the total proportion of explained variance (i.e., R^2) for the illness variable is 18% (see Table 5.1). One minus this value, $(1 - .18) = .82$, is the proportion of unexplained variance. The square root of $(1 - R^2)$ here is the square root of .82, which equals .91. This value is the residual path coefficient, and it estimates the correlation between the illness variable and its disturbance. Like any correlation, it can be squared to indicate the proportion of shared variance, $.91^2 = 82\%$. Thus, 82% of the variance of the illness variable is shared with its disturbance, which is the same value as the proportion of unexplained variance. Both representations in Figure 5.3 convey the same information, but the convention shown in Figure 5.3(a) is used throughout this book for standardized solutions.

The unstandardized estimate of the unanalyzed association between the exercise and hardiness variables of Figure 5.2 is their observed covariance, –7.56, which equals $-.03(66.50)(3.80)$, the product of their correlation and standard deviations. The unstandardized path coefficients are the unstandardized regression coefficients reported in Table 5.1. These values indicate change in the endogenous variables but in raw score units. For example, the unstandardized path coefficient for stress → illness is 27.12, which means that a 1-point increase in stress is associated with an increase of 27.12 points on the measure of illness holding all other causal variables constant. Unlike standardized path coefficients, though, the values of unstandardized path coefficients are not directly comparable across endogenous variables with different metrics, which is true of this example ($SD_{fitness} = 18.40$; $SD_{stress} = 6.70$; $SD_{illness} = 625.80$). The general relation between an unstandardized path coefficient P_{YX} for the direct effect of X on Y and the standardized path coefficient p_{YX} is as follows:

$$P_{YX} = p_{YX}(SD_Y/SD_X). \qquad (5.2)$$

(Compare Equations 5.2 and 2.16 for regression coefficients.)

Unstandardized estimates of the variances of the three disturbances for the model in Figure 5.2 equal proportions of unexplained variance times the observed variances of the endogenous variables in their original metrics. Calculated for each endogenous variable of the model of Figure 5.2, these disturbance variances are as follows:

$$D_{fitness}: \quad .84(18.40^2) = 285.39,$$

$$D_{stress}: \quad .93(6.70^2) = 41.75,$$

$$D_{illness}: \quad .82(625.80^2) = 321,133.03.$$

The first set of numerical values in each of the above expressions are proportions of unexplained variance. The second values in parentheses are the squared standard deviations (the variances) of each endogenous variable. The products of the two values are error variances. To illustrate the relation between unstandardized estimates of disturbance variances and the proportions of unexplained variance, consider the unstandardized disturbance variance for fitness calculated above, 285.39. The observed standard deviation for this variable is 18.40 (Table 5.1), which yields a variance of $18.40^2 = 338.56$. The ratio of the unstandardized disturbance variance over the observed variance of fitness is 285.39/338.56, or .84, which equals the proportion of unexplained variance $(1 - R^2)$ for fitness. As with unstandardized path coefficients, the magnitudes of unstandardized disturbance variances are not directly comparable across endogenous variables with different metrics.

Indirect and Total Effects

After the path coefficients are in hand, it is possible to calculate estimates of the indirect effects and total effects. Because regression programs do not directly calculate these values, it is necessary to do so by hand. As mentioned in Chapter 3, indirect effects involve mediator variables that "transmit" a portion of the effect of a prior variable onto a subsequent one. Indirect effects are estimated statistically as the products of the direct effects, either standardized or unstandardized, that comprise them. For example, the standardized indirect effect of fitness on illness through stress is the product of –.11 (fitness → stress) and .29 (stress → illness), or (–.11)(.29) = –.03. The rationale for this derivation is as follows: fitness has a certain direct effect on stress (–.11), but only part of this effect, .29 of it, is transmitted to illness. Indirect effects are interpreted just as path coefficients: here, illness is expected to decrease by –.03 standard deviations given a change of one full standard deviation in fitness via its effect on stress, a mediator variable.

Total effects are the sum of all the direct and indirect effects of one variable on another. For example, the standardized total effect of fitness on illness is the sum of its direct (–.26) and indirect effect (–.03), or –.29. Total standardized effects are also interpreted as path coefficients, and this value of –.29 means that increasing fitness by one standard deviation reduces illness by this amount via all direct and indirect causal links between these variables. Unstandardized estimates of total effects are calculated the same way but with the unstandardized path coefficients.

Presented in the upper part of Table 5.2 is an *effects decomposition* based on the standardized solution. An effects decomposition is a tabular summary of the direct, indirect, and total causal effects on endogenous variables. Note that some variables have more than one indirect effect on others, and that all of these are included in the total effects. Note also that stress has only a direct effect on illness, which is also its total effect. Also reported in the table are results of significance tests of the unstandardized versions of the direct effects,

TABLE 5.2. Decomposition of Standardized Effects for a Model of Illness

Causal variable	Endogenous variable		
	Fitness	Stress	Illness
Exercise			
Direct effect	.39**	–.01	.03
Indirect via Fitness	—	–.04*	–.10**
Indirect via Stress	—	—	.00
Indirect via Fitness and Stress	—	—	–.01^{nt}
Total effect	.39**	–.05	–.08
Hardiness			
Direct effect	.08	–.22**	–.07
Indirect via Fitness	—	–.01	–.02
Indirect via Stress	—	—	–.06*
Indirect via Fitness and Stress	—	—	.00^{nt}
Total effect	.08	–.23**	–.15**
Fitness			
Direct effect	—	–.11*	–.26**
Indirect via Stress	—	—	–.03
Total effect	—	–.11*	–.29**
Stress			
Direct effect	—	—	.29**

^{nt}Not tested for significance.
*$p < .05$; **$p < .01$.

the indirect effects that are made up of three variables (e.g., exercise → fitness → illness), and the total effects. Results for the direct effects are those from Table 5.1 (i.e., tests of the regression coefficients conducted by the multiple regression program). Tests of the significance of three-variable indirect effects and total effects must be calculated by hand; the steps to do so are described in Appendix 5.B. The author is unaware of a hand-calculable test of the exact significance of indirect effects that involve more than three variables (e.g., hardiness → fitness → stress → illness), but a rule of thumb is suggested in Appendix 5.B.

A brief summary of the effects decomposition presented in Table 5.2 is as follows. The direct effects of exercise and hardiness on illness are both nonsignificant. However, exercise and hardiness each has a significant indirect effect on illness, exercise through fitness and hardiness through stress, respectively. This pattern of results—significant indirect effects but nonsignificant direct ones—represent the strongest demonstration for a mediator effect, assuming, of course, that the directionality specifications are correct (Baron & Kenny, 1986). In contrast, fitness has only a significant direct effect; its indirect effect through stress is not significant. These results are generally consistent with Roth and colleagues' (1989) hypotheses described in the previous subsection and illustrated in Figure 5.2(a).

Model-Implied or Predicted Correlations

The standardized total effects of one variable on another approximate the part of their observed correlation due to presumed causal relations. The sum of the standardized total effects and all other noncausal associations (e.g., spurious) represented in the model equal *model-implied (predicted) correlations* that can be compared against the observed correlations. *Model-implied covariances* have the same general meaning, but they concern the unstandardized solution. Most model-fitting programs automatically calculate model-implied correlations and covariances. If a regression program is used, however, then predicted correlations or covariances must be derived by hand. A method for doing so is demonstrated for the just-identified model of Figure 5.2(a), but in actual practice it makes sense to use it only for overidentified models that are recursive because the implied correlations of just-identified models equal the respective observed ones. This method is based on the *tracing rule*: a model-implied correlation is the sum of the causal effects and noncausal associations from all

valid tracings between two variables in a path model. A "valid" tracing means that (1) a variable is not entered through an arrowhead
and exited by the same arrowhead, and (2) a variable is not entered
twice in the same tracing.

As an example of the application of the tracing rule to calculate
model-implied correlations with the standardized solution, look
again at Figure 5.2(b) and find the hardiness and stress variables.
There are four valid tracings between them. Two of these tracings
make up the total effect (hardiness → stress, hardiness → fitness →
stress), which equals –.23 (Table 5.2). The other two tracings involve
the unanalyzed association of hardiness with another variable, exercise, that has direct or indirect effects on stress. These two tracings
are hardiness ↔ exercise → stress and hardiness ↔ exercise → fitness
→ stress. Both are calculated in the same way as indirect effects; that
is, as the products of the relevant path coefficients and correlations.
The hardiness ↔ exercise → stress association is calculated as
–.03(–.01) = .0003, and the second association, hardiness ↔ exercise
→ fitness → stress, equals –.03(.39)(–.11) = .0013. The implied correlation between hardiness and stress thus equals the total effect (–.23)
plus both of these near-zero associations that involve unanalyzed associations between the exogenous variables, or –.2316 overall. Note
that this value rounded to two decimal places (–.23) also equals the
observed correlation between hardiness and stress (Table 5.1), which
is just what we expect because this model is just-identified.

Two other points should be noted about the tracing rule. First,
use of the tracing rule is error prone even for relatively simple models because it can be difficult to spot all of the valid tracings. For instance, there are a total of *10* valid tracings between the stress and
illness variables of Figure 5.2. All but one of these tracings are for either spurious associations or ones that involve unanalyzed associations between the exogenous variables.[2] There are other, more accurate ways to derive implied correlations or covariances by hand, but
they require knowledge of matrix algebra (e.g., Bollen, 1989, pp.
376–389; Loehlin, 1992, pp. 43–47; Pedhazur, 1982, pp. 607–614). It
is advisable to leave the tedium of deriving implied correlations and
covariances to computers, which is yet another reason to learn how
to use a model-fitting program. Second, the tracing rule as just de-

---

[2]Spurious associations between stress and illness include (1) stress ← fitness → ill-
ness, (2) stress ← exercise → illness, and (3) stress ← hardiness → illness. Connections that involve unanalyzed associations between the exogenous variables include (1) stress ← hardiness ↔ exercise → illness, (2) stress ← exercise ↔ hardiness → illness, (3) stress ← hardiness ↔ exercise → fitness → illness, (4) stress ←
fitness ← hardiness ↔ exercise → illness, (5) stress ← fitness ← exercise ↔ hardiness → illness, and (6) stress ← exercise ↔ hardiness → fitness → illness.

scribed does not apply to nonrecursive path models. Indirect and to-tal effects of nonrecursive path models are described in Chapter 6.

Assumptions

The interpretation of path coefficients derived with multiple regres-sion as indexes of causal effects requires many assumptions. Some of these assumptions include the standard statistical requirements for multiple regression, for example, linearity and residuals that are inde-pendent, normally distributed, and homoscedastic with means of zero (section 2.5). Note that these standard assumptions are needed to test whether a regression (path) coefficient differs statistically from some a priori value, usually zero; they are *not* required per se for in-terpreting the estimated coefficient as causal. Other assumptions are consequences of least squares estimation that the residuals are uncor-related with the predictor variables (e.g., Equation 2.6). In path analysis, this aspect of least squares requires the assumption that the disturbances of each endogenous variable are uncorrelated with all of the causes of that variable. This requirement explains why multiple regression cannot be used to estimate nonrecursive path models. For example, look at model (b) of Figure 5.1, which is nonrecursive be-cause it has a direct feedback loop, $Y_1 \rightleftarrows Y_2$. The causal variables of Y_2 of this model include two observed variables, X_1 and Y_1, and one un-observed variable, its disturbance, D_2. From the perspective of multi-ple regression, X_1 and Y_2 are the predictors of Y_2, and D_2 can be seen as its residuals. But note that D_2 of this model is specified to covary with D_1 ($D_1 \leftrightarrow D_2$), the disturbance of Y_1, which is one of the predic-tors of Y_2. This covariance implies that D_1 is correlated with Y_2. Thus, the consequence of least squares estimation that the residuals (distur-bances) are unrelated to the predictors (causal variables) is inconsis-tent with the implied correlations of this model. Readers are encour-aged to use the tracing rule to determine that recursive models (a) and (c) of Figure 5.1 meet this requirement and that the nonrecursive model (d) does not.

The assumption that the disturbances are unrelated to causal variables also implies all of the following: (1) there is no reverse cau-sation (i.e., the endogenous variables do not cause the exogenous variables); (2) none of the omitted causes affects the exogenous vari-ables; and (3) the exogenous variables are measured without error (i.e., they are perfectly reliable). The first two of these requirements concern the accuracy of specifications about variables included in the model and the directionalities of causal effects among them. The third requirement about measurement error is discussed in more detail in section 5.11.

5.9   Maximum Likelihood Estimation

Description

Maximum likelihood (ML) estimation is the default method in many model-fitting programs. Model-fitting programs usually offer additional estimation options (described later), but none of them are as widely used as ML. As mentioned, multiple regression and ML estimation yield identical values of path coefficients for just-identified recursive path models and generally similar ones for overidentified models. Also, the interpretation of estimates of path coefficients and disturbance variances derived with either method is the same. The two differ primarily in how they go about the task of estimation. In contrast to multiple regression, which requires a separate analysis for each endogenous variable, ML estimation is *simultaneous*. That is, estimates of all model parameters are calculated all at once. The name "maximum likelihood" describes the statistical principle that underlies their derivation: if they (the estimates) are assumed to be population values, they are ones that maximize the likelihood (probability) that the data (the observed covariances) were drawn from this population. The mathematics of ML estimation are complex, and it is beyond the scope of this section to describe them in detail (e.g., Bollen, 1989, pp. 107–111, 131–144; Eliason, 1993; less technical presentations are available in Hayduk, 1987, pp. 127–142, and Nunnally & Bernstein, 1994, pp. 147–155). The similarities between ML-based estimates and those derived with multiple regression for recursive path models is reassuring for nonstatisticians, however.

ML estimation is usually so complicated that is is often *iterative*, which means that the computer derives an initial solution and then attempts to improve these estimates through subsequent cycles of calculations. "Improvement" means that the model-implied covariances based on the estimates from each step become more similar to the observed ones. For just-identified recursive path models, the predicted covariances will eventually equal the observed ones. For overidentified models, the observed and model-implied covariances may not be equal, but iterative estimation will continue until the increments of the improvement in the solution fall below a predefined minimum value. (Recall the role of statistical criteria in arriving at a unique solution for an overidentified model.) Iterative estimation may converge to a solution quicker if the procedure is given *starting values,* which are initial estimates of a model's parameters. If these initial estimates are grossly inaccurate—for instance, the starting value for a path coefficient is positive but the actual direct effect is negative—then iterative estimation may fail to converge, which means that a stable solution has not been reached. Model-fitting programs typically issue a warning message if iterative estimation is unsuccessful. When this occurs, whatever final set of estimates were derived by the computer may warrant little confidence. Also, some model-fitting programs automatically generate their own starting values. *It is important to understand, however, that computer-derived starting values do not always lead to converged solutions.* Although the computer's "guesses" about starting values are usually pretty good, sometimes it is necessary for the researcher to provide starting values for the solution to converge. Presented in Appendix 5.C are recommendations for generating starting values for path models.

It is important to understand a couple of technical points about ML estimation of path models. First, ML estimates of the variances and covariances of the observed exogenous variables are simply the observed values, just as with multiple regression. Second, disturbances are typically represented in the syntax of model-fitting programs as latent variables that have a single indicator, the observed endogenous variable associated with it. This representation is conceptually consistent with the view of disturbances as unobserved exogenous variables that represent all omitted causes. For reasons that are explained in Chapter 7 about measurement models, most model-fitting programs require the specification that the residual path coefficient of disturbances is set to 1.0 in the program code that describes the path model. This specification convention allows the program to estimate just the variance of the disturbance.

Assumptions

With two exceptions, ML requires basically the same assumptions as does multiple regression. The first exception concerns the disturbances. Although both procedures generally assume that the exogenous variables are independent of the disturbances, ML allows model-implied correlations between endogenous variables and the disturbances of subsequent variables the endogenous variables are specified to affect. For this reason, ML estimation is appropriate for nonrecursive path models. The second exception is that ML assumes multivariate normality (section 4.7) of endogenous variables and exogenous variables that are continuous. The normality assumption does not apply to exogenous variables that are dichotomous (e.g., gender).[3] In contrast to ML, multiple regression does not require a specific distributional assumption for the observed variables. Reviewed in Chapter 7 are the results of computer simulation studies of the robustness of ML estimation against violation of the assumption of multivariate normality. Very briefly summarized, these results suggest that although the values of parameter estimates generated by ML are relatively robust against non-normality, results of significance tests tend to lead to rejection of the null hypothesis too often. Ways to deal with this problem are discussed in Chapter 7, but it can be said here that corrective measures should be taken if the data are severely non-normal.

Fit Indexes

There are literally dozens of fit indexes described in the SEM literature, more than any single model-fitting program reports. Some widely used fit indexes and recommendations for their use are described here. Perhaps the most basic fit index is the *generalized likelihood ratio,* which is sometimes called G^2 in the SEM literature. The value of the G^2 statistic reflects the sample size and the value of the ML fitting function. The fitting function is the statistical criterion that ML attempts to minimize and is analogous to the least squares criterion of regression (section 2.5). ML estimation minmizes the fitting function by deriving parameter estimates that yield predicted covariances that are as close as possible to the observed values in a particular sample. In large samples, the generalized likelihood ratio (G^2) is interpreted as a Pearson chi-square (χ^2) statistic with degrees of freedom that are equal to the difference between the number of observations and parameters. (The discussion from this point refers to χ^2 instead of G^2.) The χ^2 statistic for a just-identified model equals zero and has no degrees of freedom. For overidentified models, the number of degrees of freedom is positive; the value of the χ^2 statistic may be positive, too. Within a large sample and under the assumption of multivariate normality, the χ^2 statistic for an overidentified

---

[3]LISREL offers a "fixed-X" option that may be appropriate for dichotomous exogenous variables. Specification of this option for an exogenous variable assumes that its values are fixed rather than random. This means that the values of that exogenous variable are unchanged in all samples (e.g., the proportion of males is 50%) and there is no need to estimate something about the population distribution. The designation of an exogenous variable as "fixed-X" also implies that its variance is not considered a model parameter.

model is interpreted as a test of significance of the difference in fit between that model and a just-identified version of it. For example, suppose that the goodness-of-fit χ^2 statistic for an overidentified recursive model is 16.37 with five degrees of freedom. The number of degrees of freedom indicate that this model has five fewer parameters than observations. A $\chi^2(5)$ of 16.37 is significant at the .01 level, which indicates that the fit of this overidentified model is significantly *worse* than if it had five more paths; that is, if it were just-identified. A *nonsignificant* value of $\chi^2(5)$, however, would indicate that the overall fit of this overidentified model does not differ statistically from that of a just-identified version of it. Thus, low and nonsignificant values of the χ^2 index are desired.

There are two problems with the χ^2 statistic as a fit index. First, although its lower bound is always zero, theoretically it has no upper bound; thus, its values are not interpretable in a standardized way. Second, it is very sensitive to sample size. That is, if the sample size is large, which is required in order that the index may be interpreted as a significance test, then the χ^2 statistic may be significant even though differences between observed and model-implied covariances are slight. Also, the value of the χ^2 statistic for a particular model and its data will change simply by specifying a different sample size to the model-fitting program. (This assumes that a matrix summary of the raw data is analyzed.) Specifically, giving the computer a larger sample size but using the same covariance matrix yields a larger value of χ^2. To reduce the sensitivity of the χ^2 statistic to sample size, some researchers divide its value by the degrees of freedom (χ^2/df), which results in a lower value. Although there is no clear-cut guideline about what value of χ^2/df is minimally acceptable, a frequent suggestion is that this ratio be less than 3.

Values of other fit indexes are more standardized and may be less sensitive to sample size than the χ^2 statistic. Two of these, the Jöreskog–Sörbom *Goodness of Fit Index* (GFI) and the *Adjusted Goodness of Fit Index* (AGFI; Jöreskog & Sörbom, 1996a), were originally associated with the LISREL program but are now computed by other programs, too. Values of both indexes theoretically range from 0 (poor fit) to 1 (perfect fit). The GFI is analogous to a squared multiple correlation in that it indicates the proportion of the observed covariances explained by the model-implied covariances. In contrast, the AGFI is like a shrinkage-corrected squared multiple correlation in that it includes a built-in adjustment for model complexity. Specifically, more complex models—those with more parameters—tend to fit the same data better than do simpler ones. The AGFI takes this into account by correcting downward the value of the GFI as the number of parameters increases. It should be noted, however, that values of both the GFI and AGFI can fall outside of the range 0–1. Values greater than 1 may be found with just-identified models or with overidentified models with almost perfect fit to the data; negative values are most likely to happen when the sample size is small or when the fit of the model is very poor. Also, the AGFI has not performed especially well in some computer simulation studies (e.g., Marsh, Balla, & McDonald, 1988; see also Mulaik et al., 1989). It seems that the AGFI is used less often nowadays, perhaps due to increasing awareness of these problems.

Three other indexes with analogous rationales are the Bentler–Bonett *Normed Fit Index* (NFI), the Bentler Comparative Fit Index (CFI), and the Bentler–Bonett *Non-Normed Fit Index* (NNFI; Bentler, 1990; Bentler & Bonett, 1980). All three were originally associated with EQS but are now calculated by other programs. The value of the NFI indicates the proportion in the improvement of the overall fit of the researcher's model relative to a null model. The typical null model is an independence model, that is, one in which the observed variables are assumed to be uncorrelated. If the NFI equals .80, for example, then the relative overall fit of the researcher's model is 80% better than that of the null model estimated with the same sample data. For this reason, the NFI and other indexes scaled in a similar way are sometimes referred to as *incremental fit indexes*. The Jöreskog–Sörbom GFI, on the other hand, has a more absolute interpretation because it concerns only the researcher's model. Bentler (1990) devised a modified version of the NFI called the *Comparative Fit Index* (CFI), which is interpreted in the same way as the NFI (i.e., it is an incremental fit index) but may be less affected by sample size. The NNFI includes a correction for model complexity, much like the AGFI. (An older name for the NNFI is the Tucker–Lewis Index.) Also like the AGFI, values of the NNFI can fall outside of the range 0–1. In small samples, it is also possible for the value of the NNFI to be much lower than those of other fit indexes.

Another fairly widely used index is the *Standardized Root Mean Squared Residual* (SRMR), which is a standardized summary of the average *covariance residuals*. Covariance residuals are the differences between the observed and model-implied covariances. The SRMR is another Jöreskog–Sörbom index that was originally part of LISREL but is now printed by other programs. When the fit of the model is perfect, the SRMR equals zero. As the average discrepancy between the observed and predicted covariances increases, so does the value of the SRMR.

Because indexes like those described above reflect somewhat different facets of model fit (e.g., absolute vs. relative proportions of explained variance), researchers typically report the values of multiple indexes. A minimal set would include the χ^2 statistic and its degrees of freedom and significance level; an index that describes the overall proportion of explained variance such as the Jöreskog–Sörbom GFI, the Bentler–Bonett NFI, or the Bentler CFI; an index that adjusts the proportion of explained variance for model complexity such as the Bentler–Bonett NNFI (the Jöreskog–Sörbom AGFI may be problematic); and an index based on the standardized residuals such as the SRMR.

Whatever combination of indexes the researcher selects, three limitations of all fit indexes should be kept in mind. First, values of fit indexes indicate only the overall or average fit of a model. Thus, it is possible that some parts of the model may poorly fit the data even if the value of the index seems favorable. Second, fit indexes do not indicate whether the results are theoretically meaningful. For example, the signs of some path coefficients may be unexpectedly in the opposite direction. Even if values of fit indexes appear to be good, results so anomalous require explanation. Finally, good values of fit indexes do not indicate that the predictive power of the model is also high. For example, the disturbances of models with even perfect fit to the data can still be large, which means that the model accurately reflects the relative absence of predictive validity among the variables.

For more information about the fit indexes described here as well as information about others, readers are referred to articles by Bentler and Bonett (1980), La Du and Tanaka (1995), Marsh et al. (1988), and Mulaik et al. (1989); and to chapters by Bollen (1989, pp. 256–281), Gerbing and Anderson (1993), Hu and Bentler (1995), Marsh, Balla, and Hau (1996), Schumacker and Lomax (1996, chap. 7), and Tanaka (1993).

What Is Good Fit?

This is a natural question about fit indexes, but it is easier to approach it from the negative side; that is, what does *not* constitute evidence for good fit? Because a single index reflects only a particular aspect of fit, a favorable value of that index does not by itself indicate good fit. Even the finding of favorable values of several indexes does not necessarily demonstrate good fit. This is so because, as mentioned, fit indexes reflect only the overall fit of the model. Thus, it still necessary to inspect more detailed information about model–data correspondence even when the values of several fit indexes are favorable.

What are "favorable" values of the indexes described above? A nonsignificant goodness-of-fit χ^2 statistic is desired, but (as mentioned) this may be unlikely with large samples. The χ^2/df ratio can also be calculated, and values of less than 3 are considered favorable. Note, however, that this recommendation (i.e., $\chi^2/df < 3$) applies mainly to large sample analyses. In small samples, a χ^2/df ratio of, say, 2.5, may arise even if the overall fit of the model is poor. Values of indexes that indicate absolute or relative proportions of the observed covariances explained by the model such as the Jöreskog–Sörbom GFI, the Bentler–Bonett NFI, and the Bentler CFI should be greater than .90. Their counterparts that are corrected for the number of parameters (e.g., the AGFI and the NNFI) should also have comparably high values. A favorable value of the SRMR, which is based on the standardized covariance residuals, is less than .10.

To get some sense of the fit of specific portions of the model, researchers should also inspect the *correlation residuals,* which are differences between observed and model-implied correlations. Model-fitting programs can typically print correlation residuals in the output. There is a rule of thumb in the SEM literature that correlation residuals with absolute values greater than .10 suggest that the model does not explain the associated observed correlation very well. Although it is difficult to say how many absolute correlation residuals greater than .10 is "too many," the more there are, the worse the fit of specific portions of the model.

Thus, there is no single answer to the question about what is good fit. The more criteria listed above that a model satisfies, the better is its fit. To use the descriptor "good" about fit would require, at minimum, favorable values of numerous fit indexes *and* absolute values of correlation residuals less than .10. Considering that model fit is a multifaceted concept, it would seem advisable to use the adjective "good" very conservatively or to apply terms with more neutral connotations instead ("adequate," "satisfactory," "acceptable," etc.).

5.10   Testing Path Models

Overview

This sections concerns ways to test hypotheses about path models, recursive or nonrecursive. Perhaps the most common type of model testing involves the comparison of *hierarchical models.* (The term *nested models* is also used.) Two path models are hierarchical if one is a subset of the other. For example, if a path is dropped from Model A to form Model B, the two models are hierarchically related (i.e., B is nested under A). There are two contexts in which hierarchical models are usually compared, model trimming and model building. In the first, the researcher typically begins the analysis with a just-identified model and simplifies it by eliminating paths. The starting point for model building is usually a "bare-bones," overidentified model to which paths are added. As a model is trimmed, its fit to the data as indicated by its χ^2 statistic typically becomes progressively worse (i.e., its χ^2 increases). Likewise, the value of a model's χ^2 generally decreases as paths are added (i.e., its fit improves). The goal of both model trimming and model building is to find a parsimonious model that still fits the data reasonably well.

An alternative to the trimming or building of hierarchical models is to compare nonhierarchical models. Nonhierarchical models are not subsets of one another; instead, they usually represent competing theories about the phenomenon under study. Although this type of model testing may be conducted less often, the goal is the same as when hierarchical models are contrasted. Each strategy is discussed below.

Introduction to Model Trimming and Building

In the parlance of SEM, model trimming involves the imposition of a *constraint* on the values of one or more parameter estimates. Specifically, parameters that were previously freely estimated by the computer are constrained to equal zero, which drops the associated effect from the model. In contrast, model building involves the releasing of a constraint. Typically, a previously fixed-to-zero parameter is freely estimated, which adds that effect to the model.

Models can be trimmed or built according to one of two standards, theoretical or empirical. The first represents tests of specific, a priori hypotheses. For instance, suppose that a model contains a direct effect of X on Y_2 and an indirect effect through Y_1 ($X \rightarrow Y_2$ and $X \rightarrow Y_1 \rightarrow Y_2$). If a researcher believed that the relation of X to Y_2 is mediated entirely by Y_1, then he or she could test this hypothesis by constraining the path coefficient for $X \rightarrow Y_2$ to zero (i.e., this direct effect is trimmed from the model). If the overall fit of this constrained model is not appreciably worse than one with $X \rightarrow Y_2$ as a free parameter, then the hypothesis about a mediated relation of X to Y_2 is supported. The main point, though, is that the respecification of a model to test hierarchical versions of it is guided by the researcher's hypotheses. This is not the case, however, for empirically guided respecification, in which paths are deleted or added according to statistical criteria. For example, if the sole basis for trimming paths is that they are not significant at, say, the .05 level, then model respecification is guided by purely empirical considerations. The distinction between theoretically or empirically based respecification has implications for the interpretation of the results of model trimming or building, which are considered after a test of significance is introduced.

When one uses a model-fitting program, the *chi-square difference* ($\chi^2_{\text{difference}}$) *test* can be used to evaluate the significance of the decrement in overall fit as paths are eliminated (trimming) or the improvement in fit as paths are added (building). As its name suggests, the $\chi^2_{\text{difference}}$ statistic is simply the difference between the χ^2 values of two hierarchical models; its degrees of freedom equal the difference between the two respective values. A nonsignificant value of the $\chi^2_{\text{difference}}$ statistic suggests that the overall fits of the two models are comparable. In model trimming, a significant $\chi^2_{\text{difference}}$ test suggests that the model has been simplified too much; a significant result in model building, however, supports retention of the path that was just added. For example, suppose that the $\chi^2(5)$ statistic for an overidentified model is 18.30. Also suppose that a single path is added to model (which reduces the degrees of freedom by 1) and that the resulting $\chi^2(4)$ value is 5.10. The $\chi^2_{\text{difference}}$ statistic here equals 15.20 (18.30 – 5.10), which with a single degree of freedom (5 – 4) is significant at the .01 level. Thus, the fit of the new model is significantly better than that of the original. In this example, the $\chi^2_{\text{difference}}$ test is a univariate one because it concerned a single path. When two hierarchical models that differ by two or more paths are compared (i.e., degrees of freedom ≥ 2), then the $\chi^2_{\text{difference}}$ test is essentially a multivariate test of all the added (or deleted) paths together. If significant, then at least one of the paths is nonzero. The paths may be significant if tested individually, but this is not guaranteed.

The interpretation of the $\chi^2_{\text{difference}}$ test depends in part on whether a new model is derived empirically or theoretically. For example, if individual paths that are not significant are dropped from the model, then it is almost certain that the $\chi^2_{\text{difference}}$ test will also be not significant. But if the deleted path is also predicted in advance to be zero, then the $\chi^2_{\text{difference}}$ test is of utmost theoretical interest. Also, if model respecification is entirely driven by empirical criteria (e.g., the significance level), then the researcher has to worry about capitalization on chance variation. That is, a path may be statistically significant simply due to chance, and its inclusion in the model would be akin to a Type I error. Likewise, a path that corresponds to a true, nonzero causal effect in the population could be nonsignificant in this particular sample, and its exclusion would essentially be a Type II error. A sort of buffer against the problem of sample-specific results, though, is a greater role for theory in model trimming or building.

The issue of capitalization on chance is especially relevant when the researcher uses an "automatic modification" option that is available in some model-fitting programs. Such options drop or add paths according to empirical criteria (e.g., significance at the .05 level). In EQS, LISREL, and some other programs, paths can be automatically added to an overidentified model based on values of *modification indexes*. A modification index is calculated for every parameter that is fixed to zero. Modification indexes are actually univariate versions of something known as a *Lagrange Multiplier*, which in this case is expressed as a χ^2 statistic with one degree of freedom. The value of a univariate Lagrange Multiplier in the form of a modification index approximates the amount by which the model's overall χ^2 would *decrease* if a particular parameter were freely estimated. The greater the value of a modification index, the more the overall fit of the model would improve if that parameter were added to the model. The probability level of a modification index indicates whether this improvement in fit is significant. Although the value of a modification index may not exactly equal that of the $\chi^2_{\text{difference}}(1)$ statistic calculated for the same parameter, the two are usually very similar (e.g., Bollen, 1989, pp. 289–303). Also, some programs like EQS allow the user to generate modification indexes for specific parameters, which lends a more a priori sense to the use of this statistic. EQS also generates multivariate Lagrange Multipliers that estimate the effect of allowing a set of constrained-to-zero parameters to be freely estimated. A multivariate Lagrange Multiplier with five degrees of freedom, for instance, approximates the corresponding value of $\chi^2_{\text{difference}}(5)$ for the same five parameters (Bentler, 1995).

The Wald W statistic is a related index but one used for model trimming. A univariate Wald W statistic estimates the amount the model's overall χ^2 would *increase* if a particular free parameter were fixed to zero (i.e., dropped from the model). A nonsignificant value of a Wald W statistic thus indicates a nonsignificant decrement in overall fit when a parameter is eliminated. Model trimming that is entirely empirically based would thus delete the parameters with nonsignificant Wald W statistics. Some programs like EQS can calculate Wald W statistics for all freely estimated model parameters or for ones specified by the researcher. Multivariate Wald W statistics estimate the corresponding values of the $\chi^2_{\text{difference}}$ test for dropping a set of parameters from the model.

MacCallum (1986) and Silvia and MacCallum (1988) conducted computer simulation studies of what they called "specification searches." These authors took known structural models, imposed different types of specification errors on them (e.g., a nonzero path is omitted), and evaluated these erroneous models using data generated from populations in which the known models were true. The results of both studies are sobering. In MacCallum's study, models were modified using the empirically based procedures just described. Most of the time the changes suggested by empirically based respecification were incorrect; that is, they did not typically result in discovery of the true model. This pattern was even more apparent for small samples ($N = 100$) than for larger ones. Silvia and MacCallum followed a similar procedure except that the application of automatic modification was guided by theoretical knowledge, which improved the chances of discovering the true model. The implication of these studies is clear: learn from your data, but your data should not be your teacher.

Before an example is considered, two other points warrant mention. First, the $\chi^2_{difference}$, Lagrange Multiplier, and Wald W statistics all test only the *relative* fit of two hierarchically related (nested) models. It is possible that the fits of two nested models, both of which poorly fit the data, do not differ significantly from one another. Thus, results of these tests are more meaningful when the more complex model fits the data. Second, all three tests are sensitive to sample size; thus, even a trivial improvement in fit could be significant within a large sample. In addition to noting whether, say, a modification index is significant, one should also consider the absolute magnitude of the change in the parameter if it is allowed to be either freely estimated (model building) or constrained to equal zero (model trimming). If the absolute magnitude of the change is small, then significance of the modification index may be due more to the sample size than to the size of the effect. Readers are referred to Kaplan (1989) for more information about the role of expected parameter change in model modification.

Example of Model Trimming

Model trimming guided by both a priori and empirical considerations is demonstrated for the just-identified recursive model of health-related problems evaluated earlier. Recall that Roth et al. (1989) believed that six paths of the original just-identified model were actually zero (see Figure 5.2). To test this hypothesis, the correlations and standard deviations from Table 5.1 were analyzed with the ML procedure of a model-fitting program. The six paths hypothesized by Roth et al. to be zero were so constrained in this analysis. Reported at the top of Table 5.3 are values of selected fit indexes for this trimmed model. These results suggest that the overall fit of the mod-

TABLE 5.3. Comparison of Hierarchical Path Models of Illness

Goodness of fit summary

Model	χ^2	df	χ^2/df	$\chi^2_{\text{difference}}$	$df_{\text{difference}}$	NFI	NNFI
				Constrast with baseline model			
Baseline (six paths fixed to zero)	11.41	6	1.90	—	—	.93	.94
Five paths fixed to zero (fitness → stress-free)	6.25	5	1.25	5.16*	1	.96	.98

Correlation residuals from baseline model

Variable	1	2	3	4	5
1. Exercise	—				
2. Hardiness	−.03	—			
3. Fitness	.00	.07	—		
4. Stress	−.05	.00	**−.13**	—	
5. Illness	.02	−.09	−.04	.03	—

Modification indexes for paths fixed to zero in baseline model

Path	Modification index $\chi^2(1)$
Fitness → Stress	5.10*
Hardiness → Fitness	2.92
Hardiness → Illness	2.46
Exercise → Stress	1.27
Exercise → Illness	0.58
Exercise ↔ Hardiness	0.34

Note. NFI, Bentler–Bonett Normed Fit Index; NNFI, non-NFI.
*p < .05.

el with six constrained-to-zero paths is generally reasonable. For example, the $\chi^2(6)$ statistic (11.41) is not significant, the χ^2/df ratio (1.90) is less than 3, and the Bentler–Bonett NFI is .93. However, the constrained model's $\chi^2(6)$ statistic of 11.41 falls just short of the value required for significance at the .05 level (12.59). Thus, it may be worthwhile to more closely inspect the fit of the constrained model.

The correlation residuals for the constrained path model are also reported in Table 5.3. One correlation residual (presented in boldface in the table) has an absolute value greater than .10. This residual (−.13) is between the fitness and stress variables. According to the model with six constrained-to-zero paths, there are no valid tracings between these two variables; thus, their predicted correlation is zero. The observed correlation between them is –.13 (Table 5.1); thus, the constrained model underpredicts this observed correlation by –.13. Values of modification indexes (i.e., univariate Lagrange Multipliers) for each of the six fixed-to-zero paths are reported in the bottom part of Table 5.3. The $\chi^2(1)$ statistic for the fitness → stress direct effect is significant; values for the other five fixed paths are not. Based on these results, the fitness → stress path was added and the model was reanalyzed. Values of fit indexes for the model with five paths fixed to zero are, as expected, better than those of the more restricted model (see the table). Results of the $\chi^2_{\text{difference}}$ test between the two models are as follows:

$$\text{Model without fitness} \rightarrow \text{stress:} \quad \chi^2(6) = 11.41;$$

$$\text{Model with fitness} \rightarrow \text{stress:} \quad \chi^2(5) = 6.25;$$

$$\chi^2_{\text{difference}}(df = 6 - 5 = 1) = 11.41 - 6.25 = 5.16, \quad p < .05.$$

(Note that the values of the above $\chi^2_{\text{difference}}(1)$ statistic and of the Lagrange Multiplier for the fitness → stress path [Table 5.3] are close but not identical: 5.16 and 5.10, respectively.) Thus, the addition of the direct effect of fitness on stress results in a significant reduction in the model's χ^2. Overall, these results are consistent with Roth and colleagues' hypotheses except for the fitness → stress path, which was retained here. There is a way to test the relative fits of two hierarchical recursive path models using multiple regression. This procedure is summarized in Appendix 5.D, but it must be calculated by hand.

Comparing Nonhierarchical Models

The $\chi^2_{\text{difference}}$ statistic can be used as a test of significance only for hierarchical models. However, sometimes researchers specify alternative models that are not hierarchically related. Although the values of the χ^2 statistics from two nonhierarchical models can still be compared, the difference between them cannot be tested for significance. Any such comparison, though, should take account of the number of parameters because more complex models tend to fit the data better. Something called the Akaike (1987) Information Criterion (AIC) allows such a comparison. The AIC is a modification of the standard goodness-of-fit χ^2 statistic that includes a "penalty" for complexity.

In this sense, the AIC is analogous to indexes of model fit like the Bentler–Bonett NNFI in that it adjusts for the number of parameters. The AIC for a given model is

$$AIC = \chi^2 - 2df. \tag{5.3}$$

Models with fewer degrees of freedom—more complex ones—get larger reductions in their χ^2 values. Note that the value of the AIC can be less than zero. Given two nonhierarchical models, the one with the lowest AIC is preferred.[4] An example follows.

Romney, Jenkins, and Bynner (1992) evaluated two nonhierarchical models of the 6-month postoperative status of 469 patients admitted for coronary artery bypass or cardiac valve replacement surgery. Both of these models are presented in Figure 5.4. The one at the top of the figure, the Psychosomatic Model, represents the hypothesis that morale mediates the effect of neurological dysfunction (e.g., memory problems) and reduced income on physical symptoms and social relationships. The Conventional Medical Model, the one at the bottom of the figure, depicts different assumptions about causality among the same variables. The correlation matrix presented in Table 5.4 (Romney et al. did not report means or standard deviations) was submitted to a model-fitting program. Values of selected fit indexes for each model are presented in the table. Although the values of the overall χ^2 statistics and other fit indexes favor the Conventional Medical Model, this model is also the more complex of the two. Adjusting for the number of parameters via the AIC, however, still indicates a preference for the Conventional Medical Model: the AIC of this model is 2.76, and for the Psychosomatic Model it is 30.40.

Equivalent Models

After the researcher selects a final model from among hierarchical or nonhierarchical alternatives, then *equivalent models* should be considered (Stelzl, 1986). Equivalent models yield the same predicted corre-

---

[4]There is a variation on the AIC known as the consistent version of the AIC (CAIC) by Bozdogan (1987). The CAIC takes sample size into account and equals

$$CAIC = \chi^2 - \log_e(N + 1)df,$$

where $\log_e$ is the natural logarithm. The CAIC is used in the same way as the AIC: the nonhierarchical model with the smaller value is preferred.

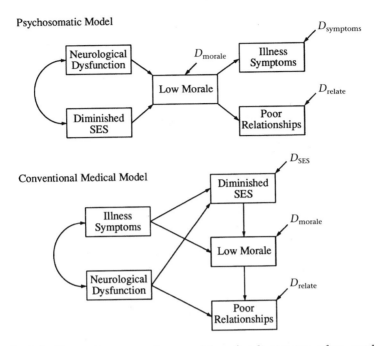

FIGURE 5.4. Alternative recursive models of adjustment after cardiac surgery.

lations or covariances, but they do so with a different configuration of paths among the same variables. For a given path model, there may be many equivalent variations; thus, it behooves the researcher to explain why his or her final model should be preferred over mathematically identical ones. Readers already know that just-identified path models perfectly fit the data. By default, any variation of a just-identified model exactly matches the data, too, and thus is an equivalent model. Now, some versions of a just-identified model may be implausible due to the nature of variables or the time of their measurement. For instance, a model that contains a direct effect from, say, an acculturation variable to gender is illogical; also, the assessment of Y_1 before Y_2 is inconsistent with the specification $Y_2 \rightarrow Y_1$. When an equivalent just-identified path model cannot be disregarded, however, it is up to the researcher to provide a rationale for preferring one over the other.

Equivalent versions of overidentified path models can be generated using the *Lee–Hershberger replacing rules* (Hershberger, 1994; Lee & Hershberger, 1990), which are summarized below (readers are re-

TABLE 5.4. Analysis of Models of Recovery after Cardiac Surgery

Correlations (Romney, Jenkins, & Bynner, 1992; $N = 469$ cardiac patients)

Variable	1	2	3	4	5
1. Low Morale	—				
2. Illness Symptoms	.53	—			
3. Neurological Dysfunction	.15	.18	—		
4. Poor Relationships	.52	.29	−.05	—	
5. Diminished SES	.30	.34	.23	.09	—

Goodness of fit summary

Model	χ^2	df	χ^2/df	AIC	CFI	NNFI	SRMR
Psychosomatic	40.40**	5	8.08	30.40	.91	.83	.07
Conventional Medical	3.24	3	1.08	2.76	.99	.99	.02

Note. SES, socioeconomic status; AIC, Akaike Information Criterion; CFI, Bentler Comparative Fit Index; NNFI, Bentler–Bonett Non-Normed Fit Index; SRMR, Standardized Root Mean Squared Residual.

**$p < .01$.

ferred to the works just cited and to MacCallum, Wegener, Uchino, & Fabrigar, 1993, for additional examples):

1. Within a block of variables at the beginning of a model that is just-identified and with unidirectional relations to subsequent variables, direct effects, correlated disturbances, and reciprocal effects are interchangeable. For example, $Y_1 \rightarrow Y_2$ may be replaced with $Y_2 \rightarrow Y_1$, $D_1 \leftrightarrow D_2$, or $Y_1 \rightleftarrows Y_2$. If two variables are specified as exogenous, then an unanalyzed association may be substituted, too.

2. At subsequent places in the model where two endogenous variables have the same causes and their relations to prior and subsequent variables are unidirectional, all of the following may be substituted for one another: $Y_1 \rightarrow Y_2$, $Y_2 \rightarrow Y_1$, $D_1 \leftrightarrow D_2$, and $Y_1 \rightleftarrows Y_2$.

Some comments are needed before an example is presented. Note mention of reciprocal relations above as replacements for other types of effects. Such substitutions would make the model nonrecursive. Nonrecursive models and the evaluation of reciprocal relations are described in Chapter 6. Also, these rules assume an equality-constrained reciprocal effect, which means that the estimates of the component direct effects are forced to be equal. Equality constraints are also described in Chapter 6.

Presented in Figure 5.5 is an example of the application of the

Lee–Hershberger replacing rules to the Romney et al. (1992) Conventional Medical Model. The first two equivalent models in the figure are recursive; the next two are nonrecursive. Equivalent model (a), for instance, features the substitution of a direct effect for an unanalyzed association between illness symptoms and neurological dysfunction; also, the direct effect between diminished socioeconomic status (SES) and low morale is reversed. Equivalent model (b) replaces unanalyzed associations for direct effects among the just-identified block of variables illness symptoms, SES, and low morale. Equivalent model (c) replaces a direct effect between SES and low morale with a disturbance correlation. Equivalent model (d) has two reversed direct

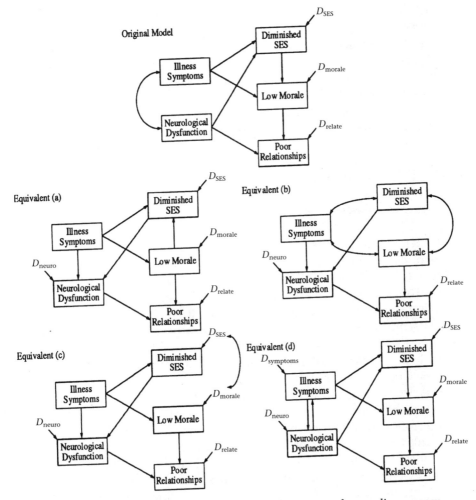

FIGURE 5.5. Five equivalent path models of adjustment after cardiac surgery.

effects and a reciprocal effect relative to the original. Because all five models in Figure 5.5 explain the data equally well, a choice among them must be based on theoretical rather than mathematical grounds. It is possible to generate even more equivalent models than those presented in the figure. For instance, application of the Lee–Hershberger replacing rules to the equivalent models of Figure 5.5 may yield even more equivalent models.

Relatively simple path models may have few equivalent versions, but more complicated ones may have hundreds or even thousands (e.g., see MacCallum et al., 1993). Thus, it may be unrealistic to expect that researchers consider all possible equivalent models. As a compromise, however, researchers should generate at least a few substantively meaningful equivalent versions of their final path model. Unfortunately, even this limited step is often neglected in the research literature. For instance, MacCallum et al. (1993) reviewed 53 studies published in educational, personality, and social psychology journals between 1988 and 1991 in which structural models were evaluated. Although nonhierarchical alternative models were considered in about a dozen works, none of the authors explicitly acknowledged the existence of equivalent models. Readers are urged to consider equivalent models in their own work.

5.11   Other Issues

What to Do after a Path Analysis

General requirements for estimating a causal model from correlations were described at the beginning of this chapter (section 5.2), all of which apply to the interpretation of results from a path analysis. The statistical procedures used in path analysis usually require additional assumptions about the distributions of either the observed variables (e.g., multivariate normality) or the disturbances (e.g., normal and homoscedastic). Given a single study, it would be almost impossible to believe that all of these logical and statistical requirements are met. Thus, the interpretation that direct effects in a path model that was not rejected must correspond to causal relations in the real world is typically unwarranted. It is usually only with the accumulation of the following types of evidence that researchers can even begin to think that the results of a path analysis may indicate causality: (1) replication of the model across independent samples; (2) corroborating evidence from experimental studies of variables in the model that are manipulable; and (3) the accurate prediction of the effects of interventions. Without such evidence, structural models, whether of observed or latent variables, are best seen as "as if" models of causality. Articles or chapters about the inference of causality in SEM by Biddle and Marlin (1987), Bollen (1989, chap. 3), Bullock, Harlow, and Mulaik (1994), Mulaik (1987), and Mulaik and James (1995) address issues raised here in more detail.

Consequences of Measurement Error

An assumption of path analysis is that the exogenous variables are measured without error. The consequences of minor violations of this requirement are not very critical. More serious violations result in biased estimates of direct effects. This bias affects not only the path coefficients of exogenous variables measured with error but also those of other exogenous variables in the model. However, it is difficult to anticipate the direction of this bias. Depending upon the intercorrelations among the exogenous variables, some path coefficients may be biased upward (i.e., they are too high) but others may be biased in the other direction. For example, a direct effect that is truly zero may have a nonzero path coefficient, a true negative direct effect may have a positive path coefficient, or the absolute value of the path coefficient may be less than the true effect (i.e., attenuation), all the result of measurement error. In an actual analysis, though, the direction of bias for individual path coefficients is difficult to predict. The amount of bias may be less if intercorrelations among measures of exogenous variables are low or if the magnitudes of the true direct effects on the endogenous variables are low.

Although there is no assumption that the endogenous variables are measured without error, the use of psychometrically deficient measures of them has somewhat different consequences than for exogenous variables. The effect of measurement error on endogenous variables is manifested in their disturbances in addition to the effects of omitted causes. This leads to a potential interpretive confound, but one that affects *standardized* estimates of direct effects on the endogenous variable but not *unstandardized* ones. *Standardized* path coefficients tend to be too small when endogenous variables are measured with error. Values of *unstandardized* path coefficients for the same direct effects, on the other hand, are not biased by measurement error. This pattern of bias due to measurement error in the endogenous variables assumes that the exogenous variables have no measurement error. If the exogenous variables are measured with error, then these effects for the endogenous variables could be amplified, diminished, or even canceled out. It is best not to hope for the latter, however.

The use of more than a single measure of a construct is the most common way to deal with the problem of measurement error; this topic is introduced in Chapter 7. Measurement with multiple indicators tends to be more reliable and valid than when a single measure is used. Path analysis does not readily accommodate a multiple approach to measurement, but other SEM techniques do. In particular, the evaluation of a hybrid model can be viewed as a type of a path analysis that allows the use of multiple indicators. Hybrid models are the subject of Chapter 8. Readers who wish to learn more about the effect of measurement error in SEM are referred to Bollen (1989, chap. 5), Kenny (1979, chap. 5), and Lomax (1986).

Other Estimation Procedures

Other estimation procedures available in some model-fitting programs may include *generalized least squares* (GLS) and *unweighted least squares* (ULS). As their names imply, GLS and ULS are based on the least squares criterion. But unlike multiple regression (sometimes called *ordinary least squares* in the SEM literature) in which the sum of squared differences between observed and predicted scores of individual subjects is minimized, ULS and GLS concern differences between observed and predicted covariances. ULS estimation is limited by its sensitivity to the measurement scales of the observed variables. In contrast, GLS and maximum likelihood (ML) estimation are more scale invariant, which means that if a variable's scale is linearly transformed, a parameter estimate for the transformed variable can be algebraically converted back to the original metric. One potential advantage of ULS and GLS over ML is that they require less computation time and presumably less computer memory.

ULS, GLS, and ML require certain assumptions about the distributions of the variables (e.g., multivariate normality). Other estimation procedures, however, make no such assumptions. One example is *asymptotically distribution-free* (ADF) estimation, which adjusts its results for the degree of kurtosis in the data (e.g., Browne, 1984). Thus, this procedure requires input of the raw data instead of a matrix summary of them. There are some significant potential costs, however, for the less restrictive distributional requirements of ADF estimation. First, it may require substantially more computer time and memory than ML estimation. Second, ADF procedures may need very large samples in order to generate stable, accurate estimates. ADF estimation is probably inappropriate for sample sizes less than 100; instead, Ns of 200–500 or larger may be required for even relatively simple models. Complex models may require sample sizes on the order of thousands of cases with ADF estimation.

There is another class of estimation methods that strike a middle ground between procedures based on *normal distribution theory* that assume multivariate normality (e.g., ML, GLS, ULS) and those based on *arbitrary distribution theory* that make no distributional assumptions (e.g., ADF). These methods are based on *elliptical distribution theory*, which requires only symmetrical distributions (e.g., Bollen, 1989; Bentler & Dijkstra, 1985; Bentler, 1987). Elliptical distribution methods allow for univariate or multivariate kurtosis but may not require as many cases as arbitrary distribution estimators like ADF. Like ADF, though, ellipitical distribution methods require the analysis of raw data and more computation time and computer memory than do normal distribution methods. We will deal in more detail with the use of normal, elliptical, or arbitrary distribution methods when the data are non-normal in Chapter 7.

An estimation procedure that is described in more detail in Chapter 6 (section 6.8) is *two-stage least squares* (2SLS). Briefly, 2SLS is a variation on multiple regression that gets around the problem of model-implied correlations between disturbances and causal variables, which makes 2SLS well suited for nonrecursive path models. Also, 2SLS estimation is noniterative, which reduces its computational demands and eliminates the need for starting values. In fact, 2SLS is used to generate starting values for some model-fitting programs (e.g., LISREL). Finally, 2SLS is available as a module in some general statistics packages (e.g., SPSS).

The availability of so many different estimation procedures can sometimes seem overwhelming to newcomers to SEM. Loehlin (1992) cites the following proverb that may describe this sensation: a person with one watch *always* knows what time it is; a person with two *never* does. Actually, the situation is not so bewildering because ML estimation works just fine for most types of structural equation models so long as the data have been properly screened and their distributions are reasonably normal. Also, these different estimation procedures tend to yield similar solutions for such "well-behaved" data. Additional references for readers who wish to learn more about the estimation procedures mentioned here include Bollen (1989), Loehlin (1992), Nunnally and Bernstein (1994), and West, Finch, and Curran (1995).

5.12 Summary

The main goal of a path analysis is to account for the covariances of observed exogenous and endogenous variables with a structural model of their presumed unanalyzed associations, spurious associations, and causal relations with each other. Causal effects can be either direct (e.g., $X \to Y$) or indirect through mediating variables (e.g., $X \to Y_1 \to Y_2$). Recursive path models assume that all causal effects are unidirectional—that no variable is both a cause and an effect of another. Recursive path models also assume independent disturbances unless there are no direct effects among the endogenous variables. Nonrecursive models have feedback loops or may have correlated disturbances. Feedback loops can be either direct (e.g., $Y_1 \rightleftarrows Y_2$) or indirect (e.g., $Y_1 \to Y_2 \to Y_3 \to Y_1$), and they represent presumed mutual causal effects among sets of concurrently measured variables.

The process by which the aforedescribed elements are combined into a model is called specification, which requires knowledge of the variables to be included in the model and the directionalities of causal effects among them. The total number of statistical effects (parameters) that can be represented in a path model is limited by the number of observations, which equals the number of variances and unique covariances among the observed variables, $v(v + 1)/2$. The parameters of path models include the variances and covariances of the exogenous variables (measured or unmeasured [disturbances]) and direct effects on endogenous variables from other observed variables. Path models with more parameters than observations are underidentified, which means that it is not possible to derive a unique estimate of each of their parameters.

It is impossible to specify a recursive model that is underidentified. In fact, recursive path models are either just-identified (having equal numbers of observations and parameters) or overidentified (having more parameters than observations). Thus, it is theoretically possible to calculate unique estimates of the parameters for any recursive path model. Data-related problems such as multicollinearity—a form of empirical underidentification—can still prevent their analysis in practice, though. Although data-related problems can also thwart the analysis of nonrecursive path models, such models must meet additional requirements for identification beyond having at least as many observations as parameters. This problem and other aspects of the analysis of nonrecursive path models are covered in Chapter 6.

Just-identified path models perfectly fit the data, which means that correlations or covariances implied by them equal the observed values. In fact, any variation of a just-identified path model also perfectly explains the same data and is thus an equivalent version. Although some equivalent versions of a just-identified path model may be implausible, others may offer reasonable alternative explanations. It is only with overidentified models that discrepancies between the model and the data are possible. Given an overidentified path model with acceptable albeit imperfect fit to the data, it may be possible to generate equivalent versions of it using the Lee–Hershberger replacing rules. Among equivalent versions of an overidentified model that are theoretically plausible, the researcher should justify why one is preferred over the rest.

The parameters of recursive path models can be estimated either with multiple regression or with other procedures that are available in model-fitting programs. The most widely used among the latter is maximum likelihood (ML) estimation. In order to estimate path coefficients with multiple regression, it is necessary to assume linearity and that the disturbances are unrelated to the causal variables. The latter implies that there are no omitted common causes of the exogenous and endogenous variables, that the endogenous variables do not cause the exogenous ones, and that the exogenous variables are measured without error. Additional assumptions about the residuals are necessary for the interpretation of significance tests of path coefficients (i.e., the residuals are normally distributed, independent, homoscedastic, and have means of zero). ML estimation has basically the same assumptions except that it allows correlations between disturbances and causal variables. This characteristic of ML estimation allows it to be used with nonrecursive path models, too. The ML method also assumes that the distributions of continuous variables are multivariate normal. Violation of this distributional requirement could lead to rejection of the null hypothesis in significance testing too often (i.e., the rate of Type I error is inflated). Estimates yielded by multiple regression and ML estimation for recursive models are virtually identical in large samples, but advantages of the latter include the automatic derivation of things like indirect and total effects, the availability of several indexes of overall model fit, and the resulting ease with which hierarchical (nested) path models can be compared. A potential drawback of ML estimation, however, is that iterative estimation can fail to converge if the computer is provided with inaccurate initial estimates (starting values) of model parameters.

Researchers often begin a path analysis with a just-identified model that is then trimmed; that is, the model is simplified by eliminating paths. As models are trimmed, their fit to the data usually becomes worse as indicated by their χ^2 statistics. At each step, though, the fit of each simplified model can be compared against that of the original, just-identified model with the $\chi^2_{\text{difference}}$ test, which is simply the difference between the χ^2 values of the models being contrasted. Researchers can also test models in the opposite direction: an initial, overidentified model can be made more complex by adding paths. The goal of both model trimming and model building is to find a parsimonious model that also fits the data reasonably well. Also, both trimming and building should be guided as much as possible by theoretical rather than empirical considerations (e.g., paths are added solely according to their significance levels).

One typically cannot conclude with confidence at the end of a path analysis that the causal relations represented in a model also exist in the real world. It would be difficult to believe that a researcher somehow measured all relevant causal variables *and* correctly specified the directionalities of their relations, all within in a single study. Instead, path analysis is probably best seen as an initial step, one that in combination with other experimental or nonexperimental methods may eventually clarify causal mechanisms.

The next chapter introduces the analysis of nonrecursive structural models with observed variables and the rationale of multiple group path analysis.

5.13   Recommended Readings

"Classical" Works on Path Analysis

These are well worth tracking down.

Blalock, H. M. (1964). *Causal inferences in nonexperimental research.* Chapel Hill, NC: University of North Carolina Press.
Heise, D. R. (1969). Problems in path analysis and causal inference. In E. Borgatta (Ed.), *Sociological methodology 1969* (pp. 38–73). San Francisco: Jossey-Bass.
Land, K. C. (1969). Principles of path analysis. In E. Borgatta (Ed.), *Sociological methodology 1969* (pp. 3–37). San Francisco: Jossey Bass.

Introductions to Path Analysis

These works are in addition to ones cited earlier in the chapter (e.g., chap. 9 of Cohen, 1983; chaps. 1, 3, and 4 of Kenny, 1979; and chap. 15 of Pedhazur, 1982).

Asher, H. B. (1983). *Causal modeling* (2nd ed.). Beverly Hills, CA: Sage.

James, L. R., Mulaik, S. A., & Brett, J. M. (1982). *Causal analysis: Assumptions, models, and data.* Beverly Hills, CA: Sage.

Klem, L. (1995). Path analysis. In L. G. Grimm & P. R. Yarnold (Eds.), *Reading and understanding multivariate statistics* (pp. 65–98). Washington, DC: American Psychological Association.

Knoke, D. (1985). A path analysis primer. In S. B. Smith (Ed.), *A handbook of social science methods* (Vol. 3, pp. 390–407). New York: Praeger.

Additional Empirical Examples

Curry, R. H., Yarnold, P. R., Bryant, F. B., Martin, G. J., & Hughes, R. L. (1988). A path analysis of medical school and residency performance: Implications for house staff selection. *Evaluation and the Health Professions, 11,* 113–129.

Ellickson, P. L., & Hays, R. D. (1991). Antecedents of drinking among young adolescents with different alcohol use histories. *Journal of Studies on Alcohol, 52,* 398–408.

Igbaria, M., & Parasuraman, S. (1989). A path analytic study of individual characteristics, computer anxiety and attitudes toward microcomputers. *Journal of Management, 15,* 373–388.

Appendix 5.A   Effect Size Interpretation of Path Coefficients

It is difficult to suggest a set of interpretive guidelines that will be useful across different research areas. This is because what may be considered a "large" effect in one area may be seen as rather modest in another. Also, some types of endogenous variables are more difficult to predict than others. For instance, the predictive validity of IQ scores against scholastic achievement is quite strong, but it is less so against other variables such as occupational success. Finally, Prentice and Miller (1992) make the point that when predictive relations of *any* type are unexpected, an effect of almost any size may be of great interest.

Within these limitations, some suggestions about the interpretation of the absolute magnitudes of path coefficients are offered. These guidelines reflect recommendations by Cohen (1988) about effect size interpretations of correlations in the social sciences. Standardized path coefficients with absolute values less than .10 may indicate a "small" effect; values around .30 a "medium" one; and "large" effects may be suggested by coefficients with absolute values of .50 or more. Now for more qualifiers: these numerical guidelines should not be rigidly interpreted (e.g., one standardized path coefficient of .49 and another of .51 should not be considered as qualitatively different because the former indicates a "medium" effect whereas the latter indicates a "large" one); also, these guidelines may need to be adjusted up or down depending upon the research area. For other recommendations about qualitative descriptions of the magnitudes of path coefficients, see Bollen (1989, pp. 137-138).

Appendix 5.B   Significance Tests of Indirect and Total Effects Using a Regression Program

Indirect Effects

Baron and Kenny (1986) described a hand-calculable significance test for indirect effects that include only three variables (e.g., $X \rightarrow Y_1 \rightarrow Y_2$) that has the following form: suppose that a is the path coefficient for the direct effect $X \rightarrow Y_1$ and that SE_a is its standard error; let b and SE_b represent the same things for the $Y_1 \rightarrow Y_2$. (Note that multiple regression programs typically print standard errors only for unstandardized coefficients; thus, unstandardized estimates are used in this example.) Let the product ab, then, be the estimate of the indirect effect of X on Y_2 through Y_1. The standard error of ab is

$$SE_{ab} = \sqrt{b^2 \, SE_a^2 + a^2 \, SE_b^2 + SE_a^2 SE_b^2} \tag{5.4}$$

In a large sample, the ratio ab/SE_{ab} is interpreted as a z statistic, which means that the indirect effect is significant at the .05 level (two-tailed) if its absolute value exceeds 1.96; the .01 level requires a value of at least 2.58.

Computation of this test is demonstrated for the exercise $\rightarrow$ fitness $\rightarrow$ illness indirect effect of the model in Figure 5.2. The two unstandardized path coefficients (from Table 5.1) and standard errors (in parentheses) of this indirect effect are .11 (.01) and -8.84 (1.75), respectively. The unstandardized estimate of the indirect effect is .11 $\times$ -8.84 = $-.97$; its standard error is thus

$$\sqrt{.11^2 \times 1.75^2 + 8.84^2 \times .01^2 + .01^2 \times 1.75^2} = .21.$$

With this standard error, $z = -.97/.21 = -5.62$. This indirect effect is thus significant at the .01 level.

For complex indirect effects that involve four or more variables, Cohen and Cohen (1983) suggested a reasonable substitute for an exact significance test: if all of its component path coefficients are significant, then the whole indirect effect can be taken as significant, too. All three path coefficients of the exercise → fitness → stress → illness indirect effect of the model in Figure 5.2 meet this requirement, so it can be considered significant. Note that the other four-variable indirect effect of this model, hardiness → fitness → stress → illness, fails to meet this standard because the path coefficient of its first direct effect is not significant.

Total Effects

Total effects can also be tested for significance. It is not necessary to calculate these tests by hand, but additional runs with a regression program are required. The test works as follows for the total effect of X on Y: enter X and other variables with direct effects on Y as predictors in a regression equation except those variables that mediate the effect of X on Y. The regression coefficient of X in this analysis is not a path coefficient; instead, it represents X's direct and indirect effects on Y, and the test of its significance is thus a test of the total effect.

Significance tests for total effects are demonstrated for the illness model of Figure 5.3. Summarized in the first accompanying table are the standardized five total effects on all endogenous variables that do not exactly equal a direct effect (e.g., exercise → fitness), abstracted from Table 5.2.

	Total effects on endogenous variables		
Predictor	Fitness	Stress	Illness
Exercise	—	−.05	−.08
Hardiness	—	−.23	−.15
Fitness	—	—	−.29

Three separate regressions are necessary to test the above five total effects; each is outlined in the second table (below). The first regression concerns the total effects of exercise and hardiness on illness. Note three things here. First, fitness and stress, which mediate some of the effects of the predictors, are omitted from the equation. Second, the beta weights (exercise, −.08; hardiness, −.15) equal the corresponding standardized total effects listed above. The second regression yields the total effects of the same two predictors on stress; fitness, a mediator of both, is excluded. The third regression concerns the total effect of fitness on illness; note that the prior variables and the mediator (stress) are omitted. Finally, the significance levels reported here in the second table are from the unstandardized regression coefficients. These probabilities may apply to the standardized values reported there, but that is not assured.

Criterion	Predictors	Regressions to derive total effects	
		Beta weight	R^2
1. Illness	Exercise	−.08	.03**
	Hardiness	−.15**	
2. Stress	Exercise	−.05	.06**
	Hardiness	−.23**	
3. Illness	Fitness	−.29**	.08**

**$p < .01$.

Appendix 5.C   Recommendations for Starting Values for Recursive Path Models

These recommendations concern the generation of starting values for path coefficients and disturbances and are based on the guidelines about "small," "medium," and "large" effects presented in Appendix 5.A. If the researcher is using different numerical definitions of these effect sizes, then they can be substituted in the following equations. Suppose that a researcher believed that the direct effect of X on Y is positive and of "moderate" magnitude. A reasonable starting value for the standardized path coefficient for $X \rightarrow Y$ would be .30; for the unstandardized coefficient, the starting value would be $.30(SD_Y/SD_X)$. If the expected magnitude were "small" or "large," then .10 or .50 (respectively) would be substituted for .30. Also suppose that a researcher believes that the predictive power of all variables with direct effects on Y (including X) is "large." A component of the starting value for Y's disturbance in standardized terms could be .75, which corresponds to 25% explained variance and 75% unexplained. (The former is the squared value of a "large" correlation, $.50^2$.) The unstandardized starting value of Y's disturbance would be $.75(s_Y^2)$. If instead the researcher believed that the predictive power is "small" or "moderate," then .99 (i.e., 1% explained variance, or $.10^2$) or .91 (i.e., 9% explained, or $.30^2$), respectively, would be substituted for .75.

Appendix 5.D   Comparing Hierarchical Recursive Path Models with Multiple Regression

Specht (1975), Pedhazur (1982, pp. 617–628), and Schumacker and Lomax (1996, pp. 44–45) described a procedure for testing the relative fit of two hierarchical recursive path models estimated with multiple regression that can be conducted by hand. This method is demonstrated here for the comparison of the just-identified model of illness of Figure 5.2 against the overidentified version of it with six deleted paths. The first step is to calculate for each model a *generalized squared multiple correlation*, R_m^2:

$$R_m^2 = 1 - (1 - R_1^2)(1 - R_2^2) \cdots (1 - R_{last}^2), \tag{5.5}$$

where R_1^2 through R_{last}^2 are the squared multiple correlations for the first endogenous variable through the last. Presented in the accompanying tables are the squared multiple correlations for each endogenous variable for both the just-identified and overidentified versions of the illness model. (Four-decimal accuracy is recommended for these calculations.)

Model	R^2 values for endogenous variables		
	Fitness	Stress	Illness
Just-identified $(df = 0)$	.1588	.0662	.1835
Overidentified $(df = 6)$	.1521	.0530	.7710

The R_m^2 values for each model are calculated as follows:

$$R_{m,\text{ just-identified}}^2 = 1 - (1 - .1588)(1 - .0662)(1 - .1835) = .3586,$$

$$R_{m,\text{ overidentified}}^2 = 1 - (1 - .1521)(1 - .0530)(1 - .1771) = .3392.$$

The next step is to derive the value of the following ratio, called Q:

$$Q = \frac{1 - R_{m,\text{ just-identified}}^2}{1 - R_{m,\text{ overidentified}}^2}. \tag{5.6}$$

Here Q indicates the relative fit of an overidentified recursive path model to that of a just-identified version of it. If the two have identical fits to the data, then Q equals 1. For this example Q is $(1 - .3586)/(1 - .3392) = .6414/.6608 = .9706$.

The final step is to convert Q to a χ^2 statistic with degrees of freedom that equal the number of paths hypothesized to be zero in the overidentified model. In general, the value of χ_Q^2 is

$$\chi_Q^2 = -(N - df)\log_e Q, \tag{5.7}$$

where N is the sample size; df are the degrees of freedom; and $\log_e Q$ is the natural logarithm of Q. For this example, $\chi_Q^2 = -(373 - 6)\log_e(.9706) =$

−367(−.0298) = 10.97. The critical value for $\chi^2(6)$ at the .05 level is 12.59. The value of χ_Q^2 (6) for this example, 10.97, falls short of the required value for statistical significance. Therefore, we conclude that the relative fits of the just-identified and overidentified models of illness are not significantly different. Note that although the value of the $\chi^2_{\text{difference}}(6)$ statistic derived using ML estimation is somewhat greater for the same comparison (11.41 vs. 10.97; see Table 5.3), both values are not significant at the .05 level.

CHAPTER SIX

Stuctural Models with Observed Variables and Path Analysis: II. Nonrecursive Models, Multiple Group Analysis

Creative people . . . do not run away from non-being, but by encountering and wrestling with it, force it to produce being. They knock on silence for answering music; they pursue meaninglessness until they force it to mean.
— ROLLO MAY (1975, p. 93)

6.1 Foreword

The specification of a recursive path model requires the restrictive assumptions that all causal effects are unidirectional and that the disturbances are independent if there are direct effects among the endogenous variables. Because nonrecursive path models do not require either assumption, they allow the researcher to test a wider range of hypotheses. This potential advantage comes at a cost, though, because nonrecursive path models are more difficult than recursive path models. One source of this problem is identification: as mentioned in the previous chapter, particular combinations of effects in a nonrecursive path model can result in the underidentification of one or more of its parameters even if the model has fewer parameters than observations. For two reasons, it is important to evaluate the identification status of a nonrecursive path model when it is specified and *before* the data are collected. First, one of the remedies for a nonidentified nonrecursive model (among others discussed later) is to add exogenous variables, which may be possible only before the study is carried out. Second, dealing with the identification issue early on may prevent a frustrating round of unsuccessful attempts with the computer to analyze a nonrecursive path model that is actually not identified. (Both of these recommendations apply to *any* type of structural equation model, not just nonrecursive path models.)

The main topic of this chapter concerns how to determine whether a nonrecursive path model is identified. These procedures are described and demonstrated for different kinds of nonrecursive models. After consideration of general issues in the estimation of nonrecursive path models, an example is presented.

Also introduced in this chapter in section 6.10 is the evaluation of *any* type of path model across independent samples. (Because the presentation of this topic does not assume knowledge of nonrecursive path models, readers who are interested mainly in multiple group path analysis can skip directly to section 6.10.) The rationale that underlies a multiple group path analysis generalizes to the multisample analysis of other kinds of structural equation models such as measurement models or hybrid models. Altogether, the topics covered in this chapter should help the reader better understand not only the full range of path models but also hybrid models with nonrecursive structural submodels and the general logic of multiple group SEM.

6.2   Overview of the Identification Status of Path Models

Presented in Table 6.1 is a summary of the identification status of path models as a function of their characteristics. Case 1 in the table refers to models considered in this book to be recursive. Recursive models do not have feedback loops; they may also have disturbance correlations only if there are no direct effects among the endogenous variables (e.g., Figure 5.1). The remaining cases (2–4) in Table 6.1 concern nonrecursive models. Unlike recursive models, nonrecursive models are not always identified. Although there are algebraic means to determine whether the parameters of a nonrecursive path model can be expressed as unique functions of its observations (e.g., Berry, 1984, pp. 27–35; Bollen, 1989, pp. 91–93; Fox, 1984, pp. 239–251),

TABLE 6.1. Requirements for the Identification of Path Models

	Model characteristics		Identification status	
Case	Pattern of disturbance correlations	Feedback loop?	Conditions for identification	Necessary or sufficient?
Models considered recursive				
1	Only if no direct effects between Ys; otherwise, none	No	Always identified	—
Models considered nonrecursive				
2	All possible pairwise	Yes or no	1. Parameters ≤ observations	Necessary
			2. Order condition	Necessary
			3. Rank condition	Sufficient
3	All possible pairwise within recursively related blocks	Yes or no	1. Parameters ≤ observations	Necessary
			2. Order condition in each block	Necessary
			3. Rank condition in each block	Sufficient
4	Any other pattern	Yes or no	1. Parameters ≤ observations	Necessary
			2. Model-fitting program yields a solution that passes checks of uniqueness	Necessary

these techniques are practical only for very simple models. Fortunately, there are alternatives that involve checking whether a nonrecursive model meets certain requirements for identification. Some of these conditions are only necessary but not sufficient for identification. A necessary condition must be satisfied, but doing so does not guarantee that the model is identified. If a nonrecursive model satisfies a sufficient condition, however, then it is identified. Remember, though, that identification concerns whether it is *theoretically* possible to derive unique estimates of each model parameter. Problems such as empirical underidentification—described in the previous chapter for recursive models (section 5.5) and discussed later for nonrecursive models—can still derail the estimation of a model that is theoretically identified.

As is indicated in Table 6.1, the nature and number of conditions for identification that a nonrecursive path model must satisfy depend upon its pattern of disturbance correlations. For example, if a nonrecursive model has unanalyzed associations between all pairs of its disturbances (case 2 in the table), then it must meet three conditions in order to be identified. Two of these conditions are necessary, but the third is sufficient. The necessary conditions include the requirement for at least as many observations as parameters (the parameters ≤ observations condition) and another one that is called the *order condition*. Readers already know how to count numbers of observations and parameters for path models (section 5.3); the order condition is described below in section 6.3. A nonrecursive model with all possible disturbance correlations that fails to meet either of these necessary conditions is not identified and thus must be respecified. The third requirement listed in Table 6.1, the *rank condition* (also described in section 6.3), provides a more stringent test of a model's identification status because it is a sufficient condition. If the evaluation of a nonrecursive model with all possible disturbance correlations against these three conditions indicates that it is not identified, then something must be done. Various corrective options are considered later.

The parameters ≤ observations, order, and rank conditions also apply to nonrecursive models described by case 3 in Table 6.1. These models have disturbance correlations but not between every pair of disturbances. Instead, they have all pairwise disturbance correlations within blocks of endogenous variables that are recursively related to each other. Also, such models may or may not have feedback loops. When at least one block has a feedback loop, some authors (e.g., Berry, 1984; Rigdon, 1995) use the term *block recursive* to describe them, even though such models are nevertheless nonrecursive. Examples of block recursive models and how to evaluate whether they are identified are presented later.

Case 4 in Table 6.1 concerns nonrecursive path models with any pattern of disturbance correlations not described by cases 2 and 3. In this sense, they could be considered as "none of the above" nonrecursive models. For example, a model with a feedback loop but no disturbance correlations would be considered such a model. Although there are two necessary conditions for the identification of "none of the above" nonrecursive models, there may be no sufficient condition, at least one that can be readily evaluated by hand. Thus, the identification status of case 4 models may be more ambiguous than for nonrecursive models with other patterns of disturbance correlations. Suggestions for how to evaluate whether "none of the above" nonrecursive path models may be identified are offered later.

With this overview in mind, let's consider how to determine whether a nonrecursive model with all possible disturbance correlations is identified.

6.3 Nonrecursive Path Models with All Possible Disturbance Correlations

This section is about nonrecursive path models described by case 2 of Table 6.1. Presented in Figure 6.1 are two models with all possible disturbance correlations. Both models satisfy the parameters ≤ observations requirement for identification. Model (a) in the figure has 10 observations (4 variables: 4(5)/2) and 10 parameters; the latter include 4 variances (of X_1, X_2, D_1, and D_2), 2 unanalyzed associations ($X_1 \leftrightarrow X_2$ and $D_1 \leftrightarrow D_2$), and 4 direct effects on the endogenous variables Y_1 and Y_2 from other observed variables, two of which make up the direct feedback loop $Y_1 \rightleftarrows Y_2$. Model (b) of Figure 6.1 has 21 observations (6 variables: 6(7)/2) and 18 parameters, including six variances (of three Xs and three Ds), 6 unanalyzed associations (3 among the Xs; 3 among the Ds), and 6 direct effects on the endogenous variables. Three of these direct effects are part of the indirect feedback loop $Y_1 \rightarrow Y_2 \rightarrow Y_3 \rightarrow Y_1$. Because the parameters ≤ observations requirement is only a necessary condition, it is not yet clear whether

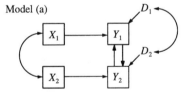

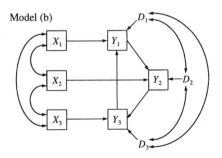

FIGURE 6.1. Two nonrecursive path models with all possible disturbance correlations.

the models in Figure 6.1 are identified. However, one can more clearly determine their identification status with the order and rank conditions.

Order Condition

The order condition is a counting rule applied to each of the endogenous variables of a nonrecursive model with all possible disturbance correlations. If the order condition is not satisfied, then the equation for that variable is underidentified. One evaluates the order condition by tallying the number of observed variables that have direct effects on each endogenous variable versus the number that do not; let's call the latter excluded variables. Excluded variables can be either endogenous or exogenous. The order condition requires that the number of excluded variables for each endogenous variable equals or exceeds the total number of endogenous variables minus 1:

Number of excluded variables $\geq$
$$\text{(Number of endogenous variables} - 1). \qquad (6.1)$$

Let's evaluate the order condition for the models of Figure 6.1. Model (a) has two endogenous variables, Y_1 and Y_2. To satisfy the order condition, there must be at least one excluded variable for each endogenous variable, which is true here: X_1 is excluded from the equation for Y_2 (i.e., $X_2 \rightarrow Y_2 \leftarrow D_2$), and X_2 is excluded from Y_1's equation ($X_1 \rightarrow Y_1 \leftarrow D_1$). Model (b) in Figure 6.1 also satisfies the order condition: with three endogenous variables, each must have at least two variables excluded from its equation; each endogenous variable of model (b) has two variables that are specified to directly affect it; with six observed variables altogether in model (b), the number of variables excluded from the equation of every endogenous variable is 4.

Rank Condition

Recall that the order condition is necessary for identification but not sufficient; therefore, we still do not know whether the nonrecursive models with all possible disturbance correlations of Figure 6.1 are in fact identified. Evaluation of the sufficient rank condition, however, will provide the answer. The rank condition is typically described in the SEM literature in matrix terms (e.g., Bekker, Merckens, & Wansbeek, 1994; Bollen, 1989; Johnston, 1984), which is fine for those with a background in linear algebra but otherwise not. Berry (1984) devised an algorithm for checking the rank condition that does not require knowledge of matrix operations, a simpler version of which is presented here. Before this method is described, though, a nontechnical description of the rank condition is outlined below.

For nonrecursive path models like those of Figure 6.1, the rank condition can be viewed as a requirement that each endogenous variable in a feedback loop has a unique pattern of direct effects on it from variables outside the loop. A unique pattern of external effects provides an "anchor" so that the parameters of variables involved in feedback loops can be estimated distinctly from one another. Look again at model (b) of Figure 6.1. Note that three variables, Y_1, Y_2, and Y_3, are involved in a feedback loop and that each has a unique pattern of direct effects on it from variables outside the loop ($X_1 \rightarrow Y_1$, $X_2 \rightarrow Y_2$, and $X_3 \rightarrow Y_3$). The same general pattern is also true for model (a) of Figure 6.1 ($X_1 \rightarrow Y_1$ and $X_2 \rightarrow Y_2$). Note that this analogy does not hold for models considered in this book to be nonrecursive that do not have feedback loops (e.g., "partially recursive" models with correlated disturbances and direct effects among the endogenous variables; see Figure 5.1). Therefore, a more formal way of evaluating the rank condition is needed.

The starting point for checking the rank condition is to construct something that Berry (1984) called a *system matrix* in which the endogenous variables are listed on the left side of the matrix (rows) and all of the variables, exogenous and endogenous, along the top (columns). In each row of a system matrix, a "0" or "1" appears in the columns that corresponds to that row. A "1" indicates that the variable represented by that column has a direct effect on the endogenous variable represented by that row. A "1" also appears in the column that corresponds to the endogenous variable represented by that row. The remaining entries in the rows of a system matrix are "0's," and they indicate excluded variables. The system matrix for model (a) of Figure 6.1 constructed according to these rules is presented here (I):

$$
\begin{array}{c}
 \\
Y_1 \\
Y_2
\end{array}
\begin{array}{cccc}
X_1 & X_2 & Y_1 & Y_2 \\
\left[\begin{array}{cccc}
1 & 0 & 1 & 1 \\
0 & 1 & 1 & 1
\end{array}\right]
\end{array}
\qquad \textbf{(I)}
$$

"Reading" this matrix for Y_1 indicates three "1's" in its row, one in the column for itself and the others in the columns of variables that, according to the model, directly affect it, X_1 and Y_2. Because X_2

is excluded from Y_1's equation, the entry in the X_2 column is a "0"; the row for Y_2 is read in a similar way.

The rank condition is evaluated using the system matrix. Like the order condition, the rank condition must be evaluated for the equation of each endogenous variable of a model with all possible disturbance correlations. The steps to do so are outlined below:

1. Begin with the first row of the system matrix (i.e., the first endogenous variable). Cross out all of the entries of that row. Also cross out any column in the system matrix with a "1" in this row. Use the entries that remain to form a new, reduced matrix. Row and column labels are not necessary in the reduced matrix.

2. Simplify the reduced matrix further by deleting any row with entries that are all zeros. Also delete any row that is an exact duplicate of another or that can be reproduced by adding other rows together.[1] The number of remaining rows is the rank. (Readers who are familiar with linear algebra may recognize this step as the equivalent of elementary row operations to find the rank of a matrix.) *The rank condition is met for the equation of this endogenous variable if the rank of the reduced matrix is greater than or equal to the total number of endogenous variable minus 1.*

3. Repeat steps 1 and 2 for every endogenous variable. *If the rank condition is satisfied for every endogenous variable, then the model is identified.*

Steps 1 and 2 applied to the system matrix for model (a) of Figure 6.1 are outlined here **(II)**. Note that we are beginning with endogenous variable Y_1.

$$\rightarrow \begin{array}{c} \\ Y_1 \\ Y_2 \end{array} \begin{array}{cccc} X_1 & X_2 & Y_1 & Y_2 \\ \left[\begin{array}{cccc} \cancel{1} & \cancel{0} & \cancel{1} & \cancel{1} \\ \cancel{0} & 1 & \cancel{1} & \cancel{1} \end{array} \right] \end{array} \rightarrow [1] \rightarrow \text{Rank} = 1. \qquad \textbf{(II)}$$

For step 1, all of the entries in the first row of the system matrix **(II)** are crossed out. Also crossed out are the three columns of the ma-

---

[1]As an example of the latter, consider the following reduced matrix:

$$\begin{bmatrix} 1 & 0 & 0 \\ 0 & 1 & 0 \\ 1 & 1 & 0 \end{bmatrix}$$

The third row above can be formed by adding the first and second rows, so it should be deleted. Therefore, the rank of this matrix is 2 instead of 3.

trix with a "1" in this row. The resulting reduced matrix has only a single value. Because this value is not zero, this matrix cannot be further simplified, so step 2 is unnecessary. The reduced matrix has a single row, which means that the rank for the equation of Y_1 is 1. This exactly equals the minimum required value, which is the total number of endogenous variables in this model minus 1 (2 − 1). The row condition is satisfied for Y_1.

We repeat this process for the second endogenous variable of model (a) of Figure 6.1, Y_2. The steps for doing so are summarized next (**III**).

$$
\begin{array}{c}
\begin{array}{cccc} X_1 & X_2 & Y_1 & Y_2 \end{array} \\
\begin{array}{c} Y_1 \\ \rightarrow \quad Y_2 \end{array}
\left[\begin{array}{cccc} 1 & 0 & 1 & 1 \\ \hline -0 & 1 & 1 & 1 \end{array}\right]
\rightarrow [1] \rightarrow \text{Rank} = 1.
\end{array} \quad \textbf{(III)}
$$

Crossing out the row of the system matrix (**III**) that corresponds to Y_2 and columns with a "1" in this row leaves a reduced matrix that cannot be further simplified. The number of rows in the reduced matrix is 1, which is the rank and also equals the minimum required value (2 − 1). *Because the rank condition is satisfied for both endogenous variables of model (a) of Figure 6.1, we conclude that the model is identified.*

The steps for evaluating the rank condition for each endogenous variable of model (b) of Figure 6.1 are summarized in Table 6.2. Readers are encouraged to follow through these steps for the sake of additional practice. Because the rank for every endogenous variable of this model equals or exceeds the number of endogenous variables minus 1 (3 − 1 = 2), model (b) of the figure is also identified.

Although evaluation of the rank condition is more laborious than for the order condition, recall that the latter is only a necessary condition for identification. Thus, it is possible that a nonrecursive model with all possible disturbance correlations could meet the order condition and still not be identified because it fails the rank condition. An example of such a model is presented next.

Respecification of Models That Fail the Order or Rank Condition

Consider the two models presented in Figure 6.2. Both models are not identified but for different reasons. Suppose that the context for the specification of model (a) is as follows: let Y_1 and Y_2 respectively represent violence on the part of protesters and police. (This example is a variation on ones presented by Berry, 1984, and Kritzer, 1977.) A

TABLE 6.2. Evaluation of the Rank Condition for Model (b) of Figure 6.1

System matrix

	X_1	X_2	X_3	Y_1	Y_2	Y_3
Y_1	1	0	0	1	0	1
Y_2	0	1	0	1	1	0
Y_3	0	0	1	0	1	1

Evaluation for Y_1

$$\rightarrow \begin{array}{c} Y_1 \\ Y_2 \\ Y_3 \end{array} \begin{bmatrix} 1 & 0 & 0 & 1 & 0 & 1 \\ 0 & 1 & 0 & 1 & 1 & 0 \\ 0 & 0 & 1 & 0 & 1 & 1 \end{bmatrix} \rightarrow \begin{bmatrix} 1 & 0 & 1 \\ 0 & 1 & 1 \end{bmatrix} \rightarrow \text{Rank} = 2$$

Evaluation for Y_2

$$\begin{array}{c} Y_1 \\ \rightarrow \ Y_2 \\ Y_3 \end{array} \begin{bmatrix} 1 & 0 & 0 & 1 & 0 & 1 \\ 0 & 1 & 0 & 1 & 1 & 0 \\ 0 & 0 & 1 & 0 & 1 & 1 \end{bmatrix} \rightarrow \begin{bmatrix} 1 & 0 & 1 \\ 0 & 1 & 1 \end{bmatrix} \rightarrow \text{Rank} = 2$$

Evaluation for Y_3

$$\begin{array}{c} Y_1 \\ Y_2 \\ \rightarrow \ Y_3 \end{array} \begin{bmatrix} 1 & 0 & 0 & 1 & 0 & 1 \\ 0 & 1 & 0 & 1 & 1 & 0 \\ 0 & 0 & 1 & 0 & 1 & 1 \end{bmatrix} \rightarrow \begin{bmatrix} 1 & 0 & 1 \\ 0 & 1 & 1 \end{bmatrix} \rightarrow \text{Rank} = 2$$

researcher believes that these variables reciprocally cause each other: as protesters become more violent, so do the police, and vice versa. Also suppose that the researcher believes that two exogenous variables, X_1 and X_2, affect protester and police violence; X_1 is the seriousness of the civil disobedience committed by the protesters, and X_2 is the availability of police riot gear (clubs, shields, tear gas, etc.). Immediately after this model is specified and *before* the data are collected, the researcher evaluates its identification status. Two problems are discovered: the model has more parameters (11) than observations (10), and the order condition is violated because there are no excluded variables for Y_2, police violence. (Readers are encouraged to verify both problems.) Because model (a) violates the order condition, it will also fail the rank condition.

What can the researcher do about this identification problem? Because the data are not yet collected, one possibility is to add exogenous variables to the model such that (1) the number of additional observations afforded by the new exogenous variables is greater than

Model (a): Too Many Parameters

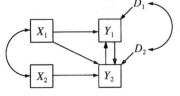

Model (b): Fails Rank Condition

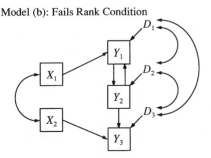

FIGURE 6.2. Two examples of nonidentified nonrecursive models.

the number of parameters they add to the model; (2) the number of excluded variables for Y_1 and Y_2 are each at least one; and (3) the modified model also satisfies the rank condition. Suppose the researcher consults relevant theory and research and decides that an appropriate new exogenous variable, X_3, would be the protesters' level of commitment to nonviolence. The addition of $X_3 \rightarrow Y_1$ (Y_1 is protester violence) and unanalyzed associations between X_3 and the other two exogenous variables to model (a) of Figure 6.2 would accomplish all three goals just listed. Thus, model (a) respecified in this way is identified. (Readers are encouraged to verify that the respecified model meets the parameters $\leq$ observations, order, and rank conditions.) Barring problems of empirical underidentification, it should be possible for the computer to derive unique estimates of its parameters.

But now suppose that the researcher did not check the identification status of model (a) of Figure 6.2 until *after* the study was carried out. Because it is now too late to add exogenous variables to the model, there is only one option: the model must be simplified. One way to do this is drop paths from the model, which is the same as constraining the value of the estimate of that path to zero. Other types of constraints such as equality or proportionality constraints (described later) reduce the number of free parameters without deleting paths. However, both options to simplify the model have potential drawbacks. For instance, deleting the path $X_1 \rightarrow Y_2$ (riot gear $\rightarrow$ police violence) would yield an identified model (cf. model (a) of Figure 6.1), but doing so forces a change in the researcher's hypotheses. That is, if the researcher believes that the availability of riot gear has a direct effect on police violence, then dropping this path from the model is akin to intentionally making a specification error. Adding an exogenous variable to the model, in contrast, does not sacrifice the original specifications about causal effects.

Model (b) of Figure 6.2 demonstrates the insufficiency of the parameters/observations ratio and the order condition to establish identification. There are 15 observations (5 variables: 5(6)/2) available to estimate this model's 14 parameters (5 variances: (2 Xs and 3 Ds), 4 unanalyzed associations, plus 5 direct effects). This model also satisfies the order condition because there are at least two excluded variables for every endogenous variable. However, this model fails the rank condition, specifically for Y_1, as is demonstrated here **(IV)**.

$$
\begin{array}{c}
\rightarrow \\
\\
\end{array}
\begin{array}{c}
Y_1 \\
Y_2 \\
Y_3
\end{array}
\begin{array}{c}
\begin{matrix} X_1 & X_2 & Y_1 & Y_2 & Y_3 \end{matrix} \\
\left[
\begin{array}{ccccc}
1 & 0 & 1 & 1 & 0 \\
0 & 0 & 1 & 1 & 0 \\
0 & 1 & 0 & 1 & 1
\end{array}
\right]
\end{array}
\rightarrow
\begin{bmatrix}
0 & 0 \\
1 & 1
\end{bmatrix}
\rightarrow \text{Rank} = 1. \quad \textbf{(IV)}
$$

The rank of the equation for Y_1 is thus only 1, which is one short of the minimum value, 2, the number of endogenous variables minus 1. In terms of the "anchor" analogy about the rank condition offered earlier, this model is not identified because Y_2 does not have a unique pattern of direct effects on it from outside its reciprocal relation with Y_1. Adding a third exogenous variable X_3 to this model with a direct effect on Y_2 results in an identified model. If it were not possible to add an exogenous variable (i.e., if the data are already collected), then adding either $X_2 \rightarrow Y_2$ or $Y_3 \rightarrow Y_2$ to this model would make it identified. Either direct effect would provide unique "anchors" for endogenous variables in feedback loops. Note that the addition of the path $X_1 \rightarrow Y_2$ instead of these other two direct effects does *not* meet the rank condition.

6.4   Nonrecursive Path Models with All Possible Disturbance Correlations within Recursively Related Blocks

This section concerns identification case 3 of Table 6.1. Consider the two models presented in Figure 6.3, which some authors would de-

Model (a)

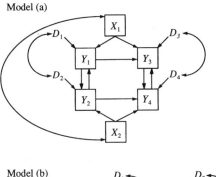

Model (b)

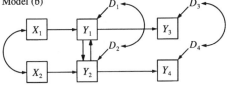

FIGURE 6.3. Examples of nonrecursive path models that are block recursive.

scribe with the term *block recursive*. Note that one can partition the endogenous variables of each model into two blocks, one with Y_1 and Y_2 and the other made up of Y_3 and Y_4. Each block contains all possible disturbance correlations (i.e., $D_1 \leftrightarrow D_2$ for the first block, $D_3 \leftrightarrow D_4$ for the second), but the disturbances across the blocks are independent (e.g., D_1 is uncorrelated with D_3). Also, causal relations within the blocks are nonrecursive (e.g., $Y_1 \rightleftarrows Y_2$), but effects between the blocks are unidirectional. For example, in both models, Y_1 of the first block is specified to affect Y_3 of the second block but Y_3 does not have an effect on back on Y_1. These two characteristics—correlated disturbances within but not between blocks and unidirectional effects between blocks—imply that the blocks are recursively related to each other; hence the term "block recursive" even though the whole model is nonrecursive. The identification of block recursive models can be evaluated with the parameters ≤ observations, order, and rank conditions. The application of the order and rank conditions must be adjusted, but the latter provides a sufficient test of identification for block recursive models.

Model (a) of Figure 6.3 has 19 parameters (6 variances and 3 covariances of observed exogenous variables or disturbances plus 10 direct effects). With 6 observed variables, there are 21 observations, which exceeds the number of parameters. The order and rank conditions are evaluated separately for each block as is demonstrated in

Table 6.3. The steps are as follows: First, construct a system matrix for each block. For example, the system matrix for the block that contains Y_1 and Y_2 of model (a) of Figure 6.3 lists only these variables plus prior variables in the model (X_1 and X_2; see Table 6.3). Variables of the second block of model (a), Y_3 and Y_4, are not included in the system matrix for the first block. The system matrix for the second block of model (a) lists only Y_3 and Y_4 in its rows but represents all of the variables in the model in its column. Second, inspect the rows of each system matrix to determine whether the order condition is met for each equation. This is accomplished by counting the number of "0's" in each row, which indicates the number of excluded variables for that endogenous variable. This value must be greater than the number of endogenous variables in each block minus 1. Endogenous

TABLE 6.3. Evaluation of the Order and Rank Conditions for Model (a) of Figure 6.3

System matrices

Block 1

$$
\begin{array}{c}
 & \begin{array}{cccc} Y_1 & Y_2 & X_1 & X_2 \end{array} \\
\begin{array}{c} Y_1 \\ Y_2 \end{array} & \left[\begin{array}{cccc} 1 & 1 & 1 & 0 \\ 1 & 1 & 0 & 1 \end{array} \right]
\end{array}
$$

Block 2

$$
\begin{array}{c}
 & \begin{array}{cccccc} Y_1 & Y_2 & Y_3 & Y_4 & X_1 & X_2 \end{array} \\
\begin{array}{c} Y_3 \\ Y_4 \end{array} & \left[\begin{array}{cccccc} 1 & 0 & 1 & 0 & 1 & 0 \\ 0 & 1 & 1 & 1 & 0 & 1 \end{array} \right]
\end{array}
$$

Evaluation for the endogenous variables of Block 1

$$
\rightarrow \begin{array}{c}
 & \begin{array}{cccc} Y_1 & Y_2 & X_1 & X_2 \end{array} \\
\begin{array}{c} Y_1 \\ Y_2 \end{array} & \left[\begin{array}{cccc} 1 & 1 & 1 & 0 \\ 1 & 1 & 0 & 1 \end{array} \right]
\end{array} \rightarrow [1] \rightarrow \text{Rank} = 1
$$

$$
\rightarrow \begin{array}{c}
 & \begin{array}{cccc} Y_1 & Y_2 & X_1 & X_2 \end{array} \\
\begin{array}{c} Y_1 \\ Y_2 \end{array} & \left[\begin{array}{cccc} 1 & 1 & 1 & 0 \\ 1 & 1 & 0 & 1 \end{array} \right]
\end{array} \rightarrow [1] \rightarrow \text{Rank} = 1
$$

Evaluation for the endogenous variables of Block 2

$$
\rightarrow \begin{array}{c}
 & \begin{array}{cccccc} Y_1 & Y_2 & Y_3 & Y_4 & X_1 & X_2 \end{array} \\
\begin{array}{c} Y_3 \\ Y_4 \end{array} & \left[\begin{array}{cccccc} 1 & 0 & 1 & 0 & 1 & 0 \\ 0 & 1 & 1 & 1 & 0 & 1 \end{array} \right]
\end{array} \rightarrow [1 \ 1 \ 1] \rightarrow \text{Rank} = 1
$$

$$
\rightarrow \begin{array}{c}
 & \begin{array}{cccccc} Y_1 & Y_2 & Y_3 & Y_4 & X_1 & X_2 \end{array} \\
\begin{array}{c} Y_3 \\ Y_4 \end{array} & \left[\begin{array}{cccccc} 1 & 0 & 1 & 0 & 1 & 0 \\ 0 & 1 & 1 & 1 & 0 & 1 \end{array} \right]
\end{array} \rightarrow [1 \ 1] \rightarrow \text{Rank} = 1
$$

variables Y_1 and Y_2 of the first block each have one excluded variable, which meets the order condition; Y_3 and Y_4 of the second block also each satisfy the order condition. Third, evaluate the rank condition for the system matrix of each block. These steps are outlined in Table 6.3. Because the rank of the equation of every endogenous variable of each system matrix for model (a) equals the number of endogenous variables in each block minus 1 (2 − 1), the rank condition for the whole model is satisfied. Model (a) of Figure 6.3 is thus identified.

Model (b) of Figure 6.3 has only a single feedback loop. Like model (a), though, it has the same pattern of disturbance correlations and recursively related blocks. Because model (b) satisfies the parameters ≤ observations, order, and rank conditions, it is identified. Readers are encouraged to verify this using the method just outlined to evaluate the order and rank conditions. For additional examples of the evaluation of whether block recursive models are identified, see Rigdon (1995).

6.5   Empirical Underidentification

Nonrecursive path models described by either cases 2 or 3 of Table 6.1 that meet the sufficient rank condition can nevertheless be empirically underidentified. Multicollinearity, which may prevent the estimation of recursive and nonrecursive path models alike, is one way this can happen. Nonrecursive models, especially those with feedback loops, are susceptible to an additional kind of empirical underidentification: if the path coefficients for certain direct effects are close to zero (e.g., .01), then the rank condition may be violated because the associated path is, practically speaking, eliminated from the model. For instance, suppose the path coefficient for $X_1 \rightarrow Y_1$ of model (a) of Figure 6.1 is about zero. The virtual absence of $X_1 \rightarrow Y_1$ from this model alters its system matrix, which in turn violates the rank condition for Y_2. This consequence is outlined here starting with a system matrix (V) for model (a) of the figure without $X_1 \rightarrow Y_1$. Working through the steps listed earlier indicates that the rank for Y_2 is zero.

$$\begin{array}{c} \\ \rightarrow \end{array} \begin{array}{c} \\ Y_1 \\ Y_2 \end{array} \overset{\begin{array}{cccc} X_1 & X_2 & Y_1 & Y_2 \end{array}}{\left[\begin{array}{cccc} 0 & 0 & 1 & 1 \\ 0 & 1 & 1 & 1 \end{array}\right]} \rightarrow [\text{-}\theta\text{-}] \rightarrow \text{Rank} = 0. \quad \textbf{(V)}$$

Model (a) of Figure 6.1 is also empirically underidentified if the path coefficient for $X_2 \rightarrow Y_2$ is close to zero. The patterns of near-zero direct effects that may result in the empirical underidentification of model (b) of Figure 6.1 are more complex. For example, if the path coefficients for any two of the direct effects from the exogenous variables are close to zero (e.g., $X_1 \rightarrow Y_1$ and $X_2 \rightarrow Y_2$), the equation for the third endogenous variable (e.g., Y_3) may fail the rank condition. (Readers are encouraged to prove this by evaluating the rank condition using system matrices for model (b) without these direct effects.)

6.6 "None of the Above" Nonrecursive Path Models and Empirical Checks for Identification

This section is about identification case 4 of Table 6.1. If a nonrecursive path model has either no disturbance correlations or less than all possible disturbance correlations such that the model is not block recursive, then the order and rank conditions are too conservative. That is, "none of the above" nonrecursive models that fail either condition could nevertheless be identified. For instance, the model $X_1 \rightarrow Y_1 \rightleftarrows Y_2$, where the disturbances of Y_1 and Y_2 are independent, is identified even though there are zero excluded variables for the equation of Y_1 (the order condition is violated) and the rank for the same is zero (the rank condition is violated). The requirement about relative numbers of parameters and observations still applies to "none of the above" models, but recall that this condition for identification is only necessary and not sufficient.

Suppose that a researcher has specified a "none of the above" nonrecursive path model and wishes to evaluate its identification status before the data are collected. Also suppose that the researcher has determined that the number of model parameters is less than the number of observations, which only means that the model *may* be identified. Is there anything else that can be done to evaluate the model? Yes, and it involves using a model-fitting program as a diagnostic tool with made-up data. The made-up data are arranged in a covariance matrix based on correlations and standard deviations that the researcher anticipates may approximate actual values. Care must be taken not to generate hypothetical correlations that are out of bounds (e.g., sections 4.4 and 4.5) or that may result in empirical underidentification due to near-zero path coefficients. (If the researcher is uncertain about a particular hypothetical covariance matrix, then others with somewhat different but still plausible values can be constructed.) The model is then analyzed with the hypothetical data. If a model-fitting program is unable to generate a converged, sensible-looking solution, then the model may not be identified. However, if the program successfully analyzes the model, then it may be identified. More about both outcomes and related cautions are outlined below. (Of course, the issues discussed below also apply to the analysis of actual data, but it is inadvisable to wait until after the study is conducted to begin to address the issue of identification.)

Some model-fitting programs automatically check some aspects of identification. Included among these automatic checks may be counts of the numbers of observations and parameters and whether certain operations such as matrix inversion can be performed. Such checks typically concern necessary but not sufficient mathematical requirements for identification. However, model-fitting programs are not yet sophisticated enough to be able to definitively determine whether a nonrecursive path model is in fact identified before attempting to analyze it.[2] Part of the problem is that there are theoretically an infinite number of nonrecursive path models (and other types of models, too, such as measurement or hybrid ones). Another is that the algebraic machinations necessary to determine whether a model's parameters can be expressed as unique functions of the observations are complex. A consequence of these limitations is that it is possible for a model-fitting program to yield a solution for a model that is not actually identified. If this happens, then the solution is not really unique. Although there are ways to empirically check the uniqueness of a solution (described momentarily), they do not guarantee that the model is identified. *Therefore, a necessary but insufficient condition for the identification of a "none of the above" nonrecursive model is that a model-fitting program generate a logical solution that passes empirical checks of its uniqueness.* Such checks are outlined below.

One empirical check for the uniqueness of a solution is to use the model-implied covariance matrix from a successful analysis of a "none of the above" nonrecursive path model as the input data for a second analysis of the same model. (Hint: Copy the predicted covariance matrix from the output file of the first analysis and paste it in the command file or window for the second analysis.) The second analysis should yield the same solution as the first because the input data (i.e., predicted covariances) were generated based on the parameter estimates from the first analysis. If not, the solution is not unique and the model is not identified. Note that this empirical check works only for models with fewer parameters than observations. If the numbers of observations and parameters are equal, then the predicted covariances must equal the observed ones, and analyses of the model with the same input data will yield the same solution.

[2] A recent text by Bekker et al. (1994) includes a disk of PASCAL programs for IBM-compatible PCs that check the identification status of not only nonrecursive path models but also of other types of structural equation models. Although the book is very technical and the computer program requires a working knowledge of matrix algebra, both are examples of a preliminary step toward having computers check the identification status of nonrecursive path models.

Another empirical test of uniqueness is to conduct a second analysis using starting values that are somewhat different than in the original. If estimation converges to the same solution working from different starting points, then the model may be identified. Remember, though, that these and other more complicated empirical checks that are based on linear algebra (e.g., Bollen, 1989, pp. 246–251) do not guarantee that a model is identified.

If a model-fitting program is unable to generate a solution or yields one with illogical values (e.g., estimates of disturbance variances that are less than 0 or of correlations with absolute values greater than 1), then the model may not be identified. Also, some model-fitting programs give warning messages about individual parameters that may not be identified. For example, Amos prints the message, "The (probably) unidentified parameters are marked," when it singles out problematic parameters; EQS issues "condition codes" that warn about problems with specific parameters; and LISREL indicates when statistics like standard errors and significance tests cannot be calculated for certain estimates. Such warnings while useful are nevertheless fallible. For instance, the parameters indicated in program warning messages may not be the actual ones that are underidentified. However, program warning messages tend to at least localize the problem to the general "neighborhood" in the path diagram of the parameters mentioned.

Because there may be no sufficient conditions for the identification of "none of the above" nonrecursive models that can be readily checked by hand, it is difficult to suggest general guidelines for the respecification of models that appear to be not identified. Sometimes constraining a disturbance correlation to zero for variables involved in a feedback loop may bring about identification. Adding exogenous variables to the model and constraining some of their direct effects on other variables to zero may also help. Although some trial and error in attempts to achieve the identification of a "none of the above" nonrecursive model may be necessary, the process should be based as much as possible on substantive considerations. For more information about how to deal with nonrecursive models that cannot be conclusively evaluated against a sufficient requirement like the rank condition, readers are referred to Rigdon (1995).

6.7 A Healthy Perspective on Identification

At first glance, the respecification of nonrecursive path models so that they are identified can seem like a shell game: add this path, drop another, and—voilà!—the model is identified or—curses!—it's not. Although one obviously needs an identified model, it is crucial to modify models in a judicious manner. That is, any change to the original specification of a model for the sake of identification should be guided by the researcher's hypotheses and sense of relevant theory. For instance, the specification that a path is zero must be made on theoretical or logical grounds, not on empirical ones. That is, one cannot estimate a model, find that a path coefficient is close to zero, and then eliminate the path in order to identify a nonrecursive model. Don't lose sight of the ideas that motivated the analysis in the first place through willy-nilly respecification.

6.8   Issues in the Estimation of Nonrecursive Path Models

Four issues in the estimation of nonrecursive path models are discussed in this section, including starting values, constraints, the derivation of indirect and total effects and the related assumption of equilibrium, and two-stage least squares (2SLS) as an alternative estimation procedure.

Starting Values

Maximum likelihood and related estimation procedures described in Chapter 5 are appropriate for nonrecursive path models. More so than for recursive models, the convergence of iterative estimation to a stable solution in the analysis of nonrecursive models requires reasonably accurate starting values. This is especially true for the direct effects of a feedback loop. If a model-fitting program does not automatically generate starting values, or if it does but the computer's initial estimates do not lead to a converged solution, then it is up to the researcher to provide better starting values. The guidelines for calculating starting values presented in Appendix 5.C may be helpful. Another tactic is to increase the program's default limit on the number of iterations to a higher value (e.g., from 30 to 100). Allowing the computer more "tries" may lead to a converged solution.

Inequality, Equality, and Proportionality Constraints

Dropping a path to achieve identification is the same as fixing the estimate of its parameter to zero. Another type of constraint on a single

parameter is an *inequality constraint* that forces the value of its estimate to be less than or greater than a specified value. The specification that the value of an unstandardized path coefficient must be at
least 5 is an example of an inequality constraint. The restriction of
the estimates of a parameter to a particular range (e.g., ≥ 5) may facilitate a converged solution, but it may be difficult to know in advance
what lower or upper bounds to specify. Perhaps for this reason, inequality constraints seem not to be used very often.[3]

An *equality constraint* means that the estimates of two or more
parameters are forced to be equal. In the analysis of nonrecursive
path models, the imposition of equality constraints on the direct effects of a feedback loop is one way to reduce the number of model
parameters without dropping paths. For example, the imposition of
an equality constraint on the reciprocal relation $Y_1 \rightleftarrows Y_2$ means that
only one path coefficient is needed rather than two. A possible drawback of equality constraints on feedback loops is that they preclude
the detection of unequal mutual influence. An example of such was
recently described by Wagner, Torgeson, and Rashotte (1994), who
found in longitudinal studies that the effect of children's phonological abilities on their reading skills is about three times the magnitude
of the effect in the opposite direction. If equality constraints are
blindly imposed when bidirectional effects differ in magnitude, then
not only may the model poorly fit the data but the researcher may
also miss an interesting finding. A *proportionality constraint*, however,
allows for unequal mutual influence but on an a priori basis. As its
name suggests, one estimate is forced to be some proportion of the
other; for example, the path coefficient for $Y_1 \rightarrow Y_2$ is forced to be
three times the value of the coefficients for $Y_2 \rightarrow Y_1$. Like equality
constraints, proportionality constraints reduce the number of parameters, one for each pair of direct effects. However, the imposition of
proportionality constraints requires prior knowledge about the relative magnitudes of the direct effects in a feedback loop.

A technical note about equality constraints and unstandardized
versus standardized solutions follows: the estimates of equality-constrained direct effects in a feedback loop are equal in the unstandardized solution, but the standardized path coefficients may be unequal.
This can occur when the two variables of the direct effect have different variances. Recall that standardized estimates are "normed" by the
standard deviations of each variable (section 2.4). Thus, it makes no

---

[3]Some model-fitting program automatically impose inequality constraints on certain parameters. EQS, for example, by default requires estimates of disturbance
variances to be greater than zero.

sense to compare standardized path coefficients from equality-constrained direct effects. The same general phenomenon occurs for proportionality constraints, which may apply as specified (e.g., 3:1) only in the unstandardized solution.

Overall, the imposition of constraints of any type in the analysis of a nonrecursive path model—or *any* type of structural equation model—should be treated like other decisions about specification: let theory and reason be your guide.

Indirect and Total Effects and the Equilibrium Assumption

Variables in feedback loops have indirect effects—and thus total effects—on *themselves,* which is apparent in effect decompositions calculated by model-fitting programs for nonrecursive path models. Consider the reciprocal relation $Y_1 \rightleftarrows Y_2$. Suppose that the standardized direct effect of Y_1 on Y_2 is .40 and that the effect in the other direction is .20. An indirect effect of Y_1 on itself would be the sequence $Y_1 \rightarrow Y_2 \rightarrow Y_1$, which is estimated as (.40)(.20), or .08. There are additional indirect effects of Y_1 on itself through Y_2, however, because cycles of mutual influence in feedback loops are theoretically infinite. The indirect effect $Y_1 \rightarrow Y_2 \rightarrow Y_1 \rightarrow Y_2 \rightarrow Y_1$ is one of these, and its estimate is (.40)(.20)(.40)(.20), or .0064. Mathematically, these product terms head fairly quickly to zero, but the total effect of Y_1 on itself is an estimate of the sum of all possible cycles through Y_2. Indirect and total effects of Y_2 on itself are derived in a similar way.

Calculation of indirect and total effects among variables in a feedback loop requires the assumption of *equilibrium*—that the constituent direct effects remain stable throughout an infinite number of causal reverberations. The mechanics of deriving indirect and total effects and the related equilibrium assumption are additional reasons why one cannot use methods developed to study recursive relations (i.e., multiple regression) to analyze a nonrecursive model. Additional examples of the calculation of indirect and total effects in nonrecursive models and more information about the equilibrium assumption are available in Kenny (1979, chap. 6) and Heise (1975).

Two-Stage Least Squares Estimation

Maximum likelihood (ML) estimation is commonly used nowadays to estimate nonrecursive path models. An older alternative is *two-stage least squares* (2SLS). As its name implies, 2SLS is a variation on multiple regression (i.e., ordinary least squares) that gets around the problem of model-implied correlations between disturbances and the causes of endogenous variables. Unlike ML estimation, 2SLS is not iterative, and thus it may require less computation time and memory. A brief description of 2SLS is presented here; more extensive presentations can be found in Berry (1984, chap. 5), Bollen (1989, pp. 409–415), James and Singh (1978), and Kenny (1979, pp. 83–92, 103–107).

The logic of 2SLS is described using the nonrecursive model presented in Figure 6.4 as an example. (This model is the same as model (a) of Figure 6.1.) The use of multiple regression—labeled ordinary least squares (OLS) in Figure 6.4—to estimate direct effects is inappropriate because the model is not recursive. As a result, some model-implied correlations between disturbances and causal variables are not zero. For example, the model in Figure 6.4 implies a correlation between the disturbance of Y_1 (D_1) and one of the observed variables specified to directly affect it (Y_3). Note that the model-implied correlation between Y_1's disturbance and its other cause (X_1) is zero. In

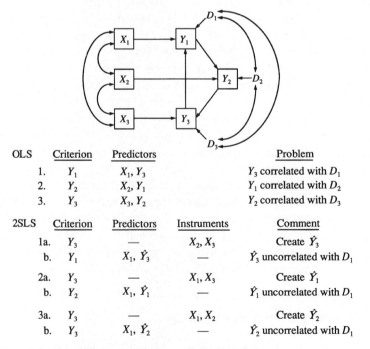

OLS	Criterion	Predictors	Problem
1.	Y_1	X_1, Y_3	Y_3 correlated with D_1
2.	Y_2	X_2, Y_1	Y_1 correlated with D_2
3.	Y_3	X_3, Y_2	Y_2 correlated with D_3

2SLS	Criterion	Predictors	Instruments	Comment
1a.	Y_3	—	X_2, X_3	Create $\hat{Y}_3$
b.	Y_1	$X_1, \hat{Y}_3$	—	$\hat{Y}_3$ uncorrelated with D_1
2a.	Y_3	—	X_1, X_3	Create $\hat{Y}_1$
b.	Y_2	$X_1, \hat{Y}_1$	—	$\hat{Y}_1$ uncorrelated with D_1
3a.	Y_3	—	X_1, X_2	Create $\hat{Y}_2$
b.	Y_3	$X_1, \hat{Y}_2$	—	$\hat{Y}_2$ uncorrelated with D_1

FIGURE 6.4. Two-stage least squares (2SLS) estimation for a model with a feedback loop. OLS, ordinary least squares (multiple regression).

2SLS, "problematic" causal variables—those correlated with the disturbances of an endogenous variable—are replaced by new variables. These new variables are created by regressing the problematic causal variable on exogenous variables that do *not* have direct effects on the endogenous variable. The predictors in this regression are called *instruments* or *instrumental variables*. From this regression analysis, a new variable is created that is substituted for the problematic causal variable in a subsequent regression. This new variable is uncorrelated with the disturbance of the endogenous variable, which remedies the problem. These steps are outlined in Figure 6.4 and are described below for the endogenous variable Y_1.

In an OLS analysis (standard multiple regression), Y_3 is the problematic causal variable because it is implied by the model to covary with D_1. In the first step of a 2SLS analysis, Y_3 is regressed on X_2 and X_3, the exogenous variables in the model that do not have direct effects on the endogenous variable Y_1; X_2 and X_3 are the instruments for Y_3. From this regression, a new variable is created, $\hat{Y}_3$, which represents the part of Y_3 that is predictable by the instruments. Because the instruments are implied by the model to be uncorrelated with the disturbance of Y_1 (D_1), the new variable $\hat{Y}_3$ has the same characteristic. In the second step of the 2SLS procedure, the endogenous variable Y_1 is regressed on X_1 and the new predictor $\hat{Y}_3$. The regression weight of $\hat{Y}_3$ in this analysis is used as the estimate of the path coefficient for the $Y_3 \rightarrow Y_1$ direct effect. Similar two-stage regressions are conducted for the other two endogenous variables, Y_2 and Y_3, as is outlined in Figure 6.4.

Given the choice between ML estimation and 2SLS, the former is preferred. This is mainly because ML estimates are derived taking the whole model into account; in contrast, 2SLS estimates are calculated for only a part of the model at a time. For this reason, ML is sometimes described in the SEM literature as a "full-information" procedure and techniques like OLS and 2SLS as "partial-" or "limited-information" methods. Also, ML estimation is better when the model is overidentified. The advantages of 2SLS are thus mainly practical instead of statistical. As mentioned, 2SLS may require fewer computing resources; also, one does not need a model-fitting program for this approach. For example, some general statistical packages like SPSS have a 2SLS module.

6.9   Example of the Analysis of a Nonrecursive Path Model

Data for this example are from a thesis by Cooperman (1996), who studied a sample of 84 mothers (47 of girls, 37 of boys) participating in a longitudinal study of psychological problems. Although the sample size here is small, the data set is interesting. When these women were in elementary school, their classmates completed peer nomination scales about aggressive and withdrawn behavior, and these subjects obtained extreme scores on either dimension. During follow-up evaluations about 10–15 years later, schoolteachers completed rating scales about externalizing and internalizing problems of the children of these women. Information about the educational levels and maternity ages of these same women was also available. Data from these six variables are summarized in Table 6.4.

The nonrecursive model presented in Figure 6.5 depicts the transgenerational relation of the adjustment problems of these mothers and their children. Some of these relations are represented as direct (e.g., mother withdrawal → child internalization), and others as mediated by the level of the mother's education and maternity age. Of the two presumed mediators, maternity age is hypothesized to be directly affected by a maternal childhood history of aggression,

TABLE 6.4. Evaluation of a Nonrecursive Path Model of
Transgenerational Transmission of Adjustment Problems

Correlations, means, and standard deviations (Cooperman, 1996; $N = 84$
mothers and children)

Variable	1	2	3	4	5	6
1. Mother Aggression (Grade School)	—					
2. Mother Withdrawal (Grade School)	.19	—				
3. Mother's Education	−.16	−.20	—			
4. Maternity Age	−.37	−.06	.36	—		
5. Child Internalization (Teacher Rating)	−.06	−.05	−.03	−.25	—	
6. Child Externalization (Teacher Rating)	.13	−.06	−.09	−.28	.41	—
M	.51	.47	10.87	20.57	.08	.15
SD	1.09	1.03	2.17	2.33	.28	.36

Goodness of fit summary

Model	χ^2	df	χ^2/df	GFI	NFI	NNFI	SRMR
Original	2.96	2	1.48	.99	.95	.83	.004
One path added (mother aggression → child internalization)	.62	1	.62	.99	.99	1.13	.002

Note. GFI, Jöreskog–Sörbom Goodness of Fit Index; NFI, Bentler–Bonett Normed Fit Index; NNFI, Non-Normed Fit Index; SRMR, Standardized Root Mean Squared Residual.

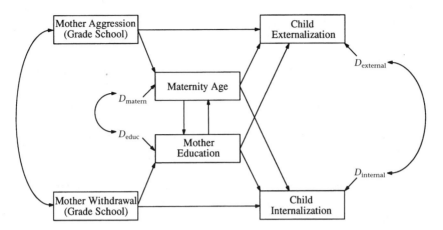

FIGURE 6.5. A nonrecursive path model of transgenerational adjustment problems.

which may manifest itself in adolescence through more frequent or careless sexual activity. Educational level, on the other hand, is assumed to be directly affected by the tendency to withdraw. The two mediator variables are specified as reciprocally related: young women may be more likely to leave school if they are pregnant, but leaving school itself could be a risk factor for early pregnancy. Also, the disturbances of each variable are assumed to covary, which reflects the hypothesis that education and maternity age have common omitted causes. The disturbances of the variables about the internalization and externalization status of the children of these women are also specified to covary. Note, however, that these disturbances are specified as unrelated to those of other endogenous variables about maternal history.

The model of Figure 6.5 does not have all possible disturbance correlations, but it does have such correlations within recursively related blocks of endogenous variables. Thus, this model corresponds to case 3 of Table 6.1, which means that the parameters ≤ observations, order, and rank conditions for identification apply. (This model is also similar to model (b) of Figure 6.3.) With 6 observed variables, there are 2 more observations than model parameters—respectively, 21 versus 19 (6 variances, 3 unanalyzed associations, plus 10 direct effects). The order and rank conditions evaluated within each block of this model are also satisfied; therefore, the nonrecursive model in Figure 6.5 is identified.

The data summarized in Table 6.4 were analyzed with the ML procedure of a model-fitting program. Some of the values of the fit indexes reported in the table indicate satisfactory overall fit (e.g., $\chi^2(2) = 2.96$, $p > .05$; $\chi^2/df = 1.48$; Jöreskog–Sörbom Goodness of Fit Index = .99), but the value of the Bentler–Bonett Non-Normed Fit Index (NNFI), which is adjusted for the number of parameters, is only .83. As mentioned in Chapter 5, though, the value of the NNFI tends to be less than those of other fit indexes in small samples. Inspection of the correlation residuals indicated only one absolute value greater than .10. This value (.15) is for the correlation between mother aggression and child internalization. Based on this result, a direct effect between these two variables was added to the model, and the model was reanalyzed. The value of the chi-square statistic for the revised model was only somewhat smaller than that of the original model ($\chi^2(1) = .62$ vs. $\chi^2(2) = 2.96$). The NNFI for the revised model was out of bounds (1.13; see Table 6.4) but the NNFI can be greater than 1 when the fit of an overidentified model is almost perfect. Also, the path coefficient for the mother aggression → child internalization path in the revised model was not significant. (The small sample size limits the power of this test, however.) For both of these reasons, the original model of Figure 6.5 was not rejected in favor of the revised model with the direct effect mother aggression → child internalization.

The unstandardized and standardized solutions are reported in Table 6.5. Only three path coefficients are significant at the .05 level. (Again, power here is low due to the small sample size.) Women who were described by their grade school peers as being aggressive tend to have their first child at a younger age (standardized path coefficient = –.38). The direct effects of maternity age and mother's education on each other are not significant but they are in the expected direction, positive; for example, lower maternity age, lower education. Lower maternity age is in turn predictive of greater internalization and externalization problems in the children of these mothers as reported by schoolteachers (the standardized path coefficients are respectively –.28 and –.25). Although the absolute magnitudes of these direct effects are only moderate, they seem more impressive given the time intervals (10–15 years) between some of these variables. The proportions of explained variance range from 7% (for child internalization) to 16% (mother's education).

6.10 Multiple Group Path Analysis

The basic rationale of a multiple group path analysis is the same whether the model is recursive or nonrecursive. The main question

TABLE 6.5. Parameter Estimates for a Model of the Generational
Transmission of Adjustment Problems

Parameter	Estimate[a]	
Path coefficients		
Effects on maternity age and education		
Mother Withdrawal → Mother Education	−.38	(−.18)
Mother Withdrawal → Child Internalization	−.01	(−.02)
Mother Aggression → Maternity Age	−.81*	(−.38)
Mother Aggression → Child Externalization	.03	(.09)
Maternity Age → Mother Education	.32	(.34)
Mother Education → Maternity Age	−.07	(−.06)
Effects on child adjustment		
Mother Education → Child Internalization	.01	(.07)
Mother Education → Child Externalization	.01	(.02)
Maternity Age → Child Internalization	−.03*	(−.28)
Maternity Age → Child Externalization	−.04*	(−.25)
Disturbance variances		
$D_{education}$	3.95**	(.84)
$D_{maternity\ age}$	4.90*	(.90)
$D_{child\ internalization}$	.01**	(.93)
$D_{child\ externalization}$	.12**	(.91)
Disturbance covariances		
$D_{education}$ ↔ $D_{maternity\ age}$	.30	(.07)
$D_{child\ internalization}$ ↔ $D_{child\ externalization}$	36.72**	(.38)

Note. D, disturbance.
[a]Unstandardized (standardized). The standardized values for the disturbance variances are proportions of unexplained variance.
*$p < .05$; **$p < .01$.

of a multisample analysis is this: do estimates of model parameters vary across groups? Another way of expressing this question is in terms of an interaction effect; that is, does group membership moderate the relations specified in the model? The simplest way to address these questions is to conduct a separate path analysis for each group and then visually inspect the solutions. (Recall that unstandardized estimates should be compared when the groups differ in their variabilities.) More sophisticated comparisons are available with model-fitting programs that perform multiple group analyses. Through the imposition of *cross-group equality constraints,* the significance of group differences on any model parameter or set of parameters can be tested. A cross-group equality constraint forces the computer to derive equal estimates of that parameter for all samples. A common tactic in a multiple group path analysis is to impose cross-group equality constraints on the path coefficients. The χ^2 of the model with its path coefficients constrained to equality is then contrasted against that of the unconstrained model. If the relative fit of the constrained model is much worse than that of the unconstrained model, one concludes that the direct effects differ across the groups.

A multiple group path analysis is demonstrated with the recursive path model of delinquency by Lynam, Moffitt, and Stouthamer-Loeber (1993) introduced in Chapter 3 (section 3.4) and re-presented in Figure 6.6. Two covariance matrices constructed from the data summarized at the top of Table 6.6 for samples of white ($N = 181$) and African-American ($N = 214$) adolescent males were submitted to a model-fitting program for estimation with a ML procedure. Because this model is just-identified, it would perfectly fit the data in each group if analyzed without constraints. With the imposition of cross-group equality constraints on the model's seven direct effects, however, this is no longer true. In this multisample analysis, the total number of observations is the sum of such across both groups; with five variables, there are $5(6)/2 = 15$ observations in each group and 30 altogether. The total number of parameters of this just-identified model evaluated across both groups is similarly calculated ($15 \times 2 = 30$), but seven—the path coefficients—are constrained to be equal. Thus, the total number of free parameters is actually 23, which means that the χ^2 for the multigroup analysis has seven degrees of freedom.

Reported in Table 6.6 are the values of selected fit indexes for the multisample analysis of the path model with equality-constrained direct effects. Although the values of the Bentler–Bonett NFI and NNFI (.96 and .95, respectively) and the χ^2/df ratio (1.67) all seem reasonable, the overall $\chi^2(7)$ statistic of 11.68 is not far from being significant at the .05 level. (The critical value is 14.07.) To check whether

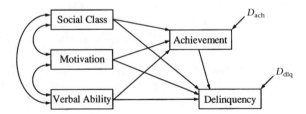

FIGURE 6.6. A path model of delinquency evaluated across multiple groups.

TABLE 6.6. Multiple Group Path Analysis of a Recursive Path Model of Delinquency

Correlations, means, and standard deviations (Lynam, Moffitt, & Stouthamer-Loeber, 1993; male adolescents, $N = 214$ African-American [above diagonal], $N = 181$ white [below diagonal])

						African-American	
Variable	1	2	3	4	5	M	SD
1. Social Class	—	.08	.28	.05	-.11	31.96	10.58
2. Motivation	.25	—	.30	.21	-.17	-.01	1.35
3. Verbal Ability	.37	.40	—	.50	-.26	93.76	13.62
4. Achievement	.27	.28	.61	—	-.33	2.51	.79
5. Delinquency	-.11	-.20	-.31	-.21	—	1.40	1.63
White M	34.64	.05	104.18	2.88	1.22		
SD	11.53	1.32	16.32	.96	1.45		

Goodness of fit summary

Model	χ^2	df	χ^2/df	NFI	NNFI
Path coefficients invariant across groups	11.68	7	1.67	.96	.95

Modification indexes for equality-constrained direct effects

		Path coefficients from separate sample analyses[a]			
Direct effect	Modification index $\chi^2(1)$	White		African-American	
Social Class → Achievement	3.81	.01	(.05)	-.01	(-.10)
Test Effort → Achievement	0.18	.03	(.04)	.04	(.07)
Verbal Ability → Achievement	1.99	.03**	(.58)	.03**	(.51)
Social Class → Delinquency	0.88	.01	(.02)	-.01	(-.07)
Test Effort → Delinquency	0.15	-.10	(-.09)	-.10	(-.08)
Verbal Ability → Delinquency	0.33	-.02**	(-.26)	-.01	(-.08)
Achievement → Delinquency	5.47*	-.04	(-.03)	-.55**	(-.27)

Note. NFI = Bentler–Bonett Normed Fit Index; NNFI = Non-Normed Fit Index.
[a]Unstandardized (standardized).
*$p < .05$; **$p < .01$.

these indexes of overall model fit were masking more specific effects, modification indexes (i.e., univariate Lagrange Multipliers) were derived to test group differences on each of the seven path coefficients. When a model is analyzed across multiple groups with equality constraints, values of modification indexes estimate the amount by which the overall χ^2 would decrease if the associated parameter were estimated freely in each sample. Statistical significance of a modification index thus indicates a group difference on that parameter. Values of modification indexes for this analysis are reported in the bottom of Table 6.6, and they indicate a significant group difference on the achievement $\rightarrow$ delinquency path and another that falls just of significance ($p = .051$) on the social class $\rightarrow$ achievement path. To investigate group differences further, each of the seven path coefficients were derived separately within each group in subsequent runs with a model-fitting program; these values are also reported in the table. (Although the standardized path coefficients are also reported in the table, recall that these values are generally appropriate only for within-group comparisons.) Within both samples, the direct effect of verbal ability on achievement is significant. Verbal ability is the only significant predictor of delinquency within the white sample. In contrast, achievement is the only significant predictor of delinquency for the African-American adolescents. Lynam and colleagues' (1993) interpretation of these results was summarized in Chapter 3. Very briefly reviewed, they speculated that school has a larger role in the development of delinquency for African-American than for white male adolescents.

Although only the coefficients for the direct effects were constrained in this example, it is theoretically possible to impose additional constraints on other parameters. For example, constraining the error variances to be equal provides a test of whether the model has comparable predictive power across the groups; equality constraints on the variances of the exogenous variables provide tests of group differences in variabilities. Some of these constraints may be implausible, though, like the expectation of equal group variances on the exogenous variables. Unless specific hypotheses demand otherwise, it is usually only the coefficients for the direct effects that are constrained to be equal across independent samples.

6.11   Summary

The quote from Rollo May at the beginning of this chapter about the pursuit of meaningfulness is a pertinent one for nonrecursive path models. Compared to recursive models, nonrecursive models pose more potential obstacles in their analysis. The most noteworthy of these possible problems is identification: recursive path models are always identified; in contrast, certain configurations of paths in nonrecursive models can render one (or more) of their parameters underidentified. Attempts to analyze a nonidentified model may be unsuccessful—the program may crash, iterative estimation may not converge, or the values of some parameter estimates may be illogical. Although less likely, it is also possible for a model-fitting program to yield a converged, sensible-looking solution for a nonrecursive path model that is not actually identified. Such solutions are not unique. Fortunately, there are ways to evaluate the identification status of nonrecursive path models. However, because adding exogenous variables is one of the remedies for modifying a model that is not identified, it is crucial to tackle the identification problem when the model is specified and before the data are collected.

Nonrecursive path models with correlations between all pairs of disturbances or with all possible disturbance correlations within recursively related blocks of variables must meet three conditions for identification. Two of these are relatively easy to check but are only necessary conditions, which do not guarantee that the model is actually identified. The necessary conditions include the by-now familiar requirement that a model not have more parameters than observations and an additional one called the order condition. For models with all possible disturbance correlations, the order condition requires that the number of variables (exogenous or endogenous) excluded from the equation of every endogenous variables equals or exceeds the overall number of endogenous variables minus 1. For models with all possible disturbance correlations within recursively related blocks, the order condition requires that the number of excluded variables equals or exceeds the number of endogenous variables in each block minus 1. The third requirement for the identification of nonrecursive path models with disturbance correlations in the patterns just described is the rank condition. Unlike the parameters ≤ observations and order conditions, the rank condition is sufficient: Models that satisfy it are identified. Like the order condition, the rank condition is evaluated for each endogenous variable. If the rank condition is violated for a particular endogenous variable, then its equation is underidentified. A method for evaluating the rank condition that does not require knowledge of linear algebra was described earlier in the chapter. The rank condition requires that the rank of the equation for every endogenous variable is greater than or equal to the total number of endogenous variables in that system matrix minus 1. If the rank condition is satisfied for every endogenous variable, then the whole model is identified.

Just as with recursive path models, nonrecursive models that are theoretically identified are still subject to empirical underidentification. Multicollinearity is one form of empirical underidentification that can impede the analysis of any type of path model, recursive or nonrecursive. Another problem more specific to nonrecursive models occurs when estimates of certain direct effects are close to zero, especially for direct effects on variables involved in feedback loops. The virtual deletion of certain paths due to near-zero path coefficients can lead to violation of the rank condition, which makes the model nonidentified.

If a nonrecursive path model has any other pattern of disturbance correlations other than all possible or all possible within recursively related blocks (e.g., it has none), then the order and rank conditions are too strict. That is, "none of the above" models that fail them may nevertheless be identified. Such models still must meet the necessary (but insufficient) parameters ≤ observations condition. Another way to evaluate the identification status of a "none of the above" nonrecursive path model is to use a model-fitting program as a diagnostic tool. Specifically, using either made-up or actual data—only the former can be used before the researcher actually carries out the study, though—he or she determines whether a model-fitting program can estimate the model. If the computer can arrive at a logical solution, then the model may be identified. Additional confidence may be warranted if the solution also passes empirical checks for uniqueness described earlier, but such tests do not guarantee identification. If the program is unable to yield a solution, then the model may not be identified. Warning messages generated by model-fitting programs about individual parameters can help to determine the source of an identification problem, but such warnings are not always accurate.

There are two basic options for dealing with nonrecursive path models that are not identified. One is to add or delete paths, which respectively is the same as freeing previously fixed-to-zero parameters or constraining previously free parameters to zero. Paths can be added either among the original variables of a model or by adding exogenous variables. The latter increases the number of available observations and may be especially useful for models that violate the order or rank conditions (i.e., assuming that the order and rank conditions apply to that model). Deleting paths may increase the number of excluded variables, which is useful for meeting the order condition. The second major option is to impose another type of constraint such as an inequality, equality, or proportionality constraint. Inequality constraints set upper or lower bounds to the values of individual parameter estimates. Equality and proportionality constraints are imposed on two or more parameters and thus reduce the overall number of parameters. It is inadvisable to automatically impose an equality constraint on the direct effects of a feedback loop because doing so may prevent the detection of unequal mutual influence. Proportionality constraints, on the other hand, allow for unequal effects but on an a priori basis. The use of either option to deal with identification problems should be guided by theoretical/logical reasons rather than empirical ones.

Maximum likelihood (ML) estimation is appropriate for nonrecursive path models. However, iterative estimation of nonrecursive models may be more likely to fail to converge than recursive path models if the starting values are not reasonably accurate. This is also true for model-fitting programs that automatically generate their own initial estimates. Thus, it may be necessary for the researcher to provide starting values in order for iterative estimation to converge. An estimation procedure that may be an alternative to ML for nonrecursive path models is two-stage least squares (2SLS): 2SLS is simply multiple regression but applied in such a way as to work around the requirement that the model must be recursive. Because 2SLS is not iterative and its mathematics are simpler than those of ML procedures, it usually requires fewer computer resources and no starting values. Also, 2SLS modules are available in some general statistical packages.

A multiple group analysis can be conducted with either recursive or nonrecursive path models. The simplest way to conduct a multisample path analysis is to estimate the model separately for each group and then compare the unstandardized solutions. A more formal way is to use a model-fitting program that allows the imposition of equality constraints on parameter estimates across the groups. A common practice is to impose cross-group equality constraints only on the path coefficients; values of other parameters (e.g., variances of the exogenous variables) are freely estimated with each sample. Tests of the significance for each constrained parameter indicate whether the fit of the constrained model is worse than the fit of the model without that constraint. If so, then a significant group difference on that parameter is indicated. If several such results are found, then whatever variable is represented by group membership may moderate the effects represented in the path model.

Given an understanding of path analysis, one knows essentially half the rationale of SEM—that of structural models. The other half concerns measurement models in which observed variables are represented as indicators of underlying latent variables, the subject of the next chapter. Once the reader also understands the principles of measurement models, then he or she will have acquired the conceptual framework from which to view the whole of SEM as variations on these two major themes, structural and measurement models.

6.12   Recommended Readings

Introductions to Nonrecursive Path Models

Bollen (1989, chap. 4) and Kenny (1979, chap. 6) deal with nonrecursive path models. Coverage by Berry (1984) of the identification problem is especially useful.

Berry, W. D. (1984). *Nonrecursive causal models.* Beverly Hills, CA: Sage.
Bollen, K. A. (1989). *Structural equations with latent variables.* New York: Wiley.
Kenny, D. C. (1979). *Correlation and causality.* New York: Wiley.

Additional Empirical Examples of Nonrecursive Path Models

Duncan, O. D. (1975). *Introduction to structural equation models.* New York: Academic Press.
Duncan, O. D., Haller, A. O., & Portes, A. (1971). Peer influences on aspirations: A reinterpretation. In H. M. Blalock (Ed.), *Causal models in the social sciences* (pp. 219–244). Chicago: Aldine-Atherton.
Gillespie, M. W., & McDonald, J. L. (1991). *Structural equation models of multiple respondent data: Mutual influence versus family factor approaches* (Research Discussion Paper no. 83). Edmonton, Alberta, Canada: University of Alberta, Department of Sociology.

CHAPTER SEVEN

Measurement Models and Confirmatory Factor Analysis

He who loves practice without theory is like the sailor who boards ship without a rudder and compass and never knows where he may be cast.

— Leonardo da Vinci

7.1 Foreword

One of the main limitations of path analysis is the use of a single measure of each construct represented in the model. Not only does this force the researcher to choose among alternative measures (if available), but also any single measure is inevitably susceptible to measurement error. One way around these problems is to use multiple measures of each construct. A multiple-indicator approach tends to reduce the overall effect of measurement error of any individual observed variable on the accuracy of the results. Although path models do not readily accommodate a multiple-indicator approach to measurement, other types of structural equation models do. These models feature the distinction between observed variables (indicators) and the underlying latent variables (constructs) that the indicators are presumed to measure, which together make up a measurement model.

This is the first of two chapters about structural equation models with latent variables. Considered in this chapter are the conceptual nature of latent variables, principles of their measurement with multiple indicators, general requirements for the specification and identification of measurement models, and their evaluation with confirmatory factor analysis (CFA). Measurement models evaluated by CFA have a particular characteristic: the latent variables in CFA models are simply assumed to covary with one another; that is, all of their associations are specified as unanalyzed. It is possible, however, to test more specific hypotheses about relations between latent variables by specifying a hybrid model. In hybrid models, some unanalyzed associations between latent variables are replaced by direct or reciprocal causal effects, which gives a hybrid model a structural as well as a measurement component. In this way, hybrid models are like path models but with multiple measures of each theoretical variable. Hybrid models are the subject of the next chapter.

7.2   Conceptual Nature of Latent Variables

Latent variables in structural equation models typically correspond to some type of hypothetical construct. Although hypothetical constructs could represent almost anything that is not directly observable—the soul, angels, or poltergeists, for instance—constructs have a very specific connotation in science. As concisely defined by Nunnally and Bernstein (1994, p. 85), a construct

> . . . reflects the hypothesis (often incompletely formed) that a variety of behaviors will correlate with one another in studies of individual differences and/or will be similarly affected by experimental manipulations.

This definition highlights four responsibilities of the researcher who wishes to represent a hypothetical construct in a statistical model: (1) A construct requires an operational definition sufficiently specific so that (2) indicators of it can be selected. Because a construct is typically not considered synonymous with any one indicator, it is usually necessary to have multiple indicators. (3) To claim that a set of indicators assesses some common construct, data from the indicators should be consistent with certain predictions. For example, indicators that supposedly measure the same construct should be at least moderately correlated; that is, they should exhibit convergent validity. By the same token, indicators of supposedly different constructs should not be so highly correlated (e.g., $r > .85$) that it is clear they really measure the same thing. (4) If the data are not consistent with these predictions, then the researcher's original theory—the operational definition of the construct—is called into question. When the initial definition of a construct is tentative, however, then some discrepancies between theory and data are not unexpected. In any event, the researcher's original assumptions about the construct and its measurement may need to be revised.

The process just described is that of *construct validation,* originally described in the psychological literature by Cronbach and Meehl (1955). The general logic of construct validation is basically the same as that underlying the representation of latent variables in SEM: Theory sets the stage for making predictions about the relations of indicators to each other based on the hypothetical constructs they are presumed to measure. These predictions are represented in the form of a measurement model analyzed with the observed covariances among the indicators. If the model-implied covariances correspond to the observed ones, then the theory is supported. If not, then a new model based on a revised theory should be tested.

It is important to avoid two logical errors when evaluating measurement models in SEM. First, failure to reject a measurement model does not prove that the indicators actually reflect the hypothetical constructs represented in the model. One reason is that just as in path analysis, there may be many equivalent versions of a particular measurement model. Recall that equivalent models generate the same predicted correlations/covariances as the original model but with a different configuration of paths. Given equivalent measurement models, the researcher must justify the preference for a particular model. (Equivalent measurement models are discussed in more detail later.) Another reason could be called the *naming fallacy.* That is, just because a latent variable in a measurement model is assigned a particular label—"social skills," "professional burnout," or "holistic reasoning," for example—does not mean that the hypothetical construct is understood or even correctly named. Latent variables require some type of designation, however, if for no other reason than communication of the results. Although verbal labels are more "user friendly" than more abstract symbols like η or ξ (both are from LISREL's matrix algebra notation), they should be viewed as conveniences and not as substitutes for critical thinking. The second logical error to avoid is *reification,* the belief that a hypothetical construct *must* correspond to a real thing. For example, a general cognitive ability factor—often called g in the mental test literature—is a type of latent, hypothetical construct. To automatically consider g as real instead of an abstract concept, however, is a potential error of reification. That is, there may not be a direct, one-to-one link between g and mental faculties that are physically based in particular regions of the brain. There could be, of course, but to assume so may affect a researcher's interpretation of his or her findings. In his engaging book *The Mismeasure of Man,* Stephen Jay Gould (1981) cites many examples of reification associated with IQ tests earlier this century. For example, in part out of the belief that IQ scores are synonymous with intelligence, some scientists proposed the of use IQ tests to screen immigrants to the United States who spoke little or no English.

With potential logical errors like the naming fallacy or reification, the representation of latent variables in SEM should not be taken lightly. Indeed, some might argue that latent variables are more trouble than they are worth. This is a rather extreme position, however, and one that may suit only a small number of investigators. Those who adhere to a strict behavioral model of science of the type advocated by B. F. Skinner may favor the banishing of latent variables to the hinterlands. Researchers who study very specific, discrete behaviors with little concern about the generalizability of their findings to situations outside the laboratory may endorse this position, too. But several factors argue for a more balanced, flexible view of latent variables. As mentioned in Chapter 1, the distinction between observed and latent variables allows researchers to test hypotheses that otherwise would be difficult if not impossible to evaluate. Also, the process of peer review in science offers some safeguards against potential interpretive errors regarding latent variables. Although this process is far from perfect, it may at least catch some blatant errors before they appear in print. Finally, the uncertainty that exists in some research areas about the relation between hypothetical constructs and observed measures could encourage creativity on the part of researchers, which might well lead to unexpected advances.

7.3 Principles of Measurement

Given an operational definition of a construct, the researcher must either make his or her own measures or select them from among existing scales. How to construct an original measure is beyond the scope of this section; readers are instead referred to general texts on psychometric theory (e.g., Kaplan & Sacruzzo, 1993; Nunnally & Bernstein, 1994) for more information about test construction. Helpful resources for selecting among published measures include compendiums of test reviews such as the *Eleventh Mental Measurements Yearbook* (Kramer & Conoley , 1992) or *Test Critiques* (Keyser & Sweetland, 1984); other useful sources are journal articles in which results with a particular measure are reported.

Whether constructed by the researcher or not, indicators of some construct should be as free as possible from the biasing effects of measurement error. In other words, indicators should be both reliable and valid. Of the two types of measurement error, random and systematic, reliability concerns random error. In contrast, the concept of validity includes both random and systematic measurement error. Reliability and validity are each reviewed below.

Reliability

Adjectives that describe reliability include consistency, precision, and repeatability. Scores on reliable measures are not greatly influenced by random error. Because there are different types of random error, it is often necessary to evaluate different aspects of a measure's reliability. There are four basic kinds of reliability: test–retest, alternate form, interrater, and the related concepts of split-half and internal consistency reliability. Each is described below.

Test–retest reliability involves the readministration of a measure to the same group of subjects on a second occasion. If the two sets of scores are highly correlated, then random error due to events that occurred in a single test session (e.g., fatigue, a noisy room) may be minimal. The length of the interval between the assessments should be appropriate to the measure. For example, a 1-year retest interval for a questionnaire about current mood may be much too long. For a test that supposedly measures a more stable trait (e.g., an IQ test), however, a 1-year interval may not be unreasonably long to expect relatively high test–retest correlations. *Alternate forms reliability* involves the administration of different versions of a test to the same subjects either within the same session (immediate administration) or within a short time interval (delayed administration). Alternate forms theoretically cover the same content but with different sets of items. If the correlation across the forms is high, then subjects' performances may be relatively unaffected by the particular items selected to assess that construct. *Interrater reliability* is mainly relevant for subjectively scored measures: if independent raters do not consistently agree in their scoring, then examiner-specific factors may contribute to the observed variability of test scores.

Split-half reliability and *internal consistency reliability* both concern the consistency of subjects' responses within a single test. The latter concerns the item-to-item consistency of subjects' responses. For example, do children who pass certain types of math problems also correctly solve similar ones? Split-half reliability concerns the stability of subjects' responses across separate halves of the test (e.g., odd vs.

even items). Both kinds of reliability reflect whether the content of a test may be so heterogeneous that it introduces inconsistency in subjects' responses. If so, then an omnibus total score may not be the best unit of analysis for the test because its items are not unidimensional.

Not all of the kinds of reliability just described may apply to a particular measure. For example, interrater reliability is not relevant for an objective test that is machine scored. (This assumes that the scoring program is correct and the machine operates correctly.) Alternate forms reliability is not applicable when there is only a single version of the test (e.g., the Rorschach). The results of a reliability study are summarized with a reliability coefficient, which is often represented by the symbol r_{XX}. Reliability coefficients range from 0 (no reliability) to 1 (perfect reliability) and estimate the proportion of observed variance that is consistent or systematic; 1 minus the reliability coefficient thus estimates the proportion of test variance that is due to random measurement error of the type indicated by that kind of reliability analysis. For example, an internal consistency coefficient of .70 means that 30% of the total variance is due to the random effects of content heterogeneity. Likewise, test–retest, alternate forms, and interrater reliability coefficients respectively reflect time-, content-, and examiner-related sources of random error.

Other factors that affect the magnitude of reliability coefficients include the length of the test and the range of individual differences. Measures with more items tend to be more reliable than shorter ones. Because reliability coefficients reflect correlations (e.g., between test scores over time), they also tend to be higher when the range of individual differences among the subjects' scores is greater. Restriction of the range of individual differences (e.g., only high-ability subjects are tested) tends to reduce the magnitudes of reliability coefficients.

Although there is no gold standard about how high coefficients should be in order to consider reliability as "good," some rough guidelines are offered: reliability coefficients around .90 can be considered "excellent," values around .80 as "very good," and values around .70 as "adequate"; those below .50 indicate that at least one-half of the observed variance may be due to random error, and measures so unreliable should be avoided. The researcher can either evaluate the reliability of a measure in his or her own samples or rely on published sources (test manuals, journal articles, etc.). Note that published reliability coefficients may not generalize to a researcher's particular sample. Be careful about using a measure of unknown reliability.

Validity

Whereas reliability concerns the consistency of test scores, validity concerns, broadly speaking, how they should be interpreted. An indicator can be reliable without being valid. For example, the brand of athletic shoes worn by world-class marathon runners could probably be reliably measured, but such observations probably would not make up a valid measure of long-distance running ability. In order for a measure to be valid, though, it must be reliable. Reliability can thus be viewed as a necessary but insufficient requirement for validity.

Just as reliability does not refer to a single attribute of a test, the concept of validity is also multifaceted. Four basic kinds of validity are described in the psychometric literature: content validity, criterion-related validity, convergent and discriminant validity, and construct validity. Construct validity is the most general type of validity and actually subsumes the other three. Construct validity concerns whether an indicator actually measures the construct the researcher believes it does. Content validity, criterion-related validity, and convergent and discriminant validity each involve particular aspects of this question and methods to evaluate it. Each type of validity is described below.

Content validity concerns whether an indicator's items are representative of the domain it is supposed to measure. The evaluation of content validity is not a statistical matter. Instead, expert opinion about the representativeness of the items provides the basis for appraising content validity. Content validity is most relevant for constructs with domains that are relatively straightforward to delineate. Examples of such constructs could include Grade 2 mathematics skills or the factual knowledge that drivers of automobiles should have in order to be granted a license. The content of both domains could probably be defined with relatively high consensus among appropriate content experts (e.g., Grade 2 teachers, professional driving instructors). The exact content of many other constructs studied by social scientists may not be so clearly delineated, however. Consider the construct "intelligence," for which only limited consensus would be expected about the various attributes and behaviors that make up the content of this domain. When the specific content of some domain is not well delineated, it is up to the researcher to articulate specific operational definitions. These definitions not only guide the selection of indicators but also allow others to evaluate whether the content of the indicators is consistent with the researcher's stated definition.

Criterion-related validity concerns whether a measure relates to an external standard against which the measure can be evaluated. These relations are typically assessed with correlations that are called validity coefficients. Validity coefficients are often represented with the symbol r_{XY}, where X stands for the predictor (i.e., the measure being evaluated) and Y for the external criterion. For example, suppose that the predictor is a relatively inexpensive screening test for the presence of a disease. The accuracy of the screening test can be evaluated against a more thorough but costly series of laboratory tests that can conclusively detect the disease. The laboratory tests are the criterion for the screening measure. Specifically, if the screening measure tends to indicate the same result as the laboratory tests, then the screening measure shows criterion-related validity. Another example would be scores on a university entrance examination (the predictor) and a later university grade point (the criterion): if the two correlate highly, then this result is positive evidence for the criterion-related validity of the entrance examination.

The term *concurrent validity* is used when scores on the predictor and on the criterion are collected at the same time (e.g., results of a screening test and lab tests for a disease); *predictive validity*, when the criterion is measured later (e.g., entrance examination scores and grade point); and *postdictive validity*, when the criterion is measured before the predictor. An example of postdictive validity would be the administration of a questionnaire (the predictor) to groups of patients who differ in their medical histories (the criterion) to determine whether the questionnaire can discriminate between the groups. Here the criterion is known before the predictor is administered. One limitation of criterion-related validity is that there is not always an obvious external standard against which the researcher can evaluate a predictor. Suppose that parents and adolescents are administered scales about their respective perceptions of the quality of their relationships with each other. Among these measures, it may be difficult to justify the selection of one (e.g., parental report) as the criterion for the other.

The magnitude of a validity coefficient r_{XY} is influenced by all of the factors mentioned in Chapter 2 (section 2.6)—the variabilities of X and Y, the relative shapes of their distributions, and the linearity of their relation—plus the reliabilities of X and Y. Unreliability in either variable, the indicator (X) or the criterion (Y), tends to attenuate the absolute value of their observed correlation. Classical measurement theory (e.g., Nunnally & Bernstein, 1994, p. 241) shows the exact relation between the reliabilities of X and Y (r_{XX} and r_{YY}) and the theoretical maximum absolute value of their observed correlation:

$$\text{Theoretical maximum absolute value of } r_{XY} = \sqrt{r_{XX} \times r_{YY}}. \quad (7.1)$$

Equation 7.1 concretely demonstrates the meaning of the statement that reliability is a prerequisite for validity. One implication of this equation is that the absolute value of a validity coefficient r_{XY} can equal 1.00 only if both X and Y are perfectly reliable. For example, if r_{XX} and r_{YY} are both .50, then the maximum absolute value of r_{XY} equals the square root of (.50)(.50), which is .50. Another implication is that if either X or Y has a reliability coefficient of zero, then their expected correlation is zero.

A variation on Equation 7.1 is the *correction for attenuation,* which estimates the theoretical correlation between X and Y that would be found if both variables were perfectly reliable. The correction for attenuation is

$$\hat{r}_{XY} = \frac{r_{XY}}{\sqrt{r_{XX} \times r_{YY}}}, \quad (7.2)$$

where $\hat{r}_{XY}$ is the predicted validity coefficient, r_{XY} is the observed correlation, and r_{XX} and r_{YY} are the reliabilities of X and Y. For example, suppose that $r_{XY} = .25$, $r_{XX} = .70$, and $r_{YY} = .80$. Using Equation 7.2, we find that $\hat{r}_{XY}$, the predicted correlation between X and Y, assuming that both are measured without error, is their observed correlation divided by the square root of the product of their reliabilities, or

$$.25/\sqrt{.70 \times .80} = .33.$$

Note that the disattenuated correlation is greater than the observed correlation (.33 vs. .25). As X or Y is less reliable, the difference between their observed and disattenuated correlations becomes larger. Also, because disattenuated correlations as per Equation 7.2 are only estimates, it can happen that their absolute values exceed 1.0. Disattenuating observed correlations is one way to take reliability into account, but note that estimates of r_{XX} and r_{YY} are required. Perhaps a better way to take reliability into account, though, is to use multiple measures of each construct and specify a measurement model.

The concepts of *convergent validity* and *discriminant validity* involve the evaluation of measures against one another instead of against an external criterion. These ideas were introduced in Chapter 3 (section 3.5) and are central to evaluation of measurement models in SEM. Briefly reviewed, a set of indicators presumed to measure the same construct shows convergent validity if their intercorrelations are at least moderate in magnitude. If the estimated correlations of the factors that underlie sets of indicators that are supposed to measure different constructs are not excessively high, then there is evidence for discriminant validity. As mentioned earlier, high intercorrelations among a set of indicators do not prove that they measure what the researcher thinks they do. Suppose that a researcher uses three different self-report questionnaires about psychological problems and finds that their scores are highly correlated. This result could be due to some artifact of their common method (e.g., a social desirability response set) rather than to measurement of a common underlying construct. For this reason, it is important to try to find multiple indicators of some construct that are based on different methods of measurement. (How to evaluate common method effects with CFA is described later.) Also, low reliability could result in low observed correlations (Equation 7.1), but such correlations could not reasonably be interpreted as evidence for discriminant validity.

All the types of validity described above are relevant to the evaluation of *construct validity*. Other methods can be used to assess construct validity including experimental manipulations of some variable to evaluate whether test scores change in a predicted way. For example, telling some subjects that their performance on a difficult task (e.g., mirror drawing) reflects their intelligence may be expected to lead to higher scores on a measure of state anxiety than those of subjects given more neutral-sounding descriptions of the task. The method of CFA is also used to evaluate construct validity. An important thing to know about construct validity is that no single method provides a definitive test of whether the researcher's specifications about measurement are correct. Also, construct validity is not typically established in a single study. Instead, several different types of studies may be required to evaluate various facets of construct validity (content validity, predictive validity, etc.).

One last point about the measurement of constructs. Although many of the constructs studied by social scientists concern human characteristics (cognitive processes, emotional states, etc.), constructs can also represent phenomena where the units of analysis are not persons. Examples of such constructs include retail availability of alcohol and alcohol-related health problems across counties (e.g., Rush, Gliksman, & Brook, 1986) and levels of police and protester violence across demonstrations (e.g., Kritzer, 1977). Whether a construct concerns characteristics of people or some other unit of analysis, the same basic principles of measurement discussed in this section apply.

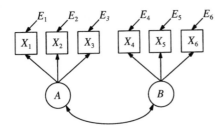

FIGURE 7.1. A standard CFA measurement model.

7.4   CFA Models and Their Specification

Presented in Figure 7.1 is an example of a standard CFA measurement model, the type evaluated most often in the social science literature; the indicators are depicted with Xs, latent variables with the letters A and B, and measurement error terms with Es. This model represents the hypothesis that X_1 through X_3 assess construct A, X_4 through X_6 measure construct B, and the two constructs covary. Standard CFA measurement models have the characteristics listed below and described afterward:

1. Each indicator is represented as having two causes, a single factor that the indicator is supposed to measure and all other unique sources of variance that are represented by the measurement error term.
2. The measurement error terms are independent of each other and of the factors.[1]
3. All associations between the factors are unanalyzed.

The single-arrowheaded line that points from a factor to an indicator (e.g., $A \rightarrow X_1$ in the figure) represents the presumed direct causal effect of the latent variable on the observed measure. The statistical estimates of these direct effects are called factor loadings. Although factor loadings in exploratory factor analysis (EFA) are typically correlations, factor loadings in CFA are more generally inter-

---

[1]The reason for assuming independence of error terms and factors is the same as the analogous one in path analysis that disturbances are uncorrelated with the exogenous variables: estimation procedures in CFA partition the variances of the indicators into two independent parts, explained by the factors and unexplained. The implication of this partition is that unique causes of scores on indicators are typically specified as unrelated to the latent variables.

preted as regression coefficients that may be in unstandardized or standardized form. (More on this point later.) Indicators assumed to be caused by latent variables are called *effect indicators*. In this sense, indicators in a standard CFA measurement model can be viewed as endogenous variables and the factors as exogenous variables.

The line that points to an indicator from its measurement error term (e.g., $X_1 \leftarrow E_1$ in Figure 7.1) reflects all other sources of variance not explained by the indicator's underlying factor. Like disturbances in path models, measurement errors in CFA models can also be seen as unmeasured exogenous variables. Measurement error terms reflect two kinds of unique variance: (1) random error of the type estimated by reliability coefficients, and (2) systematic variance due to things that the indicator measures besides its underlying factor. Variance due to an indicator's method of measurement (e.g., self-report vs. unobtrusive measurement) is an example of the latter. A specification error is another source of unique variance that is systematic. For instance, if X_1 in Figure 7.1 really measures construct B and not A, then E_1 may be large if construct A has little effect on X_1's scores and if the correlation between factors A and B is not large (i.e., the real cause of X_1, B, does not covary substantially with A).

Characteristics 2 and 3 in the above list—the specification that each indicator loads on only one factor, and the specification that the measurement error terms are independent—are described by some authors (e.g., Anderson & Gerbing, 1988) as *unidimensional measurement*. If an indicator is specified to load on more than one factor or if its measurement error is assumed to covary with that of another indicator, then measurement is represented as *multidimensional* rather than unidimensional. For example, adding a direct effect from factor B to indicator X_1 ($B \rightarrow X_1$) to the model of Figure 7.1 represents the assumption that X_1 measures two constructs instead of one. Readers should note that there is some controversy in the SEM literature about allowing indicators to load on more than one factor. One the one hand, Cattell (1978) noted that some indicators are by nature factorially complex; that is, they really measure more than one domain. Suppose that X_1 is an engineering aptitude test comprised of both text and diagrams. Such an indicator may be multidimensional in that it can measure both reading comprehension and visual–spatial reasoning. Allowing such indicators to load on more than one factor in a CFA model would be consistent with this possibility. On the other hand, Anderson and Gerbing (1988) argued that unidimensional measurement models are more useful for the interpretation of latent constructs because such models allow more precise tests of the convergent and discriminant validity of the indicators. For example, if every indicator of the model of Figure 7.1 were specified to load on both factors, then the whole model would essentially be an EFA model (e.g., Figure 3.2).

The specification of correlated measurement errors is the second way to represent indicators as multidimensional instead of unidimensional. A measurement error correlation reflects the assumption that the two indicators measure something in common that is not represented in the model. Because measurement error correlations are unanalyzed associations between unmeasured exogenous variables (e.g., $E_1 \leftrightarrow E_2$), what this "something" in common may be is unknown as far as the model is concerned. Correlated measurement errors can be included in a model as a way to test hypotheses about shared sources of variance other than that due to a common construct. For example, consider the two measurement models in Figure 7.2. Both models have correlated measurement errors but in different patterns. Model (a) has all possible measurement error correlations

(a) Within-Factor Correlated Measurement Errors

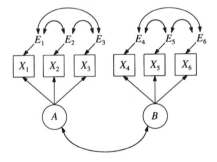

(b) Between-Factor Correlated Measurement Errors

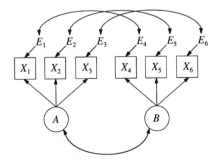

FIGURE 7.2. Examples of CFA models with correlated measurement errors.

between the indicators of each factor. This pattern may be appropriate if, say, X_1 through X_3 were all based on one method (e.g., self-report) or obtained from one informant (e.g., teachers) and X_4 through X_6 were based on another method (e.g., projective) or a different informant (e.g., parents). Model (b) of Figure 7.2 features correlated measurement errors between the indicators of different factors. Suppose that X_4 through X_6 are alternate forms of X_1 through X_3 (X_4 is the alternate form of X_1, etc.) and that X_1 through X_3 are administered at Time 1 and X_4 through X_6 are administered at Time 2. The pattern of between-factor measurement error correlations in model (b) could represent the hypothesis that the unique variances of alternate forms covary over time.

Either form of multidimensionality—indicators that load on multiple factors or measurement error correlations—has implications for the identification of a CFA measurement model, which is considered below in section 7.5. Adding either characteristic to a standard CFA model also increases the number of parameters, which reduces the parsimony of the model. As with other types of specification decisions in SEM, though, the choice between the representation of indicators as unidimensional versus multidimensional should be guided by substantive considerations.

There is another variation on standard CFA measurement models that feature hierarchical relations among the factors. Hierarchical CFA models depict at least one latent variable as a higher-order factor that is not directly measured by any indicator and is assumed to account for the correlations among lower-order factors. Hierarchical models of intelligence in which a general ability factor (g) is presumed to underlie more specific ability factors (verbal, visual–spatial, etc.) are examples of this. CFA models with higher-order factors are considered later.

A final comment about any type of CFA model is warranted before we move on. The assumption that indicators are caused by the factors is not always appropriate. That is, some indicators may be viewed as *cause indicators* that affect the latent variable instead of the reverse. Consider the following example by Bollen and Lennox (1991): Suppose that four variables are used to measure socioeconomic status (SES), education, income, occupational prestige, and neighborhood of residence. In a standard CFA model, these variables would be represented as effect indicators that are caused by an underlying SES factor (and by measurement errors). However, we usually think of SES as being "caused" by all of these variables, not the other way around. For example, a change in any one of these variables (e.g., a salary increase) may change SES. The specification of even one observed variable as a cause indicator implies that the underlying factor is endogenous instead of exogenous, which technically makes the model a hybrid model. A special type of measurement model with a single cause indicator that is an equivalent version of a one-factor CFA model is considered later.

7.5 Requirements for the Identification of CFA Models

Presented in Table 7.1 is an overview of the identification status of basic CFA measurement models. (More specialized models such as hierarchical CFA models are discussed later.) Any CFA measurement model (cases 1–3 in the table) must meet two necessary but insufficient conditions in order to be identified: (1) the number of free parameters must be less than or equal to the number of observations, and (2) every factor must have a scale. The number of observations equals

TABLE 7.1. Requirements for the Identification of CFA
Measurement Models

	Model characteristics		Identification status	
Case	Unidimensional measurement[a]	Number of factors	Conditions for identification	Necessary or sufficient?
1	Yes	1	1. Parameters ≤ observations	Necessary
			2. Scale for every factor	Necessary
			3. ≥3 indicators	Sufficient
2	Yes	≥2	1. Parameters ≤ observations	Necessary
			2. Scale for every factor	Necessary
			3. ≥2 indicators per factor	Sufficient
3	No	≥1	1. Parameters ≤ observations	Necessary
			2. Scale for every factor	Necessary
			3. Model-fitting program yields a solution that passes uniqueness checks	Necessary

[a]Each indicator loads on a single factor and measurement errors are independent.

the number of variances and covariances among the observed variables—or $v(v + 1)/2$, where v is the number of observed variables, which is the same as for path models. Parameters of CFA measurement models are counted as follows:

> *The total number of variances and covariances (i.e., unanalyzed associations) of the factors and of the measurement errors plus direct effects on the indicators from the factors (i.e., factor loadings) equals the number of parameters.*

The second necessary requirement for identification is that every latent variable must have a scale (i.e., a metric). Because latent variables are not directly measured, they require a measurement scale in order for the computer to be able to calculate estimates of effects that involve them. There are two ways to scale a latent variable. The first is to fix the variance of a factor to equal a constant. This constant is usually 1.0, which standardizes the latent variable. The second is to fix the loading of one indicator per factor to equal 1.0, which gives the latent variable the same metric as that indicator. Suppose that X_1 is specified as an indicator of factor A. If the loading of X_1 on A is fixed to 1.0, this means that a 1-point increase in the factor is associated with a 1-point increase in X_1 and that factor A is unstandardized because it has the same metric as X_1.

Either method outlined above to scale latent variables reduces the total number of parameters, one for each construct in the model. Both methods also result in the same overall fit of the model to the data. The choice between them, then, is based on the relative merits of analyzing factors in standardized versus unstandardized form. When a CFA model is analyzed in a single sample, either method described above is probably acceptable. Fixing the variance of a factor to 1.0 (i.e., the factor is standardized) has the advantage of simplicity. A shortcoming of this method, though, is that it is usually applicable only to latent exogenous variables.[2] This is not a problem for CFA models wherein all factors are exogenous, but it is for hybrid models in which some factors are endogenous. Scaling a factor by fixing the loading of one of its indicators to 1.0 (i.e., the factor is unstandardized) can be used for latent variables that are either exogenous or endogenous. The method just described has the drawback, however,

---

[2]Essentially all model-fitting programs allow the imposition of constraints on any model parameter, but the variances of endogenous variables are not considered parameters. The RAMONA program by Browne, Mels, and Cowan (1994) and version 8 of LISREL (Jöreskog & Sörbom, 1996a), however, allow the model-implied variances of endogenous variables to be fixed to 1.0, which scales the factor.

that it precludes tests of significance of factor loadings fixed to the constant 1.0. Also, a natural question about this method arises: given multiple indicators of a factor, which one should be selected to fix its loading to 1.0? Assuming that all of the indicators of a construct are of comparable reliability, the choice is arbitrary. There are some special considerations in setting scales for latent factors in multiple-group CFAs, but these issues are addressed later. However, it can be said here that standardizing factors by fixing their variances to 1.0 is generally *not* an appropriate way to scale factors in multiple-group CFAs, especially if the groups are expected to have different variabilities on the latent variables.

The requirement that every latent variable be scaled is also behind something that was mentioned in Chapter 5 (section 5.9) about path models. Recall that model-fitting programs typically require that the residual path coefficient from a disturbance to an endogenous variable be fixed to 1.0 in the program syntax that specifies a path model. If a disturbance in a path model is conceptualized as a latent exogenous variable, then it requires a scale in order for the model to be identified. From this perspective, an endogenous variable in a path model is seen as an indicator of its disturbance, and fixing the residual path coefficient to 1.0 is the same as assigning the disturbance the same scale as its indicator. Based on the same rationale, the residual path coefficient for the direct effect of a measurement error term on its indicator in CFA is also typically fixed to 1.0 in model-fitting program syntax. This specification convention scales the measurement error term, which allows the computer to estimate only its variance. As with path models, this constraint is often not shown in the diagram of a measurement model, but it is part of identifying the measurement model.

CFA models that meet both necessary requirements just discussed may nevertheless be nonidentified. Fortunately, there is a sufficient condition for identification that concerns minimum numbers of indicators that applies to standard CFA models. Recall that standard CFA models feature unidimensional measurement—each indicator loads on a single factor and the measurement error terms are independent—and all possible correlations among the factors. *If a standard CFA model with a single factor has at least three indicators, then the model is identified* (case 1 in Table 7.1). *If a standard model with two or more factors has at least two indicators per factor, then the model is identified* (case 2). Bollen (1989) described a variation of the two-indicator requirement for multifactor CFA models: if factors with only two indicators are specified to covary with at least one other factor, then the model is identified. Note, however, that models with factors that have only two indicators are more prone to empirical underidentification or other estimation problems when the sample is small. Both points are discussed later, but a minimum of three indicators per factor is recommended.

There is no comparable, easily applied sufficient condition for CFA models with multidimensional measurement (case 3 in Table 7.1). Although the identification status of such "none of the above" CFA models is more ambiguous, two suggestions for dealing with them can be offered. First, the presence of either correlated measurement errors or loadings of indicators on more than one factor in a CFA model may not be problematic. The presence of both in the same model, however, may cause identification problems. Second, a researcher can use the empirical checks for the uniqueness of a solution yielded by a model-fitting program described earlier (section 6.6) when analyzing a "none of the above" CFA model.

Let's apply the requirements for identification summarized in Table 7.1 to the CFA models presented in Figure 7.3. The 1.0s in the figure designate fixed loadings to set scales for latent variables. Model (a) is a single-factor model with only two indicators. This model is underidentified: with two observed variables, there are three observations $(2(3)/2 = 3)$ but four parameters, including three variances (of factor A and of the measurement errors E_1 and E_2) and one factor loading $(A \to X_2$; the other loading is fixed to 1.0 to scale Factor A). The imposition of a constraint such as one of equality (e.g., $A \to X_1 = A \to X_2 = 1.0$) may make the model estimable.[3] Model (b) in Figure 7.3 is a standard CFA model with a single factor and three indicators. This model has six parameters, including four variances (of factor A and of measurement errors E_1 to E_3) and two factor loadings $(A \to X_2, A \to X_3$; the other loading is fixed to 1.0). With 3 observed variables, there are $3(4)/2$, or 6, observations, so model (b) of the figure is just-identified. Note that a standard single-factor CFA model must have at least four indicators in order to be overidentified. Model (c) has two factors each with two indicators. Because model (c) represents unidimensional measurement, has more than one factor, and has at least two indicators per factor, it is identified. In fact, this model is overidentified: there are $4(5)/2$, or 10, observations and 9 parameters, including 6 variances (of the 2 factors and the 4 measurement errors), 1 unanalyzed association between the factors $(A \leftrightarrow B)$, and 2 factor loadings $(A \to X_2, B \to X_4)$.

---

[3]Kenny (1979) noted for model (a) of Figure 7.3 that if the correlation between the two indicators is negative, then the just-identified model that results by imposing an equality constraint on the factor loadings does not exactly reproduce the observed correlation.

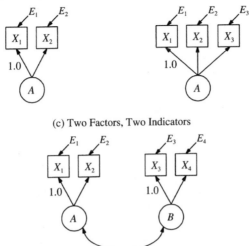

(a) Single Factor, Two Indicators   (b) Single Factor, Three Indicators

(c) Two Factors, Two Indicators

FIGURE 7.3. Identification status of three CFA models.

Just as with path models, CFA models that are theoretically identified are still susceptible to empirical underidentification which occurs when data-related problems lead to nonidentification rather than features of the model. For example, suppose that the factor loading of indicator X_2 on factor A of model (b) of Figure 7.3 is close to zero. Practically speaking, model (b) would resemble model (a) in that both have only two indicators, which is too few for a single-factor model. Model (c) in Figure 7.3 may be empirically underidentified if the estimate of the correlation between factors A and B is close to zero. The virtual elimination of the path $A \leftrightarrow B$ from this model transforms it into two single-factor, two-indicator models, each of which is underidentified.

7.6   Estimation

Interpretation of Parameter Estimates

Unstandardized estimates in CFA are interpreted as follows: Unanalyzed associations either between factors (e.g., $A \leftrightarrow B$) or measurement errors (e.g., $E_1 \leftrightarrow E_2$) are covariances. Factor loadings (e.g., $A \rightarrow X_1$) are interpreted as unstandardized regression coefficients that estimate the direct effects of the factors on the indicators. Note that factor loadings fixed to 1.0 to scale a latent variable remain 1.0 in the unstandardized solution and are not tested for significance. Unstandardized estimates of measurement error variances (e.g., of E_1) are expressed in the original metric of the associated indicator. The ratio of the unstandardized measurement error variance over the observed variance of the indicator equals the proportion of unique variance, that is, the percent of variance unexplained by the factors. Likewise, 1.0 minus this ratio is the proportion of indicator variance explained by the factors.

In the standardized solution, estimates of unanalyzed associations between either factors or measurement errors are correlations. If an indicator is specified to load on only a single factor, then the standardized estimate of its factor loading is also a correlation and the square of its factor loading equals the proportion of variance explained by the factor. For example, if the standardized factor loading of X_1 on A is .70 and X_1 loads on no other factors, then factor A accounts for $.70^2$, or 49%, of X_1's variance. The portion of explained indicator variance is sometimes referred to as *common variance* in the factor analysis literature. If X_1 is specified to load on multiple factors, however, then its standardized loadings are interpreted as standardized regression coefficients (i.e., beta weights) that take account of the correlations between the multiple factors that the indicator is supposed to measure. Recall that beta weights are not correlations, so one cannot square their values to derive the proportion of explained variance. However, 1 minus the ratio of the unstandardized variance of the measurement error term over the observed variance of an indicator always equals the proportion of explained variance regardless of whether an indicator has just one or multiple factor loadings.

Loadings of indicators fixed to 1.0 to scale latent variables typically have different values in the standardized solution. For unidimensional indicators, standardized factor loadings should have absolute values less than 1.0 because they are correlations. This result demonstrates that although the latent variable has the same scale as one of its indicators, it is not identical to that indicator. Variances of the factors and measurement errors all equal 1.0 in the standardized solution. As with disturbances in path analysis, diagrams of CFA models in which standardized estimates are reported may depict measurement errors as proportions of unexplained variance.

Estimation Methods and the Analysis of Severely Non-Normal Data

The most frequently used estimation methods in CFA are those that assume multivariate normality, including maximum likelihood (ML), generalized least squares (GLS), and unweighted least squares (ULS; section 5.11). Among the methods just listed, ML is used most often. What happens if such methods are applied to data that are clearly non-normal? The results of several computer simulation studies of the analysis of CFA models with severely non-normal data generated from known population parameters (e.g., Browne, 1984; Chou & Bentler, 1995; Curran, West, & Finch, 1997; Hu, Bentler, & Kano, 1992; Muthén & Kaplan, 1992; Satorra & Bentler, 1994; see also Bollen, 1989, and West, Finch, & Curran, 1995) generally suggest the following:

Although parameter estimates derived with methods that assume normality are fairly accurate within large samples when the data are severely non-normal, results of significance tests tend to be significant too often. For the overall goodness of fit χ^2 test, this means that true models will be rejected too often (i.e., a Type I error in this context). For example, West et al. (1995) found in some of their simulations that the actual rate of Type I error was as high as 50%, when the expected rate was 5%. Significance tests of individual parameters (e.g., factor loadings) also tend to be significant more often than they should. This occurs because estimates of standard errors tend to be too small when the data are severely non-normal. (Recall that standard errors are the denominators of significance tests; section 2.9.) The degree of underestimation of standard errors may be as much as 25–50%, depending upon the data and the model (e.g., West et al., 1995).

Unlike simulation studies in which the actual population parameters are known, it is not usually possible to know the exact amount of bias when severely non-normal sample data are analyzed with methods that assume normal distributions. There are three basic options to avoid bias when the data are severely non-normal: (1) use transformations to normalize the variables (section 4.7), and analyze the transformed data with a normal distribution method like ML; (2) analyze the original, untransformed data with a normal distribution method, but use corrected test statistics that may reduce bias; or (3) use an estimation method that does not assume normality. The second and third options require the analysis of a raw data file by the model-fitting program. Estimation methods based on elliptical or arbitrary distribution theory were described earlier (section 5.11). Recall that methods that make no distributional assumptions (e.g., asymptotically distribution-free (ADF) estimation) may require very large samples in order to be accurate.

Corrected test statistics for normal distribution methods like ML include rescaled goodness of fit χ^2s and so-called robust standard errors. An example of a rescaled χ^2 is the Satorra–Bentler statistic (e.g.,

Satorra & Bentler, 1994), which adjusts the value of the standard (normal distribution theory) χ^2 downward by a constant that reflects the degree of observed kurtosis. Results of simulation studies of this corrected χ^2 statistic are generally favorable (e.g., Chou & Bentler, 1995; Curran, et al., 1997). The Satorra–Bentler statistic is currently available only in the EQS model-fitting program. Like adjusted χ^2s, robust standard errors also feature a correction factor that takes account of the degree of non-normality. The possibility of bias when severely non-normal data are estimated with methods that assume normality without corrected test statistics highlights the importance of careful data screening.

Additional Fit Indexes

All of the indexes of overall model fit described in Chapter 5 (section 5.9) are applicable to CFA. An additional fit statistic that is used for measurement models is the squared multiple correlation (R^2) calculated for each indicator, which equals the proportion of explained variance (i.e., 1 minus the ratio of the unstandardized measurement error variance over the observed variance). Values of R^2 less than .50 mean that more than half of an indicator's variance is unique and thus unexplained by the factor(s) it is specified to measure. A related index is Jöreskog and Sörbom's (1981) *coefficient of determination*, which summarizes the overall effect of the exogenous factors on the endogenous indicators. The coefficient of determination ranges from 0 (no effect) to 1 (all indicator variance is explained). A drawback of the coefficient of determination is that its value tends to be higher than that of R^2 for any individual indicator. Some model-fitting programs print the value of the coefficient of determination, but not all programs do. The formula for the coefficient of determination is based on matrix algebra, but a way to calculate it by hand is presented in Appendix 7.A. Examples of both fit indexes are presented later.

Problems

A problem that can arise in the analysis of a CFA model is a phenomenon called a *Heywood case* (after H. B. Heywood; e.g., Heywood, 1931) that refers to an improper solution in which the absolute value of an estimated correlation between an indicator and its factor is greater than 1 or an estimated error variance is less than 0. Such improper estimates can be caused by specification errors, outlier cases that distort the solution, a combination of small sample sizes and only two indicators per factor, inaccurate starting values, or extremely high or low population correlations that result in empirical underidentification. The detection of outliers was discussed earlier (section 4.6). Presented in Appendix 7.B are recommendations for specifying starting values for standard CFA models. These suggestions may be helpful if either a researcher's model-fitting program does not automatically generate starting values or if computer-generated initial estimates do not lead to a converged solution. For more information about the causes of Heywood cases in SEM, see Dillon, Kumar, and Mulani (1987).

Other potential problems are related to sample size. Results of some computer simulation studies of CFA models (e.g., Anderson & Gerbing, 1984; Gerbing & Anderson, 1985; see also Anderson & Gerbing, 1988) indicate that problems like Heywood cases or nonconvergence of iterative estimation are more likely to occur for models with only two indicators per factor and sample sizes of less than 100–150 cases. If possible, at least three indicators per factor are recommended, especially if a researcher's sample is so small. The suggestion offered in Chapter 5 for path models that researchers think about minimum sample sizes in terms of the ratio of subjects to free model parameters (i.e., 10:1 or, even better, 20:1) also seems appropriate for CFA. For example, model (c) of Figure 7.3 has 10 parameters, so a minimum sample size of about 100 cases is recommended.

7.7 Testing CFA Models

The essentials of testing CFA models with data from single samples are covered in this section. The main example considered here was first introduced in Chapter 3 (section 3.5; Figure 3.3) and concerns the Kaufman Assessment Battery for Children (K-ABC), a cognitive ability test based on a two-process theory of intelligence (sequential processing, simultaneous processing). Also demonstrated here is respecification, the modification of an initial CFA model with mediocre or poor fit to the data.

Test for a Single Factor

When theory is not specific about the number of constructs, this is often the first stop in a series of CFAs: if a single-factor model cannot be rejected, then there is little point in evaluating more complex ones; even when theory is more precise about the number of factors such as for the K-ABC (i.e., two factors), the researcher should determine whether the fit of a simpler, one-factor model is comparable. Presented in the upper part of Table 7.2 are the intercorrelations and standard deviations of the K-ABC's eight ability subtests for 10-year-old children from the test's normative sample ($N = 200$; A. S. Kaufman & N. L. Kaufman, 1983). A covariance matrix assembled from the correlations and standard deviations summarized in Table 7.2 was submitted to a model-fitting program for a CFA to evaluate a single-factor model with independent measurement errors. The loading of the Hand Movements task was fixed to 1.0 to scale the latent variable. With this loading fixed, the one-factor model has 16 free parameters, including 7 remaining factor loadings and 9 variances (of 8 measurement errors and the latent variable). With 8 observed variables, there are $8(9)/2 = 36$ observations. According to the guidelines outlined earlier (section 7.5), this one-factor model is theoretically identified.

Values of selected fit indexes for the one-factor model of the K-ABC are reported in Table 7.2. This model's overall $\chi^2(20)$ statistic is significant at the .01 level, but this is not surprising given the reasonably large sample size (200). More informative is the χ^2/df ratio, which for this model is greater than 3 (5.25). Also, values of both the Bentler–Bonett Normed Fit Index (NFI) and the Non-Normed Fit Index (NNFI) are less than .80. Overall, these results indicate that a one-factor model inadequately accounts for the observed covariances among these eight subtests.

A brief point before we go on to evaluate a two-factor model of this cognitive ability test. The test for a single-factor model is relevant not just for CFA models. Brewer, Campbell, and Crano (1970) and Kenny (1979) suggested that such models could also be tested as part of a path analysis. The inability to reject a one-factor model in this context would mean the same thing as in CFA: the observed variables do not show discriminant validity; that is, they seem to measure only one domain. As an example of this procedure, a test for single factoredness was conducted for the five variables of the Roth et al. (1989) path model of illness discussed in Chapter 5 (Figure 5.2; Table 5.1). The results indicated that a one-factor model poorly fit these data—for example, $\chi^2(5) = 60.66$, $p < .01$, $\chi^2/df = 12.13$, NFI = .63—which provides a sort of "green light" to precede with evaluation of the structural model.

Multifactor Models

The specification of a multifactor CFA model in which each indicator loads on a single construct provides a very specific test of convergent

TABLE 7.2. Evaluation of One- and Two-Factor Models of the Kaufman Assessment Battery for Children

Correlations, means, and standard deviations (A. S. Kaufman & N. L. Kaufman, 1983; $N = 200$ 10-year-olds, nationally representative sample)

Variable	Sequential			Simultaneous				
	1	2	3	4	5	6	7	8
Sequential Processing scale tasks								
1. Hand Movements	—							
2. Number Recall	.39	—						
3. Word Order	.35	.67	—					
Simultaneous Processing scale tasks								
4. Gestalt Closure	.21	.11	.16	—				
5. Triangles	.32	.27	.29	.38	—			
6. Matrix Analogies	.40	.29	.28	.30	.47	—		
7. Spatial Memory	.39	.32	.30	.31	.42	.41	—	
8. Photo Series	.39	.29	.37	.42	.58	.51	.42	—
SD	3.40	2.40	2.90	2.70	2.70	4.20	2.80	3.00

Goodness of fit summary

Model	χ^2	df	χ^2/df	Contrast with baseline model		CFI	NNFI	SRMR
				$\chi^2_{\text{difference}}$	$df_{\text{difference}}$			
Baseline (one-factor)	104.90**	20	5.25	—	—	.82	.75	.01
Two-factor	38.13**	19	2.01	67.77**	1	.96	.94	.01

R^2s and coefficient of determination for the two-factor model

Indicator	R^2	Indicator	R^2
Hand Movements	.25	Gestalt Closure	.25
Number Recall	.65	Triangles	.52
Word Order	.65	Matrix Analogies	.43
		Spatial Memory	.35
		Photo Series	.61

Coefficient of determination = .94

Note. CFI, Bentler Comparative Fit Index; NNFI, Bentler–Bonett Non-Normed Fit Index; SRMR, Standardized Root Mean Squared Residual.

**$p < .01$.

and discriminant validity. Presented in Figure 7.4 is the two-factor model of the K-ABC. Three tasks are specified to measure one construct, five the other, and the two constructs are assumed to covary. To set scales for the latent variables, the loadings of the Hand Movements task and of the Gestalt Closure task on their respective factors were each fixed to 1.0. A total of 17 parameters remain to be estimated, including 10 variances (2 factors, 8 E terms), 6 factor loadings (2 on the one factor, 4 on the other), and 1 covariance between the factors. With 8 observed variables, there are 36 observations; thus, the overall χ^2 for the two-factor model has 19 (36 – 17) degrees of freedom. The model in Figure 7.4 not only meets the necessary requirements for identification but also the sufficient condition because every factor has at least two indicators (case 2, Table 7.1).

The two-factor model of the K-ABC was analyzed with CFA using a covariance matrix of the eight tasks as the input data (Table 7.2). Values of selected fit indexes for the two-factor model are reported in Table 7.2. The overall fit of the two-factor model is superior to that of the single-factor model for these data. For example, the χ^2/df ratio for the two-factor model is 2.01, which compares favorably to the value of 5.25 for the single-factor model. Values of fit indexes with more standardized metrics also indicate a preference for the two-factor model. For example, the NFI for the two-factor model is .92, whereas for the one-factor model the NFI is .79. Also reported in Table 7.2 is a

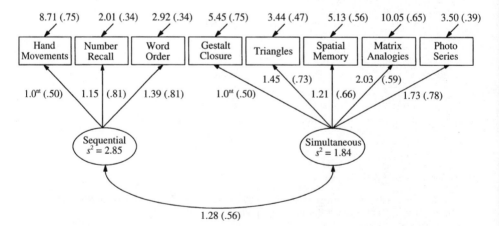

FIGURE 7.4. Two-factor model of the K-ABC with the unstandardized and standardized solutions. All unstandardized estimates are significant at the .01 level except those designated "nt," which means not tested. Standardized estimates are reported in parentheses. The standardized values for the measurement error terms are proportions of unexplained variance.

$\chi^2_{\text{difference}}(1)$ statistic that equals 38.13, which is significant at the .01 level. Remember, though, that the $\chi^2_{\text{difference}}$ statistic can be interpreted as a significance test only for hierarchial (nested) models. Is this true of the one- and two-factor models of the K-ABC? Yes, and here's why: the one-factor model is a actually a constrained version of the two-factor model. Look at again at Figure 7.4. If the correlation between the two factors is fixed to equal 1.0, then the two factors, sequential and simultaneous, are identical, which is the same as replacing both factors with just one. Thus, we can appropriately say based on the $\chi^2_{\text{difference}}(1)$ statistic of 38.13 that the fit of the one-factor model is significantly *worse* than that of the two-factor model. The comparison just described can be generalized to models with more than two factors. With a four-factor model, for instance, fixing all of the factor correlations to 1.0 generates a single-factor model that is nested under the unrestricted model.

Also reported in Table 7.2 are the squared multiple correlations (R^2) for each indicator of the two-factor model and the coefficient of determination. Some of the R^2 values are fairly low. For example, only 25% of the variance of the Hand Movements task and the Gestalt Closure task are explained by the two-factor model. The value of the coefficient of determination is .94, which is much higher than any of the individual R^2s. This is typical of this index, which means that it cannot be interpreted in the same way as are other fit indexes with more standardized metrics (e.g., the NFI and the NNFI).

The unstandardized and standardized solutions are reported in Figure 7.4. The numbers inside the ovals are the unstandardized estimates of factor variances. (The standardized estimates of variances are all 1.0.) The unstandardized estimates for the measurement error terms are also variances, but the standardized results reported in the figure for these terms are proportions of unexplained variance. For example, the estimated measurement error variance of the Hand Movements task is 8.71. The observed variance of this task is 11.56 (or 3.40^2; see Table 7.2). The ratio of the unstandardized measurement error variance over the observed variance for the Hand Movements task is 8.71/11.56, which equals .75, the proportion of unexplained variance. (Also note that the R^2 value for this indicator is .25; see Table 7.2.) The unstandardized factor loadings are interpreted as regression coefficients that indicate expected change in the indicator given a 1-point increase in the factor. For example, scores on the Number Recall task are predicted to increase by 1.15 points for every 1-point increase in the sequential factor. All of the unstandardized loadings that are not fixed to 1.0 to scale factors are significant at the .01 level. Because each indicator is specified to measure a single factor, the standardized loadings are interpreted as correlations and their squared values as proportions of explained variance. The standardized factor loading of the Hand Movements task, for instance, is .50, which means that $.50^2$, or 25%, of its variance is shared with the sequential factor. (Note that the unstandardized loading of this task is fixed to 1.0 to scale this factor.)

Overall, the evidence for the adequacy of the two-factor model of the K-ABC is mixed. On the positive side, its overall fit is reasonable. The estimated correlation between the factors is only moderate (.56), which suggests discriminant validity. Support for convergent validity is somewhat problematic, though, because the model explains less than 50% of the variance of four of eight indicators (see Table 7.2). Respecification of this model in an attempt to remedy some of these problems is discussed next.

Respecification

In the face of adversity, the protagonist of Kurt Vonnegut's novel *Slaughterhouse-Five* often remarks, "So it goes." And so it often does in CFA that an initial model does not fit the data very well. Respecification of path models was discussed in Chapter 5 (section 5.10). The respecification of a CFA model may be more difficult because there are more possibilities for change than for a path model. For instance, the number of constructs, their relations to the indicators, and patterns of unanalyzed associations among measurement error terms are all candidates for modification. Given so many potential variations, respecification of CFA models should be guided as much as possible by substantive considerations rather than solely by empirical ones. Otherwise, the process of model respecification could be like the sailor mentioned in the quotation by Leonardo da Vinci that opens this chapter—without a compass or rudder, heading to nowhere in particular. Discussed below are basic respecification options and related considerations. Their application to the two-factor model of the K-ABC (Figure 7.4) is demonstrated afterward.

There are two general classes of problems that are considered in the respecification of CFA models. The first concerns the indicators. Sometimes indicators fail to have substantial loadings on the factors to which they are originally assigned (e.g., standardized loading = .10). One option is to specify that an indicator loads on a different factor. Inspection of the correlation residuals can help to identify the other factor to which the indicator's loading may be switched. (Recall that correlation residuals are differences between observed and model-implied correlations.) Suppose that an indicator is originally specified to measure factor *A* but that the correlation residuals between it and the indicators of factor *B* are large and positive. This would suggest that the indicator may measure factor *B* more so than it does factor *A*. Note that an indicator can also have relatively high loadings on its own factor but have high correlation residuals between it and the indicators of another factor. The pattern just described suggests that the indicator in question measures more than one construct, which can be represented in the model by allowing the indicator to load on multiple factors. Another possibility consistent with this same pattern of correlation residuals is that these indicators share something that is unique to them like a particular method of measurement, which could be represented by allowing the measurement errors of the associated indicators to covary. Indicators for which none of these modifications results in a reasonably large factor loading (e.g., absolute standardized value > .50) may measure something that the other indicators do not. Indicators so orthogonal to the rest could be dropped from the model. The second class of problems often considered in respecification concerns the factors. For example, the researcher may have specified the wrong number of latent variables. Poor discriminant validity as evidenced by very high factor correlations may indicate that the model has too many factors. On the other hand, poor convergent validity among the indicators of some factors suggests that the model may have too few factors. For instance, some of the original factors may themselves be multidimensional that should be "split" into more homogeneous subfactors.

As if the aforedescribed choices were not numerous enough, there are additional considerations. First, the inclusion (or exclusion) of things like correlated measurement errors or loadings on multiple factors (i.e., multidimensional measurement) can result in equivalent models. An equivalent CFA model generates the same predicted correlations and covariances but with different specifications. (Equivalent models are discussed later.) The researcher must also decide how to decide—specifically, as to the role of empirically based information about respecification (e.g., modification indexes) versus the weight given to more rationally based considerations. As mentioned in Chapter 5, a specification search based solely on empirical strategies may be unlikely to lead to the true model (e.g., MacCallum, 1986; Silvia & MacCallum, 1988). Also, empirical indexes provide information only about the effects of freeing (or fixing) parameters in a particular CFA model. They cannot indicate whether more fundamental changes should be made such as the inclusion of additional factors.

This example concerns the analysis of the two-factor model of the K-ABC (Figure 7.4). To recap, the overall fit of this model is reasonable, but some indicators have rather high proportions of unique variance.

A starting point for respecification often includes inspection of the correlation residuals, which for this model are reported in the top part of Table 7.3. Absolute correlation residuals greater than .10 are reported in boldface. Most of these larger residuals concern one of the indicators of the sequential factor, Hand Movements, and most of the tasks specified to measure the simultaneous factor. All of these values are positive, which means that the original model generally underestimates correlations between the Hand Movements task and those that are supposed to measure the other factor. The standardized loading of the Hand Movements task on its original factor (sequential) is at least moderate (.50), however, which suggests that it may measure both factors.

Another type of information relevant for respecification are val-

TABLE 7.3. Respecification of the Two-Factor Model of the Kaufman Assessment Battery for Children

Correlation residuals

Variable	Sequential			Simultaneous				
	1	2	3	4	5	6	7	8
Sequential Processing scale tasks								
1. Hand Movements	—							
2. Number Recall	−.01	—						
3. Word Order	−.05	.02	—					
Simultaneous Processing scale tasks								
4. Gestalt Closure	.07	**−.12**	−.07	—				
5. Triangles	**.12**	−.06	−.04	.02	—			
6. Matrix Analogies	**.22**	−.01	−.02	−.03	−.01	—		
7. Spatial Memory	**.23**	.06	.04	.01	−.01	.02	—	
8. Photo Series	**.17**	−.06	.02	.03	.01	.00	−.04	—

Modification indexes

Description of parameter	Modification index $\chi^2(1)$
Allow Hand Movements to load on simultaneous factor	20.00**
Allow measurement errors of Word Order and Number Recall to covary	20.00**
Allow measurement errors of Hand Movements and Word Order to covary	6.98**
Allow Number Recall to load on simultaneous factor	6.98**
Allow measurement errors of Hand Movements and Matrix Analogies to covary	4.82**

**$p < .01$.

ues of modification indexes (i.e., univariate Lagrange Multipliers) of parameters constrained to equal zero. Recall that modification in dexes estimate the amount by which the model's overall χ^2 will decline if the associated parameter is freed. Modification indexes significant at the .05 level for the two-factor model under consideration are reported in the bottom part of Table 7.3. Note that allowing the Hand Movements task to load on the other factor (simultaneous) would reduce the model's overall χ^2 by about 20 points. However, a different change, the addition of a correlation between the measurement error terms of two other indicators—Word Order and Number Recall of the sequential factor—would result in *exactly* the same estimated decrease in the model's overall χ^2. Other changes suggested by the modification indexes would result in smaller improvements in model fit, but among these two have exactly the same estimated $\chi^2(1)$ value (see Table 7.3). Obviously, the researcher needs some rationale for choosing among these potential modifications.[4]

Additional Tests

Two additional tests for single- and multifactor CFA models are now briefly described. There is a distinction in the psychometric literature about whether indicators of a single-factor model are *congeneric, tau-equivalent,* or *parallel.* These terms reflect increasingly stringent assumptions: congeneric indicators are presumed to simply measure the same construct; tau-equivalent indicators are assumed to measure the same construct *and* have equal true score variabilities; and parallel indicators are both tau-equivalent *and* equally reliable. All three assume independent measurement errors. In CFA, one can test whether a set of indicators is congeneric, tau-equivalent, or parallel by comparing with the $\chi^2_{difference}$ test a series of hierarchical models. The CFA model for congenerity is simply a standard one-factor model with independent measurement errors and no constraints imposed on any of the estimates. If this model fits the data reasonably well, then one can proceed to test the more demanding assumptions of tau-equivalence and parallelism. The CFA model for tau-equivalence is a constrained version of the one-factor model for congenerity. By imposing equality constraints on all the factor loadings (e.g., they all equal 1.0) and comparing the relative fit of this constrained model against that of the unconstrained model (i.e., the model for congenerity), one tests whether

---

[4]Based on my familiarity with the K-ABC, allowing the Hand Movements task to load on both factors is plausible.

the indicators are tau-equivavlent. Specifically, if the fit of the model with equality–constrained factor loadings is not significantly worse than the unconstrained model, then the hypothesis of tau-equivalence is not rejected. If the model for tau-equivalence fits the data reasonably well, then additional constraints can be imposed that test for parallelism. These additional constraints consist of equality constraints imposed on all the measurement error variances. If the fit of this model is not significantly worse than that of the model for tau-equivalence, then the indicators may be parallel. Note that a covariance matrix, not a correlation matrix, must be analyzed for these tests.

It was demonstrated earlier that fixing all factor correlations to 1.0 in a multifactor CFA model generates a one-factor model that is nested under the original. In the factor analysis literature, application of the $\chi^2_{\text{difference}}$ statistic to compare the relative fits of the original and constrained (one-factor) models is sometimes referred to as a test for *redundancy*. That is, if the fit of a multifactor CFA model is not superior to that of one-factor model, then the multiple factors are redundant. A variation on this theme is to fix the factor correlations in a multifactor model to zero, which provides a test for *orthogonality*. If the model has only two factors, then this procedure is not necessary because the test of significance of the factor correlation in the unconstrained model provides the same information. For models with three or more factors, the test for orthogonality is akin to a multivariate test of whether all the factor covariances considered together are significant. Note, however, that the test for orthogonality requires that each factor has at least three indicators. Otherwise, the model may not be identified. For more information about tests of congenerity, tau-equivalence, parallelism, redundancy, and orthogonality, see Nunnally and Bernstein (1994, pp. 576–578).

Equivalent CFA Models

Just as in path analysis, there are probably equivalent versions of a researcher's preferred CFA model. There are two sets of principles about the generation of equivalent CFA models—one for single-factor models and the other for models with multiple factors. As an example of the latter, consider the two-factor model of self-perception of ability and achievement aspiration presented at the top of Figure 7.5. This model was originally evaluated by Kenny (1979) with data from 556 Grade 8 students (summarized in Table 7.4). The fit of this model is acceptable, as is apparent from the values of the fit statistics reported in the table.

The other three models presented in Figure 7.5 are equivalent

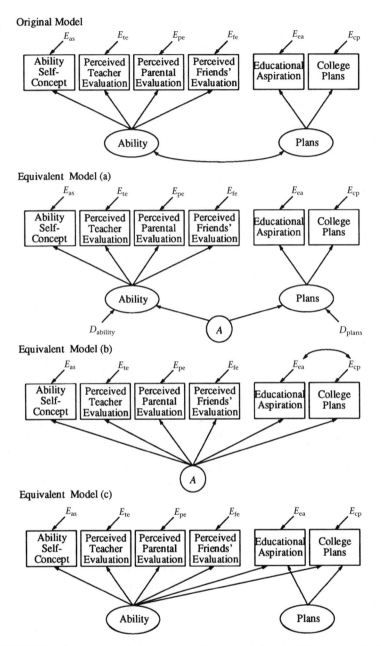

FIGURE 7.5. Original and three equivalent models of self-perceived ability and educational plans.

TABLE 7.4. Equivalent Versions of a Two-Factor Model of Perceived Ability and Education Plans

Correlations (Kenny, 1979; N = 556 Grade 8 students)

Variable	1	2	3	4	5	6
1. Ability Self-Concept	—					
2. Perceived Parental Evaluation	.73	—				
3. Perceived Teacher Evaluation	.70	.68	—			
4. Perceived Friends' Evaluation	.58	.61	.57	—		
5. Educational Aspiration	.46	.43	.40	.37	—	
6. College Plans	.56	.52	.48	.41	.72	—

Goodness of fit summary

Model	χ^2	df	χ^2/df	GFI	AGFI	NFI	NNFI	SRMR
Original two-factor and all equivalent models	9.26	8	1.16	.994	.985	.995	.999	.012

Note. GFI, Jöreskog–Sörbom Goodness of Fit Index; AGFI, Adjusted GFI; NFI, Bentler–Bonett Normed Fit Index; NNFI, Non-NFI; SRMR, Standardized Root Mean Squared Residual.

versions of the original that yield the same predicted correlations and covariances and values of fit statistics. In equivalent model (a), the unanalyzed association between the constructs of the original model is replaced by a second-order factor (A), which provides an alternative account of why the two lower-order constructs (ability, plans) covary. (Models with second-order factors are discussed later.) Two other variations are unique to models wherein some factors have only two indicators. For example, equivalent model (b) of Figure 7.5 features the substitution of the plans factor with a measurement error correlation between its indicators. Equivalent model (c) features replacement of the correlation between the ability and plans factors with the specification that some indicators are multidimensional. Although the factors are assumed to be independent in this model, all six indicators have loadings on a common factor, which accounts for their intercorrelations just as well as does the original model.[5] Altogether, the four models of Figure 7.5 provide theoretically different

[5]Two of the models in Figure 7.5 require constraints in order to be identified. In equivalent model (a), the second order factor A has only two indicators. To estimate this model, one could impose an equality constraint on the loadings of the first-order factors on the second-order factors. In equivalent model (c), the plans construct has only two indicators and the two factors are assumed to be uncorrelated. Constraining the factors loadings of the college plans and educational aspirations indicators to be equal makes this model estimable.

but mathematically identical accounts of the observed correlations among these six observed variables.

Equivalent versions of single-factor models can be derived using something that Hershberger (1994) calls the *reversed indicator rule,* which involves the specification of one of the observed variables as a cause indicator while the rest remain as effect indicators. An example is presented in Figure 7.6. The indicators of the one-factor model of reading presented in Figure 7.6(a) represent tests administered to 65 Grade 1 children, including measures of word and letter recognition, word attack (i.e., correct pronunciation of nonsense words), and phonics skills (Margolese & Kline, 1996). The fit of this model to the data is acceptable (see Table 7.5). An equivalent version of the original one-factor model is also presented in Figure 7.6(b), and it features phonics skill as a cause of reading, a specification for which there is evidence (e.g., Wagner et al., 1994). Note that the factor in this equivalent model is no longer exogenous: because a prior variable (phonics skill) has a direct effect on it, the factor here is endogenous and thus has a disturbance. Also, the phonics skill indicator is exogenous in the equivalent model (b), not endogenous as in the original (a). For

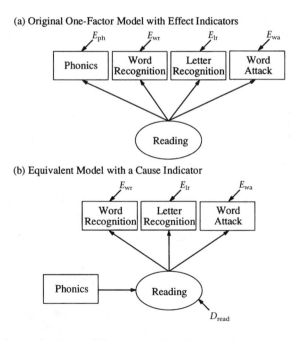

FIGURE 7.6. Application of the reversed indicator rule to generate an equivalent one-factor model of reading.

TABLE 7.5. Analysis of a One-Factor Model of Reading
and Equivalent Models

Correlations, means, and standard deviations (Margolese & Kline, 1996;
N = 65 Grade 1 students)

Variable	1	2	3	4
1. Letter Recognition	—			
2. Word Recognition	.58	—		
3. Word Attack	.44	.76	—	
4. Phonics	.31	.45	.46	—
M	100.51	102.60	99.52	88.90
SD	11.12	10.38	11.30	12.45

Goodness of fit summary

Model	χ^2	df	χ^2/df	GFI	AGFI	NFI
One-factor and all equivalent models	1.62	2	.81	.988	.939	.984

Note. GFI, Jöreskog–Sörbom Goodness of Fit Index; AGFI, Adjusted GFI; NFI, Bentler–Bonett Normed Fit Index.

these reasons, this equivalent model is actually a hybrid model. A total of three other such equivalent models could potentially be generated, one with each of the remaining indicators specified as causes of reading. Not all of these equivalent versions may be theoretically plausible, but at least the one with phonics as a cause indicator offers a logical alternative to the original one-factor CFA model. See Hershberger (1994) for additional examples.

7.8 Multiple Group CFA

The main question of a multiple group CFA concerns *measurement invariance* (sometimes called *factorial invariance*), which is whether a set of indicators assesses the same latent variables in different groups. A related concept in the psychometric literature is that of *construct bias*, which implies that a test measures something different in one group than in another (Reynolds & Kaiser, 1990). If so, then group membership moderates the relations between the indicators and latent variables specified in the measurement model. The evaluation of measurement invariance with CFA typically involves the comparison of the relative fits with the $\chi^2_{\text{difference}}$ test of two factor models, one with cross-group equality constraints imposed on some of its parameters and the other without constraints. A common practice is to constrain the factor loadings to be equal across the groups. If the fit of a CFA model with equality-constrained loadings is not significantly worse than that of the unconstrained model, then the indicators may measure the factors in comparable ways in each group. If the fit of the constrained model is significantly worse, however, then individual factor loadings should be compared across the samples to determine the extent of *partial measurement invariance*. That is, some factor loadings may vary substantially by group but the values of others may not. Although it is theoretically possible to do so, cross-group equality constraints are usually not imposed on estimates of variances or covariances. This is because groups may be expected to differ in their variabilities on either the latent factors or unique factors (i.e., the measurement errors) even if the indicators measure the latent factors in comparable ways for all groups (MacCallum & Tucker, 1991).

The example presented here concerns the two-factor model of the K-ABC (Figure 7.4). In section 7.7, this model was analyzed using data from a single nationally representative sample (Table 7.2). In this analysis, the two-factor model is analyzed across separate samples of 86 pairs of white and African-American children matched on age, gender, and socioeconomic status who were tested by Naglieri and Jensen (1987). Data from these two groups are summarized in Table 7.6. Note that although these data include group means, a regular CFA ignores the means (i.e., only the covariances are analyzed). It is possible, though, to extend the analysis of a multisample measurement model to include mean scores on both the indicators *and* the factors. The analysis of means in structural equation models is discussed in Chapter 10.

As in a single-sample CFA, scales for the latent variables must be set in order for the model to be identified, but there are special considerations in a multisample analysis. Of the two ways to set scales described earlier, fixing factor variances to 1.0 is the same as assuming that the groups are equally variable on the latent variables. If group variabilities on the underlying factors are really different, then this method may lead to inaccurate results. A better way to scale latent variables in a multiple group CFA is to fix the loading of one indicator per factor to 1.0. Note, though, that the loadings of the same indicators should be fixed to 1.0 in each sample. Although this method allows the variances of the factors to be freely estimated in each group, there are two potential complications. First, loadings fixed to 1.0 in all samples cannot be tested for group differences. The second complication follows from the first: because fixed loadings are excluded from tests of measurement invariance, it must be as-

TABLE 7.6. Multiple Group CFA of a Two-Factor Model of the Kaufman Assessment Battery for Children

Correlations, means, and standard deviations (Naglieri & Jensen, 1987; elementary school students, $N = 86$ white [below diagonal], $N = 86$ African-American [above diagonal])

	Sequential			Simultaneous					African-American	
Variable	1	2	3	4	5	6	7	8	M	SD
Sequential Processing scale tasks										
1. Hand Movements	—	.19	.26	.13	.19	.26	.22	.28	12.00	4.38
2. Number Recall	.35	—	.40	.06	.22	.24	.18	.09	10.93	1.90
3. Word Order	.36	.59	—	.08	.10	.32	.30	.11	12.86	1.54
Simultaneous Processing scale tasks										
4. Gestalt Closure	.00	−.08	−.06	—	.50	.34	.27	.21	18.36	2.79
5. Triangles	.31	.25	.31	.07	—	.41	.48	.28	13.28	2.02
6. Matrix Analogies	.39	.21	.25	.17	.44	—	.41	.35	11.91	3.47
7. Spatial Memory	.30	.09	.25	.17	.39	.29	—	.38	13.81	2.30
8. Photo Series	.33	−.02	.10	.32	.31	.14	.29	—	12.38	2.40
White M	12.65	11.01	13.03	18.72	14.48	13.00	14.87	12.80		
SD	2.73	2.06	2.04	2.45	2.28	3.36	12.80	2.12		

Goodness of fit summary

				Contrast with baseline model		
Model	χ^2	df	χ^2/df	$\chi^2_{difference}$	$df_{difference}$	CFI
Single-sample analyses						
White only	34.90*	19	1.84	—	—	.87
African-American only	22.46	19	1.18	—	—	.97
Multiple group analyses						
Baseline (no constraints)	57.36*	38	1.51	—	—	.92
Factor loadings invariant	63.83*	44	1.45	6.47	6	.91

Note. CFI, Bentler Comparative Fit Index.
*$p < .05$.

sumed that the associated indicator assesses the factor equally well in all groups. Thus, if the researcher decides to fix the loading of an indicator that is not invariant across the groups, then the subsequent results may be inaccurate. One way to deal with this dilemma is to reanalyze the model after fixing the loadings of other indicators to 1.0. If the factor loadings that were originally fixed are comparable in new analyses in which they are free parameters, then that indicator may be measurement invariant. See Reise, Widaman, and Pugh (1993) for additional information about scaling options for multiple group analyses.

To set scales for the latent variables, the loadings of the Hand Movements task (on the sequential factor) and of the Gestalt Closure task (on the simultaneous factor) were fixed to 1.0 in the white and African-American samples. Covariance matrices for each group were submitted to a model-fitting program for a multisample CFA. Reported in the middle part of Table 7.6 are values of various fit indexes for the two-factor model estimated without equality constraints. This model's overall $\chi^2(38)$ from the multisample analysis is 57.36, which, as the entries in the table indicate, is just the sum of the sample separate χ^2s (white, $\chi^2(19) = 34.90$; African-American, $\chi^2(19) = 22.46$). For the multisample analysis, the χ^2/df ratio is 1.51 and the Bentler Comparative Fit Index (CFI) is .92. The overall fit of the two-factor model evaluated across both samples is generally acceptable. The two-factor model explains the data somewhat better for African-American children than for white children. Within both groups, some of the same problems of the two-factor model found in the single-sample analyses described earlier (section 7.7) are apparent in these analyses, too (e.g., relatively low factor loadings of some indicators).

The two-factor model was analyzed again but with cross-group equality constraints on the factor loadings not already fixed to 1.0 (six altogether: two on the sequential factor; four on the simultaneous factor). Results of this analysis are also summarized in Table 7.6. The $\chi^2(44)$ statistic for the model with equality-constrained factor loadings is 63.83. The change in the overall chi-square ($\chi^2_{\text{difference}}(6) = 6.47$) is not statistically significant. This result implies that the factor loadings as a set do not differ significantly across the African-American and white samples. In addition, none of the modification indexes for the constrained factor loadings is significant, which means that no individual loadings differ significantly across the groups. Overall, these results suggest that the tasks of the K-ABC measure two factors in comparable ways for African-American and white children.

A final point before concluding this section. Suppose that the fit of an unconstrained CFA model across independent samples is reasonable but the imposition of equality constraints on the factor loadings notably worsens its fit. Also suppose that several of the individual factor loadings differ substantially by group. This pattern suggests that although the set of indicators reflects the same number of factors in each group, the measurement properties of individual indicators are group specific. It is possible to weight invariant indicators differential-ly by group in the derivation of summary scores (e.g., see Reise et al., 1993). It is only sensible to do so, however, if the unconstrained CFA model is viable for each sample. If not, then the indicators may not measure the same factors in each group. Other recent examples of multiple group CFAs include those of Keith et al. (1995), who analyzed the factor structure of the K-ABC by race, and Windle (1992), who evaluated a model of temperament by gender. Additional examples can be found in Loehlin (1992, pp. 120–130). Other contributions by Cunningham (1991) and Horn (1991) are more general in that they concern various operational definitions of measurement invariance.

7.9   Specialized Types of CFA Models

Models for Multitrait–Multimethod Data

This example concerns the application of CFA to analyze data from a multitrait–multimethod study, the logic of which was first articulated by Campbell and Fiske (1959). Briefly described, the two main purposes of such a study are to (1) evaluate the convergent and discriminant validity of a set of tests that vary in their measurement method, and (2) derive separate estimates of the effect of traits versus measurement methods on the observed scores. Although "method" has often been understood as the *format* of the test (self-report, unobtrusive, projective, etc.), the connotation can also include the source of the scores, such as informants, the subject of this example.

The data summarized in Table 7.7 concern symptom ratings completed by parents, teachers, and clinicians about 373 children referred to a psychiatric facility (Kline, Lachar, & Gdowski, 1992). Each informant completed one questionnaire about aggressive behavior, another about depression, and a third about cognitive deficits. Information about convergent validity—here, the assessment of supposedly the same trait but by different informants—is provided by the correlations reported in boldface in Table 7.7. For this sample, the assessment of aggression seems to show greater convergent validity than for the measurement of the other two traits. The underlined values in the table are discriminant validity coefficients because they represent correlations between measures of different traits by different informants. These values should be low, and most are for these data. The remaining correlations are between measures of different traits but completed by the same informant. Thus, they say something about *common method variance,* here whether there is a systematic effect of type of informant. Expressed another way: does the fact that, say, a

TABLE 7.7. Analysis of Multitrait–Multimethod Data
from Clinic-Referred Children

Correlations and standard deviations (Kline et al., 1992; $N = 373$
referred children and adolescents)

Variable	Parent			Teacher			Clinician		
	1	2	3	4	5	6	7	8	9
Parent									
1. Aggression	—								
2. Depression	.29	—							
3. Cognitive	.10	.03	—						
Teacher									
4. Aggression	**.50**	.04	.10	—					
5. Depression	.10	**.19**	.08	.03	—				
6. Cognitive	.07	.16	**.33**	.17	.05	—			
Clinician									
7. Aggression	**.48**	.01	.15	**.56**	.20	.05	—		
8. Depression	.02	**.34**	.08	.20	**.36**	.16	.06	—	
9. Cognitive	.08	.11	.33	.15	.06	**.27**	.18	.27	—
SD	17.33	18.21	20.22	7.05	2.21	3.09	3.44	2.23	1.92

Goodness of fit summary

Model	χ^2	df	χ^2/df	GFI	CFI	NNFI	SRMR
Correlated uniqueness	30.34	15	2.02	.98	.98	.94	.003

Note. Correlations in boldface indicate convergent validity, and underlined values
are discriminant validity coefficients. The other correlations indicate common method
effects. GFI, Jöreskog–Sörbom Goodness of Fit Index; CFI, Bentler Comparative Fit Index; NNFI, Bentler–Bonett Non-Normed Fit Index; SRMR, Standardized Root Mean
Squared Residual.

parent rather than a teacher completes a questionnaire itself systematically affect the scores apart from the adjustment domain being rat-
ed? The common method correlations in Table 7.7 are about the
same magnitude (low to moderate) for each type of informant, which
suggests the absence of strong informant-specific effects.

CFA offers a more systematic way to analyze multitrait–
multimethod data than simple inspection of correlations. When CFA
was first applied to this problem (in the 1970s), researchers typically
specified models like the one presented in Figure 7.7, which Marsh
and Grayson (1995) called a *correlated trait, correlated method* (CTCM)
model. Such models have separate trait and method factors that are

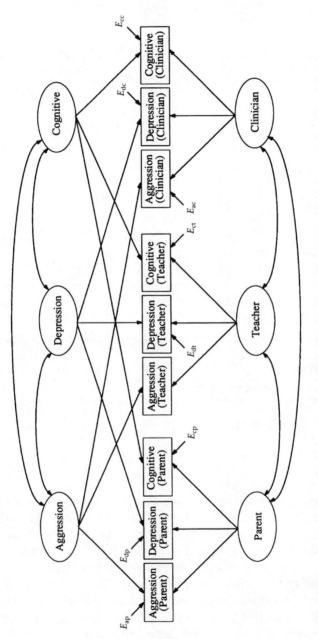

FIGURE 7.7. A correlated trait, correlated method (CTCM) model of symptom ratings of referred children.

assumed to covary, but method factors are assumed to be independent of trait factors. According to the rationale of this model, high loadings on the trait factors would suggest convergent validity, high loadings on the method factors would indicate common method variance, and moderate correlations among the trait factors would suggest discriminant validity. Although some authors have reported successful analyses of CTCM models (e.g., Bollen, 1989, pp. 190–195), others have found that analyses of such models yield improper or unstable solutions (e.g., Kenny & Kashy, 1992; Wothke, 1996). Also, Marsh and Bailey (1991) found in computer simulation studies that illogical estimates were derived about three-quarters of the time for CTCM models. Kenny and Kashy (1992) noted part of the problem: CTCM models are not identified if the loadings on the trait or method factors are equal. If the loadings are different but similar in value, then CTCM models may be empirically underidentified.

Several simpler alternative models for multitrait–multimethod data have been proposed, including ones with multiple but uncorrelated method factors, a single-method factor specified to affect all the indicators, and a model like the one presented in Figure 7.8, which Marsh and Grayson (1995) and others call a *correlated uniqueness model*. This model features measurement error correlations among the scales from the same informant. (Compare Figure 7.8 to model (a) of Figure 7.2.) In this representation, method effects are assumed to be a property of each indicator, and high correlations among their residuals are taken as evidence of a common method effect for each pair of indicators.

The correlated uniqueness model of Figure 7.8 was estimated with the data summarized in Table 7.7. The variances of the three trait factors were fixed to 1.0, which allows all factor loadings to be tested for significance. Values of fit indexes are reported in the table, and they indicate that the overall fit of the model is acceptable. For clarity's sake, only the standardized solution is presented in the figure. Estimates of measurement errors are expressed as proportions of unexplained variance. Note that the results of the significance tests reported in the figure are from the unstandardized solution and may not apply to the standardized estimates. Estimates of the correlations among the three trait factors are moderate in size (.23–.29), which indicates discriminant validity. Consistent with impressions based on inspection of the correlations (Table 7.7), the indicators of aggression show better convergent validity, a fairly typical finding in clinical research (e.g., Achenbach, McConaughy, & Howell, 1987). The measurement error correlations for measures of aggression and depression are significant for all informants, so any common method effects on the rating of these characteristics are not specific to parents,

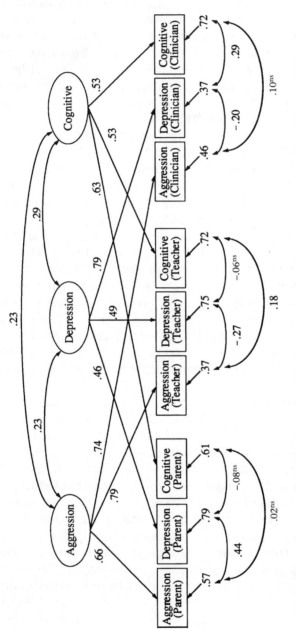

FIGURE 7.8. A correlated uniqueness model for multi-informant ratings of referred children and the standardized solution. The *unstandardized* versions of all of the above standardized estimates are significant at the .01 level except for those designated "ns," which means not significant.

teachers, or clinicians. Other patterns of significant measurement error correlations are less consistent across informant types. Overall, symptom ratings from all three sources may be subject to the about the same (small-to-moderate) amounts of common method variance.

Some very helpful works about the application of CFA to multitrait–multimethod data include those by Marsh and Grayson (1995) and Kenny and Kashy (1992); a recent chapter by Wothke (1996) is more technical but provides information about statistical techniques that are alternatives to CFA. Byrne (1994) devotes a chapter to an extended example of the analysis of many of the types of models for multitrait–multimethod data mentioned in this section with EQS. Other recent examples of the application of CFA to multitrait–multimethod data include studies by Marsh and Byrne (1993) and Byrne and Goffin (1993).

CFA Models with Higher-Order Factors

The Stanford–Binet Intelligence Scale (4th ed.—SB4; Thorndike, Hagen, & Sattler, 1986a, 1986b) is an individually administered cognitive ability battery for children and young adults. The test is based on a hierarchical model of intelligence in which general ability (g) is assumed to affect more specific ability factors (verbal, memory, etc.), which in turn are measured by the SB4's subtests. In this conceptual view of ability, g is a higher-order, more abstract construct that is not directly measured. In contrast, more specific ability areas are viewed as lower-order factors that are presumed to be caused by g.

It is possible to represent hypotheses about hierarchical relations between constructs in CFA models through the specification of higher-order factors that have direct effects on lower-order ones. A hierarchical CFA model of the SB4 for 11-year-old children is presented in Figure 7.9. SB4 subtests for children this age are represented as indicators of three *first-order factors* that correspond to a scoring system devised by Sattler (1988). Each of first-order factors have direct effects on them from a *second-order factor, g,* which represents a general ability construct that has no indicators. Unlike a standard CFA model in which associations between the factors are unanalyzed ($\leftrightarrow$), the first-order factors in Figure 7.9 are presumed to have a common cause (e.g., $g \rightarrow$ Verbal) that accounts for their intercorrelations. Accordingly, the first-order factors of this model have disturbances because they are endogenous. The second-order factor, g, however, is exogenous.

In order for a CFA model with a second-order factor to be identi-

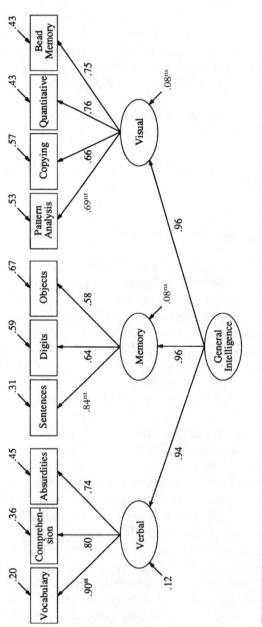

FIGURE 7.9. A second-order CFA model of the Stanford–Binet and the standardized solution. The *unstandardized* versions of the above estimates are all significant at the .01 level except for those designated "ns," which means not significant, and "nt," which means not tested. The standardized values for the disturbances of the first-order factors and for the measurement errors of the indicators are proportions of unexplained variance.

fied, there must be at least three first-order factors. Otherwise, the direct effects of the second-order factor on the first-order factors or the disturbances may be underidentified. Also, each first-order factor should have at least two indicators. The model in Figure 7.9 satisfies both of these requirements. This model was analyzed using the data summarized in Table 7.8, which are from the 11-year-old group of the SB4's normative sample ($N = 237$). To set scales for the first-order factors (verbal, memory, visual), one loading on each was fixed to 1.0. The tactic cannot be used with the second-order factor because it has

TABLE 7.8. Evaluation of a Second-Order CFA Model of the Stanford–Binet Intelligence Scale (4th ed.)

Correlations, means, and standard deviations (Thorndike et al., 1986a, 1986b; $N = 237$ 11-year-olds, nationally representative sample)

	Verbal			Visual			Memory			
Variable	1	2	3	4	5	6	7	8	9	10
Verbal										
1. Vocabulary	—									
2. Comprehension	.73	—								
3. Absurdities	.65	.59	—							
Visual										
4. Pattern Analysis	.52	.48	.54	—						
5. Copying	.48	.40	.51	.51	—					
6. Quantitative	.64	.59	.49	.49	.49	—				
7. Bead Memory	.60	.50	.58	.56	.49	.55	—			
Memory										
8. Sentence Memory	.72	.61	.55	.47	.49	.60	.57	—		
9. Digit Memory	.44	.40	.37	.43	.45	.49	.43	.55	—	
10. Object Memory	.47	.37	.42	.37	.42	.37	.43	.45	.42	—
M	27.40	28.20	25.50	32.50	23.40	22.40	25.80	25.20	12.20	7.00
SD	4.49	5.13	4.02	7.71	4.05	4.90	4.55	4.54	3.50	2.15

Goodness of fit summary

Model	χ^2	df	χ^2/df	GFI	AGFI	NFI	NNFI	SRMR
Second-order CFA	68.08**	32	2.13	.94	.90	.95	.96	.003

Note. GFI, Jöreskog–Sörbom Goodness of Fit Index; AGFI, Adjusted GFI; NFI, Bentler–Bonett Normed Fit Index; NNFI, Non-NFI; SRMR, Standardized Root Mean Squared Residual.
**$p < .01$.

no indicators. Instead, its variance was fixed to 1.0 to set its metric. Reported in Table 7.8 are values of various fit indexes, and they indicate that the overall fit of the hierarchical CFA model is satisfactory. Inspection of the standardized solution (presented in Figure 7.9) suggests reasonable overall convergent validity, especially for the first-order verbal factor. Also, the direct effects of the g factor on the lower-order factors are very strong, which results in relatively small proportions of unexplained variance for the first-order factors.

Other recent examples of the analysis of second-order factor models include the work of Windle (1992), who studied a self-report measure of temperament for adolescents; that of Byrne (1994, chap. 5), who evaluated the factor structure of a depression scale; and that of Bollen (1989, pp. 313–318), who analyzed a model of self-concept with a second-order CFA.

7.10   Other Issues

Estimated Factor Scores

When raw data are analyzed, it is possible to calculate estimated scores on the latent variables for each case. Because the latent variables are not measured directly but instead through their indicators, such scores are only estimates of subjects' relative standings on the factor. There is more than one way to compute estimated factor scores, however, and although scores derived using different methods tend to be highly correlated, they may not all yield identical rank orderings of the cases. For example, given estimated correlations between a factor and its indicators, multiple regression can be used to derive estimated factor scores that are weighted linear combinations of the indicators and the factor. The weights derived by multiple regression are those that lead to the closest correspondence between the underlying factor(s) and the estimated factor scores given estimates of correlations among the indicators and the factor(s). However, such weights are subject to capitalization on chance variation within a particular sample. An alternative to empirically derived weights is simply to add subjects' scores across the indicators, which weights each variable equally. The application of equal weights is called *unit weighting*. This method has the advantage of calculational simplicity and less susceptibility to sample-specific variation, but unit weights may not be the optimal ones within a particular sample. Given that there is no single way to derive estimated factor scores, Bollen's (1989) perspective on this matter is pertinent: researchers should probably refrain from making too fine a comparison on estimated factor scores. For more information about estimated factor scores, see Bollen (1989, pp. 305–306), Kenny (1979, pp. 131–131), Loehlin (1992, pp. 173–175), and Nunnally and Bernstein (1994, pp. 507–512).

Categorical or Ordinal Indicators (Items vs. Scales)

In most published reports of the results of CFAs, the observed variables are scales that yield interval-level, continuous scores (e.g., total scores). There are also examples in the literature of CFAs in which some or all of the indicators are items instead of scales (e.g., Byrne, 1994; Windle, 1992). Items tend to be either dichotomous (e.g., true/false, agree/disagree) or based on a Likert-type scale with a small number of ranked categories (e.g., always, sometimes, seldom, never). Although it is usually assumed in such studies that dichotomous or ordinal observed variables are indicators of continuous underlying factors, there are three problems when noncontinuous variables are analyzed with CFA. (The same problems arise in the analysis of hybrid models with noncontinuous indicators.) First, correlations between dichotomous or ordinal observed variables tend to be truncated relative to correlations between the underlying continuous latent variables (e.g., Bollen & Barb, 1981). Thus, parameter estimates derived with observed correlations or covariances of noncontinuous indicators may not accurately reflect the corresponding values for latent variables. Second, scores on categorical or ordinal indicators are not normally distributed, which may violate the distributional assumptions of methods like maximum likelihood. Failure to use estimation methods that do not assume normality or corrected test statistics with maximum likelihood may result in the rejection of correct models in favor of those with more factors. That is, when there is only a single factor in the population but the indicators are dichotomous or ordinal, one-factor models in CFAs of sample data tend to rejected more often than they should (e.g., Bernstein & Teng, 1989). Third, subjects' responses to individual items tend not to be very reliable. In contrast, the reliabilities of scales, which are usually composed of many items, are typically much higher.

Given these potential complications, what should one do if some of the indicators are not continuous? One option suggested by Bernstein and Teng (1989) is to construct miniscales that are total scores across groups of items. These "miniscales" or "parcels" are specified as the indicators instead of the original, noncontinuous items. Another option is to retain the dichotmous or ordinal indicators but use special statistical procedures to correct the observed covariances before they are analyzed in a CFA (e.g., Bollen, 1989, pp. 433–446). These corrective procedures typically yield estimated *polychoric, tetrachoric,* or *polyserial* correlations, which are correlations between the continuous variables that underlie two indicators that are both ordinal (polychoric), both dichotomous (tetrachoric), or one continuous and the other ordinal (polyserial). Some model-fitting programs such as LISCOMP (Muthén, 1987) and EQS can analyze dichotomous or ordinal indicators. With LISREL, one uses PRELIS2 (Jöreskog & Sörbom, 1996b) to prepare a corrected covariance matrix for noncontinuous variables. PRELIS2 can be used with other model-fitting programs, too.

An alternative to CFA for item-level analyses is the generation of *item-characteristic curves* (ICC) according to *item-response theory* (IRT). Briefly described, IRT yields estimates about characteristics of individual items such as their precision of measurement of a latent variable for subjects of different ability levels or about the effects of guessing on multiple-choice items. IRT also assumes that the relations between items and factors as represented by ICCs are curvilinear. For example, the probability of correctly answering a difficult item may be slight for low-ability subjects but increases geometrically at higher levels of ability. IRT is also oriented toward the development of "tailored tests," subsets of items that may optimally assess a particular person. Items from tailored tests are typically selected by a computer, and their order of presentation depends upon the subject's pattern of responses. For instance, if the subject fails initial items, then easier ones are presented. Testing stops when more difficult items are consistently failed. See Reise et al. (1993) for a comparison of CFA and IRT for item-level analyses. Nunnally and Bernstein (1994, pp. 393–415) also present an introduction to IRT.

7.11 Summary

A standard CFA model is one in which all factors are first-order ones that are assumed to covary, the observed variables are represented as effect indicators each specified to load on a single factor, and the measurement error terms are independent. The latter two characteristics describe unidimensional measurement. The specification of multidimensional measurement may be appropriate when an indicator is believed to assess more than one construct or when the unique variances of some indicators are expected to overlap.

There are two basic requirements for the identification of standard CFA models. One is the same as for any structural equation model: there should be at least as many observations as free parameters. The other is that every latent variable has a scale. There are two ways to scale a factor, including fixing the variances of each factor to 1.0, which standardizes the factor, or fixing the loading of one indicator per factor to 1.0, which gives the factor the same scale as the indicator. In a single-sample analysis, either method may be acceptable. In multiple group CFAs, however, the second method to scale the factors is preferred. If a standard CFA model with a single factor meets the two basic requirements and has at least three indicators, then it is identified. Multifactor standard CFA models that satisfy the basic requirements and have at least two indicators per factor are also identified. The specification that indicators load on more than one factor or that measurement errors terms are correlated implies that there may be no easily evaluated sufficient condition that indicates whether the model is identified.

Parameters of CFA models include the variances and covariances (i.e., unanalyzed associations) of the factors and of the measurement errors and the loadings of the indicators on the factors. Maximum likelihood (ML) estimation is the most frequently used method for CFA. In the unstandardized solution, factor loadings are interpreted as unstandardized regression coefficients. Factor loadings fixed to 1.0 to scale latent variables remain so in the unstandardized solution and not are tested for significance. In the standardized solution, factor loadings are interpreted as beta weights. Parameter estimates generated by ML are fairly robust against violation of the assumption of multivariate normality, but the results of significance tests tend to result in rejection of the null hypothesis too often because estimates of standard errors tend to be too small. Other kinds of estimation problems such as improper solutions or nonconvergence of iterative estimation are more likely with small samples, especially when some factors in the model have only two indicators.

Many types of hypotheses can be tested with standard CFA models. For example, evaluation of a single-factor model provides a test of whether a set of observed variables measures more than one construct. The evaluation of a multifactor CFA model provides a test of convergent and discriminant validity. Specifically, high loadings of sets of indicators on their common factor provides evidence for the former, and factor correlations that are no more than moderate in magnitude are evidence for the latter. More specialized CFA models such as ones for multitrait–multimethod data or hierarchical models with higher-order factors extend the range of hypotheses about measurement that can be evaluated with CFA.

It is quite common in CFA (as in other SEM methods) that an initial model does not fit the data very well. When this occurs, the model can be respecified and evaluated again. There are two broad classes of changes that can be made to CFA models. The first involves the indicators (e.g., switch loadings to another factor; allow an indicator to load on an additional factor) and the second concerns the latent variables (e.g., change the number of factors). Because there may be numerous potential changes that could be made to a CFA model, it is crucial that respecification be guided as much as possible by theoretical rather than solely empirical criteria (e.g., level of significance). Remember that empirical indexes such as modification indexes are susceptible to capitalization on chance and can only estimate the effects of freeing a parameter fixed to zero in a particular model. They cannot estimate the effect of more fundamental respecifications such as an increase (or decrease) in the number of factors.

When a researcher has selected a final CFA model, then equivalent versions that yield the same predicted correlations/covariances should be considered. Equivalent versions of single-factor CFA models can be generated with the reversed indicator rule, which means that one of the observed variables is specified as a cause indicator rather than as an effect indicator. This is accomplished by reversing the direct effect between the factor and the indicator, which also switches the roles of the two as exogenous versus endogenous. For multifactor models, it may be possible to substitute a second-order factor or multidimensional measurement for a factor correlation or to replace an entire factor with correlations among the measurement errors of its indicators. Although not all equivalent models will provide meaningful alternative accounts of the data, some may, and the researcher should explain why his or her original CFA model is preferred.

The next chapter is about hybrid structural equation models. Like CFA models, hybrid models allow the evaluation of hypotheses about measurement. Unlike CFA models, they also permit the specification and estimation of presumed causal effects among the factors. In this way, hybrid models represent the pinnacle in the SEM family for the analysis of covariances.

7.12   Recommended Readings

Works about Measurement Models

Recommended within the works listed below are Bollen (1989, chaps. 6 & 7), Kenny (1979, chaps. 7 & 8), Loehlin (1992, chaps. 5–7), Mueller (1996, chap. 2), and Nunnally and Bernstein (1994, chap. 13).

Bollen, K. A. (1989). *Structural equations with latent variables.* New York: John Wiley.

Kenny, D. A. (1979). *Correlation and causality.* New York: Wiley.

Loehlin, J. C. (1992). *Latent variable models* (2nd ed.). Hillsdale, NJ: Lawrence Erlbaum.

Mueller, R. O. (1996). *Basic principles of structural equation modeling.* New York: Springer-Verlag.

Nunnally, J. C., & Bernstein, I. H. (1994). *Psychometric theory* (3rd ed.). New York: McGraw-Hill.

Appendix 7.A   Coefficient of Determination

The formula for Jöreskog and Sörbom's (1981) coefficient of determination is presented below:

$$\text{Coefficient of determination} = 1 - \frac{|E_X|}{|S_X|},\qquad(7.3)$$

where $|E_X|$ and $|S_X|$ are the determinants of the matrices of, respectively, the unstandardized variances and covariances of the error terms and the observed variables. A determinant is essentially a numerical summary of the amount of unique information in a set of variables, and the ratio of $|E_X|$ over $|S_X|$ reflects unexplained variance across all the indicators. Determinants are awkward to calculate by hand (see Stevens, 1992, chap. 2, for a method by which to do so), but there is another way: submit each matrix to a model-fitting program or to a factor analysis program that automatically calculates determinants. The model-fitting program used to analyze the two-factor model of Figure 7.4 derived the determinant of the observed variance–covariance matrix, which equals a very large number (.30659 × 10⁷). In a second run with the program, the diagonal matrix of the unstandardized measurement error variances of the eight indicators of the model was submitted as the input data, as shown here (**A.I**).

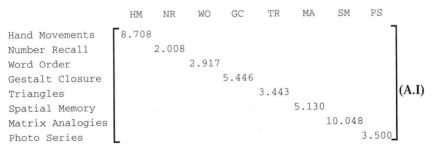

All of the off-diagonal entries of this matrix are zero, which reflects the specification of independent measurement errors. The determinant of the matrix of unstandardized measurement error variances is also a large number, $.17254 \times 10^7$. The ratio of this determinant over that of the observed covariance matrix is .06, so the coefficient of determination is 1 minus this ratio, or $(1 - .06) = .94$. Note that this value is larger than any of the R^2s or the individual indicators, which range from .25 to .65 (Table 7.2). Thus, it is difficult to recommend a value of the coefficient of determination that indicates "good" model fit. It's probably best to use the coefficient of determination as a descriptive statistic rather than as an index with more standardized values like the Jöreskog–Sörbom Goodness of Fit Index (GFI) or the Bentler Comparative Fit Index (CFI).

Appendix 7.B   Recommendations for Starting Values for CFA Models

These recommendations assume that scales for latent factors have been established by fixing the loadings of one of their indicators to 1.0 (i.e., the factors are unstandardized). Initial estimates of factor variances should not exceed the observed values of their fixed-loading indicators; a value of 90% of the observed variance seems reasonable. Starting values for factor covariances follow from the initial estimates of their variances, that is, the product of each factor's respective standard deviations (i.e., the square roots of the starting values of the variances) and the expected correlation between them (.30, .50, etc.). If the indicators of a construct have variances similar to that of the one with the loading fixed to equal 1.0, then initial estimates of their factor loadings can also be 1.0. If the indicator with the fixed loading is, say, one-tenth as variable as another indicator of the same factor, then the initial estimate of the other indicator's factor loading could be 10.0. Remember to indicate the appropriate sign (i.e., positive, negative) of these initial estimates. Conservative starting values of error terms variances would be .90 times the observed variance of each indicator, which assumes that only 10% of the variance will be explained by the factors. Keep in mind this suggestion by Bentler (1995): it is probably better to overestimate the variances of exogenous variables (i.e., the factors and the measurement errors) than to underestimate them. This advice is also appropriate for Heywood cases of the type when the estimate of a measurement error term is negative: in the reanalysis of the model, try a starting value that is greater than in the previous run.

Application of these guidelines to the two-factor model of the K-ABC presented in Figure 7.4 and the data summarized in Table 7.2 is now demonstrated (see the table below). Here, the loadings of the Hand

Movements task ($SD = 3.4$) and of the Gestalt Closure task ($SD = 2.7$) on their respective factors (sequential, simultaneous) are fixed to 1.0. Because the magnitudes of the variances of all the indicators are similar, initial estimates of the other factor loadings are 1.0. Initial estimates of the variances of the sequential and simultaneous factors are, respectively, $.90(3.4^2) = 10.4$ and $.90(2.7^2) = 6.6$; the starting value for their covariance, assuming a correlation of .50 between them, is $.50(3.2)(2.6) = 4.2$. Starting values for the error terms are all 90% of the corresponding observed variances. For example, the variance of the Triangles task is 2.7^2; 90% of this value is 6.6. All of the starting values for this problem and final estimates from the unstandardized solution are summarized in the accompanying table.

	Factor or error variances		Loadings	
Factor or task	Starting value	Final estimate	Starting value	Final estimate
Sequential	10.4	2.85	—	—
Simultaneous	6.6	1.84	—	—
(Factor covariance)	4.2	1.28	—	—
Hand Movements	10.4	8.71	1.0 (fixed)	1.0
Number Recall	5.2	2.01	1.0	1.15
Word Order	7.6	2.92	1.0	1.39
Gestalt Closure	6.6	5.45	1.0 (fixed)	1.0
Triangles	6.6	3.44	1.0	1.45
Spatial Memory	7.1	5.13	1.0	1.21
Matrix Analogies	15.9	10.05	1.0	2.03
Photo Series	8.1	3.50	1.0	1.73

CHAPTER EIGHT

Hybrid Models with Structural and Measurement Components

It is enormously easier to present in an appealing way the wisdom distilled from centuries of patient and collective interrogation of Nature than to detail the messy distillation apparatus. The method of science, as stodgy and grumpy as it may seem, is far more important than the findings of science.
— CARL SAGAN (1996, p. 22)

8.1 Foreword

Hybrid structural equation models can be viewed as syntheses of path and measurement models. They are the most general of all the types considered up to this point. As in path analysis, the specification of a hybrid model allows tests of hypotheses about direct and indirect causal effects. Unlike path models, though, these effects can involve latent variables because a hybrid model also incorporates a measurement model that represents observed variables as indicators of underlying constructs, just as in confirmatory factor analysis (CFA). The capability to test hypotheses both about structural and measurement relations with a single model affords much flexibility. Discussed in this chapter are the characteristics of hybrid models, requirements for their identification, and strategies for their estimation. Two examples of the analysis of hybrid models are also presented. Many of the advanced SEM techniques described in Chapter 10 extend the basic rationale of hybrid models to other kinds of analyses, including the estimation of nonlinear (curvilinear and interaction) effects, means of latent variables, and models for incomplete data. With command of the concepts outlined below, readers will be better prepared for the next part of their journey.

8.2 Characteristics of Hybrid Models

The models presented in Figure 8.1 illustrate the basic features of hybrid models. Model (a) is a structural model with observed variables—a path model—that features the use of a single measure of each construct. The observed exogenous variable X_1 of this model is assumed to be measured without error, an assumption usually violated in practice. The same assumption is not required for the observed endogenous variables of this model, but measurement error in Y_1 or Y_3 is manifested in their disturbances. Model (b) in Figure 8.1 is a hy-

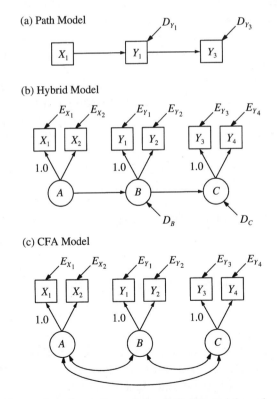

FIGURE 8.1. Examples of a path model, a hybrid model, and a CFA model.

brid model with both structural and measurement components. Its measurement model has the same three observed variables represented in the path model, X_1, Y_1, and Y_3. Unlike the path model, each of these three observed variables is specified as one of a pair of indicators of underlying factors. Consequently, all of the observed variables in the hybrid model have measurement error terms. This hybrid model also has a structural component that depicts the same basic pattern of causal effects as the path model does but with latent variables instead of observed variables. The latent endogenous variables of this hybrid model each has a disturbance. Unlike the path model, the disturbances of the hybrid model reflect only omitted causes and not measurement error. Model (c) in Figure 8.1 is a standard CFA measurement model. It features the same multi-indicator approach to measurement as represented in the hybrid model, but CFA models assume that all associations among the factors are unanalyzed.

Model (b) of Figure 8.1 could be described as "fully latent" because every variable in its structural model is a latent variable. Although this characteristic is desirable because it implies multi-indicator measurement, it is also possible to represent in hybrid models observed variables that are the sole measure of a construct. Such hybrid models could be called "partially latent" because at least one variable in their structural model is observed rather than latent. Two examples of partially latent hybrid models are presented in Figure 8.2. The observed variable X_1 in model (a) is represented as the only measure of an exogenous construct. Model (b) features a single observed measure of an endogenous mediator construct. Models (a) and (b) of Figure 8.2 both have the same limitations as those of path models concerning their single indicators. For instance, exogenous variable X_1 in model (a) is assumed to be measured without error. Likewise, the disturbance of Y_2 in model (b) reflects measurement error and omitted causes. How to address these limitations of partially latent hybrid models is dealt with later. The discussion that follows assumes a fully latent hybrid model.

8.3   Analysis of Hybrid Models

Overview

If one understands the fundamentals of path analysis and CFA, then there is little new to learn about hybrid models because their analysis can be decomposed into two parts. The specification of the structural portion of a hybrid model follows the same basic rationale as in path

(a) Single Indicator of an Exogenous Variable

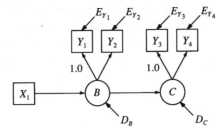

(b) Single Indicator of an Endogenous Variable

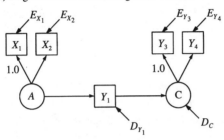

FIGURE 8.2. Two examples of hybrid models with single indicators.

analysis (section 5.3). Likewise, the specification of the measurement component of a hybrid model requires consideration of basically the same issues as in CFA (section 7.4). Also, the evaluation of whether a hybrid model is identified and its subsequent estimation should both be conducted separately for each submodel, structural and measurement. Requirements for identification and strategies for estimation are considered below, but there is a theme common to both issues: a valid measurement model is needed before the structural component of a hybrid model can be evaluated.

Requirements for Identification

Any hybrid model must satisfy the same two necessary requirements for identification that apply to CFA measurement models: The number of observations ($v(v + 1)/2$, where v is the number of observed variables), must equal or exceed the number of free parameters; and each latent variable must have a scale (section 7.5). Briefly summarized, latent exogenous variables can be scaled either through standardization by fixing their variances to 1.0 or by assigning them the same scale as one of their indicators by fixing one loading per factor to 1.0. Most model-fitting programs allow only the second method just mentioned for scaling latent endogenous variables. Recall also that standardizing factors may be inappropriate in multiple group analyses.

The parameters of hybrid models are counted according to the following rule:

The total number of (1) variances and covariances (i.e., unanalyzed associations) of the exogenous latent factors, measurement errors, and disturbances; (2) direct effects on the indicators from the factors (i.e., factor loadings); and (3) direct effects on latent endogenous factors from other factors (i.e, path coefficients) equal the number of parameters.

It is generally assumed for hybrid models that the exogenous factors are uncorrelated with the disturbances of the endogenous factors and that the factors (exogenous or endogenous) and the measurement errors are independent. These assumptions parallel similar ones for path models and CFA measurement models. It is also typically assumed that the residual path coefficients for the disturbances and the measurement errors are all fixed to 1.0 so that only their variances need to be estimated (section 7.5).

Let's apply the above rule for counting parameters to the fully latent hybrid model (b) of Figure 8.1. With 6 observed variables, there are $6(7)/2 = 21$ observations. A total of nine variances must be estimated for this model, including that of the exogenous factor A, the measurement error terms of the indicators (six in total), and the disturbances of the latent endogenous factors, B and C. There are no covariances to be estimated because this model has no unanalyzed associations. Each of the three factors of this model is assigned the same scale as one of its indicators via the loadings that are fixed to 1.0 (e.g., $A \to X_1$). These three fixed factor loadings are not free parameters, but the remaining three factor loadings are (e.g., $A \to X_2$). The other parameters include the two direct effects on the latent endogenous factors, $A \to B$ and $B \to C$. The total number of parameters for this model is 14 (9 variances, 0 covariances, 3 factor loadings, 2 path coefficients), which is 7 less than the number of observations, 21.

As with CFA measurement models, meeting the necessary requirements that every factor is scaled and that the number of free parameters is not greater than the number of observations does not guarantee identification. An additional requirement for identification reflects the view that the analysis of a hybrid model is essentially a path analysis conducted with estimated covariances among the latent variables. Thus, it must be possible to derive unique estimates of the factor covariances before more specific causal effects can be estimated. Stated another way: in order for the structural portion of a hybrid model to be identified, its measurement model must be identified. Bollen (1989) described this requirement for identification as the *two-step rule,* and the steps to evaluate whether a hybrid model meets it are outlined below:

1. Respecify the hybrid model as a CFA measurement model with all possible unanalyzed associations among the factors. Evaluate this CFA measurement model against the requirements for identification outlined in Chapter 7 (section 7.5; Table 7.1).
2. Now examine only the structural portion of the hybrid model. View this structural model as a path model. If it is recursive, then the structural model is identified. If it is nonrecursive, then evaluate the structural model against the requirements for identification (e.g., the order and rank conditions) reviewed in Chapter 6 (section 6.2; Table 6.1).

If both the measurement and structural portions of a hybrid model are identified, then the whole model is identified. The two-step rule is thus a sufficient condition: hybrid models that meet both parts of it are in fact identified. Evaluation of the two-step rule is demonstrated for the hybrid model (a) presented at the top of Figure 8.3. (This hybrid model is identical to model (b) of Figure 8.1.) We demonstrated earlier that every latent variable of this model has a scale and that there are more observations (21) than parameters (14), but these features are not sufficient to identify the model. The respecification of this hybrid model as a CFA measurement model is presented as model (b) in the middle of the Figure 8.3. This CFA model is a standard measurement model because each indicator loads on a single factor and the measurement errors are independent. This model also meets the sufficient requirement for standard multifactor CFA models that every latent variable must have at least two indicators (section 7.5). Therefore, this CFA measurement model is identified, which satisfies the first part of the two-step rule.

The structural portion of the hybrid model is presented as model (c) at the bottom of Figure 8.3. Because this structural model is recursive, it too is identified. Because the hybrid model at the top of Figure 8.3 meets both necessary conditions for identification (i.e., scales for latent variables, and the number of parameters ≤ the number of ob-

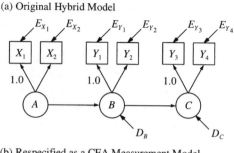

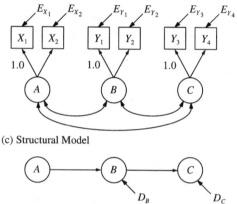

(c) Structural Model

FIGURE 8.3. Evaluation of the two-step rule for identification.

servations) and satisfies the sufficient two-step rule, it is identified (specifically, overidentified).

Two important points about the two-step rule for identification for hybrid models. First, the estimation of hybrid models that are identified can still be foiled by empirical underidentification. Suppose that the estimated correlation between any pair of factors in the CFA measurement model of Figure 8.3 is close to zero. The consequence is that one of the factors may be underidentified because it has only two indicators and is essentially independent of the other two factors. Single-factor models with only two indicators are not identified without constraints (section 7.5). Second, it is not always possible to determine the identification status of every hybrid model using the two-step rule. For example, suppose that the structural portion of a hybrid model is nonrecursive. The rank condition is a sufficient requirement for the identification of nonrecursive structural models but only if the model has all pairwise disturbance correlations or if it is block recursive (sections 6.3 and 6.4). If not, the rank condition is too strict because a nonrecursive structural model could fail it and still be identified. Likewise, if either the measurement or structural portions of a hybrid model are "none of the above" such that their identification cannot be clearly established, then the two-step rule may be too strict. Partially latent hybrid models with single indicators that are actually identified may also fail the two-step rule, which is demonstrated later. If the researcher is uncertain about whether a hybrid model is identified, then the tactics suggested in Chapter 6 can be tried. Very briefly reviewed, these include estimating the model with a model-fitting program using made-up data before the actual data are collected and using empirical checks for the uniqueness of the solution in the actual analysis (section 6.6). Readers can find more information about the identification of hybrid structural equation models in Bollen (1989, pp. 326–333) and Kenny (1979, chap. 9).

Two-Step Modeling

To introduce Anderson and Gerbing's (1988) rationale of *two-step modeling*, let's consider the following scenario: A researcher has specified a hybrid model that is identified. The data are collected and the researcher uses one-step modeling to estimate the model, which means that the measurement and structural components of the hybrid model are analyzed simultaneously in a single analysis. The results indicate that the overall fit of the hybrid model is poor. Now, where is the problem? Is the measurement portion of the hybrid model misspecified?— the structural model?—or both? With one-step modeling, it is difficult to precisely localize the source of poor model fit.

Two-step modeling parallels the two-step rule for identification. In two-step modeling, a hybrid model is first respecified as a CFA measurement model. The CFA model is then analyzed in order to determine whether it fits the data. If the fit of this CFA model is poor, then not only are the researcher's hypotheses about measurement most likely wrong, but the fit of the original hybrid model to the data may be even worse if its structural model is overidentified. For example, look again at Figure 8.3. Suppose that the fit of the three-factor CFA measurement model (b) in the middle of the figure is poor. Note that this CFA model has three paths among the factors that represent all possible pairwise unanalyzed associations ($A \leftrightarrow B, A \leftrightarrow C, B \leftrightarrow C$). In contrast, the structural portion of the hybrid model (a) in Figure 8.3 has only two paths among the latent variables ($A \rightarrow B \rightarrow C$). If the fit of CFA model with three paths among the factors is poor, then the fit of the whole hybrid model with only two paths among the factors may be even worse.

The first part of two-step modeling thus involves finding an acceptable CFA measurement model. If the initial measurement model is rejected, then the suggestions reviewed in Chapter 7 (section 7.7) for respecification can be followed. Given an acceptable measurement model, the second stage of two-step modeling is to compare the fits of the original hybrid model and those with different structural models to one another and to the fit of the CFA measurement model with the $\chi^2_{\text{difference}}$ test. The procedure is as follows: if the structural portion of a hybrid model is just-identified, then the fits of the original hybrid model and the CFA respecification of it are identical; in fact, these models are equivalent versions that generate the same predicted correlations and covariances. For example, if a direct effect from factor A to C is added to the hybrid model (a) of Figure 8.3, then it will have as many parameters as does the CFA model (b) beneath it. The original hybrid model of Figure 8.3 with its overidentified structural model is thus nested under the CFA model. However, it may be possible to trim a just-identified structural portion of a hybrid model without a significant deterioration in the overall fit of the whole model. In general, structural portions of hybrid models can be trimmed (or built) according to the same principles as in path analysis (section 5.10). The goal is also the same: to find a parsimonious structural model that still explains the data (here, estimated covariances among the factors) reasonably well.

One other point about two-step modeling: given an acceptable measurement model, one should observe only slight changes in the factor loadings as hybrid models with alternative structural models are tested. If so, then the assumptions about measurement may be relatively invariant to changes in the structural relations among the latent variables. If the factor loadings change markedly when different structural models are specified, however, then the measurement model is not invariant. This phenomenon may lead to *interpretational confounding* (Burt, 1976), which in this context means that the definitions of the latent variables as quantified by the factor loadings change depending upon the structural model. This is another potential advantage of two-step over one-step modeling: it is easier to avoid interpretational confounding with two-step modeling.

8.4   Detailed Example of the Analysis of a Hybrid Model

This example was introduced in Chapter 3 (section 3.6, Figure 3.4) and concerns the relation of familial risk for psychopathology to the cognitive and scholastic adjustment of children. Briefly reviewed, Worland, Weeks, Janes, and Strock (1984) measured within a sample of 158 junior and senior high school students two indicators of familial risk (parental psychopathology, low family socioeconomic status (SES)), three indicators of student cognitive ability (verbal, visual-spatial, memory), three indicators of scholastic achievement (reading, spelling, and arithmetic), and four indicators of classroom adjustment (teacher reports of scholastic motivation, extroversion, harmony of social relationships, and emotional stability). Data from these 12 measures are summarized in Table 8.1. Worland et al. did not report standard deviations or the means of all variables. The authors of this study used path analysis to test their hypothesis that family risk affects classroom adjustment only indirectly first through child cognitive status and then through achievement. An alternative is to specify a hybrid model that represents the use of multiple indicators and takes account of measurement error. Such a model was presented in Figure 3.4. The evaluation of this hybrid model with four factors (familial risk, cognitive ability, achievement, classroom adjustment) is demonstrated below.

Let's consider whether the four-factor hybrid model of Figure 3.4 is identified. Presented in Figure 8.4(a) is the measurement portion of this hybrid model expressed as a four-factor CFA model. If it is assumed that the variances of the factors are fixed to 1.0 to scale them, then the CFA measurement model of Figure 8.4 has 30 free parameters. These include the variances of the 12 measurement errors, of the 6 covariances among the factors, and the loadings of the 12 indicators on the factors. With 12 observed variables in the model, there are $12(13)/2 = 78$ observations, which exceeds the number of free parameters (78 vs. 30). Because this is a standard CFA model that has at least two indicators per factor, we can say that it is identified (section 7.5). The structural portion of the four-factor hybrid model of Figure 3.4 is presented in Figure 8.4(b). This structural model is recursive, so it's identified, too. Because the sufficient two-step rule indicates that both the measurement and structural models of Figure 8.4 are identified, we conclude that the original four-factor hybrid model (Figure 3.4) is identified.

The fit of the four-factor hybrid model to Worland and colleagues' data was evaluated in two steps. In the first, the correlations of Table 8.1 were submitted to a model-fitting program for a CFA with maximum likelihood (ML) estimation of the measurement model presented in Figure 8.4. (Recall that the analysis of correlations instead of covariances is not ideal.) Values of selected fit indexes are reported in the lower part of Table 8.1, and they all indicate

TABLE 8.1. Evaluation of a Hybrid Model of Familial Risk for Psychopathology and Child Cognitive and Scholastic Status

Correlations and means (Worland et al., 1984; N = 158 junior and senior high school students)

Variable	Familial risk		Cognitive ability			Achievement			Classroom adjustment			
	1	2	3	4	5	6	7	8	9	10	11	12
Familial risk												
1. Parental Psychopathology	—											
2. Low Family SES	.42	—										
Cognitive ability												
3. Verbal	−.43	−.50	—									
4. Visual–Spatial	−.40	−.40	.66	—								
5. Memory	−.35	−.38	.67	.60	—							
Achievement												
6. Reading	−.39	−.43	.78	.56	.73	—						
7. Arithmetic	−.24	−.37	.69	.49	.70	.73	—					
8. Spelling	−.31	−.33	.63	.49	.72	.87	.72	—				
Classroom adjustment												
9. Scholastic Motivation	−.25	−.25	.49	.32	.58	.53	.60	.59	—			
10. Extraversion	−.14	−.17	.18	.09	.17	.14	.15	.15	.25	—		
11. Harmony	−.25	−.26	.42	.25	.46	.42	.44	.45	.77	.19	—	
12. Emotional Stability	−.16	−.18	.33	.27	.35	.36	.38	.38	.59	−.29	.58	—
M	—	—	11.64	11.40	11.15	103.52	93.30	99.08	3.49	3.17	3.76	3.53

Goodness of fit summary

Model	χ^2	df	χ^2/df	Constrast with baseline model		GFI	AGFI	SRMR
				$\chi^2_{difference}$	$df_{difference}$			
Measurement models								
CFA four-factor	188.05**	48	3.92	—	—	.85	.76	.07
CFA three-factor with correlated errors	71.92**	35	2.05	—	—	.92	.85	.04
Hybrid models								
Baseline (just-identified structural model)	71.92**	35	2.05	—	—	.92	.85	.04
Overidentified structural model (without familial risk → classroom adjustment)	72.31**	36	2.01	.39	—	.92	.85	.04

Note. GFI, Jöreskog–Sörbom Goodness of Fit Index; AGFI, Adjusted GFI; Standardized Root Mean Squared Residual.
**p < .01.

(a) Measurement Model

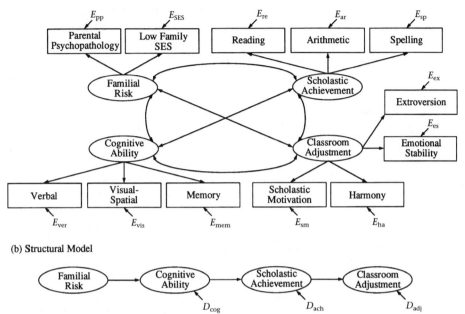

(b) Structural Model

FIGURE 8.4. The measurement and structural models of a hybrid model of familial risk for psychopathology and child adjustment.

that the correspondence of the four-factor measurement model to the data is problematic. For example, the χ^2/df ratio is somewhat high (3.92) and values of fit indexes with more standardized values are all less than .90 (e.g., the Jöreskog–Sörbom Goodness of Fit Index = .85). Inspection of the standardized parameter estimates and correlation residuals indicated three specific problems: First, the loading of the teacher-rated extroversion scale on the classroom adjustment factor is very low (.22), which suggests that this indicator has a high proportion of unique variance. The correlation residuals of the extroversion scale with indicators of other factors were not high, which suggests that switching the loading of this indicator to another factor would not substantially improve model fit. Second, the estimated factor correlations suggest poor discriminant validity. Specifically, the correlation between the cognitive ability and scholastic achievement factors is so high (.91) as to suggest that these factors are not distinct. This result is consistent with views that ability and achievement tests may not really measure distinct cognitive processes among children (e.g., Kline, Snyder, & Castellanos, 1996). Finally, some of the correlation residuals among the three indicators of cognitive ability and the three achievement measures were relatively high. This pattern suggests that the measurement errors within each set of tasks may covary. Considering that all three cognitive ability tasks are from one test and that three achievement tasks are from another test, such measurement error correlations may reflect common method variance.

Based on the results just described, the measurement model of Figure 8.4 was respecified so that (1) the cognitive ability and academic achievement factors were merged; (2) the measurement errors within each set of ability and achievement tasks were allowed to covary; and (3) the extroversion scale of the classroom adjustment factor was excluded from the analysis. The respecified measurement model was analyzed with CFA, and its overall fit to the data seems satisfactory (see Table 8.1). For instance, the χ^2/df ratio for the three-factor model is 2.05, which is about half that of the original four-factor measurement model (3.92). Also, the values of most of the standardized indexes of model fit reported in Table 8.1 for the three-factor measurement model are greater than .90. The three-factor measurement model with the standardized solution is presented in Figure 8.5. Note that all of the standardized factor loadings exceed

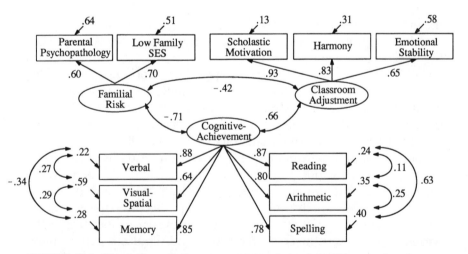

FIGURE 8.5. Final three-factor measurement model with correlated measurement errors and the standardized solution. All results are significant at the .05 level except for the measurement error covariance between reading and arithmetic. The standardized values for the measurement errors are proportions of unexplained variance.

.50 and that the absolute values of the factor correlations are not excessively high. (Even though all of the estimates in the figure except one are significant at the .05 level, the results of these significance tests should be viewed with caution because a correlation matrix was analyzed instead of a covariance matrix.)

With a satisfactory measurement model, the second stage of two-step modeling—the evaluation of the structural model—can proceed. The CFA model of Figure 8.5 was respecified as a hybrid model in which (1) the familial risk factor is exogenous and the omnibus cognitive–achievement factor and the classroom adjustment factor are both endogenous, and (2) the structural model has the following form:

Familial Risk → Cognitive–Achievement → Classroom Adjustment.

This structural model is overidentified because there is no direct effect from the familial risk factor to the classroom adjustment factor. Because the three-factor CFA measurement model of Figure 8.5 is an equivalent version of a hybrid model with a just-identified structural model, the version of the hybrid model with the overidentified structural portion presented above is nested under the CFA model. Thus, the $\chi^2_{\text{difference}}$ statistic can be used to test the significance of the difference in their relative fits.

Reported in Table 8.1 are values of fit indexes for the three-factor hybrid model with the overidentified structural model. The overall fit of this model is essentially identical to that of the CFA measurement model for these data. For example, the value of the $\chi^2(36)$ statistic for the hybrid model without a direct effect from the family risk factor to the classroom adjustment factor is 72.31. This value is only .39 greater than the $\chi^2(35)$ statistic of the CFA measurement model for these data, 71.92. Thus, the $\chi^2_{\text{difference}}$ (1) statistic of .39 is not significant, which here indicates that the path familial risk → classroom adjustment does not differ significantly from zero. The standardized path coefficient for the familial risk → cognitive–achievement direct effect is –.70 and for the cognitive–achievement → classroom adjustment direct effect is .65. As expected, higher familial risk for psychopathology is associated with lowers levels of cognitive–achievement skills, which in turn is predicts worse classroom adjustment. If the tracing rule is used (section 5.8), then the model-implied correlation between the familial risk and classroom adjustment factors equals the standardized indirect effect, which is –.70(.65) = –.46. This predicted correlation is very close to the estimated correlation between these factors from the CFA model, –.42 (see Figure 8.5). Thus, the overidentified structural portion of the final hybrid model can essentially reproduce the estimated factor correlation, which supports Worland and colleagues' (1984) hypothesis that the effect of familial risk on classroom adjustment is entirely indirect through child cognitive–achievement status. Also, the estimated factor loadings for the final hybrid model are virtually identical to those of the three-factor CFA model, which is a desired result.

8.5   Modeling Two-Wave Longitudinal Data

This example concerns the data that were screened in Chapter 4 (section 4.10). Briefly reviewed, a sample of junior high school students were administered questionnaires on two occasions 8 months apart about their expectancies of the behavioral effects of alcohol and patterns of drinking and related problems. Screening of the data resulted in the elimination of four variables due to distributional problems or poor reliability. The final sample size is 403 after multivariate outlier cases were dropped, univariate outliers were made less extreme, and missing observations were replaced with group means. For this analysis, the single expectancy scale about anticipated negative consequences of drinking was excluded, which leaves four positive expectancy scales. The other two observed variables are reports of the quantity and frequency of alcohol use. The data for this example are summarized in Table 8.2. Note that although mean scores seem to show little change over time, information about means is not represented in this analysis. (The analysis of means is considered in Chapter 10, section 10.4.)

Consider the hybrid model for these longitudinal data that is presented in Figure 8.6. The measurement portion of this model assumes that the six observed variables at each time measure two latent variables, a global positive expectancy factor and a drinking quantity–frequency factor. The 1.0s in the figure represent fixed factor loadings that scale the latent variables. The model also includes measurement error correlations between each pair of Time 1–Time 2 observed variables. This pattern of correlated measurement errors over time is a relatively common feature of hybrid models for longitudinal data. This specification reflects the hypothesis that the measurement errors of repeated measures variables covary. The structural portion of the model in Figure 8.3 is nonrecursive, with a covariance between the two disturbances. This structural model assumes that the factors at Time 2 reciprocally affect each other, are each caused by their own Time 1 counterparts, and have at least one common omitted cause.

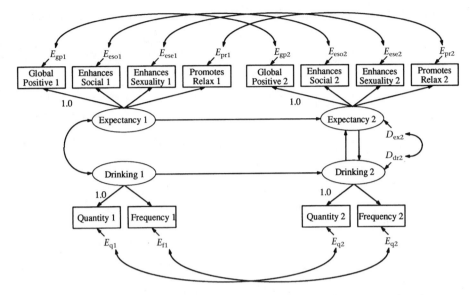

FIGURE 8.6. A model of the longitudinal relations of alcohol-related expectancies and drinking quantity and frequency.

With 12 observed variables (6 at each time), there are 12(13)/2 = 78 observations with which to estimate this model's 36 parameters. Because the model in Figure 8.6 is complex, its parameters are summarized in the accompanying table (note that factor loadings fixed to 1.0 to scale the latent variables are not included in the overall tally).

Variances		Covariances		Factor loadings	Path coefficients
Exogenous factors	2	Exogenous factors	1	8	4
Disturbances	2	Disturbances	1	(4 each time)	
Measurement errors	12	Measurement errors	6		
					Total: 36

The hybrid model in Figure 8.6 meets the two necessary conditions for identification (scales for latent variables; number of parameters ≤ number of observations). However, the measurement portion of this model is nonstandard in that it has correlated measurement errors. Nonstandard measurement models are technically "none of the above" models for which there may be no easily applied sufficient test of their identification (section 7.5). Because each indicator

TABLE 8.2. Evaluation of the Longitudinal Relation between Alcohol-Related Expectancies and Drinking

Correlations, means, and standard deviations (N = 403 Grade 6, 7, and 8 students)

| | Time 1 | | | | | | Time 2 | | | | | |
| | Expectancy | | | | Drinking | | Expectancy | | | | Drinking | |
Variable	1	2	3	4	5	6	7	8	9	10	11	12
Time 1												
Expectancy scales												
1. Global Positive	—											
2. Enhances Sociability	.47	—										
3. Enhances Sexuality	.52	.29	—									
4. Promotes Relaxation	.61	.42	.48	—								
Drinking scales												
5. Quantity	.11	.40	−.19	.12	—							
6. Frequency	.12	.36	.11	.17	.75	—						
Time 2												
Expectancy scales												
7. Global Positive	.64	.39	.08	.44	.16	.14	—					
8. Enhances Sociability	.34	.70	.21	.27	.39	.31	.42	—				
9. Enhances Sexuality	.47	.28	.61	.38	.12	.12	.60	.33	—			
10. Promotes Relaxation	.53	.41	.34	.63	.09	.13	.66	.38	.56	—		
Drinking scales												
11. Quantity	.10	.37	−.13	.11	.55	.48	.14	.42	−.04	.17	—	
12. Frequency	.10	.31	.07	.10	.46	.47	.15	.40	.14	.19	.84	—
M	6.92	5.60	4.33	9.13	2.17	2.04	7.19	5.43	4.46	9.35	2.11	1.95
SD	3.39	3.18	1.92	2.94	.88	.81	3.81	3.10	2.12	3.11	.90	.78

Goodness of fit summary

| | | | | Contrast with baseline model | | | |
Model	χ^2	df	χ^2/df	$\chi^2_{\text{difference}}$	$df_{\text{difference}}$	GFI	CFI
Baseline (unconstrained)	151.51**	42	3.61	—	—	.95	.96
Factor loadings invariant over time	171.19**	46	3.72	19.68**	4	.95	.96
Factor loadings and measurement errors invariant over time	198.32**	52	3.81	46.81**	10	.94	.95

Note. GFI, Jöreskog–Sörbom Goodness of Fit Index; AGFI, Adjusted GFI; CFI, Bentler Comparative Fit Index.

**$p < .01$.

of this model is specified to load on a single factor, however, the presence of measurement error correlations may not be problematic. In fact, the analysis of the model of Figure 8.6 respecified as a four-factor CFA measurement model ran without apparent problems and the solution passed empirical tests of uniqueness (section 6.6), which suggests that it may be identified. The nonrecursive structural portion of the hybrid model is straightforward: because it has all possible disturbance correlations and meets the rank condition (section 6.3), it is identified; overall, it seems that the whole hybrid model of Figure 8.6 may be identified.

To reduce the length of this presentation, two-step evaluation of the hybrid model of Figure 8.6 is not described in detail. This is because the nonrecursive structural model of this hybrid model is just-identified, which means that the overall fit of the hybrid model is identical to that of the CFA respecification of it. To evaluate the hybrid model in Figure 8.6, a covariance matrix based on the data summarized in Table 8.2 was submitted to a model-fitting program for ML estimation. The analysis ran without apparent problems, and the solution passed empirical tests of uniqueness. Values of fit indexes reported in the bottom part of Table 8.2 indicate marginally acceptable overall fit. For example, although the χ^2/df ratio is somewhat large (3.61), values of other fit indexes such as the Jöreskog–Sörbom Goodness of Fit Index (GFI) and the Bentler Comparative Fit Index (CFI) are .90 or higher. Although it may be possible to improve the overall fit of the model with some relatively minor modifications, the main point of this example is to demonstrate a strategy for testing hybrid models for longitudinal data.

Given a hybrid model with acceptable correspondence to longitudinal data, a common analysis strategy is to then compare with the $\chi^2_{\text{difference}}$ test the relative fits of more constrained versions of the model to that of the original. One way to constrain a hybrid model for longitudinal data is to test for measurement invariance over time. For example, imposing equality constraints on the factor loadings of each repeated measures indicator provides a test of whether the indicators assess the factors in the same way each time. If the relative fit of the model with this constraint does not differ significantly from that of the unconstrained model, then the factor loadings of each indicator may not differ notably over time. It is also possible to impose additional equality constraints on the measurement error variances of each repeated measures indicator, which tests whether the residual variances are invariant over time.

Reported in the bottom part of Table 8.2 are values of fit indexes of two constrained versions of the original hybrid model. The first version features equality-constrained factor loadings for each pair of repeated measures indicators. A total of four pairs of loadings are constrained, three for indicators of the expectancy factors (enhances sociability, enhances sexuality, promotes relaxation) and one for an indicator of the drinking factors (frequency). The second constrained model features additional equality constraints over time on all six pairs of measurement error terms. Results of the $\chi^2_{\text{difference}}$ test indicate that the fits of both constrained models are significantly worse than that of the unconstrained model. For example, the $\chi^2_{\text{difference}}(4)$ statistic for the comparison of the unconstrained model against the version with equality-constrained factor loadings equals 19.68, which is significant at the .01 level. However, the sample size here is fairly large (403), which means that the absolute magnitudes of differences in factor loadings or measurement error variances may be small.

Reported in Table 8.3 are the unstandardized and standardized parameters estimates for the unconstrained version of the model in Figure 8.3. A lot of information is summarized in this table, but let's review results first for the measurement model and then for the structural model. With one exception, all of the standardized factor loadings are greater than .50, which suggests reasonable convergent validity at both times. Also, the factor loadings of each indicator are quite similar at Time 1 and Time 2. The same is generally true for the measurement error variances. The similarity of these estimates over time suggests that the statistically significant differences in the relative fits of the unconstrained model and two constrained versions (see Table 8.2) may be more due to the large sample size than to lack of measurement invariance. Estimates of measurement error correlations range from .34 to .65, and all are significant at the .05 level except one. These results suggest that the unique variances of the respective repeated measures indicators indeed overlap. Other results for the measurement model concern discriminant validity. For example, the estimated correlation between the expectancy and drinking factors at Time 1 is only .23. Also, the model-implied correlation between these factors at Time 2 is almost identical, .24. These moderate-sized correlations indicate that the expectancy and drinking factors are relatively distinct.

The direct effects of the Time 1 expectancy and drinking factors on their Time 2 counterparts are both significant and large in absolute value; the respective standardized path coefficients are .76 and .58. This result is not surprising and suggests that the students generally maintained their rank orders on each factor over time. More surprising are the estimates of the reciprocal effects between these factors at Time 2. Both of these path coefficients are not significant and have stan-

TABLE 8.3. Parameter Estimates for a Hybrid Model of the Longitudinal Relation between Alcohol-Related Expectancies and Drinking

Parameter	Time 1	Time 2	Time 1 to Time 2
Exogenous factor variances and covariance			
Expectancy	7.93** —	—	—
Drinking	.51** —	—	—
Expectancy ↔ Drinking	.47** (.23)	—	—
Disturbance variances and covariance			
$D_{\text{expectancy}}$	—	·3.94** (.40)	—
D_{drinking}	—	.40** (.64)	—
$D_{\text{expectancy}} \leftrightarrow D_{\text{drinking}}$	—	.11 (.09)	—
Measurement error variances and covariances[b]			
$E_{\text{global positive}}$	3.57** (.31)	4.55* (.32)	1.36** (.34)
$E_{\text{sociability}}$	6.88** (.70)	7.24** (.78)	4.55** (.65)
$E_{\text{sexuality}}$	2.30** (.61)	2.21** (.48)	1.22** (.54)
$E_{\text{relaxation}}$	3.94** (.46)	3.54 (.36)	1.73** (.46)
E_{quantity}	.26** (.34)	.19* (.23)	.10* (.45)
$E_{\text{frequency}}$	.10 (.15)	.05 (.08)	.03 (.46)
Factor loadings			
Expectancy → Global Positive	1.00[nt] (.83)	1.00[nt] (.83)	—
Expectancy → Sociability	.61** (.55)	.46** (.47)	—
Expectancy → Sexuality	.43** (.62)	.49** (.72)	—
Expectancy → Relaxation	.77** (.74)	.80** (.80)	—
Drinking → Quantity	1.00[nt] (.81)	1.00[nt] (.88)	—
Drinking → Frequency	1.05** (.92)	.95** (.96)	—
Direct effects			
Expectancy 1 → Expectancy 2	—	—	.85** (.76)
Drinking 1 → Drinking 2	—	—	.64** (.58)
Expectancy 2 → Drinking 2	—	.01 (.04)	—
Drinking 2 → Expectancy 2	—	.24 (.06)	—

Note. D, disturbance; E, measurement error.

[a]Unstandardized (standardized). The standardized values for the disturbance and measurement error variances are proportions of unexplained variance.

[b]The entries in the third column are the covariances.

[nt]Not tested for significance because this loading is fixed to 1.0 to scale a factor.

*$p < .05$;   **$p < .01$.

dardized values less than .10, which suggests small effects. Also, the estimated disturbance correlation is only .09, which indicates that omitted causes of Time 2 expectancies and drinking may not substantially covary. Altogether, results from the structural model suggest that although there is a positive relation between expectancies of beneficial effects of alcohol and levels of drinking, the magnitude of their estimated relation is relatively small. Other reports in the alcohol literature about the general topic of this example include those of Henderson, Goldman, and Coovert (1994) and Kline (1996).

8.6   Other Issues

Equivalent Hybrid Models

Just as in path analysis and CFA, it is often possible to generate equivalent versions of a hybrid model. For instance, suppose that the structural portion of a hybrid model has as many paths as possible (i.e., it is just-identified). An equivalent version of such a hybrid model was mentioned earlier: the measurement portion of the hybrid model expressed as a CFA model, which also has all possible paths among the factors but in the form of unanalyzed associations. Regardless of whether the structural model is just-identified or not, it may be possible to generate equivalent versions of it using the Lee–Hershberger replacing rules described for path models in Chapter 5 (section 5.10). Given no change in the measurement model, alternative hybrid models with equivalent structural models generate the same model-implied correlations and covariances. Holding the structural model constant, it may also possible to generate equivalent versions of the measurement model using Hershberger's reversed indicator rule, which involves reversing the direction of the direct effect between a factor and one of its indicators. That is, one indicator is specified as a cause indicator rather than as an effect indicator (section 7.7). Given no change in the structural model, alternative hybrid models with equivalent measurement models also yield the same predicted correlations and covariances. See Hershberger (1994) for several examples of the generation of equivalent hybrid models.

Single Indicators in Partially Latent Hybrid Models

There are times when a researcher has only one measure of some construct. A single observed measure, however, is unlikely to have no measurement error, that is, to be both perfectly reliable and have no systematic variance that measures something other than the underlying construct. There is an alternative to representing a single observed variable in the structural portion of a hybrid model as one would in path analysis (e.g., Figure 8.2), that is, without a measurement error term. This alternative requires an a priori estimate of the proportion of variance of the single observed measure that is due to measurement error (10%, 20%, etc.). The estimate may be based on the researcher's experience with the measure or on results reported in the research literature. Suppose that observed variable Y_1 is the only measure of construct B and that the researcher estimates that 20% of Y_1's variance is due to measurement error. Given this estimate, it is possible to specify a hybrid model like the one presented in Figure 8.7. Note that Y_1 is specified as the single indicator of factor B and that Y_1 has a measurement error term. The variance of this measurement error term is fixed to equal .20 times Y_1's observed variance, .20$(s_{Y_1}^2)$, which is is the estimated error variance expressed in the original metric of Y_1. Because factor B must have a scale in order for the model to be identified, the loading of Y_1 on B is fixed to equal 1.0. With the specification of a residual term for Y_1, the disturbance for endogenous factor B is estimated controlling for measurement error in its single indicator.

Three other points should be noted about the strategy just described for single indicators: First, why not simply specify the measurement error variance for a single indicator as a free parameter and let the computer estimate it? Such a specification may result in an identification problem (e.g., see Bollen, 1989, pp. 172–175). A safer

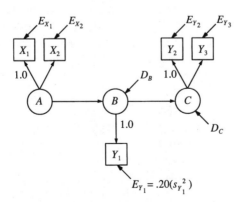

FIGURE 8.7. Example of a single indicator with a measurement error term fixed to equal 20% of its observed variance.

tactic with a single indicator is to fix the value of its measurement error term based on an a priori estimate. Second, what if the researcher is uncertain about his or her estimate of the measurement error variance of a single indicator? The model can be analyzed with a range of estimates, which allows the researcher to evaluate the impact of different assumptions about measurement error on the solution. Finally, the model in Figure 8.7 illustrates why hybrid models with single indicators that are identified may nevertheless fail the two-step rule for identification: when this model is respecified as a CFA measurement model, factor B has only one indicator, which—according to the requirements in Chapter 7 (section 7.5)—is one less than the minimum. Fixing the measurement error of Y_1 to a constant, however, identifies the model.

Cause Indicators

Observed variables of measurement models are usually represented as effect indicators that are presumed to be affected by underlying factors and by their measurement errors. The representation of observed variables as cause indicators reflects a different assumption about directionality—that the latent variable is affected by its indicators instead of the other way around. Cause indicators were introduced in Chapter 7 in the context of CFA: the specification of one indicator in a single-factor CFA model as a cause indicator instead of as an effect indicator generates an equivalent model (section 7.7).

There are examples in the literature of the analysis of hybrid models with factors that have both effect and cause indicators. Sometimes used to describe such factors is the term MIMIC, which stands for *M*ultiple *I*ndicators and *M*ult*I*ple *C*auses. A MIMIC factor is always endogenous. Stapleton (1977) analyzed a MIMIC model in which the latent variables represented the propensity to participate in various political activities (e.g., voting; working in a campaign), the effect indicators were reports about the frequencies of particular political activities, and the cause indicators were background characteristics such as age and education. Hershberger (1994) described a MIMIC depression factor with indicators that represented various symptoms. Some of these indicators such as "crying" and "feeling depressed" were specified as effect indicators because it was assumed that they are symptoms of depression. However, another indicator, "feeling lonely" was specified as a cause indicator of depression. Hershberger speculated that "feeling lonely" may be something that causes depression rather than vice versa.

It is also theoretically possible to specify that all of the indicators of a factor are cause rather than effect indicators. The example cited in Chapter 7 (section 7.4) that indicators such as education, income, and occupational prestige could all be causes of a socioeconomic status (SES) factor rather than its effects is one example. It turns out that the analysis of models with some factors that have only cause indicators can be very tricky because such models require very specific patterns of direct effects among the latent variables in order to be identified. MacCallum and Browne (1993) discuss these requirements and present a detailed example. For additional information about models with cause indicators, see also Bollen and Lennox (1991) and Kenny (1979, chap. 9).

8.7   Summary

The evaluation of a hybrid structural equation model is essentially a simultaneous CFA and a path analysis. Multiple indicator assessment of constructs is represented in the measurement portion of a hybrid model, and presumed causal relations among the latent variables are represented in the structural part. The analysis of a hybrid model can be broken down into these two models. In order for the structural component of a hybrid model to be identified, the measurement model must be identified. To evaluate whether the measurement model is identified, respecify the original model as a CFA model with all possible covariances among the factors. If the identification status of the CFA model can be determined, next look only at the structural portion of the hybrid model. Evaluate whether the structural model is identified by using the same criteria as for path models. If this two-step process indicates that both the measurement and structural models are identified, then the whole hybrid model is identified.

It is also recommended that a hybrid model be estimated in two steps. In the first step, the hybrid model is respecified as a CFA measurement model. If the fit of the measurement model is unsatisfactory, then the fit of the original hybrid model may be even worse if its structural model is overidentified. With an acceptable measurement model, however, one can then test the hybrid model with alternative structural models. If the alternative models are nested, their relative fits can be compared with the $\chi^2_{\text{difference}}$ test. The hybrid model with the most parsimonious structural model that still fits the data reasonably well and is also theoretically plausible is preferred. The researcher should also consider equivalent versions of his or her preferred hybrid model. Equivalent versions of the structural part of a hybrid model can be generated using the same rules as for path models, and equivalent measurement models can be created according to the same principles as in CFA.

Hybrid models for longitudinal data may have correlations between the measurement errors of each repeated measures indicator. A common strategy to test a model for longitudinal data is to compare the relative fits of an unconstrained model against constrained versions that test measurement invariance over time. For example, the imposition of an equality constraint on the factor loadings of each repeated measures indicator provides a test of whether the factors are measured in the same way over time. Similar equality constraints can also be placed on the measurement error variances of each repeated measures indicator.

If the researcher does not have multiple indicators of each construct, it may still be possible to specify a hybrid model that takes account of measurement error in all of the observed variables. Given an estimate of the proportion of the variance due to measurement error, one can include in a hybrid model a measurement error term for a single measure of some construct. The observed variable is specified as the sole indicator of an underlying factor. The loading of the single indicator is fixed to 1.0 to scale the factor. The measurement error variance for the single indicator is fixed to equal the estimated proportion of error variance times the observed variance of that indicator. If the latent variable on which the single indicator loads is endogenous, then it is specified to have a disturbance that is freely estimated. The estimate of this factor disturbance controls for measurement error in its single indicator.

Hybrid models represent the apex in the SEM family for the analysis of covariances. After a review of ways to fool yourself with SEM in Chapter 9, Chapter 10 elaborates ways in which hybrid models can be modified to represent nonlinear effects or means of observed or latent variables, among other types of more advanced analyses.

8.8 Recommended Readings

General Readings about Hybrid Models

Recommended among the following works are Bollen (1989, chap. 7), Kenny (1979, chap. 9), Loehlin (1992, chaps. 4 & 5), Mueller (1996, chap. 3), and Schumacker and Lomax (1996, chaps. 4, 5, 8, & 9). The chapter by MacCallum concerns the specification of hybrid models.

Bollen, K. A. (1989). *Structural equations with latent variables*. New York: Wiley.

Kenny, D. A. (1979). *Correlation and causality*. New York: Wiley.

Loehlin, J. C. (1992). *Latent variable models* (2nd ed.). Hillsdale, NJ: Erlbaum.

MacCallum, R. C. (1995). Model specification: Procedures, strategies, and related issues. In R. H. Hoyle (Ed.), *Structural equation modeling* (pp. 16–36). Thousand Oaks, CA: Sage.

Mueller, R. O. (1996). *Basic principles of structural equation modeling*. New York: Springer-Verlag.

Schumaker, R. E., & Lomax, R. G. (1996). *A beginner's guide to structural equation modeling*. Mahwah, NJ: Erlbaum.

Additional Empirical Examples of the Analysis of Hybrid Models

Brown, S. P., & Leigh, T. W. (1996). A new look at psychological climate and its relationship to job involvement, effort, and performance. *Journal of Applied Psychology, 81,* 358–368.

McFatter, R. M. (1987). Use of latent variable models for detecting discrimination in salaries. *Psychological Bulletin, 101,* 120–125.

Wagner, R. K., Torgesen, J. K., & Rashotte, C. A. (1994). Development of reading-related phonological processing abilities: New evidence of bidirectional causality from a latent variable longitudinal study. *Developmental Psychology, 30,* 73–88.

PART THREE

AVOIDING MISTAKES; ADVANCED TECHNIQUES; SOFTWARE

CHAPTER NINE

How to Fool Yourself with SEM

Scientific knowledge is an enabling power to do either good or bad—but it does not carry instructions on how to use it. Such power has evident value—even though the power may be negated by what one does with it. . . . [There is] a proverb of the Buddhist religion: To every man is given the key to the gates of heaven; that same key opens the gates of hell.
—RICHARD P. FEYNMAN (1988, p. 241)

9.1 Foreword

SEM is a marvelously flexible analytical tool. But as with any complex statistical procedure, its use must be guided by reason. Although many ways to mislead oneself with SEM were mentioned in previous chapters, they are summarized altogether here. Potential pitfalls are discussed under four categories: specification, data, analysis and respecification, and interpretation. These categories are not mutually exclusive, but they correspond to the usual sequence in which researchers should address these issues. Readers are encouraged to use the points presented in this chapter as a checklist to guide the conduct of their own SEMs.

Here they are: 35 ways to take leave of your senses in SEM. This list is not exhaustive, but it contains many of the more common mistakes.

9.2 Tripping at the Starting Line: Specification

Despite all the statistical machinations of SEM, specification is the most important part of the process. Occasionally, though, researchers spend the least amount of time on it. Listed below are several ways not to do your homework in this crucial area.

1. *Specify the model after the data are collected rather than before.* Potential problems caused by placing the data horse before the theory cart are described under other points that follow, but they include the realization that key variables are omitted or that the model is not identified. With the data already collected, it may be too late to do anything about the former. Also, the addition of exogenous variables is one way to remedy an identification problem, especially for a nonrecursive structural model.

2. *Omit causes that are correlated with other variables in a stuctural model.* If an omitted cause is uncorrelated with variables already in the model, then the estimates of the direct effects are not biased due to this omission. It is rare, however, that the types of causal variables studied by social scientists are independent. Depending upon the pattern of correlations between an omitted variable and those in the model, estimates of causal effects can be too high or too low.

3. *Fail to have sufficient numbers of indicators of latent variables.* Measurement models with more than one factor typically require only two indicators per factor for identification. However, having only two indicators per factor may lead to problems. Such models may be more likely to be empirically underidentified than models with at least three indicators per factor. Other estimation problems such as nonconvergence of iterative estimation are more likely to occur for models with only two indicators per factor, especially in small samples. Finally, it may be difficult to estimate measurement error correlations when there are only two indicators per factor, which may result in a specification error. Kenny's (1979) rule of thumb about numbers of indicators is apropos: "Two *might* be fine, three is better, four is best, and anything more is gravy" (p. 143; emphasis in original).

4. *Use psychometrically inadequate measures.* The analysis of variables with a lot of measurement error can lead to inaccurate results. The general effect of measurement error in path analysis is to underestimate causal effects, but—depending upon the intercorrelations—estimates can also be too high. Although measurement error is taken into account in the analysis of a measurement or hybrid model, estimates about latent variables are more precise when the indicators are psychometrically sound.

5. *Fail to give careful consideration to the question of directionality.* Directionality is a critical feature not only of structural models but

also of measurement models. In the former, specifications of direct and indirect effects are explicit statements about the expected sequence of causality. Assumptions about directionality in measurement models are expressed by the specification of observed variables as either effect indicators or cause indicators. If solid reasons cannot be provided for the specification of directionality, then either use another type of statistical procedure (e.g., multiple regression) or test alternative models with different causal sequences. However, some of the latter may be equivalent models that generate the same predicted correlations or covariances.

6. *Specify feedback effects in structural models (e.g., $Y_1 \rightleftarrows Y_2$) as a way to mask uncertainty about directionality.* Not only do feedback relations have their own assumptions (e.g., stationarity), their presence makes a structural model nonrecursive, which introduces potential problems (e.g., identification) in analyzing the model.

7. *Overfit the model (i.e., forget the goal of parsimony).* Any model, even theoretically nonsensical ones, will perfectly fit the data if they are specified to be as complex as possible. Models that exactly fit the data test no particular hypothesis, however. It is only more parsimonious models in which some effects are intentionally constrained to be zero that allow tests of specific ideas. The goal of model parsimony is also important in respecification. Here one must be careful not to modify the model solely for the sake of improving fit.

8. *Add disturbance or measurement error correlations without substantive reason.* This is a variation on the previous point. When there is justification (e.g., repeated measurement, a common measurement method), specification of these types of unanalyzed associations may be appropriate. Otherwise, they can be a way to improve fit simply by making a model more complex.

9. *Specify that indicators load on more than one factor without substantive reason.* This is a second variation on point 7 above. This specification may be appropriate if you really believe that an indicator measures more than one construct. Just like unanalyzed associations between residual terms, however, adding factor loadings makes a measurement model less parsimonious.

9.3   Improper Care and Feeding: Data

The potential missteps presented in this section involve leaping before you look, that is, not carefully screening the data before analyzing them.

10. *Don't check the accuracy of data input or coding.* Data entry mistakes are so easy to make, whether in recording the raw data or typing the values of a correlation or covariance matrix. Even machine-based data entry is not error free (e.g., smudges on forms can "fool" electronic scanners). Mistaken specification of codes in statistical programs is also common (e.g., "9" for missing data instead of "–9").

11. *Ignore whether the pattern of data loss is random or systematic.* If the pattern of missing observations is systematic rather than random, there is no statistical correction, SEM based or otherwise, that can eliminate potential bias in results based on the nonmissing observations. The researcher should try to understand the implications of systematic data loss for interpretation of the results.

12. *Fail to examine distributional characteristics.* The most widely used estimation procedure in SEM—maximum likelihood (ML)—assumes normal distributions. Although values of parameter estimates are relatively robust against non-normality, tests of significance are positively biased (i.e., Type I error rate is inflated). If the data are severely non-normal, then use an estimation method that does not assume normality or use corrected statistics (e.g., robust standard errors) when normal distribution methods are applied to non-normal data.

13. *Don't screen for outliers.* Even a few extreme outliers in a relatively small sample can distort the results. If it is unclear whether outlier cases are from a different populations, the analysis can be run with and without these cases in the sample. This strategy makes very clear the effect of outliers on the results.

14. *Assume that all relations are linear without checking.* A standard assumption in SEM is that variable relations are linear. Nonlinear relations can be readily represented with product terms (more about this point in Chapter 10), but such variables must be created by the researcher and then included in the model. Simple visual scanning of scatterplots can detect bivariate relations that are obviously curvilinear, but there is no comparably easy visual check for interaction effects.

9.4   Checking Critical Judgment at the Door: Analysis and Respecification

15. *Respecify a model based entirely on statistical criteria.* A blind specification search guided entirely by statistical criteria such as modification indexes may be unlikely to lead to the correct model. Use

your knowledge of relevant theory and research results to inform the use of such statistics.

16. *Fail to check the accuracy of your programming.* Just as with data entry, it is very easy to make a programming error. Although model-fitting programs have become easier to use, no computer program of any type can detect a mistake that is a logical rather than a syntax error, that is, an error that does not cause the program to fail but instead results in an unintended specification (e.g., $Y_1 \rightarrow Y_2$ instead of the reverse). Carefully check to see that the model that was analyzed was actually the model that you attempted to specify.

17. *Analyze a correlation matrix when it is clearly inappropriate.* These situations include the analysis of a model across independent groups with different variabilities, longitudinal data characterized by changes in variances over time, or a type of SEM that requires the analysis of means (e.g., a latent growth model; Chapter 10), which requires the input of not only means but covariances, too.

18. *Analyze variables so highly correlated that the solution is unstable.* If very high correlations (e.g., $r > .85$) do not a cause a model-fitting program to "crash," then extreme multicollinearity may cause the results to be statistically unstable.

19. *Estimate a very complex model with a small sample.* As the ratio of the number of cases to the number of parameters is smaller, the statistical stability of the estimates becomes more doubtful. Cases/parameters ratios less than 10:1 may be cause for concern, as are absolute sample sizes less than 100.

20. *Set scales for latent variables inappropriately.* In multisample analyses, the tactic of fixing factor variances to 1.0 is incorrect if the groups differ in their variabilities. Fixing the loading of an indicator to 1.0 is preferable, but note that (1) the same loading must be fixed for all groups, and (2) indicators with fixed loadings are assumed to be measurement invariant across all samples. In single-sample analyses, fixing to 1.0 the variances of factors measured over time is also inappropriate if factor variability is expected to change.

21. *Ignore the problem of starting values or provide grossly inaccurate ones.* Iterative estimation may fail to converge due to poor initial estimates, which is more likely with complex models. Although some model-fitting programs can automatically generate their own starting values, these values do not always lead to converged solutions. When this happens, the researcher should try to generate his or her own initial estimates.

22. *When identification status is uncertain, fail to conduct tests of solution uniqueness.* The identification of only some types of models can be clearly determined without resorting to algebraic manipulation of

their equations. If it is unknown whether a model is theoretically identified but a model-fitting program yields a converged, sensible-looking solution, then the researcher should conduct empirical tests of the solution's uniqueness. These tests do not prove that a solution is absolutely unique, but if they lead to derivation of a different set of estimates, then the model is probably not identified.

23. *Fail to recognize empirical underidentification.* Estimation of models that are identified can nevertheless fail due to data-related problems such as multicollinearity or estimates of key parameters that are close to zero. Modification of the model when the data are the problem may lead to a specification error.

24. *Fail to separately evaluate the measurement and structural portions of a hybrid model.* Two-step estimation of hybrid models can determine whether the source of poor fit of the whole model lies in the measurement model or in the structural model. These sources of poor fit may be confounded in one-step estimation.

9.5   The Garden Path: Interpretation

Potential mistakes described in this section concern the (mis)interpretation of the output of a model-fitting program. Some of these may be consequences of mistakes listed in the previous sections.

25. *Look only at indexes of overall model fit; ignore other types of information about fit.* This refers to "fit index tunnel vision," a condition that is fortunately curable by looking through the entire output. It is possible that the fit of some portion of a model is poor despite impressive-looking values of indexes of its overall correspondence to the data. Inspection of the correlation residuals can help to identify particular observed associations that are poorly explained by the model.

26. *Interpret good fit as meaning that the model is "proved."* Good model fit could reflect any of the following (not all mutually exclusive) possibilities: the model accurately reflects reality; the model is an equivalent version of one that corresponds to reality but itself is incorrect; the model fits the data from a nonrepresentative sample but does not reflect reality for the whole population; the model has so many parameters that it cannot have poor fit even if it is blatantly wrong. In a single study, it is usually impossible to determine which of these scenarios explains the good fit of the researcher's model. Thus, SEM is more useful for rejecting false models than for somehow "proving" whether a given model is in fact true.

27. *Interpret good fit as meaning that the endogenous variables are*

strongly predicted. If the exogenous variables account for small proportions of the variances of the endogenous variables and a model accurately reflects this lack of predictive validity, then the overall fit of the model may be good. Indexes of overall fit indicate whether the model can reproduce the observed correlations or covariances, not whether substantial portions of the variance of the endogenous variables are explained.

28. *Rely too much on significance tests.* This entry covers several kinds of errors. One is to interpret statistical significance as evidence for effect size, especially with large samples. Another is to place too much emphasis on significance tests of individual parameters that may not be of central interest in model testing (e.g., whether the variance of an exogenous variable differs significantly from zero when such is expected). A third is to forget that tests of significance tend to result in rejection of the null hypothesis too often when nonnormal data are analyzed by procedures that assume normality.

29. *Interpret the standardized solution in inappropriate ways.* This is a relatively common mistake in multisample analyses—specifically, to compare standardized estimates across groups that differ in their variabilities. In general, standardized solutions are fine for comparisons within each group (e.g., the relative magnitudes of direct effects on *Y*), but only unstandardized solutions are usually appropriate for cross-group comparisons. A related error is to interpret group differences in the standardized estimates of equality-constrained parameters: the unstandardized estimates of such parameters are forced to be equal, but their standardized counterparts may be unequal if the groups have different variabilities.

30. *Fail to consider equivalent models.* Essentially all structural equation models have equivalent versions that generate the same predicted correlations or covariances. Researchers should be prepared to offer reasons why their models are preferred to some obvious equivalent versions of it.

31. *Fail to consider (nonequivalent) alternative models.* When there are competing theories about some phenomenon, it may be possible to specify alternative models that reflect them. Not all of these alternatives may be equivalent versions of one another. If the overall fits of some of these alternative models are comparable, then the researcher must explain why a particular model is preferred.

32. *Reify factors.* Believe that constructs represented in your model *must* correspond to things in the real world. Perhaps they do, but do not assume it.

33. *Believe that a strong analytical method like SEM can compensate for poor study design or slipshod ideas.* No statistical procedure can

make up for inherent logical or design flaws. For example, expressing poorly thought out hypotheses with a path diagram does not give them more credibility. The specification of direct and indirect effects in a structural model cannot be viewed as a replacement for a longitudinal design. As mentioned earlier, the inclusion of a measurement error term for an observed variable that is psychometrically deficient cannot somehow transform it into a good measure.

34. *As the researcher, fail to report enough information so that your readers can reproduce your results.* There are still too many reports of SEMs in the literature in which the authors do not give sufficient information for readers to re-create the analyses or to evaluate models not considered by the authors. At minimum, authors should generally report all relevant correlations, standard deviations, and means. Also describe the specification of the model(s) in enough detail so that a reader can reproduce the results.

35. *Interpret estimates of large direct effects from a structural model as "proof" of causality.* As discussed earlier in the book, it would be almost beyond belief that all of the conditions required for the inference of causality from covariances have been met in a single study. In general, it is better to view structural models as "as if" models of causality that may or may not correspond to causal sequences in the real world.

9.6 Summary

Many of the ways to mislead oneself just listed are not unique to SEM but apply to essentially any analytical method that (1) requires certain assumptions about the integrity of the data and the researcher's hypotheses, and (2) exacts a price of complexity for its potential advantages. That it is possible to misuse or misinterpret the results of a statistical tool like SEM, however, may not be so much a criticism of the procedure itself but of its user, who has the responsibility to learn both the strengths and limitations of SEM and to provide a complete account of its application.

9.7 Recommended Readings

Describing SEMs in Research Reports

Hoyle, R. H., & Panter, A. T. (1995). Writing about structural equation models. In R. H. Hoyle (Ed.), *Structural equation modeling* (pp. 158–176). Thousand Oaks, CA: Sage.

Criticisms of Bad Practice in SEM

The authors of the following works discuss potential pitfalls of both statistical modeling in general and SEM in particular.

Cliff, N. (1983). Some cautions concerning the application of causal modeling methods. *Multivariate Behavioral Research, 18,* 115–126.

Freedman, D. A. (1992). Statistical models and shoe leather. *Sociological Methodology, 22,* 291–313.

Contexts for Limitations of SEM

The authors of the works listed below discuss limitations of SEM from broader perspectives that include the quality of graduate-level training in quantitative techniques and some of the difficulties in using other methods (e.g., quasi-experimental designs) in the study of variables that are inherently non-manipulable.

Berk, R. A. (1992). Toward a methodology for mere mortals. *Sociological Methodology, 22,* 315–324.

Blalock, H. M. (1992). Are there really any constructive alternatives to causal modeling? *Sociological Methodology, 22,* 325–335.

Mason, W. M. (1992). Freedman is right as far as he goes, but there is more, and it's worse: Statisticians could help. *Sociological Methodology, 22,* 337–351.

CHAPTER TEN

Other Horizons: Overview of Advanced Techniques

*Imagine: In Florida the wind is rattling the chimes. You look
over the alligators and the sea grass and water. There it is: The
rocket's burn. The best century ever. We were here. But now it's
time to go.*
                    —Douglas Coupland (1995, p. 81)

10.1 Foreword

And so this journey of learning about the principles and practice of
SEM is about to draw to a close. The conclusion of any voyage, however, leaves the traveler at the threshold of other potential journeys.
Because the SEM family is a large and growing one, there is no short-
age of other horizons to explore. Some are described in this chapter,
including the estimation of nonlinear effects, the analysis of means,
the representation in models of latent categorical variables, among
other topics. It is beyond the scope of this chapter to describe these
more advanced techniques in detail. Instead, the main goal here is to
make readers aware of the existence of these facets of SEM and to provide them with relevant references and other resources for further
study.

10.2   Nonlinear (Curvilinear and Interactive) Effects

All of the effects in models considered up to this point have been assumed to be linear. This section offers an overview of the estimation of nonlinear effects in SEM. Recall that there are two kinds of nonlinear effects—curvilinear relations that involve only two variables, and interactive effects that concern at least three (e.g., section 2.6, Figure 2.1). Interaction effects are also called moderator effects that occur when, in their simplest form, the relation of one variable to another changes across the levels of a third. Although any multisample SEM can be viewed as a test of whether group membership is a moderator variable, the interaction effects considered in this chapter can be estimated within a single group. Discussed below are methods to analyze curvilinear and interactive effects of observed variables and of latent variables.

Observed Variables

Nonlinear effects of observed variables are estimated by creating power or product variables that are entered along with the original variables in a statistical model. Presented below are examples of using this method in multiple regression. This same basic method not only underlies the analysis of trend and interaction effects in the analysis of variance (recall that ANOVA is just a special case of multiple regression), it can also be used to represent nonlinear effects in path models or in portions of partially latent hybrid models that concern single indicators.

Consider the raw scores on variables X and Y that are presented at the top of Table 10.1. The relation between X and Y is obviously not linear. In fact, it is curvilinear—specifically a quadratic relation: scores on Y decline and then rise as scores on X increase. Regressing Y on X yields a correlation of only $-.10$ and a nonsignificant unstandardized regression coefficient of $-.04$. These results occur because the simple regression of Y on X reflects only the linear aspect of their relation, which for these data is very weak. To also represent the quadratic relation of X to Y, all that is necessary is to create the variable X^2 (which is often called a "power" term because the original variable is raised to a higher power— here, 2) and enter it along with X as a predictor of Y in a multiple regression equation. The presence of X^2 in the equation adds one bend

TABLE 10.1. Nonlinear Effects of Observed Variables Represented with Product Variables

Curvilinear (quadratic) effect

	Variable	Power	Criterion
Subject	X	X^2	Y
A	5	25	15
B	7	49	14
C	10	100	11
D	13	169	9
E	15	225	9
F	17	289	5
G	19	361	8
H	23	529	11
I	25	625	14
J	26	676	14
Unstandardized regression coefficients:	−.04	—	$r_{XY} = -.10$
	−2.20**	.07**	$R_{Y \cdot X, X^2} = .93**$

Interaction (XW) effect

	Variables		Product	Criterion
Subject	X	W	XW	Y
A	2	10	20	5
B	4	12	60	7
C	6	12	60	9
D	8	13	104	11
E	11	10	110	10
F	2	22	44	10
G	4	24	96	11
H	7	19	95	9
I	8	18	144	7
J	11	25	275	5
Unstandardized regression coefficients:	−.01	.02	—	$R_{Y \cdot X, W} = .05$
	1.18*	.47*	−.07*	$R_{Y \cdot X, W, XW} = .83*$

$*p < .05;$ $**p < .01.$

to the regression line, and its regression coefficient estimates the magnitude of the quadratic aspect of X's relation to Y. For the data in Table 10.1, the multiple correlation with both X and X^2 in the equation is .93 and both regression coefficients are significant. Even higher-order curvilinear effects can be represented with the appropriate power term. For example, the variable X^3 represents the cubic relation of X to Y, X^4 represents the quartic relation, and so on.[1]

The same basic method can be extended to interactive effects, too. The example discussed below concerns an interaction between two continuous variables, but interaction effects of categorical variables can also be represented with product terms (e.g., Aiken & West, 1991; Cohen & Cohen, 1983). Consider the scores on variables X, W, and Y that are presented at the bottom of Table 10.1. If X and W are the only predictors of Y in a regular multiple regression analysis, then neither has a significant regression coefficient and the overall multiple correlation is only .05. The analysis just described is sensitive only to linear relations between the predictors and the criterion, but inspection of the raw scores in Table 10.1 indicates a more complex pattern. For example, the relation of X to Y is linear and *positive* for subjects with low scores on W (≤ 12) but is linear and *negative* at higher levels of W. Although it is not as apparent, there is a similar change in the direction of the linear relation between W and Y: positive at higher levels of X; negative at lower levels. Now look again at Table 10.1 to see what happens when X, W, and the product variable XW are all specified as predictors in the regression equation: the overall multiple correlation increases to .83 (from just .05 without XW), and the regression coefficients of all three predictors are significant. These results indicate that W moderates the relation of X to Y. Because an interactive effect is a joint one, however, X can also be described as moderating the relation of W to Y. Also, the use of multiple regression with product variables like XW to estimate interactions is sometimes called *moderated multiple regression.*

Although it exceeds the scope of this section to cover this topic in detail, the basic method just described can also be used to estimate higher-order interactions. For example, the product XW for the data of Table 10.1 represents the linear × linear interaction of X and W. If significant (as it is for these data), it means that the linear relation between X and Y changes uniformly (i.e., in a linear way) across the levels of W. In contrast, the product term XW^2 represents a linear × quadratic interaction, which means that the linear relation of X to Y changes faster at higher (or lower) levels of W. Because the estimation of higher-order interactive (and curvilinear) effects may require

---

[1]Power terms such as X^2, X^3, etc. (which are sometimes called *power polynomials*) can be so highly intercorrelated with each other and with X that multicollinearity may be a problem. Cohen and Cohen (1983, pp. 237–238, 242–249) describe methods to reduce multicollinearity like rescaling X so that its mean is zero before higher-order power terms are computed.

(a) Quadratic Relation of X to Y

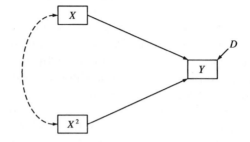

(b) Interactive Relation of X and W to Y

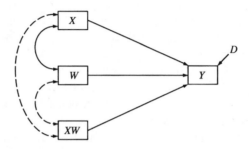

FIGURE 10.1. Path models with power or product variables that represent nonlinear effects of observed variables.

the analysis of numerous product variables, very large samples may be necessary.

Nonlinear effects of observed variables are represented in structural models with the appropriate product terms. Consider the two path models presented in Figure 10.1.[2] Model (a) represents variables X and X^2 as exogenous and Y as endogenous. Path coefficients for the direct effects $X \rightarrow Y$ and $X^2 \rightarrow Y$ of this model respectively estimate the linear and quadratic causal effects of X on Y. Path model (b) of Figure 10.1 depicts X, W, and the product variable XW as causes of Y. Estimates of the direct effects of model (b) reflect the linear causal effects of X and W on Y ($X \rightarrow Y$, $W \rightarrow Y$) and their interactive causal effect ($XW \rightarrow Y$). The former ($X \rightarrow Y$, $W \rightarrow Y$) are analogous to main effects in ANOVA and have a lower interpretive priority than does the

---

[2]The dashed curved lines in Figure 10.1 stand for unanalyzed associations between the product variables and their component variables and represent the possibility that the former can be created such that they have low or zero correlations with the latter (e.g., Lance, 1988).

interaction effect ($XW \rightarrow Y$). That is, a large and significant interaction term means that the effect of one variable (e.g., X) on Y is conditional on the other variable (e.g., W).

Examples of structural models with curvilinear effects of observed variables can be found in McArdle (1994), who studied the linear, quadratic, and cubic effects of age to latent cognitive ability factors; and in Loehlin, Horn, and Willerman (1990), who included quadratic effects of age in models of the stability of extroversion, socialization, and emotional lability among adopted and biological children of adoptive parents. Path models with interactive effects are described by Cohen and Cohen (1983), who analyzed a model of university faculty salary and productivity; and by Lance (1988), who evaluated factors that moderate social recall. Some of the models analyzed by Lance featured both interaction effects and indirect effects, which demonstrates that moderator and mediator effects can be represented in the same model. See Baron and Kenny (1986) and James and Brett (1984) for additional information and examples.

Latent Variables

The estimation of nonlinear effects of observed variables is limited by the use of a single indicator of each theoretical variable and the resulting inability to take account of measurement error. The second limitation just mentioned may be especially critical for power or product variables because they reflect the combined measurement errors of their component variables. For example, if either X or W is unreliable, then the reliability of XW must also be poor. Although there are ways to adjust path coefficients of power or product terms for measurement error (e.g., Jaccard & Wan, 1995; Ping, 1996b), the only way to overcome the first limitation just mentioned is to use multiple indicators of each construct. The estimation of nonlinear effects of latent variables within a multiple indicator approach to measurement is outlined below. Readers should be aware that such analyses may require very large samples because even relatively simple models with nonlinear effects of latent variables may have many parameters. Also, the example presented below features a quadratic effect of a latent variable, but the same principles apply to interactive effects, too.

Consider model (a) of Figure 10.2, which represents the linear effect of exogenous factor A on the observed exogenous variable Y. (The rationale outlined here also applies to the use of multiple indicators to measure an endogenous construct.) Factor A has two indicators, X_1 and X_2. The measurement model for these two observed variables can also be represented with the following two structural equations:

$$X_1 = A + E_1$$
$$X_2 = L_2A + E_2,$$

(10.1)

where the loading of X_1 is fixed to 1.0 to scale the factor, and the loading of X_2 is a free parameter represented by L_2. The only other parameters of this measurement model are the variances of factor A and of the two measurement error terms, E_1 and E_2.

Suppose that a researcher wished to estimate the *quadratic* effect of factor A on the endogenous variable. This calls for adding to model (a) of Figure 10.2 the latent product variable A^2 that represents this effect, which is estimated by the path coefficient for the direct effect $A^2 \rightarrow Y$. Like its linear counterpart, A^2 is a latent variable that is measured only indirectly through its indicators. What are the indicators

(a) Standard Hybrid Model with Linear Effect of X on Y

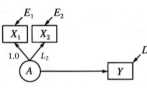

(b) Hybrid Model with Linear and Quadratic Effects of X on Y

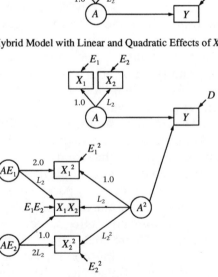

FIGURE 10.2. (a) A standard hybrid model with a linear effect of factor A. (b) The complete hybrid model with linear and quadratic effects of factor A.

of a latent product factor? The appropriate products of the corresponding observed variables. For this example, the indicators of A^2 are all the products of the indicators of A that represent a quadratic effect, which are X_1^2, X_2^2, and X_1X_2. (Note that X_1X_2 does *not* here represent an interaction because its components, X_1 and X_2, are specified to measure the same factor.) By squaring or taking the product of the relevant equations above (10.1), the measurement model for the product indicators is

$$X_1^2 = A^2 + 2AE_1 + E_1^2$$

$$X_2^2 = L_2^2A^2 + 2L_2AE_2 + E_2^2 \qquad (10.2)$$

$$X_1X_2 = L_2A^2 + L_2\,AE_1 + AE_2 + E_1E_2.$$

Equations 10.2 show that the measurement model for the product indicators involves not just the latent product factor A^2 but also five additional latent product terms, AE_1, AE_2, E_1^2, E_2^2, and E_1E_2. (The latter three product factors are error terms for the product indicators.) Note that all of the factor loadings of the measurement model of Equations 10.2 are either constants or functions of L_2, the loading of X_2 on factor A. In fact, the only free parameters of this measurement model are the variances of A^2 and the other five latent product factors that underlie the product indicators. (How to estimate these values is considered momentarily.) Presented as model (b) in Figure 10.2 is the hybrid model that includes the measurement models for A and A^2 (i.e., Equations 10.1 and 10.2) and the structural model for causal effects on Y. Among estimates for this hybrid model, of greatest interest here are probably the two path coefficients of the structural model, which respectively estimate the linear $(A \rightarrow Y)$ and quadratic $(A^2 \rightarrow Y)$ causal effects on the endogenous variable.

There are two general methods for estimating models with product indicators like model (b) of Figure 10.2, one by Kenny and Judd (1984) and the other by Ping (1996a). Ping's method can be seen as an approximation of the Kenny–Judd method for the estimation of nonlinear effects of latent variables. Both are based on basically the same assumptions—that the linear latent variables (A in the figure) and the measurement errors of their indicators (E_1 and E_2) are normally distributed and have means of zero.[3] Given these assumptions,

---

[3]With actual data, one evaluates the normality assumption by inspecting the distributions of the observed variables. The assumption that the means are zero is usually handled by subtracting the mean from each raw score before creating product variables.

Kenny and Judd (1984) demonstrated that the parameters of the measurement model of the product indicators (Equations 10.2) are functions of the parameters of the measurement model of the non-product indicators (Equations 10.1). For example, the variance of the latent quadratic factor A^2 equals two times the squared variance of the latent linear factor A (Var A^2 = 2(Var X)^2), and the variance of the product factor AE_1 is the product of the variance of A and E_1 (Var AE_1 = Var A Var E_1). To estimate model (b) of Figure 10.2, the Kenny–Judd method involves the imposition of *nonlinear constraints* on the parameters of the measurement model of the product indicators that reflect the relations just mentioned and others. With all relevant nonlinear constraints in place, it is then possible to estimate the effects of interest, the path coefficients for $A \to Y$ and $A^2 \to Y$.

The main drawback to the Kenny–Judd method for estimating nonlinear effects of latent variables is that it requires a model-fitting program that accepts nonlinear constraints. LISREL 8 (Jöreskog & Sörbom, 1996a), the COSAN subroutine of CALIS (Hartmann, 1992), and the Mx program (Neale, 1994) accommodate nonlinear constraints, but not all model-fitting programs do. Ping (1996a) described a method to estimate curvilinear or interactive effects of latent variables that is an approximation of the Kenny–Judd procedure that does not require nonlinear constraints, which means that Ping's method can be used with essentially any model-fitting program. Ping's method is analogous to two-step estimation of a hybrid model (section 8.3). In the first step, the model is analyzed *without* the product indicators. One records parameter estimates from this analysis and calculates by hand the parameters of the measurement model of the product indicators. These calculated values are then specified as fixed parameters in the subsequent analysis of all variables, product and nonproduct alike. From this second analysis one obtains the path coefficients for the linear and nonlinear causal effects of the latent variables. Applied to Figure 10.2, one would first analyze model (a) to obtain estimates of the loading of X_2 on factor A and the variances of A and the two measurement errors. Using these values to calculate estimates for the measurement model of the product indicators X_1^2, X_2^2, and $X_1 X_2$, one then specifies the calculated estimates as fixed parameters in the analysis of a simplified version of model (b) in Figure 10.2. The path coefficients for the linear and quadratic effects of latent variable A on the endogenous variable ($A \to Y$, $A^2 \to Y$) are obtained from this second analysis.

Examples of the application of the Kenny–Judd method to estimate nonlinear effects of latent variables can be found in Bollen (1989), Kenny and Judd (1984), and Jöreskog and Yang (1996). See

Ping (1996a) and Schumaker and Lomax (1996) for examples of Ping's method.

10.3   Latent Categorical Variables

Factors in all the models considered earlier in the book have represented continuous latent variables. It is also possible, however, to represent latent variables that are categorical. Some of the principles for doing so are extensions of *latent class analysis,* which is a type of factor analysis but for categorical observed and latent variables (e.g., Goodman, 1977). A related topic is that of item response theory (IRT), which was described earlier (section 7.10) and concerns the relation of items to latent variables that can be either continuous or categorical. Some examples of the analysis of models with latent categorical variables are described below. For additional examples, see von Eye and Clogg (1994, Pt. 3). (Note that special software programs may be required for these types of analyses.)

Macready and Dayton (1994) tested models with latent dichotomous variables that represented mastery versus nonmastery of four arithmetic operations performed with fractions—addition, subtraction, multiplication, and division. The indicators of each mastery latent variable were dichotomously scored items (e.g., $\frac{4}{5} \times \frac{1}{8}$). Students who have acquired mastery of a particular operation should theoretically be able to solve any exemplary problem. In reality, though, they may fail on some items due to things like inattentive mistakes. By the same token, students who have not yet mastered an operation may occasionally get a related item correct but are unable to repeat their success with similar items. Both types of errors just described, those of omission (the first type) and of intrusion (the second type), imply that the indicators (a set of problems) do not perfectly measure their underlying latent dichotomous variable (mastery/nonmastery). In a study described by Macready and Dayton (1994), junior high school students were assigned to one of three instructional conditions in which the four arithmetic operations were taught in different orders. Also, the students were tested on three occasions as they progressed through the instructional programs. The longitudinal design permitted (1) the modeling of the transition from nonmastery to mastery in each arithmetic operation and (2) the evaluation of whether the rates of these transitions varied by instructional condition.

Models estimated by Macready and Dayton (1994) contained terms that represented omission and intrusion errors. Following the basic rationale of a multiple group SEM, the authors tested a series of models with different numbers of cross-group equality constraints that represented different orders of transition between nonmastery and mastery (e.g., forward only from nonmastery to mastery; change in either direction) and assumptions about error variance. The results indicated that estimated rates of mastery of some arithmetic operations differed by instructional condition, but the pattern of these differences was complex. For example, no single condition was clearly superior to the others, and some instructional sequences associated with lower rates of estimated mastery of certain arithmetic operations had higher rates with others. Other examples of the specification of models with latent dichotomous variables that represent changes in qualitative states over time can be found in Collins (1991) and Langeheine (1994).

McCutcheon (1994) evaluated a model in which three categorical exogenous variables were represented as the predictors of a dichotomous latent variable about attitude toward legal abortion (approve/disapprove). Two of the predictor variables were dichotomous (religion: Catholic/Protestant; attitude toward euthanasia: approve/disapprove), but the third, attitude about premarital sex, was trichotomous (always/sometimes/not wrong). Indicators of the latent variable were three items about respondents' approval or disapproval of legal abortion in different situations (e.g., the woman is married or single). McCutcheon tested a series of nested models ranging from just-identified ones with interaction effects to simpler ones with constraints imposed on the estimates of some parameters. The final model contained only the individual predictors (and their unanalyzed associations) with no interactive effects between them. McCutcheon transformed the parameter estimates into probabilities of either approving or disapproving of legal abortion as a function of the predictor variables. For example, Protestants were about twice as likely to approve of legal abortion as were Catholics; subjects who approved of euthanasia were about four times as likely to also approve of legal abortion; and respondents who stated that premarital sex is "not wrong" were about six times as likely to approve of legal abortion as were those who said premarital sex was "always wrong."

McArdle and Hamagami (1996) evaluated a model in which the outcome variable was dichotomous, whether students on full athletic scholarships eventually completed a college degree (yes/no). This binary variable was represented in a structural model as a latent logit variable with a disturbance term. A logit is a type of natural logarithm transformation of a probability that usually makes the relation between the variable and other variables (e.g., continuous ones) more linear. The predictors included information about the individual students and the colleges they attended (e.g., graduation rates for all students). Using a multiple group analysis of this model, McArdle and Hamagami (1996) found that although rates of graduation varied across colleges, student test scores and high school grade points predicted graduation rates in the same way across different colleges.

10.4   Analysis of Means

Introduction

The basic datum of SEM, the covariance, does not convey information about means. If only covariances are analyzed, then all observed variables are mean-deviated (centered) so that latent variables must have means of zero. Sometimes this loss of information (i.e., the means) is too restrictive. For example, means of repeated measures variables or of variables measured across independent samples may be expected to differ. Means are estimated in SEM by adding what is known as a *mean structure* to the model's basic covariance structure (i.e., its structural or measurement model(s)). The input data for the analysis of a model with a mean structure are covariances *and* means (or the raw scores). The SEM approach to the analysis of means is distinguished by the capability to test hypotheses about the means of latent variables. In contrast, other statistical methods such as ANOVA are concerned mainly with the means of observed variables. The rationale for the representation of means in structural equation models is outlined below. Following this introduction, various types of applications of the analysis of means in SEM are described.

The representation of means in structural equation models is based on the general principles of regression. For instance, consider the scores on variables X and Y presented in Table 10.2. (For the moment ignore the column in the table labeled $\triangle$.) To the right of these scores are descriptive statistics and the regression equation for predicting Y from X for these data. This equation is

$$\hat{Y} = .41(X) + 15.36,$$

where $\hat{Y}$ is a predicted score on Y; .41 is the unstandardized regression coefficient; and 15.36 is the intercept, which equals $\hat{Y}$ when X is zero. The regression coefficient (.41) can be seen as the covariance structure of the regression equation for these data. This coefficient says something about the association between X and Y, but it conveys no information about the mean of either variable. In contrast, the intercept (15.36) reflects the means of both variables *and* the regression

TABLE 10.2. Derivation of the Intercept in Regression

Case	Raw scores X	Raw scores Y	Constant △	Descriptive statistics Variable	X	Y
A	90	46	1	X	—	
B	78	40	1	Y	.64	—
C	57	32	1			
D	65	42	1	M	72.00	45.00
E	80	61	1	SD	15.09	9.79
F	75	46	1			
G	45	32	1	Regression equation: $\hat{Y} = .41(X) + 15.36$		
H	91	51	1			
I	67	55	1			

Regression analyses with the intercept term omitted

Regression	Predictor(s)	Unstandardized coefficient(s)
1. Y on X and △	X	.41
	△	15.36
2. X on △	△	72.00

coefficient, albeit with a single number. Specifically, the intercept can be expressed as a function of B, the regression coefficient from the regression of Y on X, and M_X and M_Y, the means of X and Y:

$$\text{Intercept} = M_Y - B(M_X). \tag{10.3}$$

For the data of Table 10.2,

$$\text{Intercept} = 15.36 = 45.00 - .41(72.00).$$

How a computer calculates the intercept of a regression equation for unstandardized variables provides a key to understanding the analysis of means in SEM. Look again at Table 10.2 and in particular at the column labeled △, which is a constant that equals 1 for every case. The results of two regression analyses with the constant △ are summarized in the lower part of the table. Both analyses were conducted by instructing the computer to omit from the analysis the intercept term it would otherwise automatically calculate. (This is an option in most regression modules.) In the first analysis summarized in Table 10.2, Y is regressed on both X and the constant △. Note that the unstandardized regression coefficient for X is the same as before, .41, and for the constant $\triangle$ is 15.36, which equals the intercept. This result indicates a general principle: *When a criterion is regressed on a predictor and a constant, the unstandardized coefficient for the constant is the intercept.* The second analysis summarized in the table concerns the regression of X on the constant. Note that the unstandardized regression coefficient in this analysis is 72.00, which equals the mean of X. A second principle is thus: *When a predictor is regressed on a constant, the unstandardized coefficient is the mean of the predictor.*

A path analytic representation of the regression analyses just described is presented in Figure 10.3. Unlike a standard path model, the one in figure has both a covariance structure and a mean structure. The covariance structure includes the direct effect of exogenous variable X on endogenous variable Y and the disturbance. Estimating this covariance structure with the data from Table 10.2 yields an unstandardized path coefficient of .41 (the same as the unstandardized regression coefficient) and a disturbance variance of 56.59. The ratio of the unstandardized disturbance variance over the observed variance of Y is 56.59/95.84 = .59, the proportion of unexplained variance. Note that no information about the means of X or Y is represented in this covariance structure.

The mean structure of the path model of Figure 10.3 consists of the direct effects of the constant $\triangle$ on both observed variables. Although the constant is depicted as exogenous in the figure, it is not an exogenous variable in the usual sense because it has no variance. The unstandardized path coefficient for the direct effect of the constant on the exogenous variable X is 72.00, which is the mean of X and the same value obtained by regressing X on the constant (Table 10.2). The mean of X is thus explicitly represented in the mean structure of this model in the form of an unstandardized path coefficient. (The standardized path coefficient for $\triangle \rightarrow X$ is zero because the means of standardized variables are zero.) Also note that because the

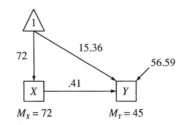

FIGURE 10.3. A path model with a mean structure.

constant has no indirect effect on X through other variables, the path coefficient for $\triangle \rightarrow X$ of 72.00 is also a total effect. The unstandardized path coefficient for the direct effect of the constant on the endogenous variable Y is 15.36, which is the intercept. In addition to this direct effect, the constant $\triangle$ also has an indirect effect on Y through X. Using the tracing rule for this model, we obtain the following equation:

$$\text{Total effect of } \triangle \text{ on } Y = \text{direct effect} + \text{indirect effect}$$
$$= 15.36 + (.41)72.00 = 45.00,$$

which equals the mean of Y. A third principle about mean structures can thus be expressed in path analytic language: *The mean of an endogenous variable Y is a function of three parameters: the intercept* (15.36 for the data of Table 10.2), *the unstandardized path coefficient* (.41), *and the mean of the exogenous variable* (72.00).

When a model-fitting program analyzes means, it automatically creates a constant on which variables in the model are regressed.[4] A variable is included in the mean structure by specifying in the program's syntax that the constant has a direct or indirect effect on it. This leads to a fourth principle: *For exogenous variables, the unstandardized path coefficient for the direct effect of the constant is a mean. For endogenous variables, though, the direct effect of the constant is an intercept but the total effect is a mean.* If a variable is excluded from the mean structure, then the mean of that variable is assumed to be zero. Note that error terms (disturbances and measurement errors) are *not* included in a mean structure because their means are typically assumed to be zero. In fact, the mean structure may not be identified if the mean of an error term is inadvertently specified as a free parameter.

The parameters of a model with a mean structure include the means of the exogenous variables (e.g., $\triangle \rightarrow X$ in Figure 10.3), the intercepts of the endogenous variables (e.g., $\triangle \rightarrow Y$), and the number of parameters in the covariance portion of the model counted in the usual way for that type of model (e.g., $X \rightarrow Y$ and the variances of X and the disturbance). There is a simple rule for counting the total

---

[4]In the syntax of EQS, this constant is called V999. In Amos, the constant is specified in text mode with the $Mstructure command and in graphics mode by clicking on the "Means" button. Mean structures in the SIMPLIS language of LISREL are specified with the CONST (constant) term and in LISREL's matrix-based syntax with the τ_x, τ_y, α, and κ matrices (tau x, tau y, alpha, and kappa). See Chapter 11 for more information about these programs.

number of observations available to estimate the parameters of a model with a mean structure, which is

$$\text{Number of observations} = v(v + 3)/2, \qquad (10.4)$$

where v is the number of observed variables. Equation 10.4 above gives the total number of variances, nonredundant covariances, and means of the observed variables. For example, if there are 5 observed variables, then there are $5(8)/2 = 20$ observations, which include 5 means and 15 variances and covariances (i.e., $5(6)/2$). In order for the mean structure of a model to be identified, the number of its parameters (i.e., exogenous variable means, endogenous variable intercepts) cannot exceed the total number of means of the observed variables. Also, the identification status of a mean structure must be considered separately from that of the model's covariance structure. That is, an overidentified covariance structure will not identify a nonidentified mean structure. Likewise, an overidentified mean structure cannot remedy a nonidentified covariance structure.

Some examples of structural equation models with mean structures are reviewed next. In each example, the symbol $\triangle$ is used in model diagrams to represent the mean structure. Readers should note, however, that there is no standard symbol in the SEM literature for mean structures. The symbol $\triangle$ for a constant is used by some authors (e.g., McArdle & Epstein, 1987) but not all. In fact, it is not absolutely necessary to represent mean structures in model diagrams. For instance, some authors present just the covariance structure in the diagram and report estimates about means either in the figure or in tables (e.g., Arbuckle, 1996). Thus, the symbol $\triangle$ is used in diagrams here mainly as a heuristic devise so that readers can quickly recognize the presence of a mean structure and determine which variables it includes.

Structured Means in Measurement Models

Presented in Figure 10.4 is a hypothetical measurement model with a mean structure. The covariance structure of this model assumes that the observed variables (X_1 to X_4) measure a single factor (A). For instance, the four indicators of this model may be alternate forms of a masculinity–femininity questionnaire. The mean structure of this model, which is represented by the direct effects that point from the constant $\triangle$ to the indicators and the factor, includes means in the analysis along with covariances. Based on the principles just dis-

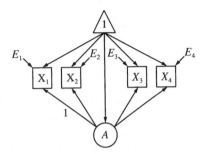

FIGURE 10.4. A hypothetical single factor measurement model with a mean structure.

cussed, the unstandardized path coefficient for the regression of exogenous factor A on the constant should theoretically equal the mean of the factor. Also, because the indicators are endogenous, their means should be estimated by the total effect of the constant on each indicator. Estimation of the model of Figure 10.4 would thus seem to allow the researcher to simultaneously test two sets of hypotheses, one about measurement (i.e., the single-factor model) and the other about means.

Unfortunately, the model of Figure 10.4 is not identified if estimated with data from a single sample. This is because its mean structure is underidentified: there are only four observations—the means of X_1 through X_4—but the mean structure has five parameters, including the mean of the exogenous factor and the intercepts of the four indicators. Perhaps the simplest way to deal with this problem is to exclude the factor from the mean structure, that is, to assume that its mean is zero. This assumption results in the elimination of one path from the model ($\triangle \to A$), which yields a just-identified mean structure. By imposing equality constraints on the four intercepts (i.e., $\triangle \to X_1 = \triangle \to X_2 = \triangle \to X_3 = \triangle \to X_4$), one can test whether the means of the four indicators are equal. Specifically, if the fit of the equality-constrained model is not significantly worse than that of the unconstrained model *and* the overall fit of the constrained model is acceptable, then one concludes that (1) the four indicators seem to measure a single factor and (2) the means of the indicators are equal within statistical error. Arbuckle (1996) presents an example of the evaluation of a single-factor, four-indicator measurement model with a mean structure that excludes the mean of the factor. The four indicators were scores from quizzes in a university course, and Arbuckle analyzed the covariances and means of the quizzes. Additional examples of the estimation of measurement models with mean structures within single samples can be found in Bollen (1989, pp. 306–311).

The mean of the factor of the model in Figure 10.4 can be included in the mean structure if the model is evaluated across multiple groups as long as certain constraints are imposed on some of the parameter estimates. Although it is beyond the scope of this section to describe these constraints in detail, one strategy is to fix the mean of the factor to zero in one of the groups. This constraint establishes that group as a reference sample. The factor means in the other samples are freely estimated, and their values estimate *relative* differences on the latent variable compared to the reference sample. Additional constraints may also include cross-group equality constraints on the factor loadings (e.g., $A \rightarrow X_2$ in Figure 10.4) and on the intercepts (e.g., $\triangle \rightarrow X_2$), which together test for invariance in measurement and in regressions of the indicators on the factors. Examples of such multisample analyses are presented by Bollen (1989), Byrne (1994), Kinnunen and Leskinen (1989), and in the manuals for Amos, EQS, and LISREL (Arbuckle, 1997; Bentler, 1995; Jöreskog & Sörbom, 1993, 1996a).

Analysis of Incomplete Data

Traditional ways to deal with missing data involve either deleting incomplete cases (listwise or pairwise) or the imputation of missing observations with estimated scores. SEM offers some additional ways to analyze data sets that are incomplete, but it is important to say up front that both the traditional and SEM-based approaches assume that the data are missing at random (MAR). As discussed earlier in the book (section 4.4), this implies that subjects' true status on some variable is unrelated to the presence versus absence of scores on that variable. If the pattern of incomplete data is systematic instead of MAR, then there is essentially no statistical procedure, SEM or otherwise, that can ameliorate potential bias in results based on the complete cases.

One option afforded by SEM to deal with the problem of missing data is to estimate a model across multiple groups, one with complete data on all variables and the others with particular patterns of missing observations. In general, the total number of possible patterns of complete versus missing observations equals 2^v where v is the number of observed variables. If there are three variables, for instance, then there are 2^3 (or eight) possible patterns: complete records with scores on all three variables; incomplete records with missing observations on just one variable (there are three ways this can occur); cases with missing data on two variables (three ways this can happen); and cases with missing observations across all variables, for eight in total. Excluding the pattern of missing on all variables, there are in general ($2^v - 1$) possible patterns of complete versus incomplete records. For this example with three variables, then, there are ($2^3 - 1$) = 7 patterns. For the multisample SEM approach to be feasible, it is necessary that there are sufficient numbers of subjects with complete records *and* with at least one pattern of missing data to each constitute a distinct group. If not, then there is another SEM-based option that involves the use of a special maximum likelihood (ML) estimation procedure that accommodates missing observations within a single sample; this method is described later.

As an example of the multiple group SEM approach to the analysis of incomplete data, suppose that there are four observed measures, X_1 through X_4, that are all thought to measure a common latent variable. Two of the indicators, X_1 and X_2, are relatively inexpensive to administer, but the other two indicators, X_3 and X_4, are much more costly or time consuming to use. The more expensive measures may require individual administration, for example, but the less expensive ones may be group-administered questionnaires. A researcher has a sample of 1,000 cases. All subjects have scores on the less expensive measures (X_1 and X_2). Due to resource limitations, the researcher can only test 100 subjects (10% of the sample) with X_3 and X_4, the more costly measures. These 100 cases are randomly selected from the total sample, which means that the missing data pattern (i.e., 900 missing scores on X_3 and X_4) is probably not systematic.

The researcher in the example just described wishes to evaluate the hypothesis that X_1 through X_4 measure a common factor. Although it would be possible to conduct a standard confirmatory factor analysis (CFA) with the 100 cases that have complete data on all four variables, this tactic would ignore the 900 cases with scores on only two of the indicators. (This option is the same as listwise deletion of incomplete cases.) A better alternative is to specify a model like the one illustrated in Figure 10.5 and to evaluate it across the two groups of this example—the smaller one with scores on all four indicators (complete; $N = 100$), and the much larger group with data from only two indicators (incomplete; $N = 900$). The model in Figure 10.5 has three key characteristics. First, its covariance structure is a standard CFA model with one factor and four indicators. Second, the model has a mean structure that includes the indicators (the factor mean is assumed here to be zero), which allows the analysis of all possible kinds of data (i.e., covariances and means). Third, the pat-

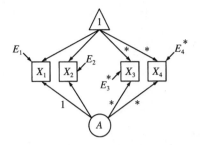

FIGURE 10.5. A hypothetical measurement model with a mean structure evaluated across samples with complete and incomplete data (* = constrained to zero in group with incomplete data).

tern of constraints depicted in the figure permits the model to be analyzed using data from all subjects, that is, those with both complete and incomplete data on the four indicators (N = 1,000 altogether). For instance, the loadings of the expensive indicators (X_3 and X_4), the variances of their measurement errors (E_3 and E_4), and their intercepts ($\triangle \rightarrow X_3$, $\triangle \rightarrow X_4$) are all fixed to zero in the incomplete sample (N = 900). In contrast, the remaining parameters—except for the loading of X_1 that is fixed to 1.0 to scale the factor—are free parameters that are estimated with data from both groups, complete and incomplete. To test whether these estimates are equal across the complete and incomplete samples, the relative fits of a model with and without these parameters constrained to be equal across the groups can be compared. If the fits of these models are not appreciably different and the overall fit of the constrained model is acceptable, then (1) the four indicators may indeed measure a common factor and (2) the measurement model for X_1 and X_2 is invariant across the complete and incomplete groups.

The input data for the analysis of the model presented in Figure 10.5 would be two matrices, one for each group (complete, incomplete). Two hypothetical matrices for this problem are presented in Table 10.3. Note that the matrix summary for the incomplete group has pseudoestimates for missing correlations, means, and standard deviations. These pseudoestimates together with actual values for the nonmissing observations make the matrix summary of the data for the incomplete group the same "size" (i.e, for four variables) as for the group with complete data. Missing correlations and means in the matrix for the incomplete group are represented by the pseudoestimate "0" and missing standard deviations by the pseudoestimate "1."

TABLE 10.3. Hypothetical Input Matrices for a Multiple Group Analysis of Incomplete Data

Data	Variable	Complete (N = 100)				Incomplete (N = 900)			
		X_1	X_2	X_3	X_4	X_1	X_2	X_3	X_4
r	X_1	—				—			
	X_2	.64	—			.43	—		
	X_3	.44	.51	—		**0**	**0**	—	
	X_4	.32	.30	.42	—	**0**	**0**	**0**	—
M		16.62	6.65	17.39	6.75	16.98	6.83	**0**	**0**
SD		13.45	4.03	14.75	3.89	14.74	4.02	**1**	**1**

Note. Entries in boldface are pseudoestimates that represent missing observations.

The pseudoestimate "1" was used here for missing standard deviations because some computer programs may err if they encounter a variable with no variance. Otherwise, any non-negative pseudoestimate may be used. Readers can find examples of the evaluation of models for incomplete data across multiple groups in Allison (1987), Bollen (1989), S. E. Duncan and T. E. Duncan (1994), and McArdle and Hamagami (1991, 1992).

The multiple group SEM approach to the analysis of incomplete data is not practical if either the total sample size is small or the number of possible patterns of missing data is large and there are only few cases for each one. An alternative approach that can be applied to data within a single group is to use a modification of standard ML estimation that handles incomplete raw data. Although it has been known for some time that ML can analyze data sets with missing observations (e.g., Wilks, 1932), the implementation of this capability used to require extensive computer resources. With the increasing sophistication of relatively inexpensive desktop computers, however, ML estimation of incomplete data is gradually becoming more accessible. Two model-fitting programs that offer this method include Amos (Arbuckle, 1997), which is reviewed in Chapter 11, and another program called Mx by Neale (1994). These special ML estimation routines typically require the analysis of a raw data file and the presence of a mean structure that includes the observed variables. These procedures also require more computation time. For example, Arbuckle (1996) reported relative times for the analysis of a two-factor, three-indicator model with different rates of missing data with the special ML procedure of the Amos program. At a 10% level of missing observations, the computation time was about four times longer compared to analyses with no missing data. At a 30% level of missing data, computation times were about 7–10 times longer than those for analyses of complete data. Examples of fitting models to incomplete raw data with special ML procedures are available in Arbuckle (1996) and McArdle and Hamagami (1996).

Results of recent computer simulation studies by Arbuckle (1996), McArdle (1994), McArdle and Hamagami (1991), and Muthén, Kaplan, and Hollis (1987) suggest the following about the performance of SEM-based methods when used to analyze incomplete data relative to casewise or pairwise deletion: When the data are missing at random and the rate of missing observations is relatively high (e.g., 30%), SEM-based parameter estimates may be more efficient than those derived using deletion of incomplete cases. (Greater efficiency means that the variability of parameter estimates from sample to sample is less.) However, when the data loss pattern is systematic rather than random, then results based on SEM methods or case deletion are all biased, although the magnitude of the bias may be somewhat less with the SEM-based approaches. As mentioned earlier, there is no magical "fix" for data loss patterns that are systematic; thus, it is imperative for the researcher to try to understand the nature of the data loss process and how it affects the interpretation of the results regardless of the method of analysis. For information about additional SEM methods for incomplete data, see R. L. Brown (1994).

Latent Growth Models

The term *latent growth model* refers to a class of models for longitudinal data that can be analyzed with SEM or other statistical procedures (e.g., hierarchical linear modeling; Byrk & Raudenbush, 1992). The particular kind of latent growth model briefly outlined below has been described by several authors in the SEM literature (e.g., Curran, Harford, & Muthén, 1996; McArdle & Epstein, 1987; Willett & Sayer, 1994, 1996), is specified as a hybrid model with a mean structure, and can be analyzed with standard model-fitting programs. These analyses typically require (1) at least three measurement occasions; (2) a dependent measure that is continuous and at the interval level of measurement; (3) scores that have the same units across time (e.g., percent correct), can be said to measure the same construct at each assessment, and are *not* standardized; and (4) data that are *time structured*, which means that the subjects are all tested at the same intervals. These intervals need not be equal. For example, a sample of young children may be observed at 3, 6, 12, and 24 months of age. However, all subjects must be tested at these same four ages. If some children are tested at, say, 4, 10, 15, and 30 months, then their data cannot be analyzed together with those tested at the other four intervals.

To demonstrate the rationale of latent growth models in SEM, consider the data summarized in Table 10.4, which were collected by Raudenbush and Chan (1992) and analyzed by Willett and Sayer (1994). These data are from an annual survey of 168 adolescents over the 5-year period from ages 11 through 15 about tolerance of deviant behaviors of varying seriousness (e.g., stealing something worth less than $5 vs. $50, hitting someone without reason, selling drugs). Higher scores on this survey indicate greater overall tolerance of such behavior. There are three noteworthy patterns evident in these data. First, the means increase over time, which indicates that these adolescents became increasingly more tolerant of deviant behavior as they matured. These increases in average deviance tolerance from year to year are fairly consistent, which suggests that the overall trend in the increase is linear. Second, the standard deviations also increase over time, which indicates that the range of individual differences in deviance tolerance becomes progressively wider. A pattern of increasing levels and ranges of individual differences on a repeated measures variable is called a *fan spread,* and it suggests growth trajectories of individual subjects that become more divergent over time. The third noteworthy characteristic is that intercor-

TABLE 10.4. Data for Latent Growth Models of Change in Tolerance of Deviant Behavior

Correlations, standard deviations, and means (These transformed data are from Willett & Sayer, 1994; the original data were collected by Raudenbush & Chan, 1992; N = 168 adolescents.)

Variable		1	2	3	4	5
Log tolerance of deviant behavior						
1. Age 11		—				
2. Age 12		.3760	—			
3. Age 13		.3653	.4788	—		
4. Age 14		.4088	.4058	.6742	—	
5. Age 15		.4373	.3968	.6024	.7665	—
	M	.2008	.2263	.3255	.4168	.4460
	SD	.1780	.1987	.2691	.2927	.2955

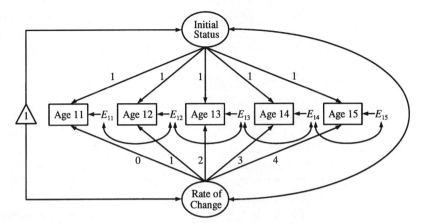

FIGURE 10.6. Latent growth model of change in tolerance of deviant behavior.

relations are higher at older ages than younger ages. For instance, the correlation of deviance tolerance between ages 11 and 12 is only .38 but between ages 14 and 15 is .77 . Although increasing correlations over time suggest that the individual differences in deviance tolerance become more stable, an alternative explanation is that there is more measurement error for younger subjects that attenuates the observed correlations.

One of the latent growth models analyzed by Willett and Sayer (1994) with the data summarized in Table 10.4 is presented in Figure 10.6. This model has the following four essential characteristics:

First, each assessment of deviance tolerance is represented as an indicator of two underlying factors, Initial Status and Rate of Change. As its name suggests, the Initial Status factor represents subjects' baseline levels of deviance tolerance at age 11.[5] Because the Initial Status factor is analogous to the intercept in a regression equation (e.g., Equation 10.3), the loadings of the repeated measures indicators on this factor are all fixed to 1.0. In contrast, loadings on the Rate of Change factor are fixed to constants that correspond to the times of measurement, beginning with 0 for the initial measurement at age 11 and ending with 4 for age 15. Because these loadings are evenly spaced (i.e., 0, 1, 2, 3, 4), the Rate of Change factor thus represents linear change over time. (It is also possible to include higher-order

---

[5]It is possible to set the initial level at other ages. In their analyses, for example, Willett and Sayer (1994) set the initial level of deviance tolerance at age 13 and evaluated relative change from this point.

factors that represent nonlinear effects such as quadratic change over time.)

Second, the Initial Status and Rate of Change factors are specified to covary. The estimate of this covariance indicates whether initial levels of deviance tolerance are related to rates of subsequent change. If this covariance is positive, it suggests that subjects with high initial levels of deviance tolerance show greater rates of subsequent change. A negative covariance would indicate just the opposite—that higher initial levels are associated with lower rates of change.

Third, the latent growth model of Figure 10.6 has a mean structure in which the constant $\triangle$ has direct effects on the exogenous Initial Status and Rate of Change factors. This specification includes the means of the factors as model parameters. The mean of the Initial Status factor is the average level of deviance tolerance at age 11 adjusted for measurement error. This average is a characteristic of the whole sample. In contrast, the *variance* of the Initial Status factor reflects the range of individual differences in deviance tolerance around the average initial level. The mean of the Rate of Change factor also reflects a group-level characteristic: Its value indicates the average amount of year-to-year change in mean levels of deviance tolerance (also adjusted for measurement error). If the mean of the Rate of Change factor is zero, then there is no overall linear change in the levels of deviance tolerance. The variance of the Rate of Change factor provides information about the range of individual differences in linear year-to-year changes as subjects mature.

The fourth key characteristic of the model in Figure 10.6 concerns measurement error. In this model, the measurement errors of adjacent years are assumed to covary (e.g., $E_{11} \leftrightarrow E_{12}$), which yields a total of four error covariances. Other patterns are also possible, including no measurement error covariances (i.e., the errors are independent over time) or the specification of additional error covariances (e.g., $E_{11} \leftrightarrow E_{13}$). The capability to explicitly model measurement error is a potential advantage of SEM over other, more traditional methods for repeated measures data. For example, ANOVA assumes that the error variances of repeated measures variables are equal and independent. MANOVA (multivariate analysis of variance) can also be applied to longitudinal data (e.g., Stevens, 1992, chap. 13). Although assumptions about error variance are less restrictive in MANOVA (e.g., errors may covary; see Cole, Maxwell, Avery, & Salas, 1993), MANOVA shares with ANOVA a crucial limitation: both techniques analyze changes only in group means and consequently treat differences among individual subjects in their growth trajectories as error variance. In contrast, one of the points of the analysis of a latent growth model in SEM is to explicitly estimate the range of individual differences in change over time.

The results of Willett and Sayer's (1994) analysis of the model of Figure 10.6 with the data of Table 10.4 indicated that the variance of the Initial Status factor did not differ significantly from zero, which suggests that the adolescents were fairly homogeneous in their initial levels of deviance tolerance. Both the mean and variance of the Rate of Change factor were significant, which together suggest that the overall rate of annual increase in deviance tolerance for the whole sample is not zero and that there are individual differences in the slopes of these increases over time. The estimate of the covariance of the Initial Status and Rate of Change factors did not differ significantly from zero, which means that the adolescents' level of deviance tolerance at age 11 did not predict their rates of subsequent change. All of the estimated error covariances differed significantly from zero. Also, the variances of the measurement error terms were less at older ages than at younger ages, which suggests that the assessment of deviance tolerance is more reliable for older adolescents, a possibility raised earlier. Fortunately, estimates of other model parameters are corrected for unequal measurement error variances and for the pairwise error covariances.

A basic analysis of change in a single variable over time as described above can be expanded in many ways in the SEM framework for latent growth models. For example, Willett and Sayer (1994) added two variables to the model of Figure 10.6 that may predict individual differences in increases in deviance tolerance, gender and previous exposure to deviant behavior at age 11. They found that although boys and girls show generally similar rates of increases in deviance tolerance over time, adolescents who reported greater exposure to deviant behavior at age 11 had significantly steeper subsequent increases in their acceptance of such behavior. Given the relevant parameter estimates, it is also possible to construct growth curves for hypothetical male and female adolescents who vary in their levels of exposure to deviant behavior, something that is demonstrated by Willett and Sayer (1994). Other ways to extend the evaluation of latent growth models in SEM include the analysis of cross-domain change in more than one variable and the analysis of models across multiple groups. Recent examples of such analyses include those of Curran et al. (1996), who analyzed data from an annual survey of young adults about their frequencies of heavy drinking and patronage of bars over a 3-year period; and Willett and Sayer (1996), who evaluated changes in reading and arithmetic skills in three groups of children, healthy, asthmatic, and those with a seizure disorder. For additional information, articles by Francis, Fletcher, Stuebing, Davidson, and Thompson (1991) and Willett, Ayoub, and Robinson (1991) about latent growth models in clinical research are recommended.

10.5   Power Analysis

The concept of the power of tests of statistical significance was introduced in Chapter 2 (section 2.9). Briefly reviewed, power is the probability that the results of a significance test will lead to rejection of the null hypothesis when there is a true effect in the population. Five basic factors influence power: (1) the general design of the study such as the sample size and the representation of an independent variable as a between- or within- subject factor (e.g., the use of independent samples vs. repeated measurement of the same subjects to test a treatment effect); (2) the particular test of significance used; (3) the level of significance at which the null hypothesis is rejected (e.g., .05 or .01); (4) the directionality of the test of the alternative hypothesis (i.e., one- or two-tailed); and (5) the magnitude of the true effect in the population. In a typical power analysis, the researcher varies one of the first four factors or estimates of the true population effect and observes its effect on power. For example, given an estimate about the magnitude of the effect in the population, it is possible to estimate power for a hypothetical study with a particular sample size, directionality of the alternative hypothesis, and level of significance for a particular test statistic. If the estimated power is low, then the effect of changing one or more of the aforementioned factors can be determined (e.g., increase sample size from 100 to 200 cases; use the .05 level instead of the .01).

Conducting a power analysis *before* the data are collected can be very useful for planning a study. For example, if the researcher wants at least a 75% chance of detecting a true effect of a certain magnitude with a significance test, then he or she can determine with a power analysis, say, the minimum sample size needed to do so. A power analysis conducted *after* the data are collected may be too late and more like an autopsy than a diagnostic procedure. A potential drawback of power analysis, however, is that it requires a reasonable estimate about the magnitude of the effect in the population. This requirement need not be an insurmountable problem, though. For instance, if the researcher is unable to formulate a particular guess about the effect with confidence, then power analyses can be conducted with a range of a priori estimates of its size.

For conventional statistics such as the t test and the F ratio (and many others), researchers can either consult special power tables (e.g., Cohen, 1988) or use computer programs that conduct power analyses. Power analysis in SEM, however, is a relatively new topic. One application concerns the ability of the $\chi^2_{\text{difference}}$ test to yield a significant result for a particular parameter that is nonzero in the population given a certain sample size, level of significance, and directionality of the test. For the sake of illustration, let's consider a power analysis of the significance test of the direct effect of X on Y. One method for this type of analysis (e.g., Matsueda & Bielby, 1986; Satorra & Saris, 1985) requires the researcher to provide a priori values of the parameters of a model that contains all effects of interest. The example that follows illustrates the rationale of this procedure.

Suppose that a researcher believed that the unstandardized direct effect of X on Y is 5.0 (i.e., a 1-point increase in X leads to an increase of Y of 5 points holding all other causal variables constant). Using this and the other a priori values of the parameters of a model that contains all effects of interest, his or her next step in a power analysis is to generate a predicted covariance matrix by employing the tracing rule (section 5.8) or methods based on matrix algebra (e.g., Bollen, 1989). The model-implied covariances are then analyzed with a model-fitting program specifying a particular sample size and that $X \rightarrow Y$ is a free parameter. Using procedures outlined in Bollen (1989, pp. 338–349) and in Saris, den Ronden, and Satorra (1987), the researcher utilizes information from this output about the standard error of the estimate of $X \rightarrow Y$ to calculate something known as a *noncentrality parameter*. A noncentrality parameter adjusts the distribution of the $\chi^2_{\text{difference}}$ statistic (here, $df = 1$ for the freely estimated path $X \rightarrow Y$) to reflect the assumption that the associated effect is not zero in the population (here, it is 5.0—standard significance tests assume nil effects). Using the noncentrality parameter as a correction factor, one finds the percentile equivalent of a significant value of $\chi^2_{\text{difference}}$ at the level of significance specified by the researcher (e.g., .01): 1 minus this percentile yields the estimated power, that is, the probability of obtaining a $\chi^2_{\text{difference}}$ value that leads to rejection of the null hypothesis assuming that the true size of the direct effect $X \rightarrow Y$ is 5. If estimated power is low, then the effect of increasing the sample size or changing the level of significance (e.g., to .05) can be determined in another power analysis. Also, the researcher can conduct this procedure with different a priori parameter values for $X \rightarrow Y$, which yields estimates of power under different assumptions about the size of this effect.

Saris and Satorra (1993) have developed a procedure for power analysis in SEM that does not require a priori values of individual model parameters. Unlike the method described above that can be implemented with essentially any model-fitting program, this one requires special computer programs that are yet not widely available. Only the general rationale of Saris and Satorra's (1993) method is described here; readers are referred to their work for computational details and examples. As with the method described above, the researcher must specify a model that contains all effects of interest. Instead of the researcher providing particular parameter values, special power analysis programs described by Saris and Satorra (1993) are used to derive sets of parameter estimates that correspond to conditions of low power (e.g., 10% chance of rejecting a false null hypothesis) versus high power (90%). The latter set of values inform the researcher about how large various effects must be in the population in order to have high probabilities of detecting them with significance tests conducted within a sample of a certain size.

10.6 Bootstrapping

Bootstrapping is a technique that provides empirical information about the variability of parameter estimates and fit indexes. The method of bootstrapping is associated mainly with the work of B. Efron, and a very readable account of its general rationale is available in a *Scientific American* article (Diaconis & Efron, 1983; also see the more recent work by Efron & Tibshirani, 1993). Although there are variations on the basic theme, bootstrapping is essentially a resampling procedure in which the researcher's data set is treated as the population. Cases from the original data file are randomly selected with replacement to generate other data sets, usually with the same numbers of cases as the original. Due to sampling with replacement, (1) the same case can appear more than once in a generated data set and (2) the composition of cases will vary somewhat across the generated samples.[6] When repeated many times with a computer (e.g., 500), bootstrapping simulates the drawing of numerous samples from a population. Of course, the "population" is merely the researcher's original sample. Thus, if the original sample is small or

---

[6]There is a related resampling procedure known as the *jackknife* in which one case is excluded from each replication of an original sample. For example, the first case is omitted in the first generated sample, the second case is excluded from the second generated sample, and so on. The maximum total number of generated samples using a jackknife procedure thus equals the total number of cases.

nonrepresentative, bootstrapping cannot somehow ameliorate these problems. Also, bootstrapping cannot be considered a substitute for cross-validating a model with an independent sample.

With the aforementioned limitations in mind, the basic principle of bootstrapping is illustrated with a simple example before its application to SEM is described. Suppose that the mean of X within a sample of 500 cases is 10.0 and that its standard error is 5.0. Recall that the standard error estimates the variability of sample means (each based on 500 cases and randomly drawn from the same population as that of the original sample) around the population mean. If a sample mean exceeds this expected variability by a factor of at least 2.0 (here, 10.0/5.0 = 2.0), then the sample mean differs statistically from zero at the .05 level of significance, assuming normality (section 2.9). Bootstrapping provides an additional way to estimate the variability of a sample mean. Here's how it works: Suppose that a computer generates 100 samples of 500 cases each by randomly selecting cases with replacement from the original sample. The computer records these 100 means from the generated samples, averages them, and calculates a standard error. This empirically derived mean and standard error can be compared to the corresponding values from the original sample (i.e., 10.0 and 5.0). A large discrepancy between these two sets of values would suggest that the estimate of the mean and standard error from the original sample may be not be statistically stable.

In SEM, bootstrap estimates can be derived for every model parameter using basically the same method as was just described. The average bootstrap parameter estimates and their standard errors can be compared with the corresponding values from the analysis of the original sample. Depending upon the bootstrap capabilities of the model-fitting program, it may also be possible to inspect distributions of fit indexes for the whole model from a large number of generated samples and to compare these values against the ones from the original sample. It may also be possible to compare two hierarchically related models by inspecting the frequency distribution of $\chi^2_{\text{difference}}$ statistics calculated within each generated sample. For instance, if the clear majority of the bootstrap $\chi^2_{\text{difference}}$ statistics exceed the value required for statistical significance, then the relative fits of the two models may not be equal. Of the three model-fitting programs reviewed in Chapter 11, Amos and EQS offer options for bootstrapping, as does LISREL when used with its companion program, PRELIS2.

For the reasons mentioned earlier, bootstrapping is not some type of magical technique that can somehow compensate for small or unrepresentative samples, distributions that are severely non-normal, or the absence of independent samples for the cross-validation of a model. Instead, it is probably best viewed as a useful diagnostic tool, one to add to the researcher's repertoire of SEM-related skills. For more information and examples of the application of bootstrapping in SEM, readers are referred to Bollen and Stine (1993), Schumaker and Lomax (1996), and Yung and Bentler (1996).

10.7   Internet Resources for SEM

In addition to the published works cited in this book, researchers can also find information about SEM on the Internet. For example, there is a an electronic mailing list called SEMNET that serves as a discussion forum for subscribed participants. Information about SEMNET is presented in the footnote below.[7] There are also many SEM-related sites on the World Wide Web. You can find them using Internet search engines such as *Yahoo!, Excite, Lycos,* and *WebCrawler,* among others, that may be available through the service that provides your Internet connection. By searching on keywords such as "structural equation modeling," "covariance structure analysis," or the name of a model-fitting program, you may be able to find something interesting. For instance, some research groups with interests in SEM have homepages on the Web. Other sites offer summaries of SEM concepts, course outlines for classes about SEM, or information about particular software packages. Considering the rapid recent growth of the Internet, it seems likely that resources for SEM will also continue to expand.

10.8   Summary

With the exception of the next chapter about software for SEM, so concludes this journey of discovery about SEM. As on any guided tour, you may have found some places along the way more interest-

---

[7]A description of SEMNET is available at the following World Wide Web site:
        HTTP://WWW.GSU.EDU/~MKTEER/SEMNET.HTML
To subscribe to SEMNET, send the following message via e-mail:
        SUBSCRIBE SEMNET *first-name last-name*
to LISTSERV@UALVM.UA.EDU.

ing than others. Also, you may decide to revisit certain sites by using some of the related techniques in your own work. Overall, I hope that the reading of this book has given you new ways of looking at your data and testing a broader range of hypotheses. Use SEM to address new questions or to provide new perspectives on older ones, but use it guided by your good sense and knowledge of your research area. Go do me proud!

CHAPTER ELEVEN

Software for SEM: Amos, EQS, and LISREL

Causal modeling provides no certain path to knowledge. In fact, causal models are maximally helpful only when good ideas are tested. Good ideas do not come out of computer packages, but from people's heads.
                                    —DAVID A. KENNY (1979, p. 8)

11.1   Foreword

Amos, LISREL, and EQS are all comprehensive model-fitting programs that can analyze the full range of standard structural equation models. In addition to traditional text-based modes in which models are specified with lines of program code, all three of these packages feature graphical interfaces that allow models to be specified by drawing them on the screen. After the drawing is complete, each program automatically interprets it and begins the analysis. These graphical interfaces allow new users to conduct SEMs almost immediately. In addition, these drawing-based program front ends also make it easier to determine whether the model analyzed is the one the user intended to specify, which helps to catch a mistake. As users become more experienced with a particular program, they can either continue to use its graphical interface or use its text-based programming language or both.

   The features of the most current releases of Amos, EQS, and LISREL as of mid-1997 are described below. (Because the features of computer programs may change with new versions, readers should contact the organizations listed below for current descriptions of each package.) Also summarized for each package are the symbols and syntax of their text-based programming languages. Annotated examples of the specification of the same hybrid model in each program's text-based programming language are also presented. Readers should note that the numbers in parentheses that appear on the right side of each example are *not* part of the program code. Instead, they designate comments about parts of the code that follow each example. Also, all three programs accept code in either upper or lower case. The particular case presented in the examples that follow are consistent with those used in each program's manual.

11.2   Amos

SmallWaters Corporation
1507 E. 53rd St., #452
Chicago, IL 60615
Voice: (773) 667-8635
Fax: (773) 955-6252
E-mail: INFO@SMALLWATERS.COM
Web site: HTTP://WWW.SMALLWATERS.COM

Description

Amos 3.6 (Arbuckle, 1997) runs under 32-bit implementations of Windows (or with a 32-bit Windows emulator on a Macintosh computer) and is available either as a stand-alone program or as SPSS Amos that installs itself into the Statistics menu of SPSS. Amos runs in two modes, Amos Graphics and Amos Text. As its name suggests, Amos Graphics provides a graphical interface through which the user conducts an analysis by drawing the model on the screen. Amos Text is for users who are already familiar with Amos's programming language. In the Amos Text mode, the user directly enters lines of code that describe the data, specify the model, and control the analysis.

Amos Graphics presents the user with a palette of tools for drawing the model. Some of these tools include shapes for drawing squares or rectangles (for observed variables), circles or ovals (for latent variables, disturbances, or measurement errors), and paths such as unanalyzed associations ($\leftrightarrow$) or direct effects ($\rightarrow$). A click of the right mouse button when the cursor is in select mode and on an object brings up a properties box in which the user can add a label, impose a constraint, or edit the object (e.g., move, copy). A mean structure is specified simply by pressing the "Means" button in the tool palette. Amos Graphics attempts to prevent mistakes in the specification of a model in two ways. First, the program does not allow the user to make illogical specifications among objects on the screen (e.g., connecting two endogenous variables with ↔, the symbol for an unanalyzed association). Second, the program also gives warnings about the omission of certain objects such as the disturbance of an endogenous variable when the analysis is run.

When the analysis is executed, Amos reports the progress of the estimation (e.g., number of iterations) and then displays the output in a text file. Amos Graphics can also display either the unstandardized or standardized estimates in their proper places in the diagram of the model along with values of fit indexes selected by the user in a figure caption. Amos Graphics also offers a feature called the Modeling Laboratory (accessed through the "Lab" button) in which the user can select an individual parameter, change its value, and observe how this change affects the fit of the whole model.

When Amos Text is started, it offers a menu through which users can edit program or data files, run an analysis, or view output files. Amos Text uses the Windows Notepad accessory as its editor for opening and saving files, so multiple program and data files can be open simultaneously. When the analysis is run, the same windows described earlier that indicate the progress of the analysis and contain the output appear on the screen.

Special Features

In addition to its very sophisticated graphical interface and comprehensive suite of model-oriented drawing tools, Amos also has extensive bootstrapping capabilities. For example, commands in Amos Text such as $Bootml (ml = maximum likelihood) can generate frequency distributions of statistics that indicate discrepancies between observed and model-implied covariances for particular estimation methods. These histograms allow the user to compare the performance of different estimation procedures applied to the same data and model. Another command, $Bootbs, generates a histogram of the goodness of fit χ^2 statistic across replication samples from centrality-corrected data, according to a procedure described by Bollen and Stine (1993). Amos is unique among the programs reviewed here in that it has a special ML procedure that fits models to incomplete raw data within a single sample (section 10.4) without the need for case deletion or imputation of missing values.

Symbols and Basic Syntax of Amos Text

Amos Text does not use a fixed set of symbols to designate things like observed versus latent variables or error terms. Instead, labels for all variables (up to 29 characters) are supplied by the user. The syntax for Amos Text is straightforward. All commands begin with the symbol "$." Although some command names are quite long (e.g., $Mindecimalplaces for minimum number of decimal places), abbreviated versions of all command names are also available. An Amos Text program file typically consists of lines that request different types of output (e.g., $Standardized for the standardized solution), describe the data (e.g., $Samplesize = 200), and specify the model.

Models are specified in Amos Text under two main headings, $Structure and $Mstructure: the former refers to the model's covariance structure; the latter, to its mean structure, if any. Starting values and constraints are also specified under these headings. Suppose that the exogenous variable of a path model is interest and that the endogenous variables are motivation and achievement. The model could be described with the following lines of Amos Text code:

```
$Structure
  interest (10?)
  dis_mot (2?)
  dis_ach (4?)
  motivation = interest + (1) dis_mot
  achievement = (5?) interest + (2?) motivation + (1) dis_ach
```

The first line above under $Structure specifies the observed exogenous variable, interest, and provides a starting value for its variance, 10. Starting values are optional and designated by a question mark. Omission of the question mark in the parentheses would fix the variance of the exogenous interest variable to 10. If more than one exogenous variable is listed, Amos Text assumes by default that they covary. The second and third lines under $Structure provide starting values for the disturbance variances for motivation and achievement (respectively, 2 and 4). These lines are optional. Also, the names of the disturbances are provided by the user. The last two lines in the above section of code specify in the form of a regression equation the direct effects and the disturbances. The notation "(1)" before the disturbances fixes the residual path coefficients to 1.0, which allows the program to estimate only the variances of the disturbances. Note that optional starting values are provided for the direct effects on achievement from interest and motivation (respectively, 5 and 2).

Consider the following Amos Text descriptions of a single-factor, three-indicator measurement model:

```
$Structure
  reading
  word_knowledge = (1) reading + (1) err_word
  sentence_comp  =     reading + (1) err_sent
  speed          =     reading + (1) err_speed
```

In the above code, reading is specified as an exogenous latent variable with three indicators, word_knowledge, sentence_comp (comprehension), and speed (of reading). The factor loading of word_knowledge is fixed to 1.0 to scale the underlying reading factor, but the other factor loadings are free parameters. Measurement error terms for each indicator are also specified.

The $Structure and $Mstructure commands specify a mean structure. Consider the following example:

```
$Structure
  reading
  word_knowledge = () + (1) reading + (1) err_word
  sentence_comp  = () +     reading + (1) err_sent
  speed          = () +     reading + (1) err_speed
$Mstructure
  reading (0)
```

These lines describe a single-factor, three-indicator measurement model with a mean structure. The empty parentheses to the right of the equals sign for the indicators adds an intercept term to each equation. The exogenous reading factor is listed under the $Mstructure command, but note that its mean is constrained to equal zero. With only three observed means, this constraint identifies the model (e.g., section 10.4).

Example of Amos Text Code

```
Amos example: The final three-factor hybrid model of
the effects of familial risk for psychopathology
on child adjustment (Table 8.1, section 8.4) estimated
with data from Worland et al. (1984)
$Standardized                                          (1)
```

```
$Smc
$Allimpliedmoments
$Residualmoments
$Inputvariables                                                    (2)
 verbal
 visual
 memory
 read
 arith
 spell
 motivate
 extraver
 harmony
 emotstab
 parpsych
 ses
$Structure
 err_ver <> err_vis (.1?)                                          (3)
 err_ver <> err_mem (.1?)
 err_vis <> err_mem (.1?)
 err_rea <> err_ari (.1?)
 err_rea <> err_spe (.1?)
 err_ari <> err_spe (.1?)
 parpsych = (1) famrisk  + (1) err_par                             (4)
 ses      =     famrisk  + (1) err_ses
 verbal   = (1) cogach   + (1) err_ver
 visual   =     cogach   + (1) err_vis
 memory   =     cogach   + (1) err_mem
 read     =     cogach   + (1) err_rea
 arith    =     cogach   + (1) err_ari
 spell    =     cogach   + (1) err_spe
 motivate = (1) classadj + (1) err_mot
 harmony  =     classadj + (1) err_har
 emotstab =     classadj + (1) err_emo
 cogach   = famrisk + (1) dis_cog                                  (5)
 classadj = cogach  + (1) dis_sch
$Samplesize = 158                                                  (6)
$Correlations
 1.00
  .66 1.00
  .67  .66 1.00
  .78  .56  .73 1.00
  .69  .49  .70  .73 1.00
  .63  .49  .72  .87  .72 1.00
  .49  .32  .58  .53  .60  .59 1.00
  .18  .09  .17  .14  .15  .15  .25 1.00
  .42  .25  .46  .42  .44  .45  .77  .19 1.00
  .33  .27  .35  .36  .38  .38  .59 -.29  .58 1.00
```

```
 -.43 -.40 -.35 -.39 -.24 -.31 -.25 -.14 -.25 -.16 1.00
 -.50 -.40 -.38 -.43 -.37 -.33 -.25 -.17 -.26 -.18  .42 1.00
$Standarddeviations
  1.0  1.0  1.0  1.0  1.0  1.0  1.0  1.0  1.0  1.0  1.0  1.0
```

(1) These four lines request the standardized solution, squared multiple correlations, model-implied correlations and covariances, and correlation and covariance residuals.

(2) Names the observed variables and indicates their order in the input data.

(3) The first six lines under $Structure specify measurement error covariances and starting values (all .10).

(4) These three groups of lines specify loadings of the observed variables on their respective factors.

(5) These two lines define the structural model among the family risk, cognitive-achievement, and classroom adjustment factors and the disturbances of the latter two factors.

(6) Specifies the sample size and reads the input data.

11.3   EQS

Multivariate Software, Inc.
4924 Balboa Blvd., #368
Encino, CA 91316
Voice: (818) 906-0740
Fax: (818) 906-8205
E-mail: SALES@MVSOFT.COM
Web site: HTTP://WWW.MVSOFT.COM

Description

EQS 5 for Windows and for the Macintosh (Bentler, 1995; Bentler & Wu, 1995a, 1995b) is designed not only as a model-fitting program but also has many features for the general management and analysis of data. Thus, it is possible to use EQS for essentially all stages of an analysis from data entry and screening to exploratory statistical analyses to SEM. Raw data entered directly into EQS, read from an external file (e.g., a dBase file) or pasted from another active program (e.g., a spreadsheet), are handled by EQS's Data Editor. The Data Editor has many of the features of a general statistical package. These include the use of logical operators (e.g., IF, AND, OR) to select cases and the capabilities to create composite variables, transform variables (e.g., logarithmic), recode variables to partition subjects into groups, specify codes for missing data, and join or merge cases from two existing files. EQS's Data Editor also offers numerous tools for data screening, including capabilities for graphical displays (e.g., histograms), the detection of outliers, and analysis of the pattern of missing observations.

There are three ways to interact with EQS. Although all three require that the user understand the program's basic symbols (presented later), two ways of running EQS do not require knowledge about its programming language:

One of these is to use EQS's Diagrammer, which offers graphical templates and tools to draw the model on the screen. Included among its built-in drawing tools are squares/rectanges and circles/ovals for observed and latent variables (respectively); lines with one or two arrowheads ($\rightarrow$, $\leftrightarrow$) for direct effects, factor loadings, or unanalyzed associations; and a special template for drawing a factor and its indicators. Like Amos Graphics, the EQS Diagrammer also prevents the user from making illogical specifications with its drawing tools. Double-clicking on an object once it is drawn brings up a properties box that permits the specification of whether the associated parameters are fixed or free, starting values (if any), and labels that can optionally appear on the screen. Captions or titles that describe the model can also be added to the figure. After the drawing is complete, the user pulls down the "Build_EQS" menu and answers "yes" to the prompt about whether to invoke "Easy Build," which automatically generates program code for the model. Easy Build also offers a series of dialogue boxes that allow the user to perform such tasks as impose constraints or request optional types of output. Each of these dialogue boxes automatically adds the appropriate lines of code to the program. After all selections in Easy Build are complete, the user executes the program by selecting the "Run EQS" command under the "Build_EQS" menu. Program output appears in a separate window. The user can also request that unstandardized or standardized parameter estimates appear in their appropriate places in the figure on the screen. Summary statistics such as values of fit indexes can also be posted to the figure.

A second way to run EQS is to bypass the Diagrammer and use Easy Build to generate the program code from scratch. Accessed this way, Easy Build provides a series of dialogue boxes that prompt the user to specify the model. After the model is specified, Easy Build then presents the same boxes described above that control the analysis, output, and program default settings. After all selections are complete, the program generated by Easy Build is executed with the "Run EQS" command.

The third way to run EQS is for users who already know its programming syntax. Lines of code that describe the data, model, and analysis can be entered directly into a window that EQS saves as an ASCII (text) file. Program code entered directly by the user is then executed through the "Run EQS" command of the "Build_EQS" menu. For experienced users who are well versed in EQS's programming language, this third way to run the program may be the most efficient.

Special Features

In addition to its extensive data management and graphics capabilities, EQS also offers very flexible test procedures for model respecification. For example, EQS calculates both univariate and multivariate Lagrange Multipliers (the former are modification indexes) with its /LMTEST procedure. In single-sample analyses, /LMTEST can be run either empirically or in an a priori way by specifying the particular constraints that are to be evaluated. It is also possible to specify a particular order in which constraints are released, which is analogous to a hierarchical regression in which predictors are added to the equation in a particular order. In a multisample analysis, /LMTEST is typically used to test cross-group equality constraints imposed on certain parameters. Releases of EQS since 5.1 include a RETEST feature that automatically modifies a model based on results indicated by the modification indexes. (Readers already know that such automatic modification procedures should be used with caution; sections 5.10 and 7.7.)

EQS also features special estimation procedures and statistics that may be especially useful for non-normal data. Two classes of estimation methods in EQS do not assume multivariate normality. Some of these methods, based on elliptical distribution theory, allow for kurtosis in the univariate or multivariate distributions. Other procedures are based on arbitrary distribution theory, under which distributions can assume any form. Among the latter is asymptotically distribution-free (ADF) estimation, which in EQS is called arbitrary distribution generalized least squares, or AGLS. Although ADF/AGLS ordinally requires very large samples in order for its χ^2 test to be accurate (section 5.11), release 5.5 of EQS calculates a corrected test, called the Yuan–Bentler test (Yuan & Bentler, 1997), which improves on the uncorrected ADF/AGLS χ^2 test. EQS also calculates for most methods (including ML) robust standard errors and the Satorra–Bentler scaled χ^2 statistic (Satorra & Bentler, 1994). As discussed earlier (section 7.6), these statistics correct for the tendency of tests of significance to result in rejection of the null hypothesis too often when the data are severely non-normal. EQS is unique among the programs reviewed in this chapter in the derivation of these corrected tests and statistics. Some other special features of EQS include bootstrapping capabilities and the ability to analyze categorical observed variables that are specified as indicators of latent continuous variables (section 7.10). Note that all of the special procedures just mentioned require the analysis of raw data.

Symbols and Basic Syntax of EQS

EQS is based on the Bentler–Weeks representational system (e.g., Bentler & Weeks, 1980) in which the parameters of any linear structural model are regression coefficients for effects on dependent variables and the variances and covariances of independent variables. In the Bentler–Weeks model, independent variables include observed or latent exogenous variables, disturbances, and measurement errors. A dependent variable in the Bentler–Weeks model is any variable that has an error term such as an effect indicator of a latent variable in a measurement model or an endogenous variable (observed or latent) in a structural model. All types of models in EQS are thus set up in a consistent way. The symbol set of EQS is very straightforward and includes the symbols shown in the accompanying table.

Symbol	Meaning
V	Observed variable
E	Disturbance or measurement error of an observed variable
F	Latent variable (i.e., a factor)
D	Disturbance of a factor
V999	A constant that includes either the mean of an exogenous variable or the intercept of an endogenous variable in a mean structure

Models are represented in EQS code as a series of equations that are grouped together according to whether the variables described are independent or dependent as per the Bentler–Weeks model. In equations that describe the model, an asterisk (*) designates a free parameter. EQS calculates default starting values for all parameters (e.g., variances of E variables are .9 times the variance of the associated V variables). If EQS's default starting values do not lead to a converged solution, then the user can supply an initial estimate by inserting the value to the left of the asterisk in the equation for that parameter.

Equations for dependent variables in EQS appear under the heading /EQUATIONS and for independent variables under the headings /VARIANCES and /COVARIANCES. (There are abbreviations for all EQS headings including, among others, /EQU, /VAR, and /COV.) All equations—indeed, all program code in EQS except headings and data—end with a semicolon. Consider the following equations for a three-variable, just-identified recursive path model:

```
/EQUATIONS
V2 =   *V1 + E2;
V3 = 5*V1 + 2*V2 + E3;
/VARIANCES
V1 = 10*; E2 = 2*; E3 = 4*;
```

The first of these two equations specify that V2 and V3 are endogenous. The equation for V2 lists variables that, according to the model, directly affect it (V1 and V2's disturbance, E2). The asterisk before V1 in this equation means that this direct effect is a free parameter. If the user does not specify a numerical value before the asterisk, EQS assumes that the starting value for a path coefficient is 1.0. However, note that no asterisk appears before E2 in the equation for V2. Because disturbances and measurement errors are considered independent variables in EQS, any user-supplied information about them is presented in another section. The equation for V3 is read as follows: V1 and V2 are specified to directly affect V3; the path coefficients for each of these direct effects is a free parameter; and the starting value for the V1→V3 effect is 5.0 and the initial estimate for V2→V3 is 2.0. Endogenous variable V3's disturbance, E3, is also represented in this equation. The /VARIANCE section above lists V1, E2, and E3. The starting value for the variance of V1 (the exogenous variable) is specified as 10.0 and for the two error terms as 2.0 and 4.0, respectively.

Consider the following equations for a single-factor, three-indicator measurement model:

```
/EQUATIONS
V1 =   F1 + E1;
V2 = *F1 + E2;
V3 = *F1 + E3;
/VARIANCES
F1 = *;
```

The expressions under the /EQUATIONS section above represent observed variables V1, V2, and V3 as the indicators of factor F1. The loading of V1 on F1 is fixed to 1.0, which scales the factor. In contrast, loadings for V2 and V3 on F1 are specified as free parameters. Because no numerical values appear before the asterisks in these equations, EQS assumes that the starting values for the nonfixed loadings are all 1.0. The variance of the factor is specified as a free parameter with the starting value 1.0 under the /VARIANCES section. Although the three measurement error terms do not appear in the /VARIANCES section, they are by default considered free parameters with starting values equal to 1.0

A mean structure is specified in EQS by including V999 as a causal variable in the /EQUATIONS section. Consider the following example:

```
/EQUATIONS
V1 = *V999 +  F1 + E1;
V2 = *V999 + *F1 + E2;
V3 = *V999 + *F1 + E3;
/VARIANCES
F1 = *;
```

These lines specify a single-factor, three-indicator measurement model with a mean structure. Inclusion of "*V999" in the equations of the indicators V1 to V3 includes their intercepts as free model parameters. The latent variable F1 is not included in the mean structure. In general, though, variables that are exogenous in the covariance structure become dependent in EQS when their means are specified as parameters of the mean structure.

An example of EQS code is presented next (additional examples can be found in Byrne, 1994; Mueller, 1996; and Schumaker & Lomax, 1996).

Example of EQS Code

```
/TITLE
 EQS EXAMPLE: THE FINAL THREE-FACTOR HYBRID MODEL OF
 THE EFFECTS OF FAMILIAL RISK FOR PSYCHOPATHOLOGY ON CHILD
 ADJUSTMENT (TABLE 8.1, SECTION 8.4) ESTIMATED WITH
 DATA FROM WORLAND ET AL. (1984)
/SPECIFICATIONS                                              (1)
 VARIABLES=12; CASES=158; MATRIX=CORRELATION;
/LABELS                                                      (2)
```

```
 V1=VERBAL; V2=VISUAL; V3=MEMORY; V4=READ; V5=MATH; V6=SPELL;
 V7=MOTIVATE; V8=EXTRAVER; V9=HARMONY; V10=EMOTSTAB;
V11=PARPSYCH; V12=SES;
 F1=FAMRISK; F2=COG-ACH; F3=CLASSADJ;
/EQUATIONS
 V1 =  F2 + E1;    V2 = *F2 + E2;  V3 = *F2 + E3;              (3)
 V4 = *F2 + E4;    V5 = *F2 + E5;  V6 = *F2 + E6;
 V7 =  F3 + E7;    V9 = *F3 + E9; V10 = *F3 + E10;
V11 =  F1 + E11; V12 = *F1 + E12;
 F2 = *F1 + D2;    F3 = *F2 + D3;
/VARIANCES
 F1 = *; E1 TO E7 = *; E9 TO E12 = *; D2 = *; D3 = *;         (4)
/COVARIANCES
E1,E2 = .1*; E1,E3 = .1*; E2,E3 = .1*;                        (5)
E4,E5 = .1*; E4,E6 = .1*; E5,E6 = .1*;
/MATRIX                                                       (6)
1.00
 .66 1.00
 .67   .66 1.00
 .78   .56   .73 1.00
 .69   .49   .70   .73 1.00
 .63   .49   .72   .87   .72 1.00
 .49   .32   .58   .53   .60   .59 1.00
 .18   .09   .17   .14   .15   .15   .25 1.00
 .42   .25   .46   .42   .44   .45   .77   .19 1.00
 .33   .27   .35   .36   .38   .38   .59 -.29   .58 1.00
-.43 -.40 -.35 -.39 -.24 -.31 -.25 -.14 -.25 -.16 1.00
-.50 -.40 -.38 -.43 -.37 -.33 -.25 -.17 -.26 -.18   .42 1.00
/PRINT
FIT=ALL;
/END
```

(1) Defines the number of variables, cases, and the type of matrix read into the program.

(2) Labels the observed and latent variables.

(3) These equations specify both the measurement and structural components of this hybrid model.

(4) Specifies the variances of the exogenous factor, measurement errors, and disturbances of the endogenous factors as model parameters.

(5) These terms specify correlated measurement errors for indicators of the cognitive–achievemement factor and provide starting values.

(6) Reads the input data in matrix form.

11.4   LISREL

Scientific Software International
7383 N. Lincoln Ave., Suite 100
Chicago, IL 60646-1704
Voice: (800) 247-6113; (847) 675-0720
Fax: (847) 675-2140
E-mail: INFO@SSICENTRAL.COM
Web site: HTTP://WWW.SSICENTRAL.COM

Description

LISREL was one of the first computer programs for SEM. The original programming language for LISREL is based on matrix algebra. Its symbol set consists of numerous double-subscripted Greek characters that correspond to elements of various matrices that define the parameters of the model. This programming language is not easy to use until after one has memorized the whole system. Although the original language is still available in LISREL 8 (Jöreskog & Sörbom, 1996a), versions for Macintosh and IBM-compatible personal computers have two new features that make the program much easier to learn for beginners: a graphical interface that allows models to be specified by drawing them on the screen, and a new programming language called SIMPLIS (Jöreskog & Sörbom, 1993). SIMPLIS is not based on matrix algebra or Greek characters, nor does it generally require familiarity with LISREL's original matrix-based language. Programming in SIMPLIS requires little more than naming the observed and latent variables and specifying the paths with equation-type statements. Because SIMPLIS is so much more straightforward than LISREL's original matrix-based language, only the former is described in detail below. Introductions to LISREL's matrix-algebra syntax are available in Mueller (1996) and Schumaker and Lomax (1996, chap. 11).

LISREL 8 opens into the program's editor. The editor accepts lines of code that specify the model either in LISREL's matrix-based programming language or in the SIMPLIS language. On-line help about the syntax of either language is available. Program code in the editor window is executed by clicking on either the "L" (LISREL) icon or selecting "Run LISREL8" from the menu bar. After a moment the output appears in a window that replaces the editor window.

The graphical interface of LISREL is activated by including the line "Path Diagram" in a program written either in SIMPLIS or

LISREL's matrix-based syntax. With this command, the unstandardized estimates appear in their appropriate places in an on-screen diagram after the analysis is complete. Other information can be presented in the diagram by selecting "Kind" from the menu bar. For example, LISREL's path diagram window can show the t statistics (which are actually z statistics in large samples) for every model parameter instead of the unstandardized estimates. Significant values of t statistics are displayed in one color (e.g., red) and nonsignificant values in another color (e.g., black), which makes scanning the individual results very easy. LISREL's path diagram window also offers other displays that may be especially useful for complex models that take up a lot of space on the screen. These displays are selected under the "Model" option from the menu bar of this window. For example, a "Y-Model" display shows the unstandardized estimates, t statistics, modification indexes, or estimated parameter changes only for indicators of latent endogenous variables. The "X-Model" display shows the same information but only for indicators of exogenous factors. The combination of various views (whole model, structural model, measurement models, etc.) and types of information (t statistics, modification indexes, etc.) allows one to quickly get a sense of the results.

Models can also be respecified in LISREL's path diagram window. For example, to add a direct effect between X and Y, one places the mouse cursor on X and then, keeping the mouse button depressed, the path is added to the model by moving the mouse cursor to Y. (Paths are removed by using the same procedure.) When a path is added, an estimated unstandardized coefficient appears alongside the path. Paths can also be added to the model by deleting a path from the modification index display. LISREL either prevents or warns against the addition of a path that is illogical such as one drawn from an endogenous to an exogenous variable. The respecified model is analyzed by selecting "Re-Estimate" from the menu bar of the path diagram window.

SIMPLIS offers an additional way to use the graphical interface. Instead of specifying the entire model in SIMPLIS code, the user can enter just enough lines to label the observed or latent variables and define the input data. Clicking on either the path diagram icon or selecting "PathDiagram" from the menu bar produces a figure that contains only the variables with no paths between them. Paths can be added to the model by using the methods described above. In this way, one needs to know very little about SIMPLIS in order to conduct an analysis.

Very briefly described, PRELIS2 (Jöreskog & Sörbom, 1996b) is a companion program to LISREL 8 that is designed to screen raw data and prepare covariance matrices for analysis with LISREL (or any other model-fitting program). Although its capabilities for managing raw data are not as extensive as those of general statistical packages, PRELIS2 has some relatively unique features. For example, PRELIS2 can replace missing observations with values from other cases that have a similar pattern of scores over a set of variables. PRELIS2 can also be used to generate bootstrap samples and estimates, conduct computer simulation studies with variables that are specified to have certain distributional characteristics, and produce corrected covariance matrices when some of the indicators are not continuous (section 7.10).

Special Features

As befitting for one of the senior programs for SEM, the features and capabilities of LISREL are very comprehensive. For example, unique among the programs reviewed in this chapter, LISREL allows latent endogenous variables to be scaled by standardizing them, which makes the factor loadings of all of their indicators free parameters that are tested for significance. LISREL accepts nonlinear constraints on parameter estimates, which is part of the Kenny–Judd method for estimating nonlinear effects of latent variables (section 10.2). LISREL also has a "fixed-x" (unconstrained x) option for observed exogenous variables, which specifies the variable as fixed rather than random and excludes its variance as a model parameter. The designation of an exogenous variable as fixed assumes that its values do not change across samples. It also means that no assumptions are made about the distributional characteristics of that variable. For example, specification of gender as a fixed rather than as a random exogenous variable might be appropriate in some circumstances. The capabilities of LISREL are extended even further when it is used in combination with the PRELIS2 program. For instance, LISREL can analyze dichotomous or ordinal variables that are assumed to be indicators of continuous latent variables. However, the raw data must be processed by PRELIS2 in order to prepare a proper covariance matrix that is passed to LISREL (or to another model-fitting program; see section 7.10). LISREL can also analyze covariance matrices from bootstrap-generated samples or from Monte Carlo samples generated by PRELIS2.

Symbols and Basic Syntax of SIMPLIS

With one exception, the names of all observed and latent variables are supplied by the user in SIMPLIS. The exception is CONST (for constant), which is used to specify a mean structure. Variable labels in SIMPLIS can be any length, but the program reads and retains only the first eight characters. Readers should note that variable names in SIMPLIS are case sensitive. For instance, SIMPLIS interprets "factor" and "Factor" as indicating two different variables. One does not specify disturbances or measurement errors in SIMPLIS because these terms are automatically generated. Models are specified in SIMPLIS in the form of equation-like statements that correspond to paths in the model diagram. The structure of these statements are quite similar to those for Amos Text. For example, suppose that the exogenous variable of a path model is interest and that the endogenous variables are motivation and achievement. A structural model for these three variables in SIMPLIS could be specified as follows:

```
Equations
 MOTIVATION = INTEREST
 ACHIEVEMENT = (5)*INTEREST + (2)*MOTIVATION
```

The first line under Equations specifies interest as a cause of motivation. The second line indicates that achievement is caused by interest and motivation. The numbers in parentheses next to the asterisks are starting values for the unstandardized path coefficients for the direct effects interest → achievement and motivation → achievement.

Consider the following SIMPLIS specification of a single-factor, three-indicator measurement model with a mean structure:

```
Observed Variables
 WORDKNOW   SENTCOMP   SPEED
Latent Variables: Reading
Equations
 WORDKNOW = (1)Reading + CONST
 SENTCOMP =    Reading + CONST
 SPEED    =    Reading + CONST
```

In the above code, reading is specified as an exogenous latent variable with three indicators, word knowledge (WORDKNOW), sentence comprehension (SENTCOMP), and speed of reading (SPEED). The factor loading of WORDKNOW is fixed to 1.0 to scale the underlying reading factor, but the other factor loadings are free parameters. The CONST (constant) term, which is included in all of the equations, specifies the intercepts of the indicators as parameters of the mean structure. (Note that the reading factor is not included in the mean structure.)

Error covariances and equality constraints are specified in SIMPLIS with sentence-like commands. For example, the command

```
Let the Errors between MOTIVATION and ACHIEVEMENT Correlate
```

specifies a correlated disturbance between the endogenous variables motivation and achievement. Likewise, the command

```
Let the Error Variances of MOTIVATION and ACHIEVEMENT be Equal
```

imposes an equality constraint on the disturbance variances of these two endogenous variables.

An example of SIMPLIS code for a hybrid model is presented next (see Schumaker & Lomax, 1996, for additional examples):

Example of SIMPLIS Code

```
SIMPLIS example: The final three-factor hybrid model of
  the effects of familial risk for psychopathology on child
  adjustment (Table 8.1, section 8.4) estimated with
  data from Worland et al. (1984)
Observed Variables                                         (1)
  VERBAL     VISUAL     MEMORY
  READ       ARITH      SPELL
  MOTIVATE   EXTRAVER   HARMONY    EMOTSTAB
  PARPSYCH   SES
Latent Variables: Famrisk  Cogach  Classadj
Correlation Matrix                                         (2)
  1.00
   .66 1.00
   .67  .66 1.00
   .78  .56  .73 1.00
   .69  .49  .70  .73 1.00
   .63  .49  .72  .87  .72 1.00
   .49  .32  .58  .53  .60  .59 1.00
   .18  .09  .17  .14  .15  .15  .25 1.00
   .42  .25  .46  .42  .44  .45  .77  .19 1.00
   .33  .27  .35  .36  .38  .38  .59 -.29  .58 1.00
  -.43 -.40 -.35 -.39 -.24 -.31 -.25 -.14 -.25 -.16 1.00
  -.50 -.40 -.38 -.43 -.37 -.33 -.25 -.17 -.26 -.18  .42 1.00
Sample Size is 158
Equations
  PARPSYCH = 1*Famrisk                                     (3)
  SES      =   Famrisk
  VERBAL   = 1*Cogach
  VISUAL   =   Cogach
```

```
MEMORY     =    Cogach
READ       =    Cogach
ARITH      =    Cogach
SPELL      =    Cogach
MOTIVATE = 1*Classadj
HARMONY    =    Classadj
EMOTSTAB =      Classadj
Cogach = Famrisk                                        (4)
Classadj = Cogach
Let the Errors of VERBAL and VISUAL correlate           (5)
Let the Errors of VERBAL and MEMORY correlate
Let the Errors of VISUAL and MEMORY correlate
Let the Errors of READ and ARITH correlate
Let the Errors of READ and SPELL correlate
Let the Errors of ARITH and SPELL correlate
LISREL Output: SC EF RS                                 (6)
Path Diagram                                            (7)
End of Program
```

(1) Names the observed variables and the latent variables.

(2) Reads the input data and specifies the sample size.

(3) Specifies the three-factor measurement model.

(4) These lines specify the structural model among the latent variables.

(5) Specifies correlated errors among the three tasks of the IQ battery and among the three tasks of the achievement battery.

(6) Requests the standardized solution, indirect and total effects, and correlation and covariance residuals.

(7) Draws a path diagram after the analysis is complete.

References

Achenbach, T. M., McConaughy, S. H., & Howell, C. T. (1987). Child/adolescent behavioral and emotional problems: Implications of cross-informant correlations for situational specificity. *Psychological Bulletin, 101*, 213–232.

Aiken, L. S., & West, S. G. (1991). *Multiple regression: Testing and interpreting interactions*. Newbury Park, CA: Sage.

Akaike, H. (1987). Factor analysis and AIC. *Psychometrika, 52*, 317–322.

Allison, P. D. (1987). Estimation of linear models with incomplete data. In C. C. Clogg (Ed.), *Sociological methodology* (pp. 71–103). San Francisco: Jossey-Bass.

Anderson, J. C., & Gerbing, D. W. (1984). The effects of sampling error on convergence, improper solutions and goodness-of-fit indices for maximum likelihood confirmatory factor analysis. *Psychometrika, 49*, 155–173.

Anderson, J. C., & Gerbing, D. W. (1988). Structural equation modeling in practice: A review and recommended two-step approach. *Psychological Bulletin, 103*, 411–423.

Arbuckle, J. L. (1996). Full information estimation in the presence of incomplete data. In G. A. Marcoulides & R. E. Schumacker (Eds.), *Advanced structural equation modeling* (pp. 243–277). Mahwah, NJ: Erlbaum.

Arbuckle, J. L. (1997). *Amos user's guide*. Chicago: SmallWaters.

Armitage, P., & Berry, G. (1987). *Statistical methods in medical research*. New York: Academic Press.

Asher, H. B. (1983). *Causal modeling* (2nd ed.). Beverly Hills, CA: Sage.

Austin, J. T., & Calderón, R. F. (1996). Theoretical and technical contributions to structural equation modeling: An updated bibliography. *Structural Equation Modeling, 3*, 105–175.

Austin, J. T., & Wolfe, L. M. (1991). Annotated bibliography of structural equation modeling: Technical work. *British Journal of Mathematical and Statistical Psychology, 44*, 93–132.

Bacon, D. R. (1995). A maximum likelihood approach to correlational outlier identification. *Multivariate Behavioral Research, 30,* 125–148.

Barnett, V., & Lewis, T. (1978). *Outliers in statistical data.* New York: Wiley.

Baron, R. M., & Kenny, D. A. (1986). The moderator–mediator variable distinction in social psychological research: Conceptual, strategic, and statistical considerations. *Journal of Personality and Social Psychology, 51,* 1173–1182.

Bekker, P. A., Merckens, A., & Wansbeek, T. J. (1994). *Identification, equivalent models, and computer algebra.* New York: Academic Press.

Bentler, P. M. (1980). Multivariate analysis with latent variables: Causal modeling. *Annual Review of Psychology, 31,* 419–456.

Bentler, P. M. (1987). Drug use and personality in adolescence young adulthood: Structural models with non-normal variables. *Child Development, 58,* 65–79.

Bentler, P. M. (1990). Comparative fit indexes in structural models. *Psychological Bulletin, 107,* 238–246.

Bentler, P. M. (1995). *EQS structural equations program manual.* Encino, CA: Multivariate Software.

Bentler, P. M., & Bonett, D. G. (1980). Significance tests and goodness of fit in the analysis of covariance structures. *Psychological Bulletin, 88,* 588–606.

Bentler, P. M., & Dijkstra, T. (1985). Efficient estimation via linearization in structural models. In P. R. Krishnaiah (Ed.), *Multivariate analysis VI* (pp. 9–42). Amsterdam: North-Holland.

Bentler, P. M., & Lee, S. Y. (1983). Covariance structures under polynomial constraints: Applications to correlation and alpha-type structural model. *Journal of Applied Statistics, 8,* 207–222.

Bentler, P. M., & Weeks, D. G. (1980). Linear structural equations with latent variables. *Psychometrika, 45,* 289–308.

Bentler, P. M., & Wu, E. J. C. (1995a). *EQS for Macintosh users' guide.* Encino, CA: Multivariate Software.

Bentler, P. M., & Wu, E. J. C. (1995b). *EQS for Windows users' guide.* Encino, CA: Multivariate Software.

Berk, R. A. (1992). Toward a methodology for mere mortals. *Sociological Methodology, 22,* 315–324.

Bernstein, I. H., & Teng, G. (1989). Factoring items and factoring scales are different: Spurious evidence for multidimensionality due to item categorization. *Psychological Bulletin, 105,* 467–477.

Berry, W. D. (1984). *Nonrecursive causal models.* Beverly Hills, CA: Sage.

Biddle, B. J., & Marlin, M. M. (1987). Causality, confirmation, and structural equation modeling. *Child Development, 58,* 4–17.

Blalock, H. M. (1964). *Causal inference in nonexperimental research.* Chapel Hill: University of North Carolina Press.

Blalock, H. M. (1992). Are there really any constructive alternatives to causal modeling? *Sociological Methodology, 22,* 325–335.

Block, J. (1995). On the relation between IQ, impulsivity, and delinquency: Remarks on the Lynam, Moffitt, and Stouthamer-Loeber (1993) interpretation. *Journal of Abnormal Psychology, 104,* 395–398.

Bollen, K. A. (1989). *Structural equations with latent variables.* New York: Wiley.

Bollen, K. A., & Barb, K. H. (1981). Pearson's R and coarsely categorized measures. *American Sociological Review, 46,* 232–239.

Bollen, K., A., & Lennox, R. (1991). Conventional wisdom on measurement: A structural equation perspective. *Psychological Bulletin, 110,* 305–314.

Bollen, K. A., & Stine, R. A. (1993). Bootstrapping goodness-of-fit measures in structural equation models. In K. A. Bollen & J. S. Long (Eds.), *Testing structural equation models* (pp. 111–135). Newbury Park, CA: Sage.

Boomsma, A. (1983). *On the robustness of LISREL (maximum likelihood estimation) against small sample size and nonormality.* Amsterdam: Sociometric Research Foundation.

Bourque, L. B., & Clark, V. A. (1992). *Processing data: The survey example.* Newbury Park, CA: Sage.

Bozdogan, H. (1987). Model selction and Akaike's information criteria (AIC): The general theory and its analytical extensions. *Psychometrika, 52,* 345–370.

Breckler, S. J. (1990). Applications of covariance structure modeling in psychology: Cause for concern? *Psychological Bulletin, 107,* 260–273.

Brewer, M. B., Campbell, D. T., & Crano, W. D. (1970). Testing a single factor model as an alternative to the misuse of partial correlations in hypothesis-testing research. *Sociometry, 33,* 1–11.

Brown, R. L. (1994). Efficacy of the indirect approach for estimating structural equation models with missing data: A comparison of five methods. *Structural Equation Modeling, 1,* 287–316.

Brown, S. P., & Leigh, T. W. (1996). A new look at psychological climate and its relationship to job involvement, effort, and performance. *Journal of Applied Psychology, 81,* 358–368.

Browne, M. W. (1982). Covariance structures. In D. M. Hawkins (Ed.), *Topics in multivariate analysis* (pp. 72–141). Cambridge, England: Cambridge University Press.

Browne, M. W. (1984). Asymptotically distribution free methods for the analysis of covariance structures. *British Journal of Mathematics and Statistical Psychology, 37,* 62–83.

Browne, M. W., Mels, G., & Cowan, M. (1994). *Path analysis: RAMONA. SYSTAT for DOS advanced applications* (Version 6, pp. 167–224.). Evanston, IL: SYSTAT.

Bryant, F. B., & Yarnold, P. R. (1995). Principal components analysis and exploratory and confirmatory factor analysis. In L. G. Grimm & P. R. Yarnold (Eds.), *Reading and understanding multivariate statistics* (pp. 99–136). Washington, DC: American Psychological Association.

Bullock, H. E., Harlow, L., L., & Mulaik, S. A. (1994). Causation issues in structural equation modeling. *Structural Equation Modeling, 1,* 253–267.

Burt, R. S. (1976). Interpretational confounding of unobserved variables in structural equation models. *Sociological Methods and Research, 5,* 3–52.

Byrk, A. S., & Raudenbush, S. W. (1992). *Hierarchical linear models.* Newbury Park, CA: Sage.

Byrne, B. M. (1994). *Structural equation modeling with EQS and EQS/Windows.* Thousand Oaks, CA: Sage.

Byrne, B. M., & Goffin, R. D. (1993). Modeling MTMM data from additive and multiplicative covariance structures: An audit of construct validity. *Multivariate Behavioral Research, 28,* 67–96.

Campbell, D. T., & Fiske, D. W. (1959). Convergent and discriminant validation by the multitrait–multimethod matrix. *Psychological Bulletin, 56,* 81–105.

Cattell, R. B. (1978). *The scientific use of factor analysis in behavioral and life sciences.* New York: Plenum Press.

Chou, C.-P., & Bentler, P. M. (1995). Estimates and tests in structural equation modeling. In R. H. Hoyle (Ed.), *Structural equation modeling* (pp. 37–55). Thousand Oaks, CA: Sage.

Cliff, N. (1983). Some cautions concerning the application of causal modeling methods. *Multivariate Behavioral Research, 18,* 115–126.

Cohen, J. (1988). *Statistical power analysis for the behavioral sciences* (2nd ed.). New York: Academic Press.

Cohen, J., & Cohen, P. (1983). *Applied multiple regression/correlation for the behavioral sciences* (2nd ed.). Hillsdale, NJ: Erlbaum.

Cole, D. A. (1987). Utility of confirmatory factor analysis in test validation research. *Journal of Consulting and Clinical Psychology, 55,* 584–594.

Cole, D. A., Maxwell, S. E., Avery, R., & Salas, E. (1993). Multivariate group comparisons of variable systems: MANOVA and structural equation modeling. *Psychological Bulletin, 114,* 174–184.

Collins, L. M. (1991). Measurement in longitudinal research. In L. M. Collins & J. L. Horn (Eds.), *Best methods for the analysis of change* (pp. 137–148). Washington, DC: American Psychological Association.

Cook, R. D. (1977). Detection of influential observations in linear regression. *Technometrics, 19,* 15–18,

Cooperman, J. M. (1996). *Maternal aggression and withdrawal in childhood: Continuity and intergenerational risk transmission.* Unpublished master's thesis, Concordia University, Montreal, Quebec, Canada.

Coupland, D. (1995). *Microserfs.* New York: HarperCollins.

Cronbach, L. J., & Meehl, P. E. (1955). Construct validity in the psychological literature. *Psychological Bulletin, 52,* 281–302.

Cudeck, R. (1989). Analysis of correlation matrices using covariance structure models. *Psychological Bulletin, 105,* 317–327.

Cunningham, W. R. (1991). Issues in factorial invariance. In L. M. Collins & J. L. Horn (Eds.), *Best methods for the analysis of change* (pp. 107–113). Washington, DC: American Psychological Association.

Curran, P. J., Harford, T. C., & Muthén, B. O. (1996). The relation between heavy alcohol use and bar patronage: A latent growth model. *Journal of Studies on Alcohol, 57,* 410–418.

Curran, P. J., West, S. G., & Finch, J. F. (1997). The robustness of test statistics to nonnormality and specification error in confirmatory factor analysis. *Psychological Methods, 1,* 16–29.

Curry, R. H., Yarnold, P. R., Bryant, F. B., Martin, G. J., & Hughes, R. L. (1988). A path analysis of medical school and residency performance: Implications for house staff selection. *Evaluation and the Health Professions, 11,* 113–129.

Diaconis, P., & Efron, B. (1983). Computer-intensive methods in statistics. *Scientific American, 248*(5), 116–130.

Dillon, W. R., Kumar, A., & Mulani, N. (1987). Offending estimates in covariance structure analysis: Comments on the causes of and solutions to Heywood cases. *Psychological Bulletin, 101,* 126–135.

Dodge, Y. (1985). *Analysis of experiments with missing data.* New York: Wiley.

Duncan, O. D. (1966). Path analysis: Sociological examples. *American Journal of Sociology, 72,* 1–16.

Duncan, O. D. (1975). *Introduction to structural equation models.* New York: Academic Press.

Duncan, O. D., Haller, A. O., & Portes, A. (1971). Peer influences on aspirations: A reinterpretation. In H. M. Blalock (Ed.), *Causal models in the social sciences* (pp. 219–244). Chicago: Aldine-Atherton.

Duncan, S. C., & Duncan, T. E. (1994). Modeling incomplete longitudinal substance use using latent growth curve methodology. *Multivariate Behavioral Research, 29,* 313–338.

Dunlap, J. W., & Cureton, E. E. (1930). On the analysis of causation. *Journal of Educational Psychology, 21,* 657–680.

Efron, B., & Tibshirani, R. J. (1993). *An introduction to the bootstrap.* New York: Chapman & Hall.

Elias, M. F., & Robbins, M. A. (1991). Where have all the subjects gone? Longitudinal studies of disease and cognitive function. In L. M. Collins & J. L. Horn (Eds.), *Best methods for the analysis of change* (pp. 264–304). Washington, DC: American Psychological Association.

Eliason, S. R. (1993). *Maximum likelihood estimation.* Newberry Park, CA: Sage.

Ellickson, P. L., & Hays, R. D. (1991). Antecedents of drinking among young adolescents with different alcohol use histories. *Journal of Studies on Alcohol, 52,* 398–408.

Feynman, R. P. (1988). *What do you care what other people think?* New York: Norton. (Original work published 1984)

Fox, J. (1984). *Linear statistical models and related methods.* New York: Wiley.

Francis, D. J., Fletcher, J. M., Stuebing, K. K., Davidson, K. C., & Thompson, N. M. (1991). Analysis of change: Modeling individual growth. *Journal of Consulting and Clinical Psychology, 59,* 27–37.

Freedman, D. A. (1992). Statistical models and shoe leather. *Sociological Methodology, 22,* 291–313.

Gerbing, D. W., & Anderson, J. C. (1985). The effects of sampling error and model characteristics on parameter estimation for maximum likelihood confirmatory factor analysis. *Multivariate Behavioral Research, 20,* 255–271.

Gerbing, D. W., & Anderson, J. C. (1993). Monte Carlo evaluations of goodness-of-fit indices for structural equation models. In K. A. Bollen & J. S. Long (Eds.), *Testing structural equation models* (pp. 40–65). Newbury Park, CA: Sage.

Gillespie, M. W., & McDonald, J. L. (1991). *Structural equation models of multi-*

ple respondent data: Mutual influence versus family factor approaches (Research Discussion Paper No. 83). Edmonton, Alberta, Canada: University of Alberta, Department of Sociology.

Goodman, L. A. (1974). The analysis of systems of qualitative variables when some of the variables are unobservable. Part I—A modified latent structure approach. *American Journal of Sociology, 79,* 1179–1259.

Gould, S. J. (1981). *The mismeasure of man.* New York: Norton.

Gravetter, F. J., & Wallnau, L. B. (1996). *Statistics for the behavioral sciences* (4th ed.). New York: West.

Hartmann, W. M. (1992). *The CALIS procedure: Extended user's guide.* Cary, NC: SAS Institute.

Hartwig, F., & Dearing, B. E. (1979). *Exploratory data analysis.* Beverly Hills, CA: Sage.

Hayduk, L. A. (1987). *Structural equation modeling with LISREL.* Baltimore: John Hopkins University Press.

Heise, D. R. (1969). Problems in path analysis and causal inference. In E. Borgatta (Ed.), *Sociological methodology* (pp. 38–73). San Francisco: Jossey-Bass.

Heise, D. R. (1975). *Causal analysis.* New York: Wiley.

Henderson, M. J., Goldman, M. S., & Coovert, M. D. (1994). Covariance structure models of expectancy. *Journal of Studies on Alcohol, 55:* 315–326.

Hershberger, S. L. (1994). The specification of equivalent models before the collection of data. In A. von Eye & C. C. Clogg (Eds.), *Latent variables analysis* (pp. 68–105). Thousand Oaks, CA: Sage.

Hesse, H. (1969). *The glass bead game* (R. Winston & C. Winston, Trans.). New York: Holt, Rinehart & Winston. (Original work published 1943)

Heywood, H. B. (1931). On finite sequences of real numbers. *Proceedings of the Royal Society of London, 134,* 486–501.

Hoaglin, D., & Welsch, R. (1978). The hat matrix in regression and ANOVA. *American Statistician, 32,* 17–22.

Horn, J. L. (1991). Comment on "Issues in factorial invariance." In L. M. Collins & J. L. Horn (Eds.), *Best methods for the analysis of change* (pp. 114–125). Washington, DC: American Psychological Association.

Hoyle, R. H., & Panter, A. T. (1995). Writing about structural equation models. In R. H. Hoyle (Ed.), *Structural equation modeling* (pp. 158–176). Thousand Oaks, CA: Sage.

Hu, L.-T, & Bentler, P. M. (1995). Evaluating model fit. In R. H. Hoyle (Ed.), *Structural equation modeling* (pp. 76–99). Thousand Oaks, CA: Sage.

Hu, L.-T., Bentler, P. M., & Kano, Y. (1992). Can test statistics in covariance structure analysis be trusted? *Psychological Bulletin, 112,* 351–362.

Igbaria, M., & Parasuraman, S. (1989). A path analytic study of individual characteristics, computer anxiety and attitudes toward microcomputers. *Journal of Management, 15,* 373–388.

Jaccard, J., & Wan, C. K. (1995). Measurement error in the analysis of interaction effects between continuous predictors using multiple regression:

Multiple indicator and structural equation approaches. *Psychological Bulletin, 117*, 348–357.

James, L. R., & Brett, J. M. (1984). Mediators, moderators and tests for mediation. *Journal of Applied Psychology, 69*, 307–321.

James, L. R., Mulaik, S. A., & Brett, J. M. (1982). *Causal analysis: Assumptions, models, and data.* Beverly Hills, CA: Sage.

James, L. R., & Singh, B. K. (1978). An introduction to the logic, assumptions, and basic analytic procedures of two-stage least squares. *Psychological Bulletin, 85*, 1104–1122.

Johnston, J. (1984). *Econometric methods.* New York: McGraw-Hill.

Jöreskog, K. G. (1973). A general method for estimating a linear structural equation system. In A. S. Goldberger & O. D. Duncan (Eds.), *Structural equation models in the social sciences* (pp. 85–112). New York: Academic Press.

Jöreskog, K. G. (1993). Testing structural equation models. In K. A. Bollen & J. S. Lang (Eds.), *Testing structural equation models* (pp. 294–316). Newbury Park, CA: Sage.

Jöreskog, K. G., & Sörbom, D. (1981). *Analysis of linear structural relationships by maximum likelihood and least squares methods* (Research Report No. 81-8). Uppsala, Sweden: University of Uppsala.

Jöreskog, K. G., & Sörbom, D. (1993). *LISREL 8: Structural equation modeling with the SIMPLIS command language.* Chicago: Scientific Software International.

Jöreskog, K. G., & Sörbom, D. (1996a). *LISREL 8: User's reference guide.* Chicago: Scientific Software International.

Jöreskog, K. G., & Sörbom, D. (1996b). *PRELIS2: User's reference guide.* Chicago: Scientific Software International.

Jöreskog, K. G., and Yang, F. (1996). Nonlinear structural equation models: The Kenny–Judd model with interaction effects. In G. A. Marcoulides & R. E. Schumacker (Eds.), *Advanced structural equation modeling* (pp. 57–88). Mahwah, NJ: Erlbaum.

Judd, C. M., & Kenny, D. A. (1981). *Estimating the effects of social interventions.* New York: Cambridge University Press.

Kamphaus, R. W., & Reynolds, C. R. (1987). *Clinical and research applications of the K-ABC.* Circle Pines, MN: American Guidance Service.

Kaplan, D. (1989). Model modification in covariance structure analysis: Application of the expected parameter change statistic. *Multivariate Behavioral Research, 24*, 285–305.

Kaplan, R. M., & Saccuzzo, D. P. (1993). *Psychological testing* (3rd ed.). Pacific Grove, CA: Brooks/Cole.

Kaufman, A. S., & Kaufman, N. L. (1983). *K-ABC interpretive manual.* Circle Pines, MN: American Guidance Service.

Kazantzakis, N. (1963). *The rock garden* (R. Howard, Trans.). New York: Simon & Schuster. (Original work published 1959)

Keith, T. Z., Fugate, M. H., DeGraff, M., Diamond, C. M., Shadrach, E. A., & Stevens, M. L. (1995). Using multi-sample confirmatory factor analysis to test for construct bias: An example using the K-ABC. *Journal of Psychoeducational Assessment, 13*, 347–364.

Kenny, D. A. (1979). *Correlation and causality.* New York: Wiley.

Kenny, D. A., & Judd, C. M. (1984). Estimating the nonlinear and interactive effects of latent variables. *Psychological Bulletin, 96,* 201–210.

Kenny, D. A., & Kashy, D. A. (1992). Analysis of the multitrait–multimethod matrix by confirmatory factor analysis. *Psychological Bulletin, 112,* 165–172.

Keppel, G., & Zedeck, S. (1989). *Data analysis for research designs.* New York: W. H. Freeman.

Keyser, D. J., & Sweetland, R. C. (Eds.). (1984). *Test critiques* (Vol. I). Kansas City, MO: Test Corporation of America.

Kinnunen, U., & Leskinen, E. (1989). Teacher stress during the school year: Covariance and mean structure analyses. *Journal of Occupational Psychology, 62,* 111–122.

Klem, L. (1995). Path analysis. In L. G. Grimm & P. R. Yarnold (Eds.), *Reading and understanding multivariate statistics* (pp. 65–98). Washington, DC: American Psychological Association.

Kline, R. B. (1991). Latent variable path analysis in clinical research: A beginner's tour guide. *Journal of Clinical Psychology, 47,* 471–484.

Kline, R. B. (1996). Eight-month predictive validity and covariance structure of the Alcohol Expectancy Questionnaire for Adolescents (AEQ-A) for junior high school students. *Journal of Studies on Alcohol, 57,* 396–405.

Kline, R. B., Guilmette, S., Snyder, J., & Castellanos, M. (1994). Evaluation of the construct validity of the Kamphaus–Reynolds supplementary scoring system for the K-ABC. *Assessment, 1,* 301–314.

Kline, R. B., Lachar, D., & Gdowski, C. L. (1992). Clinical validity of a Personality Inventory for Children (PIC) profile typology. *Journal of Personality Assessment, 58,* 591–605.

Kline, R. B., Snyder, J., & Castellanos, M. (1996). Lessons from the Kaufman Assessment Battery for Children (K-ABC): Toward a new assessment model. *Psychological Assessment, 8,* 7–17.

Knoke, D. (1985). A path analysis primer. In S. B. Smith (Ed.), *A handbook of social science methods* (Vol. 3, pp. 390–407). New York: Praeger.

Kramer, J. J., & Conoley, J. C. (Eds.) (1992). *The eleventh mental measurements yearbook.* Lincoln: Buros Institute of Mental Measurements of the University of Nebraska–Lincoln.

Kritzer, H. M. (1977). Political protest and political violence: A nonrecursive causal model. *Social Forces, 55,* 630–640.

La Du, T. J., & Tanaka, J. S. (1995). Incremental fit indexes for nested structural equation models. *Multivariate Behavioral Research, 30,* 289–316.

Lance, C. E. (1988). Residual centering, exploratory and confirmatory| moderator analysis, and decomposition of effects in path models containing interaction effects. *Applied Psychological Measurement, 12,* 163–175.

Land, K. C. (1969). Principles of path analysis. In E. Borgatta (Ed.), *Sociological methodology* (pp. 3–37). San Francisco: Jossey-Bass.

Langeheine, R. (1994). Latent variables Markov models. In A. von Eye & C. C. Clogg (Eds.), *Latent variables analysis* (pp. 373–395). Thousand Oaks, CA: Sage.

Lee, S., & Hershberger, S. (1990). A simple rule for generating equivalent models in covariance structure modeling. *Multivariate Behavioral Research, 25,* 313–334.

Licht, M. H. (1995). Multiple regression and correlation. In L. G. Grimm & P. R. Yarnold (Eds.), *Reading and understanding multivariate statistics* (pp. 19–64). Washington, DC: American Psychological Association.

Little, R. J. A., & Rubin, D. B. (1982). Missing data in large data sets. In T. Wright (Ed.), *Statistical methods and the improvement of data quality* (pp. 215–243). Orlando, FL: Academic Press.

Little, R. J. A., & Rubin, D. B. (1987). *Statistical analysis with missing data.* New York: Wiley.

Little, R. J. A., & Rubin, D. B. (1989). The analysis of social science data with missing values. *Sociological Methods and Research, 18,* 292–326.

Loehlin, J. C. (1992). *Latent variable models* (2nd ed.). Hillsdale, NJ: Erlbaum.

Loehlin, J. C., Horn, J. M., & Willerman, L. (1990). Heredity, environment, and personality change: Evidence from the Texas Adoption Project. *Journal of Personality, 58,* 221–243.

Lomax, R. G. (1986). The effect of measurement error in structural equation modeling. *Journal of Experimental Education, 54,* 157–162.

Lynam, D. R., & Moffitt, T. (1995). Delinquency and impulsivity and IQ: A reply to Block (1995). *Journal of Abnormal Psychology, 104,* 399–401.

Lynam, D. R., Moffitt, T., & Stouthamer-Loeber, M. (1993). Explaining the relation between IQ and delinquency: Class, race, test motivation, or self-control? *Journal of Abnormal Psychology, 102,* 187–196.

MacCallum, R. C. (1986). Specification searches in covariance structure modeling. *Psychological Bulletin, 100,* 107–120.

MacCallum, R. C. (1995). Model specification: Procedures, strategies, and related issues. In R. H. Hoyle (Ed.), *Structural equation modeling* (pp. 16–36). Thousand Oaks, CA: Sage.

MacCallum, R. C., & Browne, M. W. (1993). The use of causal indicators in covariance structure models: Some practical issues. *Psychological Bulletin, 114,* 533–541.

MacCallum, R. C., & Tucker, L. R. (1991). Representing sources of error in common factor analysis: Implications for theory and practice. *Psychological Bulletin, 109,* 501–511.

MacCallum, R. C., Wegener, D. T., Uchino, B. N., & Fabrigar, L. R. (1993). The problem of equivalent models in applications of covariance structure analysis. *Psychological Bulletin, 114,* 185–199.

Macready, G. B., & Dayton, C. M. (1994). Latent class models for longitudinal assessment of trait acquisition. In A. von Eye & C. C. Clogg (Eds.), *Latent variables analysis* (pp. 245–273). Thousand Oaks, CA: Sage.

Mardia, K. V. (1970). Measures of multivariate skewness and kurtosis with applications. *British Journal of Mathematical and Statistical Psychology, 28,* 205–214.

Margolese, S. K., & Kline, R. B. (1996, August). *Prediction of early reading success in multilingual children.* Paper presented at the 104th Annual Meeting of the American Psychological Association, Toronto, Ontario, Canada.

Marsh, H. W., & Bailey, M. (1991). Confirmatory factor analysis of multi-trait–multimethod data: A comparison of alternative models. *Applied Psychological Measurement, 15,* 47–70.

Marsh, H. W., Balla, J. R., & Hau, K.-T. (1996). An evaluation of incremental fit indices: A clarification of mathematical and empirical properties. In G. A. Marcoulides & R. E. Schumacker (Eds.), *Advanced structural equation modeling* (pp. 315–353). Mahwah, NJ: Erlbaum.

Marsh, H. W., Balla, J. R., & McDonald, R. P. (1988). Goodness-of-fit indices in confirmatory factor analysis: The effect of sample size. *Psychological Bulletin, 103,* 391–410.

Marsh, H. W., & Byrne, B. M. (1993). Confirmatory factor analysis of multi-trait–multimethod self-concept data: Between-group and within-group invariance constraints. *Multivariate Behavioral Research, 28,* 313–349.

Marsh, H. W., & Grayson, D. (1995). Latent variable models of multitrait–multimethod data. In R. H. Hoyle (Ed.), *Structural equation modeling* (pp. 177–198). Thousand Oaks, CA: Sage.

Mason, W. M. (1992). Freedman [1992] is right as far as he goes, but there is more, and it's worse. Statisticians could help. *Sociological Methodology, 22,* 337–351.

Matsueda, R. L., & Bielby, W. T. (1986). Statistical power in covariance structure models. In N. B. Tuma (Ed.), *Sociological Methodology 1986* (pp. 120–158). Washington, DC: American Sociological Association.

Mauro, R. (1990). Understanding L.O.V.E. (left-out variables error): A method for estimating the effects of omitted variables. *Psychological Bulletin, 108,* 314–329.

May, R. (1975). *The courage to create.* New York: Norton.

McArdle, J. J. (1994). Structural factor analysis experiments with incomplete data. *Multivariate Behavioral Research, 29,* 409–454.

McArdle, J. J., & Epstein, D. (1987). Latent growth curves within developmental structural equation models. *Child Development, 58,* 110–133.

McArdle, J. J., & Hamagami, F. (1991). Modeling incomplete longitudinal and cross-sectional data using latent growth structural models. In L. M. Collins & J. L. Horn (Eds.), *Best methods for the analysis of change* (pp. 276–304). Washington, DC: American Psychological Association.

McArdle, J. J., & Hamagami, F. (1992). Modeling incomplete longitudinal and cross-sectional curves using latent growth structural models. *Experimental Aging Research, 18,* 145–166.

McArdle, J. J., & Hamagami, F. (1996). Multilevel models from a multiple group structural equation perspective. In G. A. Marcoulides & R. E. Schumacker (Eds.), *Advanced structural equation modeling* (pp. 89–124). Mahwah, NJ: Erlbaum.

McCutcheon, A. L. (1994). Latent logit models with polytomous effects variables. In A. von Eye & C. C. Clogg (Eds.), *Latent variables analysis* (pp. 353–372). Thousand Oaks, CA: Sage.

McFatter, R. M. (1987). Use of latent variable models for detecting discrimination in salaries. *Psychological Bulletin, 101,* 120–125.

Merton, T. (1965). *The way of Chuang Tzu.* New York: New Directions.

Minium, E. E., King, B. M., & Bear. G. (1993). *Statistical reasoning in psychology and education* (3rd ed.). New York: Wiley.

Morris, R. J., Bergan, J. R., & Fulginiti, J. V. (1991). Structural equation modeling in clinical assessment research with children. *Journal of Consulting and Clinical Psychology, 59,* 371–379.

Mosteller, F., & Tukey, J. W. (1977). *Data analysis and regression.* Reading, MA: Addison-Wesley.

Mueller, R. O. (1996). *Basic principles of structural equation modeling.* New York: Springer-Verlag.

Mulaik, S. A. (1987). Toward a conception of causality applicable to experimentation and casual modeling. *Child Development, 58,* 18–32.

Mulaik, S. A., & James, L. R. (1995). Objectivity and reasoning in science and structural equation modeling. In R. H. Hoyle (Ed.), *Structural equation modeling* (pp. 118–137). Thousand Oaks, CA: Sage.

Mulaik, S. A., James, L. R., Alstine, J. V., Bennett, N., Lind, S., & Stilwell, C. D. (1989). Evaluation of goodness-of-fit indices for structural equation models. *Psychological Bulletin, 105,* 430–445.

Muthén, B. (1987). LISCOMP: Analysis of linear structural equations with a comprehensive measurement model. Mooresville, IN: Scientific Software.

Muthén, B., & Kaplan, D. (1992). A comparison of some methodologies for the factor analysis of non-normal Likert variables: A note on the size of the model. *British Journal of Mathematical and Statistical Psychology, 45,* 19–30.

Muthén, B., Kaplan, D., & Hollis, M. (1987). On structural equation modeling with data that are not missing completely at random. *Psychometrika, 52,* 431–462.

Myers, R. (1990). *Classical and modern regression with applications* (2nd ed.). Boston: Duxbury Press.

Naglieri, J. A., & Jensen, A. R. (1987). Comparison of black–white differences on the WISC-R and the K-ABC: Spearman's hypothesis. *Intelligence, 11,* 21–43.

Neale, M. C. (1994). *Mx: Statistical modeling* (2nd ed.). Richmond: Medical College of Virginia, Department of Psychology.

Nesselroade, J. R. (1995). Exploratory factor analysis with latent variables and the study of processes of development and change. In A. von Eye & C. C. Clogg (Eds.), *Latent variables analysis* (pp. 131–154). Thousand Oaks, CA: Sage.

Nunnally, J. C., & Bernstein, I. H. (1994). *Psychometric theory* (3rd ed.). New York: McGraw-Hill.

Pedhazur, E. J. (1982). *Multiple regression in behavioral research* (2nd ed.). New York: Holt, Rinehart & Winston.

Ping, R. A. (1996a). Interaction and quadratic effect estimation: A two-step technique using structural equation analysis. *Psychological Bulletin, 119,* 166–175.

Ping, R. A. (1996b). Latent variable regression: A technique for estimating interaction and quadratic coefficients. *Multivariate Behavioral Research, 31,* 95–120.

Prentice, D. A., & Miller, D. T. (1992). When small effects are impressive. *Psychological Bulletin, 112,* 160–164.

Rand, A. (1985). *Atlas shrugged.* New York: Penguin. (Original work published 1957)

Raudenbush, S. R., & Chan, W. S. (1992). Growth curve analysis in accelerated longitudinal designs. *Journal of Research in Crime and Delinquency, 29,* 387–411.

Raymond, M. R., & Roberts, D. M. (1987). A comparison of methods for treating incomplete data in selection research. *Educational and Psychological Measurement, 47,* 13–26.

Reise, S. P., Widaman, K. F., & Pugh, R. H. (1993). Confirmatory factor analysis and item response theory: Two approaches for exploring measurement invariance. *Psychological Bulletin, 114,* 552–566.

Reynolds, C. R. & Kaiser, S. M. (1990). Bias in assessment of aptitude. In C. R. Reynolds & R. W. Kamphaus (Eds.), *Handbook of psychological and educational assessment of children: Intelligence and achievement* (pp. 611–653). New York: Guilford Press.

Rigdon, E. E. (1995). A necessary and sufficient identification rule for structural models estimated in practice. *Multivariate Behavioral Research, 30,* 359–383.

Romney, D. M., Jenkins, C. D., & Bynner, J. M. (1992). A structural analysis of health-related quality of life dimensions. *Human Relations, 45,* 165–176.

Roth, D. L., Wiebe, D. J., Fillingim, R. B., & Shay, K. A. (1989). Life events, fitness, hardiness, and health: A simultaneous analysis of proposed stress-resistance effects. *Journal of Personality and Social Psychology, 57,* 136–142.

Roth, P. L. (1994). Missing data: A conceptual review for applied psychologists. *Personnel Psychology, 47,* 537–560.

Rubin, D. B. (1976). Inference and missing data. *Biometrika, 63,* 467–474.

Rush, B. R., Gliksman, L., & Brook, R. (1986). Alcohol availability, alcohol consumption, and alcohol-related damage. I. The distribution of consumption model. *Journal of Studies on Alcohol, 47,* 1–10.

Sagan, C. (1996). *The demon-haunted world.* New York: Random House.

Saris, W. E., den Ronden, J., & Satorra, A. (1987). Testing structural equation models. In P. Cuttance & R. Ecob (Eds.), *Structural modeling by example* (pp. 202–221). Cambridge, England: Cambridge University Press.

Saris, W. E., & Satorra, A. (1993). Power evaluations in structural equation models. In K. A. Bollen & J. S. Long (Eds.), *Testing structural equation models* (pp. 181–204). Newbury Park, CA: Sage.

Satorra, A., & Bentler, P. M. (1994). Corrections to test statistics and standard errors on covariance structure analysis. In A. von Eye & C. C. Clogg (Eds.), *Latent variables analysis* (pp. 399–419). Thousand Oaks, CA: Sage.

Satorra, A., & Saris, W. E. (1985). The power of the likelihood ratio test in covariance structure analysis. *Psychometrika, 50,* 83–90.

Sattler, J. M. (1988). *Assessment of children* (3rd ed.). San Diego: Author.

Schumaker, R. E., & Lomax, R. G. (1996). *A beginner's guide to structural equation modeling.* Mahwah, NJ: Erlbaum.

Silvia, E. S. M., & MacCallum, R. C. (1988). Some factors affecting the success of specification searches in covariance structure modeling. *Multivariate Behavioral Research, 23,* 297–326.

Smith, R. L., Ager, J. W., & Williams, D. L. (1992). Suppressor variables in multiple regression/correlation. *Educational and Psychological Measurement, 52,* 17–29.

Spearman, C. (1904). General intelligence, objectively determined and measured. *American Journal of Psychology, 15,* 201–293.

Specht, D. A. (1975). On the evaluation of causal models. *Social Science Research, 4,* 113–133.

Stapleton, D. C. (1978). Analyzing political participation data with a MIMIC model. In K. F. Schuessler (Ed.), *Sociological Methodology* (pp. 52–74). San Francisco: Jossey-Bass.

Steiger, J. H. (1995). SEPATH. In *Statistica 5.0.* Tulsa, OK: StatSoft.

Stelzl, I. (1986). Changing the causal hypothesis without changing the fit: Some rules for generating equivalent path models. *Multivariate Behavioral Research, 21,* 309–331.

Stevens, J. (1992). *Applied multivariate statistics for the social sciences* (2nd ed.). Hillsdale, NJ: Erlbaum.

Tabachnick, B. G., & Fidell, L. S. (1996). *Using multivariate statistics* (3rd ed.). New York: Harper Collins.

Tanaka, J. S. (1993). Multifaceted conceptions of fit in structural equation models. In K. A. Bollen & J. S. Long (Eds.), *Testing structural equation models* (pp. 10–39). Newbury Park, CA: Sage.

Thorndike, R. L., Hagen, E. P., & Sattler, J. M. (1986a). *Stanford–Binet Intelligence Scale: Guide for administering and scoring the Fourth Edition.* Chicago: Riverside.

Thorndike, R. L., Hagen, E. P., & Sattler, J. M. (1986b). *Stanford–Binet Intelligence Scale Fourth Edition: Technical manual.* Chicago: Riverside.

Tukey, J. W. (1977). *Exploratory data analysis.* Reading, MA: Addison-Wesley.

von Eye, A., & Clogg, C. C. (Eds.) (1995). *Latent variables analysis.* Thousand Oaks, CA: Sage.

Wagner, R. K., Torgeson, J. K., & Rashotte, C. A. (1994). Development of reading-related phonological processing abilities: New evidence of a bidirectional causality from a latent variable longitudinal study. *Developmental Psychology, 30,* 73–87.

Ward, T. J., & Clark, H. T. (1991). A reexamination of public- versus private-school achievement: The case for missing data. *Journal for Educational Research, 84,* 153–163.

West, S. G., Finch, J. F., & Curran, P. J. (1995). Structural equation models with non-normal variables: Problems and remedies. In R. H. Hoyle (Ed.), *Structural equation modeling* (pp. 56–75). Thousand Oaks, CA: Sage.

Wiley, D. E. (1973). The identification problem for structural equation models with unmeasured variables. In A. S. Goldberger & O. D. Duncan (Eds.), *Structural equation models in the social sciences* (pp. 69–83). New York: Academic Press.

Wilks, S. S. (1932). Moments and distribution of estimates of population parameters from fragmentary samples. *Annals of Mathematical Statistics, 3,* 163–195.

Willett, J. B., Ayoub, C. C., & Robinson, D. (1991). Using growth modeling to examine systematic differences in growth: An example of change in the functioning of families at risk of maladaptive parenting, child abuse, or neglect. *Journal of Consulting and Clinical Psychology, 59,* 38–47.

Willett, J. B., & Sayer, A. G. (1994). Using covariance structure analysis to detect correlates and predictors of individual change over time. *Psychological Bulletin, 116,* 363–381.

Willett, J. B., & Sayer, A. G. (1996). Cross-domain analyses of change over time: Combining growth modeling and covariance structure analysis. In G. A. Marcoulides & R. E. Schumacker (Eds.), *Advanced structural equation modeling* (pp. 125–157). Mahwah, NJ: Erlbaum.

Windle, M. (1992). Revised Dimensions of Temperament Survey (DOTS-R): Simultaneous group confirmatory factor analysis for adolescent gender groups. *Psychological Assessment, 4,* 228–234.

Worland, J., Weeks, G. G., Janes, C. L., & Stock, B. D. (1984). Intelligence, classroom behavior, and academic achievement in children at high and low risk for psychopathology: A structural equation analysis. *Journal of Abnormal Child Psychology, 12,* 437–454.

Wothke, W. (1993). Nonpositive definite matrices in structural modeling. In K. A. Bollen & J. S. Long (Eds.), *Testing structural equation models* (pp. 256–293). Newbury Park, CA: Sage.

Wothke, W. (1996). Models for multitrait–multimethod matrix analysis. In G. A. Marcoulides & R. E. Schumacker (Eds.), *Advanced structural equation modeling* (pp. 5–56). Mahwah, NJ: Erlbaum.

Wright, S. (1921). Correlation and causation. *Journal of Agricultural Research, 20,* 557–585.

Wright, S. (1934). The method of path coefficients. *Annals of Mathematical Statistics, 5,* 161–215.

Yuan, K.-H., & Bentler, P. M. (1997). Mean and covariance structure analysis: Theoretical and practical improvements. *Journal of the American Statistical Association 92,* 767–774.

Yung, Y.-F., & Bentler, P. M. (1996). Bootstrapping techniques in analysis of mean and covariance structures. In G. A. Marcoulides & R. E. Schumacker (Eds.), *Advanced structural equation modeling* (pp. 195–226). Mahwah, NJ: Erlbaum.

Index

Italicized page numbers indicate tables and figures.